Service Failures and Recovery in Tourism and Hospitality: A Practical Manual

This book is enhanced with supplementary resources.
To access the customizable lecture slides please visit:
www.cabi.org/openresources/90677

Service Failures and Recovery in Tourism and Hospitality: A Practical Manual

Edited by

Erdogan Koc
Bandirma Onyedi Eylul University, Turkey

CABI is a trading name of CAB International

CABI
Nosworthy Way
Wallingford
Oxfordshire OX10 8DE
UK

CABI
745 Atlantic Avenue
8th Floor
Boston, MA 02111
USA

Tel: +44 (0)1491 832111
Fax: +44 (0)1491 833508
E-mail: info@cabi.org
Website: www.cabi.org

T: +1 (617) 682 9015
E-mail: cabi-nao@cabi.org

A catalogue record for this book is available from the British Library, London, UK.

Library of Congress Cataloging-in-Publication Data

Names: Koc, Erdogan, editor.
Title: Service failures and recovery in tourism and hospitality : a practical
    manual / edited by Erdogan Koc.
Description: Wallingford, Oxfordshire, UK ; Boston, MA : CABI, 2017. |
    Includes bibliographical references and index.
Identifiers: LCCN 2017022424 (print) | LCCN 2017044734 (ebook) | ISBN
    9781786390691 (ePDF) | ISBN 9781786390684 (ePub) | ISBN 9781786390677
    (hbk : alk. paper)
Subjects: LCSH: Tourism--Management. | Hospitality industry--Management. |
    Customer services--Management. | Consumer satisfaction.
Classification: LCC G155.A1 (ebook) | LCC G155.A1 S437 2017 (print) | DDC
    910.68--dc23
LC record available at https://lccn.loc.gov/2017022424

ISBN-13: 978 1 78639 067 7

Commissioning editor: Claire Parfitt
Editorial assistant: Emma McCann
Production editor: Tim Kapp

Typeset by SPi, Pondicherry, India
Printed and bound in the UK by CPI Group (UK) Ltd, Croydon, CR0 4YY

Contents

List of Contributors

Aybeniz Akdeniz Ar, School of Advanced Vocational Studies, Bandirma Onyedi Eylul University, Bandirma, Balikesir, Turkey. E-mail: aarqbandirma.edu.tr

Umut Avci, Department of Business Administration, Faculty of Economics and Administrative Sciences, Mugla Sitki Kocman University, Mugla, Turkey. E-mail: aumut@mu.edu.tr

Gulnil Aydin, Department of Business Administration, Faculty of Economics and Administrative Sciences, Bandirma Onyedi Eylul University, Bandirma, Balikesir, Turkey. E-mail: gaydin@bandirma.edu.tr

Melissa A. Baker, Department of Hospitality and Tourism Management, Isenberg School of Management, University of Massachusetts Amherst, Massachusetts, USA. E-mail: mbaker@isenberg.umass.edu

Kemal Birdir, Faculty of Tourism, Mersin University, Mersin, Turkey. E-mail: kemalbirdir@ mersin.edu.tr, kemalbirdir@yahoo.com

Huey Chern Boo, School of Business Management, Nanyang Polytechnic, Singapore. E-mail: hueychern@yahoo.com

Hakan Boz, Faculty of Applied Sciences, Usak University, Usak, Turkey. E-mail: hakan. boz@usak.edu.tr

Ugur Caliskan, Faculty of Tourism, Mugla Sitki Kocman University, Mugla, Turkey. E-mail: ugurcaliskan@mu.edu.tr

A. Celil Cakici, Faculty of Tourism, Mersin University, Mersin, Turkey. E-mail: celilcakici@mersin.edu.tr

Ali Dalgic, Faculty of Tourism, Mersin University, Mersin, Turkey. E-mail: alidalgic@ mersin.edu.tr

Christina K. Dimitriou, State University of New York at Plattsburgh, New York, USA. E-mail: cdimi001@plattsburgh.edu

Mariangela Franch, Department of Economics and Management, University of Trento, Trento, Italy. E-mail: mariangela.franch@unitn.it

Ozan Guler, Faculty of Tourism, Mersin University, Mersin, Turkey. E-mail: ozanguler@ mersin.edu.tr

Anna Irimiás, Tourism Department, Kodolányi University of Applied Sciences, Székesfehérvár, Hungary. E-mail: annairimias@hotmail.com, irimias@kodolanyi.hu

Petranka Kelly, Dublin Institute of Technology, Dublin, Ireland. E-mail: petranka15@ gmail.com

Jong-Hyeong Kim, School of Tourism Management, Sun Yat-sen University, Guangzhou, P. R. China. E-mail: jhkim96@gmail.com

Kawon Kim, School of Hospitality, Restaurant and Tourism Management, College of Hospitality, Retail and Sport Management, University of South Carolina, South Carolina, USA. E-mail: kawonkathykim@gmail.com

Erdogan Koc, Department of Business Administration, Faculty of Economics and Administrative Sciences, Bandirma Onyedi Eylul University, Bandirma, Balikesir, Turkey. E-mail: ekoc@bandirma.edu.tr, erdogankoc@yahoo.co

Jennifer Lawlor, Dublin Institute of Technology, Dublin, Ireland. E-mail: jennifer.lawlor@dit.ie

Minwoo Lee, Conrad N. Hilton College of Hotel and Restaurant Management, University of Houston, USA. E-mail: mlee37@central.uh.edu

Poh Theng (Beatrice) Loo, Department of International Tourism and Hospitality, I-Shou University, Taiwan. E-mail: pohtheng83@hotmail.com

Gábor Michalkó, Geographical Institute of the Hungarian Academy of Sciences and Corvinus University of Budapest, Budapest, Hungary. E-mail: michalko.gabor@csfk.mta.hu

Michael Mulvey, Dublin Institute of Technology, Dublin, Ireland. E-mail: michael.mulvey@dit.ie

Isil Arikan Saltik, Faculty of Tourism, Mugla Sitki Kocman University, Mugla, Turkey. E-mail: isilas@mu.edu.tr

Dallen J. Timothy, School of Community Resources and Development, Arizona State University, Phoenix, Arizona, USA. E-mail: dallen.timothy@asu.edu

Derya Toksöz, Faculty of Tourism, Mersin University, Mersin, Turkey. E-mail: deryatoksoz@mersin.edu.tr

1 Introduction: Service Failures and Recovery

Erdogan Koc

A service failure is any type of error, mistake, deficiency or problem occurring during the provision of a service. The consumption of tourism and hospitality services involves a high degree of uncertainty and risk (Namasivayam and Hinkin, 2003). The inherent variability in tourism and hospitality services is attributable primarily to two factors: the heavy reliance on human service providers and the near impossibility of quality inspections prior to consumption (Zeithaml *et al.*, 1990; Chan *et al.*, 2007).

Service-quality problems or service failures in service businesses occur due to the following service-quality gaps (Parasuraman *et al.*, 1991):

- The knowledge or perception gap: Difference between the customers' service expectations and service managers' perceptions of the customers' service expectations.
- The standards gap: Difference between service managers' perceptions of customer expectations and the service procedures, standards and specifications established.
- The delivery gap: Difference between service-quality specifications and the actual service delivered to the customers.
- The communications gap: Difference between what is communicated to the customer and the actual service delivered.

Service-quality models such as SERVQUAL are widely used to identify and measure the probable causes of the above gaps (Parasuraman *et al.*, 1991; Koc, 2006). The SERVQUAL model focuses on the service-quality elements of reliability, assurance, tangibles, empathy and responsiveness (Parasuraman *et al.*, 1988).

No matter how good service-quality systems are, it is believed that service failures are inevitable (Goodwin and Ross, 1992; Levesque and McDougall, 2000), but dissatisfied customers are not (Michel, 2001). This is mainly to do with the service characteristics of intangibility, inseparability, heterogeneity and perishability.

As service failures cause customer dissatisfaction, they threaten the survival and growth of service businesses (Koc, 2006; Coulter, 2009; Weber, 2009; Koc, 2010, 2013; Wang *et al.*, 2014). Service failures trigger negative emotions and negative behavioural intentions for customers (Gregoire *et al.*, 2009; Ha and Jang, 2009; Wen and Chi, 2013). These negative emotions and ensuing behavioural intentions may include customer dissatisfaction (Kelley *et al.*, 1993; Koc, 2017), negative word-of-mouth (Mattila, 2001), customer switching (Keaveney, 1995; Pranić and Roehl, 2013), increased costs (Armistead *et al.*, 1995), and lower employee performance and morale (Bitner *et al.*, 1994; Lee *et al.*, 2013).

Tourism and hospitality can be considered as highly service failure-prone industries because of the increased customer–employee contact and the service features of inseparability, heterogeneity and perishability (Koc, 2006). Additionally, tourism and hospitality industries require constant and intense contact with customers (Koc, 2003; Kim *et al.*, 2007), and as a result they are usually described as *people businesses*. Together with constant and intense contact, interaction or social exchange, the general service characteristics make tourism and hospitality more susceptible to service failures (Koc, 2013). General service characteristics that may increase the likelihood of service failures are:

- inseparability: the fact that consumption and production of hospitality services often take place simultaneously;
- heterogeneity: the difficulty of standardizing service performance elements;
- intangibility: the inability to see or touch the 'product' of service; and
- perishability: the difficulty in synchronizing supply and demand.

Koc and Boz (2014) offer a psychoneurobiochemistry perspective to the marketing and management of tourism and hospitality so as to be able to ensure customer satisfaction. This perspective proposes that minute details, such as jet lag in tourists who have travelled across several time zones, may be sufficient alone to cause dissatisfaction with the overall service provided at a particular tourism or hospitality establishment.

Service failures may prove to be extremely costly for tourism and hospitality businesses, because customers quite often switch providers after experiencing service failures (Carley and Lin, 1995; Bernardo *et al.*, 2013; Roschk and Gelbrich, 2014; Van Vaerenbergh *et al.*, 2014). The consequences of service failures may be visible, as in the case of a customer making a formal complaint, and not visible, as in the case of the alienation of potential customers through the negative word-of-mouth referrals by dissatisfied customers. It must be remembered that while a satisfied customer may express her/his content to only four or five people on average, a dissatisfied customer may express her/his discontent to as many as nine or ten people (Brown and Reingen, 1987). This means that the weighting of a dissatisfied customer is greater than a satisfied customer. In other words, one dissatisfied customer is not equal to one satisfied customer. In Chapter 3 (this volume), the emotional implications of satisfaction and dissatisfaction are explained.

Moreover, it is estimated that 96% of all dissatisfied customers switch to other providers without making a complaint (Mariani, 1993; TARP, 2007). This may mean that for every complaint received there could be 24 silent unhappy customers. Table 1.1 summarizes some of the research findings relating to customer satisfaction, service failures and service recovery.

The above explanations show the importance of service failures and recovery from both practical and theoretical perspectives. The importance of service failures and recovery is reflected in the growing number of research publications. A basic Google Scholar search of the terms 'service failure' and 'service recovery' returns a total of about 29,000 and 24,000 results, respectively. More than half of the results belong to publications produced in the past five years. This finding shows that there is a growing interest among scholars in service failures and recovery. Furthermore, a Google Scholar search of the term 'service quality', a term closely related to service failures and recovery, returns a total of over one million results.

Against this backdrop, an extensive review of the literature has been made and it has been determined that there is no specific book devoted to service failures and recovery in

Table 1.1. A summary of Research Findings on Customer Satisfaction, Service Failures and Service Recovery.

Findings	Authors
A 5% decrease in the customer defection rate can increase profits from 25% to 95%. In other words, the retaining of 5% more of the customers means the business can increase its profits from 25% to 95%.	Jacob (1994); Reichheld and Schefter (2000); Reichheld (2003)
A 1% increase in customer satisfaction may increase customer loyalty as much as 10%.	Bowen and Chen (2001)
Attracting a new customer can be three to five times costlier than retaining an existing one.	Orr (1995); Fierman (1994); O'Brien and Jones (1995).
A 1% increase in customer satisfaction may cause a 12% increase on return on investment.	Anderson, Fomell and Lehmann, (2004)
A drop in the customer defection rate from 20% to 10% may increase profits per customer per year from $134 to $300, i.e. a 166% increase. A further 5% decrease in customer defection rate increases profits from $300 to $525, i.e. a further increase of 225%.	Reicheld and Sasser (1990)
A 1% decrease in customer defection resulted in an increase of $41 million a year for the BFI company.	Brown (2006)
Having a customer retention rate of 20% ensures a 10% decrease in costs and hence increases profitability.	Power (1992)
The implementation of a service quality system can increase shareholder value as much as 56%.	Rucci, Kim and Quinn (1998)
The value of a satisfied business travel customer for an airline (Canadian Airlines) can be as much as $915,000 over a ten-year period.	Jenkins (1992)
The cost of retaining a customer is about 25% of the cost of acquiring a new customer.	Riecheld and Sasser (1990)
Businesses with high levels of loyalty tend to have over 75% net-promoter scores.	Reichheld (2003)
A loyal guest at Club Med visits the resorts an average of four times after the initial visit and spends about $1000 each time. The contribution margin is 60%. When a Club Med customer does not return after the first visit, the company loses $2400, i.e. 60% of $4000.	Hart, Heskett and Sasser (1990)

tourism and hospitality. Hence, this practical manual, as a textbook, is original and unique in that it is the only textbook available that focuses on service failures and recovery in tourism and hospitality. Therefore, the book fills an important void in the field.

The above explanations show the need for a more comprehensive and systematic education of prospective tourism and hospitality employees on service failures and recovery. Tourism and hospitality sectors are increasingly demanding graduates who can deal with service failures effectively and establish and implement efficient recovery systems.

The book is written for a number of audiences. First, the book is written for academics teaching tourism and hospitality programmes at universities. In line with the increasing importance of service failures and recovery, academics in tourism and hospitality programmes may wish to offer and develop a new elective or compulsory course in service failures and recovery to increase both the scope and depth of their undergraduate and postgraduate programmes. Additionally, academics teaching service-quality courses in tourism and hospitality programmes can use the book as a supplementary text to support their teaching. Second, practitioners in tourism and hospitality (e.g. marketing and human resources managers) can use the book to design and implement training programmes in their respective businesses. The professionals providing training to tourism and hospitality businesses may also benefit from using the book. Last but not least, the book could be used as a reference for researchers looking for original ideas for research.

As the book has been written with the above audiences in mind, chapters contain many student aids such as real-life examples, case studies, links to websites, activities and discussion questions, recent research findings from top-tier journals and presentation slides for in-class use by teaching staff.

A total of 25 prominent researchers and authors have worked diligently for over a year to bring this much-needed volume to life. Although service failures and recovery take place during service encounters, the stages before and after the service encounters matter significantly. Almost all subsystems and people in service businesses and customers come together and play a role in the occurrence of service failures and in the ensuing recovery actions. Therefore, service failures and recovery activities are dyadic in nature, involving both customers and service people (Koc, 2013; Boz and Yılmaz, 2017; Koc *et al.*, 2017). This means that service failures and recovery require a multidisciplinary perspective, e.g. marketing, human resources management. Hence, while some chapters have a strong marketing and consumer behaviour background, other chapters have a human resources management and organizational behaviour background. Also, some chapters have a combination of the above backgrounds.

As mentioned above, service-quality gaps (service failures) occur because of a wide range of deficiencies. Thus, in addition to human resources management and marketing implications, service failures and recovery are intertwined with other business functions too, such as operations management and accounting and finance. With these perspectives in mind, the book is divided into four parts.

PART 1 Understanding Service Failures and Recovery

Chapter 1 Introduction: Service Failures and Recovery
Chapter 2 Understanding and Dealing with Service Failures in Tourism and Hospitality
Chapter 3 Service Failures and Recovery: Theories and Models
After this introductory chapter by the editor explaining the rationale for the book and an outline, Chapter 2, written by Christina Dimitriou, provides a comprehensive review of the concept of service failure and the types of service failures. In Chapter 3, theories and models on service failures and recovery are explained and discussed by Melissa A. Baker.

PART 2 Understanding Emotions in Service Encounters, Service Failures and Recovery

Chapter 4 Emotions and Emotional Abilities in Service Failures and Recovery
Chapter 5 Memorable Service Experiences: A Service Failure and Recovery Perspective
Chapter 6 Customer Attribution in Service Failures and Recovery
Tourism and hospitality decisions are often strongly emotion-laden and understanding customers' and employees' behaviours in service encounters is of paramount importance. Chapter 4 explains and discusses emotions in service failures and recovery. Authors Erdogan Koc, Gulnil Aydin, Aybeniz Akdeniz Ar and Hakan Boz explore theories of emotional intelligence and emotional labour and discuss how emotions can be measured to understand customers' responses to service encounters and service failures.

Jong-Hyeong Kim, in Chapter 5, provides a comprehensive review of memorable tourism and hospitality experiences from the viewpoint of service failures and recovery. In Chapter 6, Beatrice P.T. Loo and Huey Chern Boo explain how tourism and hospitality customers make attributions and how they perceive events in different service failure and recovery contexts. The chapter also discusses the concepts of customer participation and co-production in parallel with customer perceptions of service failures and recovery.

PART 3 The Influence of Technology, Systems and People

Chapter 7 Technology, Customer Satisfaction and Service Excellence
Chapter 8 Self-Service Technologies: Service Failures and Recovery
Chapter 9 The Influence of Other Customers in Service Failure and Recovery
Chapter 10 Emotional Contagion and the Influence of Groups on Service Failures and Recovery
This part contains four chapters. The first two chapters are on the influence of technology and systems, while the latter two are on the influence of other customers.

In Chapter 7, Minwoo Lee and Melissa A. Baker provide a comprehensive review and discussion of the role and potential of technology in service failures and customer satisfaction and dissatisfaction. In Chapter 8, Petranka Kelly, Jennifer Lawlor and Michael Mulvey focus on self-service technologies from the perspective of service failures and recovery in tourism and hospitality.

Chapters 9 and 10 focus on the influence of in-group and out-group in tourism and hospitality service encounters, service failures and recovery. In Chapter 9, Kawon Kim and Melissa A. Baker explain the influence of other customers (out-group) in service failure and recovery perceptions of tourism and hospitality customers. Celil Cakici and Ozan Guler focus in Chapter 10 on the concept of emotional contagion (in-group) in service failures and recovery, as tourism and hospitality services are frequently consumed in participation with friends and relatives.

PART 4 Training for Service Failures and Recovery

Chapter 11 Staff Training for Service Failures and Recovery
Chapter 12 The Role of Empowerment, Internal Communication, Waiting Time and Speed in Service Recovery

Chapter 13 *Cross-Cultural Aspects of Service Failures and Recovery*

Chapter 14 *Disappointment in Tourism and Hospitality: the Influence of Films on Destinations*

Although various educational and training aspects of service failures and recovery are explained and discussed in almost all of the chapters, this part of the book specifically concentrates on education and training in relation to service failures and recovery. Written by Isil Arikan Saltik, Ugur Caliskan and Umut Avci, Chapter 11 provides an introduction to staff training for service failures and recovery. In Chapter 12, Ali Dalgic, Derya Toksöz and Kemal Birdir explain employee empowerment and the role of speed in efficient and effective service recoveries. Chapter 13 explores the cross-cultural aspects of service failures and recovery. In this chapter Erdogan Koc reviews some of the important cross-cultural theories on service failures and recovery and recent research findings on the topic.

In Chapter 14, Anna Irimiás, Gábor Michalkó, Dallen J. Timothy and Mariangela Franch provide a case study example of how films as a marketing communications tool may cause disappointment (service failure perception) for destinations.

My wholehearted thanks go to all the contributors who have worked so hard to produce this exceptionally useful and original book. I also would like to acknowledge the support and assistance of CABI, in particular, Claire Parfitt, Emma McCann, Rebecca Stubbs and Tim Kapp, and Alison Foskett for copy-editing work. I hope readers will find the book both interesting and useful.

Erdogan Koc
Professor of Services Marketing and Management
Bandirma Onyedi Eylul University, Turkey

References

Armistead, C.G., Clarke, G. and Stanley, P. (1995) *Managing Service Recovery*. Cranfield School of Management, Cranfield, England.

Bernardo, M., Llach, J., Marimon, F. and Alonso-Almeida, M.M. (2013) The balance of the impact of quality and recovery on satisfaction: the case of e-travel. *Total Quality Management & Business Excellence* 24, 1390–1404.

Bitner, M.J., Booms, B.H. and Mohr, L.A. (1994) Critical service encounters: the employee's viewpoint. *Journal of Marketing* 58, 95–105.

Boz, H. and Yılmaz, O. (2017) An eye tracker analysis of the influence of applicant attractiveness on employee recruitment process: a neuromarketing study. *Ecoforum Journal* 6, 354–361.

Brown, J.J. and Reingen, P.H. (1987) Social ties and word-of-mouth referral behaviour. *Journal of Consumer Research* 14, 350–362.

Carley, K.M. and Lin, Z. (1995) Organizational designs suited to high performance under stress. *IEEE Transactions on Systems, Management and Cybernetics* 25, 221–230.

Chan, H., Wan, L.C. and Sin, L.Y. (2007) Hospitality service failures: who will be more dissatisfied? *International Journal of Hospitality Management* 26, 531–545.

Coulter, K.S. (2009) Enough is enough! Or is it? Factors that impact switching intentions in extended travel service transactions. *Journal of Travel & Tourism Marketing* 26, 144–155.

Goodwin, C. and Ross, I. (1992) Consumer responses to service failures: influence of procedural and interactional fairness perceptions. *Journal of Business Research* 25, 149–163.

E. Koc

Gregoire, Y., Tripp, T.M. and Legoux, R. (2009) When customer love turns into lasting hate: the effects of relationship strength and time on customer revenge and avoidance. *Journal of Marketing* 73, 18–32.

Ha, J. and Jang, S. (2009) Perceived justice in service recovery and behavioral intentions: the role of relationship quality. *International Journal of Hospitality Management* 28, 319–327.

Keaveney, S.M. (1995) Customer switching behavior in service industries: an exploratory study. *Journal of Marketing* 59, 71–82.

Kelley, S.W., Hoffman, K.D. and Davis, M.A. (1993) A typology of retail failures and recoveries. *Journal of Retailing* 4, 429–452.

Kim, H.J., Shin, K.H. and Umbreit, W.T. (2007) Hotel job burnout: the role of personality characteristics. *International Journal of Hospitality Management* 26, 421–434.

Koc, E. (2003) The role and potential of travel agency staff as a marketing communications tool. *Tourism Analysis* 8, 105–111.

Koc, E. (2006) Total quality management and business excellence in services: the implications of all-inclusive pricing system on internal and external customer satisfaction in the Turkish tourism market. *Total Quality Management & Business Excellence* 17, 857–877.

Koc, E. (2010) Services and conflict management: cultural and European integration perspectives. *International Journal of Intercultural Relations* 34, 88–96.

Koc, E. (2013) Power distance and its implications for upward communication and empowerment: crisis management and recovery in hospitality services. *The International Journal of Human Resource Management* 24, 3681–3696.

Koc, E. (2017) *Hizmet Pazarlaması ve Yönetimi, Global ve Yerel Yaklaşım*, 2. Baskı, Seçkin Yayıncılık, Ankara.

Koc, E. and Boz, H. (2014) Psychoneurobiochemistry of tourism marketing. *Tourism Management* 44, 140–148.

Koc, E., Ulukoy, M., Kilic, R., Yumusak, S. and Bahar, R. (2017) The influence of customer participation on service failure perceptions. *Total Quality Management & Business Excellence* 28, 390–404.

Lee, Y.L., Sparks, B. and Butcher, K. (2013) Service encounters and face loss: issues of failures, fairness, and context. *International Journal of Hospitality Management* 34, 384–393.

Levesque, T. and McDougall, G. (2000) Service problems and recovery strategies: an experiment. *Canadian Journal of Administrative Sciences* 17, 20–37.

Mariani, B. (1993) The importance of customer service. *The Professional Skier* 51–52.

Mattila, A.S. (2001) The effectiveness of service recovery in a multi-industry setting. *Journal of Services Marketing* 15, 583–596.

Michel, S. (2001) Analyzing service failures and recoveries: a process approach. *International Journal of Service Industry Management* 12, 20–33.

Namasivayam, K. and Hinkin, T.R. (2003) The customer's role in the service encounter: the effects of control and fairness. *Cornell Hotel and Restaurant Administration Quarterly* 44, 26–36.

Parasuraman, A., Zeithaml, V.A. and Berry, L.L. (1988) SERVQUAL: a multiple-item scale for measuring consumer perceptions of service quality. *Journal of Retailing* 64, 12–40.

Parasuraman, A., Berry, L.L. and Zeithaml, V.A. (1991) Understanding customer expectations of service. *MIT Sloan Management Review* 32, 39.

Pranić, L. and Roehl, W.S. (2013) Development and validation of the customer empowerment scale in hotel service recovery. *Current Issues in Tourism* 16, 369–387.

Roschk, H. and Gelbrich, K. (2014) Identifying appropriate compensation types for service failures: a meta-analytic and experimental analysis. *Journal of Service Research* 17, 195–211.

TARP (Technical Assistance Research Programs Institute) (2007) *Consumer Complaint Handling in America: An Update Study*. White House Office of Consumer Affairs, Washington, DC.

Van Vaerenbergh, Y., Orsingher, C., Vermeir, I. and Larivière, B. (2014) A meta-analysis of relationships linking service failure attributions to customer outcomes. *Journal of Service Research* 17, 381–398.

Wang, K.Y., Hsu, L.C. and Chih, W.H. (2014) Retaining customers after service failure recoveries: a contingency model. *Managing Service Quality* 24, 1–1.

Weber, K. (2009) Service failure and recovery in an all-suite hotel serviced apartment context: a case study. *Journal of Travel & Tourism Marketing* 26, 195–199.

Wen, B. and Chi, C.G.Q. (2013) Examine the cognitive and affective antecedents to service recovery satisfaction: a field study of delayed airline passengers. *International Journal of Contemporary Hospitality Management* 25, 306–327.

Zeithaml, V.A., Parasuraman, A. and Berry, L.L. (1990) *Delivering Quality Service: Balancing Customer Perceptions and Expectations*. Free Press, New York.

2 Understanding and Dealing with Service Failures in Tourism and Hospitality

Christina K. Dimitriou

Learning Objectives

After reading this chapter, you should be able to:

- Define and explain a service failure.
- Explain when and why a service failure occurs.
- List and describe the different types of service failures.
- Describe how hospitality managers can learn from service failures.
- Explain how to properly deal with a service failure in a hospitality setting.
- Describe the important steps that lead to selecting the most appropriate recovery strategy for a specific service failure.

2.1 Introduction

Ideally, tourism and hospitality businesses would run smoothly most of the time according to set plans, free from service failures. Customers would always be happy because of the absence of problematic situations and there would be no reason to complain or become dissatisfied about the services provided. However, in reality this is not feasible because the hospitality industry has unique characteristics that mean that it has to deal with the unexpected and with external factors that are out of hospitality organizations' control, such as the weather, ever-changing customer needs and the so-called 'impossible customer'. Therefore, it is critical to understand service failure, its types, when and how it happens and how it can be handled more effectively. This will help increase awareness of the importance of recognizing and accepting service failure and that service failure is a valuable tool that will help the hospitality organization improve, build stronger, better, long-lasting relationships with affected customers and take the hospitality organization to higher levels of success that would never have been achieved had this service failure not taken place.

2.2 Service Failures in Tourism and Hospitality

Service failures in hospitality settings are inevitable, can be caused by a variety of different factors and could happen at any time. Tourism and hospitality managers should be aware of the major types of service failures in order to be able to identify immediately the source of the problem when it occurs on their property. However, the key when dealing with service failures is to handle them delicately, tactfully, in good time and with a high level of professionalism. Too often, hospitality managers fall into the trap of making common mistakes that worsen the situation instead of providing solutions and lead to irreparable damage on tangible (lost profits) and intangible (loss of loyal guests) levels. The purpose of this chapter is to shed some light on these critical issues and to address the art of evaluating the severity of the situation and selecting effective recovery strategies that will not only remedy a bad situation and compensate those affected but, if planned right, also impress the guest and bring positive results.

'When something goes wrong in the delivery of a service, it is called a service failure' (Ford *et al.*, 2012, p. 438). In the hospitality industry, when a tourism or hospitality business falls short of the customer's expectations a service failure has occurred. Service failures are quite common in hospitality settings because there is a high level of interaction between customers, passengers, patrons and the hospitality employees (waitresses, flight attendants, servers, bartenders, front desk agents, etc.). In fact, 'the success or failure of the customer experience strongly depends on how a single moment of truth between a hospitality employee and the customer is handled' (Ford *et al.*, 2012, p. 5).

Lovelock and Wright defined the moment as a 'point in service delivery where customers interact with service employees or self-service equipment and the outcome may affect perceptions of service quality' (2002, p. 55). 'These interactions can be face to face, over the phone, on the Web, or by mail, e-mail, or texting' (Ford *et al.*, 2012, p. 16). For example, the moment that a tired customer arrives at the front desk of a hotel after a long day of extensive travel and is warmly greeted and welcomed by a kind and smiling front desk agent who quickly and effectively checks the customer in and provides assistance with his/her luggage as he/she heads to the hotel guestroom. It is the hospitality management's duty to fully prepare its staff for successfully handling each moment of truth through careful hiring and training of quality employees so that each customer has a satisfying, or better yet an amazing, 'beyond expectations', outcome.

Most tourism and hospitality businesses identify when and where these moments of truth occur and ensure they are managed well. Since they usually involve a customer co-producing an experience with a hospitality employee, well-organized hospitality organizations 'make a special commitment to ensuring that their hospitality employees know how to deliver on the many make-or-break moments of truth each time they occur not only by delivering a flawless service, but also by doing so in a way that is memorable to the guest' (Ford *et al.*, 2012, p. 16). Many hospitality businesses, such as Gaylord Hotels, Hyatt and Disney, ask their employees to identify such moments of truth and record them in a database so they can be used to teach other employees about their service culture.

2.3 Service Failures and Service Characteristics

Services are more prone to failures and dissatisfaction (Koc, 2010). Even the best planning and training might still not prevent a tourism and hospitality business from facing a service failure because the very nature of services creates its own set of challenges.

C.K. Dimitriou

The general service characteristics increase the likelihood of service failures. There are four characteristics of services: intangibility, inseparability, heterogeneity/variability and perishability.

2.3.1 Intangibility

Unlike physical products, the hospitality product 'cannot be seen, tasted, felt, heard, or smelled before it is purchased' (Kotler *et al.*, 2017, p. 35). The hospitality product is experiential and guests, travellers, passengers, patrons, etc. will not know the quality of the product until after they have experienced it. A family planning a vacation or a hotel stay will not know if the destination for their vacation and the choice of their resort was a good one until they have had their vacation experience. They can only rely on what they read on the resort hotel's brochure and website, customer reviews, the photos of the hotel property or a virtual tour they might see online. This can be quite problematic because, if well planned and advertised, it could set customer expectations too high and run the risk of letting them down, for example if one of the hotel products or services turns out to be different from what was promised or of lower quality. Perhaps a restaurant that supposedly caters to families with young children has no high chairs or specialized menus to meet the needs of infants or young children. Or a hotel indicates that it can accommodate customers with disabilities, but when a customer arrives in a wheelchair there is no ramp giving access to the front desk, the elevator cannot take a wheelchair or, even worse, although the wheelchair can fit into the guest room, the bathroom door is too narrow and prevents the customer from accessing that facility.

2.3.2 Inseparability

Unlike physical goods that are produced, then stored, later sold and even later consumed, the hospitality product is first sold and then produced and consumed simultaneously (Kotler *et al.*, 2017). An airline promises outstanding service, but mostly consists of poorly trained, negative and unhappy flight attendants who hate their job and their only motivation to stay with that airline is simply because it 'pays their bills'. So, passengers are treated in a rude and unacceptable manner because there is nobody to monitor flight attendants' unprofessional behaviour. A couple may have chosen a restaurant because it is quiet and romantic, but if other customers include a group of loud and boisterous conventioneers seated in the same room, these customers will spoil the couple's experience. The second implication of inseparability is that customers and employees must understand that service-delivery system because they are co-producing the service. The concepts of co-production and customer participation are explained in Chapter 6 (this volume).

Kotler *et al.* (2017) describe an incident in which a waitress reached the point of exhaustion after working for 10 hours on a particularly hard day, and responded in a very unpredictable and unacceptable way to a customer complaint. The customer shouted that his baked potato was bad. The waitress picked up the potato, slapped it a couple of times, yelling 'Bad potato, bad potato', put the potato back on the customer's plate and walked away. Although this is an amusing story, the customer did not find the incident funny. 'When employees are overworked emotionally, service suffers' (Kotler et al., 2017, p. 282). To add more pressure and stress on hospitality employees, they often have managers or supervisors with very poor management skills who shout at them before a shift and then send them out to work with customers. They may have managers who never reward a job done well, but are always quick and ready to criticize them for any omissions or mistakes. It takes a really strong person to be able to keep their cool, put a smile on their face and remain professional in these circumstances.

2.3.3 Heterogeneity/variability

'Services are highly variable and heterogeneous as they depend on who provides them, when and where and for whom they are provided' (Koc, 2006, p. 861). Service variability can arise for a number of reasons. Services are produced and consumed simultaneously, which limits quality control. Fluctuating demand makes it difficult to deliver consistent products during periods of peak demand.

The high degree of contact between the service provider and the customer means that product consistency depends on the service provider's skills and performance at the time of the exchange. Organizational systems must be carefully designed to ensure the service is consistently produced so that each customer has a high-quality experience that both meets expectations and is nearly equal to that experienced by every other customer (except for differences supplied by servers in response to each customer's unique needs and co-production capabilities). The experience must also be at least equal to the one the same customer had during previous visits.

Lack of communication and heterogeneity of customer expectations can also cause service variability. A restaurant customer ordering a medium steak may expect it to be cooked all the way through, whereas the chef may define medium as having a warm pink centre. In the case of this service failure, the customer will be dissatisfied when he/she cuts into the steak and sees pink meat.

'The heterogeneity characteristic of services is largely connected with the vagaries of human interaction between and among service contact employees and consumers' (Koc, 2006, p. 861). No two services will be exactly alike because the person who delivers the service could have a different attitude or be in a different mood during that time. For example, the same server who is refreshed, well-rested and upbeat at the beginning of his/her shift will provide a better and higher quality of service, but could become ruder or impatient towards the end of a long shift where he/she had an argument with the manager or a fellow employee and is now both tired and angry. It should also be highlighted that no two customers are exactly alike because each will have different wants, needs or expectations and will experience the service in his/her own particular way.

2.3.4 Perishability

'Services cannot be stored' (Kotler et al., 2017, p. 38). A 200-room hotel that sells only 130 rooms on a particular night cannot inventory the 70 unused rooms and then sell 270 rooms the next night. The same rule applies to a plane that leaves the airport with empty seats, a restaurant that has a slow night with many empty tables, etc. Revenue lost from not selling the rest of the rooms, tables or seats is lost forever. Tourism and hospitality businesses have come up with other ways to tackle this issue, such as charging customers holding guaranteed reservations when they fail to arrive or selling their product at a very low rate rather than letting them go unsold. For example, a flight that normally costs US$330 may suddenly sell for as little as US$90 to ensure that it is a full flight on departure.

2.4 Types of Service Failures in the Hospitality Industry

Knowledge about the types of service failures is necessary to understand service failure contexts and to develop systems for service failures and recovery. A basic classification of service failures is outcome and process failures.

An outcome failure takes place when the basic or core service is not performed or delivered. An outcome failure results in customers incurring economic/financial losses in terms of money, time, etc. (Bhandari, 2010; Roschk and Gelbrich, 2014; Van Vaerenbergh *et al.*, 2012). A restaurant customer faces an outcome failure when the table he/she reserved earlier is unavailable because of overbooking or a system failure (Bao and Zhang, 2011).

A process failure is about the way a service is delivered and it takes place when the core service is delivered in an unsatisfactory manner. In this case the process failures cause customers social losses such as esteem, status, etc. (Roschk and Gelbrich, 2014). For example, a restaurant customer goes through a process failure when the hot meal he/she has ordered arrives cold and when the waiter is rude (Roschk and Gelbrich, 2014).

According to Ford *et al.* (2012, pp. 440–441), service failures can be further classified into four categories: (i) service product failures; (ii) failures to meet explicit or implicit customer requests; (iii) failures caused by employees' action or inaction; and (iv) failures caused by other customers, random events or circumstances beyond the control of the organization.

2.4.1 Service product failures

These include any failure in the core service products (e.g. cold or poorly prepared food, unavailable hotel room or broken attraction), service settings (e.g. dirty or smelly rooms, no directional signs or overly worn carpets) and service systems (e.g. out-of-stock items, inoperative credit card machines or disorganized servers). Unavailable service can be quite frustrating, but slow service can also disappoint a customer and ruin the customer experience, especially at times when that customer is in a hurry because his/her schedule is tight. To that customer, time is money and delays are a strong 'deal-breaker'.

2.4.2 Failure to meet explicit or implicit customer requests

These include inability to provide what customers ask for, such as special requests on menu items, a non-smoker being put in a smoking room or not honouring a reservation.

Special needs and preferences cannot be ignored. For example, if a customer has clearly stated that he/she prefers fluffy pillows, then it would be a disappointment to return tired and exhausted after a long day to his/her guestroom to lie on a flat and hard pillow. Customer errors also belong to this category and should not be overlooked – there are occasions when the customers themselves are to blame.

CASE STUDY

Suppose that a customer reserves a hotel room from Monday to Thursday on the first week of a specific month. He/she arrives at the hotel on Monday, but suddenly on Thursday morning realizes that according to his/her schedule the departure date should be Friday. He/she should have booked that room until Friday. Thinking that it is not a big deal and the problem can easily be fixed, the customer approaches the front desk agent, but is shocked when the agent refuses to extend his/her stay because the hotel is fully booked on that day. In this case, the customer may be angry at himself/herself, but does not have any right to accuse the hotel of being irresponsible or blaming the hotel management for not being able to keep the room or find other accommodation inside that hotel. For whatever reason, the customer did not check the dates carefully and now has to face the consequences of his/her actions.

Activity

How would you have felt and responded if you had been (i) the guest and (ii) the agent?

2.4.3 Failures caused by employee actions and inactions

These include both intentional and unintentional acts, such as showing rudeness or a bad attitude or not presenting a meal or bill in a timely manner. Other examples include the level of attention, unusual action, cultural norms and adverse conditions.

2.4.4 Failures caused by other customers, random events or circumstances beyond the control of the organization

As explained in Chapter 9 (this volume), tourism and hospitality businesses are often faced with the problem of disruptive behaviour by other customers. Customers arguing loudly, fighting or misbehaving near others in a guestroom or at a table are characteristic examples of such a service failure. Another common example, especially in hotel settings, is guests walking around the hotel property yelling, laughing loudly and creating a lot of noise late at night while most guests are asleep, waking them up. Disruptive behaviour also includes drunkenness, verbal and physical abuse, breaking company policies and rules, and uncooperative guests. It can become a huge challenge because this behaviour sets a bad example for other guests to follow; a situation can easily get out of hand because what started as one isolated incident can quickly turn into a big group of guests misbehaving and making it much harder for hotel management and staff to control.

Additionally, a combination of factors can lead to undesirable service failures. For example, a customer who ordered a medium steak with French fries receives a well-done steak with mashed potatoes and a totally different kind of wine from the one he requested, served at the wrong temperature. Moreover, the waiter is wearing a dirty uniform, his hair is untidy and his behaviour towards the customer is impolite and offensive. As a result, the customer gets angry, is extremely rude to the waiter and causes a scene in front of other customers. A big argument takes place and the restaurant manager is called to calm things down. In the meantime, customers who are witnessing this incident become very irritated and dissatisfied that they are experiencing a situation like this in an upscale restaurant that positions itself as an ideal place to enjoy excellent food and impeccable service in a nice atmosphere.

Activity

Visit the following websites and identify two examples of each of the service failures mentioned above.
www.tripadvisor.com/
www.yelp.com/writeareview/
www.airlinecomplaints.org/
How did the tourism and hospitality businesses respond to customer complaints?

2.4.5 Other types of service failures

In addition to the types of service failures explained above, types of failures can be extended to provide deeper insight. Hoffman *et al.*'s (1995) study on the restaurant industry revealed further, more detailed types of service failures. Under the category 'service delivery system failures', they list five different types.

- Product defect failures involving incidents with food described as cold, soggy, raw, burnt or spoilt, and incidents in which inanimate objects were found in the customer's food, such as hair, glass, adhesive bandages, bag ties and cardboard.
- Slow/unavailable service failures involving situations in which customers waited an excessive amount of time for service or were not able to find assistance when they needed it.
- Failures deriving from facility problems concerning cleanliness issues such as bad smells, dirty eating utensils and animate objects found in food or crawling across the table (e.g. insects).
- Failures relating to unclear policies that were not clearly stated by the restaurant or its representatives and as a result were perceived by the customers as unfair, e.g. restaurants that would not accept cheques or certain credit cards.

- Failures relating to out-of-stock conditions such as inadequate supply of menu items. Under the category 'implicit/explicit customer requests', there are two different types:
    - Food not cooked to order. These failures occur when the customer explicitly asks for the food to be prepared in a specific manner (e.g. medium-rare, no mustard) and the request is not honoured on delivery.
    - Failures related to seating problems such as seating smokers in non-smoking sections and vice versa, lost or disregarded reservations, denied requests for special tables and unruly customers.

Under the category 'unprompted/unsolicited employee actions', failures occurred because of employee behaviour such as rudeness, inappropriate verbal exchanges and poor attitudes associated with unpleasant behaviours.

Service failures can also occur as a result of incorrect orders, such as the delivery of the wrong food to the table, or in the case of fast food, packing an incorrect food item that was only discovered when the customer was no longer on the restaurant premises; lost orders, where the customer's order was misplaced and never fulfilled; and customers being mischarged, such as charged for items that were never ordered, charged incorrect prices for items that were ordered or given incorrect change.

Service failures can vary considerably across the dimensions of frequency, timing and severity. They could happen to a customer who is visiting the hospitality establishment for the very first time or to a loyal customer who has been trusting and enjoying the services of this same establishment for a number of years. Either way, the impact could be equally strong and significant. Service failures to newcomers can be so unpleasant that they discourage them from giving the hospitality business a second chance.

First impressions are important and set the scene for the kind of relationship that the hospitality business will develop with the customer. Service failures to loyal customers can ruin a great long-lasting friendship, create serious trust issues and cause irreparable damage to the hospitality business. Small mistakes are not as detrimental as big ones and are much more likely to be forgiven and forgotten quickly. Failing the customer just once during his stay can be overcome more easily than letting that customer down multiple times. For example, the customer who requested a soft, fluffy pillow for his bed, but got a flat and hard one. Normally, that should be easy to address. However, the following morning his room service order for breakfast was mixed with the order for the room next door. So, instead of receiving his favourite omelette with pancakes and coffee, he got eggs sunny-side up with apple juice and fruit salad. Later that day, he was overcharged for the towel and drink he requested at the swimming pool and hotel employees were rude to him, both at the front desk and at the restaurant. Failing the customer on so many levels can not only lead to lost business, but also severely damage the hotel's image and reputation, especially if it happens to more than one customer.

2.5 Customers' Responses to Service Failures in Hospitality Settings

The responses of customers to service failures may or may not be visible (Koc *et al.*, 2017). Visible consequences include the loss of a loyal customer; invisible consequences include the loss of prospective customers because they will be strongly influenced by dissatisfied customers' negative word-of-mouth. However, as in the heterogeneity characteristics of services, customers' reactions to service failures may vary immensely. For instance, Koc *et al.*'s (2017) study showed that, depending on the type of hospitality services and customers' age, responses to service failures differed significantly.

The severity of the service failure could be another major factor determining how customers react and respond. Generally speaking, if customers are unhappy or dissatisfied with a product or service, they express their concerns face-to-face with the hospitality employee, supervisor or manager on duty. On certain occasions, they will even demand to speak directly to the general manager the very instant the service failure occurs or at some point before leaving the premises. If they feel their voice has not been heard, then they will most likely turn to social media or websites like Trip Advisor or Yelp to write a review, submit their complaint and inform others about their experience. Some customers will choose a less confrontational way of registering their complaint, such as sending an e-mail or writing a letter when they return home, which will include all the details of what went wrong. Others prefer to fill out a comment or feedback card on their departure, knowing that it will be sent to management and hoping for a swift reply. Some choose to phone the customer service line or contact the headquarters directly and submit a formal complaint through the company's online complaint form so the problem can be resolved by higher management. Others will bypass any sort of interaction with the hotel management or staff and go directly to the internet to report their complaint.

As a general rule, those customers who express their complaint to the hospitality business are customers who are loyal or truly care about the company. These customers would like to let the management of the service business know about the service failure in the hope that the problem gets resolved and they do not need to worry about facing that problem in the future. Another explanation would be that they address the complaint to help the company improve and become more successful. However, there are also customers who do not want to be bothered; they let go of the bad situation or experience, move on and usually never return to that hospitality business. Research shows that there are three main reasons why people do not complain: (i) they think it is not worth it; (ii) they do not know where or how to complain; and (iii) they believe that nothing will be done even if they do complain (Shoemaker *et al.*, 2007).

2.6 Most Common Mistakes When Dealing with Service Failures in Hospitality Settings

There are several common mistakes that hospitality businesses make when dealing with service failures (Koc, 2013; Guchait *et al.*, 2014). This is why Part 4 of the book is assigned to training for service failures and recovery.

2.6.1 Not listening to customers' concerns

Wise hospitality businesses not only listen carefully to their customers' complaints and feedback but also have several methods in place to seek and collect that information because it will help them improve. It is likely that many other customers have faced the same issue but they didn't report it.

2.6.2 Not taking customer concerns or complaints seriously

Some tourism and hospitality businesses may take the time to listen to a customer complaint, but think that it is not important or serious enough to deal with. As a result, they may treat that customer without any empathy or respect, which will only make matters worse. Each and every customer's issue (whether big or small, seemingly odd or unbelievable) should be investigated and addressed immediately. It may be something minor or the key to preventing a major disaster for the company. However, businesses will never know unless they take the time to actually look into it.

2.6.3 Doing nothing about service failures

The complaint or concern will come to their desk, but they will just archive it, give it a reference number and put it in a folder in the bottom drawer. Indeed, this is probably the least effective or appropriate way to deal with a customer complaint. Kotler *et al.* argued that 'the worst thing a company can do is send out a form letter or e-mail that shows no empathy to the customer's problem or not respond at all' (2014, p. 47).

2.6.4 Not realizing the urgency of resolving a complaint or service failure as quickly as possible

Tourism and hospitality businesses need to understand that they not only have to resolve customer complaints, but also do so quickly. 'Resolving customer complaints quickly is a critical component of customer retention and can really work to their advantage. One study by the Technical Research Programs Institute found that if a customer had a major complaint but was resolved quickly, 82% of those customers will return. The complaint resolution drops the customer defection from 91 out of 100 to 18 out of 100' (Kotler *et al.*, 2017, p. 43).

More importantly, though, as Timm states: 'a customer complaint is an opportunity to cement a relationship and create customer loyalty' (2001, p. 41). Ritz-Carlton, which is a hotel chain renowned for outstanding service, has understood this principle and dictates that anyone who receives a customer complaint owns that complaint until it's resolved. Its employees are trained to prioritize helping customers, no matter what they're doing or what their department. They are empowered to handle problems on the spot, without consulting management. Each employee can spend up to US$2000 to redress a customer grievance and is allowed to break from his/her routine for as long as needed to make a customer happy. Therefore, tourism hospitality businesses must realize that successfully resolving customer complaints can boost profits by increasing loyalty.

2.6.5 Resolving the specific customer complaint, but not taking any measures to ensure it will not happen again

If a customer has clear proof that an item is not working properly or an employee is being disrespectful, drunk, abusive to customers, etc., it is not enough to just compensate the affected customer for that service failure. The defected item should be replaced or the employee involved should receive a form of discipline or termination for their careless or unacceptable actions. Otherwise, it is just another service failure waiting to happen.

2.6.6 Refusing to receive customer complaints

Not welcoming customer complaints is probably one of the poorest and most immature strategies that hospitality managers could ever use. Refusal to acknowledge and deal with a situation because it is considered difficult or unpleasant will not eliminate the problem and will not allow the tourism and hospitality business to make changes that will help it become more successful. On the contrary, it will create feelings of frustration and will encourage the customer to find other avenues to express their dissatisfaction and disappointment.

Putting things in a broader perspective, it is much better to have the decency to identify a weakness or problem through the customer, accept responsibility for the service failure and take care of it in a professional and timely manner internally rather than having to face this issue in the presence of the mass media, reporters and probably a judge at a court. By that time, it will have turned into a notorious scandal that will attract a great deal of bad publicity that will even risk the reputation and the image of the tourism and hospitality business involved, especially in this era when a picture or video can capture in detail the service failure and who is at fault.

2.6.7 Inability to identify the most appropriate way to respond to a customer complaint and how to properly handle it

It is important for hospitality managers to be able to figure out the most appropriate way to respond to a customer complaint and know how to handle it most effectively. For example, if there is written correspondence involved, such as a letter or e-mail, hospitality managers must be effective writers by applying the same human skills they would use in a face-to-face encounter. If they choose to respond to a letter with a phone call, they must make sure to have the letter in front of them and to refer to the specific points as written.

Notes should also be taken of what the customer says and how the hospitality manager responds. If hospitality managers choose to respond to a customer's letter with a letter of their own, it is critical that the response letter conveys a problem-solving attitude, projects goodwill and conveys professionalism (Timm, 2001). If a customer posts a bad review and addresses the complaint(s) on a website such as Trip Advisor or social media, Craig (2013) contends that it is crucial to always respond and never ignore them. Reviews drive the demand and hospitality managers must be honest and truthful about the source of the reported problem(s).

Responding as quickly as possible and explaining what has been done to fix the problem or how it will be solved is critical. Regardless of the method that will be used to address a customer complaint, hospitality managers must be sensitive to people's feelings, interests, wants and needs. Failure to do this creates unnecessary strains on relationships and leads to further, potentially uncontrollable, damage.

2.6.8 Inability to identify the most appropriate recovery strategy to follow

When faced with a service failure, the next step is to come up with a recovery strategy that will help fix the problem. Many possible strategies could be followed, but the challenge is to choose the one that will be most beneficial to everyone involved. This requires careful examination and consideration of the factors, events and people involved, especially if there are more than two people that have been treated badly.

CASE STUDY

An event planner makes a mistake and double books a meeting space to two different customers. The first customer is a brand new customer who is bringing a lot of good business, pays well and expects to receive the high-quality service that he/she was promised. The second is a loyal customer who comes several times a year, brings recognition to the tourism and hospitality business through his/her prestigious company choosing the specific tourism and hospitality business and spends a lot of money each time he/she organizes an event. They both reserved the meeting space at the same time, so there is not even the possibility of simply following a 'first come, first served' policy. It is a very delicate matter to not only choose who stays and who goes, and how to make all the necessary arrangements, but also how to say this in an agreeable, professional way that will be appreciated and help the affected customer to welcome the selected recovery strategy more easily. While certain service recoveries fix the customers' problems, others can make things even worse.

Activity

How would you have approached the problem and tried to solve it?

2.6.9 Avoiding responsibility and shifting blame

Too often, when a service failure occurs, hospitality employees try to avoid taking responsibility for the wrongdoing and blame it on someone else. There are a lot of issues that need to be addressed in this case. Precious time is lost as time is of the essence when it comes to customer complaints. It is important to make things right and do so quickly. It does not matter who is to blame at this point. The only thing that matters is that everybody works together to solve the customer's concern.

Once the service failure is resolved, then there will be plenty of time to deal with those who were responsible for the actions that led to the problem. For example, if a customer at a restaurant does not receive the dish or cocktail he/she ordered, the most important thing is to make sure that he/she gets what they ordered. It does not help to start shifting blame from the waiter, to the chef, to the guy who entered the order into the hotel's point of sale system or even worse have the hotel employees get into a heated argument and totally ignore the customer who is still waiting to be served.

C.K. Dimitriou

2.7 Evaluating the Severity of the Situation

Service failures are opportunities for a tourism and hospitality business to review, evaluate and change ineffective policies, procedures and other weaknesses and get on the path to success by showing how much it appreciates its clientele and that it is both a service- and customer-oriented company. Learning from one's mistakes prevents their repetition and it is a win-win situation for everyone involved. Above all, it is also a golden opportunity for hospitality managers to review how they handled a situation to help improve their personal management and recovery skills. A careful reflection of Timm's (2001, p. 47) checklist may be helpful for evaluating a service failure situation:

- What was the nature of the problem?
- How did the customer and the hospitality manager see the problem? What were their perspectives on this matter?
- What did the hospitality manager say to the customer that helped the situation?
- What did the hospitality manager say that seemed to aggravate the situation?
- How did the hospitality manager show his/her concern to the customer?
- What would the hospitality manager do differently if the situation arose again?
- Does the hospitality manager think this customer will do business with the company again? Why or why not?

Regardless of the reason or combination of reasons that may lead to a service failure, it can dramatically reduce customer satisfaction and have severe negative consequences for the tourism and hospitality business. Therefore, tourism hospitality managers must be prepared and have the right attitude to deal with service failures of any kind. The following are important issues for developing the right attitude towards service failures (Shoemaker *et al.*, 2007, p. 105).

2.7.1 Service failures are inevitable

The diversity of the hospitality customer and the heterogeneity of the hospitality product absolutely ensure that there will be complaints even in the most well-planned and organized tourism and hospitality business. Of course, for those more disorganized tourism and hospitality businesses, additional problems should be expected that will further complicate things.

2.7.2 Service failures are healthy

A lack of customer complaints could be an indication that hospitality managers are doing something wrong: it is not possible to make all customers happy all of the time. The fact that complaints are not reaching the management could simply mean that the doors of communication are closed and there is a lack of connection between customers and the tourism and hospitality business. It is vital that hospitality employees are trained to also look out for any potential dissatisfied or unhappy customers and report them to management.

2.7.3 Service failures are opportunities

Service failures are opportunities to learn of customers' problems, whether they are idiosyncratic or caused by the operation itself. If something is broken as they say, then hospitality managers have opportunities to fix it; and if it is not yet broken, then they still have the opportunity to make it better, to be creative, to develop a new product, to learn new needs and to keep old customers.

2.7.4 Service failures can be used as a marketing tool

The success of service businesses primarily depends on knowing what customers need and want. Many tourism and hospitality businesses go to extreme lengths and invest large sums of money in customer surveys, statistical information, forecasts, and market research and development.

2.7.5 Service failures are advertising

The advertising is negative if the tourism and hospitality business does not resolve the problem, and there is nothing more devastating in the hospitality business than negative word-of-mouth. It is positive if the tourism and hospitality business fixes the problem. Research has shown that one of the best and most loyal customers is the one who had a complaint that was successfully resolved. And this customer loves to tell others about it.

'Service failure comes in degrees, ranging from catastrophic failures that make newspaper headlines to those that are annoying, to insignificant slip-ups that are barely noticed' (Ford et al., 2012, p. 442). Their frequency varies from those that happen often to those that are rare. Additionally, since customers are so different when it comes to their needs, wants, expectations, beliefs and attitudes, it is only natural that they will also perceive differently the severity of a service failure (Ford et al., 2012). For example, one particular customer may not mind having to wait 30 minutes to be seated at a restaurant, whereas for another customer this may be grounds for never setting foot in that place again.

When a service failure occurs, the hospitality manager should carefully evaluate the situation, make sure to ask the right questions, conduct a thorough investigation of what really happened and gather all the facts to have a clear picture of the incident in order to determine the most appropriate service recovery strategy. Some of the key questions that the hospitality manager should be concerned with at that point include (Timm, 2001): What is the nature of the customer's complaint? Is it primarily value-, systems- or people-generated? Who is that customer (a loyal one, a new one, etc.)? Is he/she a chronic complainer? How does the customer see the problem? Who is to blame? What irritated the customer the most? Why is he/she angry or frustrated? Is the customer partially to blame? Has this problem occurred before?

Fully understanding all the key ingredients of the service failure and categorizing its severity and causes is a great method to reveal the type of recovery strategy that should be used to achieve the desired results. The analysis of service failures and service recoveries is beneficial to service businesses because it allows management to identify common failure situations and categorize them. This will help the tourism and hospitality business know exactly where it is lacking and use this information as a guide to minimize the occurrence of service failures, and improve its service recovery efforts through employee training programmes.

2.8 Service Recovery Strategies

According to Michael *et al.*, service recovery is 'the integrative actions a company takes to re-establish customer satisfaction and loyalty after a service failure (customer recovery), to ensure that failure incidents encourage learning and process improvement (process recovery) and to train and reward employees for this purpose (employee recovery)' (2009, p. 267). Miller *et al.* noted that 'service recovery involves those actions designed to resolve problems, alter negative attitudes of dissatisfied customers and to ultimately retain these customers' (2000, p. 388). Kotler *et al.* argued that 'good service recovery can turn angry customers into loyal ones' and it 'can win more customer purchasing and loyalty than if things had gone well in the first place' (2017, p. 42).

'Establishing good customer relations involves creating an atmosphere in which customers' complaints are sincerely addressed' (Shoemaker *et al.*, 2007, p. 115). This is called value recovery and it can be achieved by talking to the customer and making it easy for the customer to talk back. Great communication in these instances is critical and pays off in the end. In fact, Timm (2001) argues that in the case of chronic complainers, the best strategy to follow is trying to understand their motives and then encourage them to propose an acceptable solution. 'The best news is that all customers who have their complaints handled well are very likely to do business with the tourism hospitality business again' (Timm, 2001, p. 42).

When it comes to dealing with service recovery, the following eight steps (Shoemaker *et al.*, 2007, p. 107) must be followed:

- Thank the customer for sharing this valuable information with you.
- Explain why you appreciate the complaint. Let the customer know how grateful you are to learn about this problem and to have the chance to resolve it.
- Apologize to the customer about the incident and any inconvenience it may have caused. It is crucial to add that you sincerely hope you will be given a chance to serve them again in the future.
- Promise to do something about the problem immediately.
- Ask the customer all the essential information about the incident, so you can more effectively try to resolve it.
- Correct the mistake promptly. This allows you to ensure that the customer will walk out satisfied and remember what an effective recovery system your tourism hospitality business has.
- Check customer satisfaction. Before the customer leaves, check once more if they are entirely satisfied with the outcome and see if and/how you can be of help. Thank them again for the opportunity they gave you.
- Ensure that appropriate action will be taken to prevent this incident from happening again in the future.

Thinking that only monetary strategies can fix a problem and make customers happy is a naïve and narrow-minded approach when it comes to managing service recoveries. There are other acts of kindness such as a warm smile, a sincere promise and empathy that could also help. The most important lesson learned, though, which applies to every sector of the hospitality industry, is to fix the problem quickly and fix it well. For example, Park and Park's (2016) study on the airline industry in South Korea revealed that among the recovery quality elements, promptness had a positive influence on the airline's image. They also found that a recovered image of the airline had a positive influence on the recovery satisfaction and behavioural intention.

Based on the author's experience and expertise in the hotel industry, when it comes to hotel guests, there are two types of service recovery strategies: (i) those that can be implemented while the guest is still staying at the hotel; and (ii) those that will take place after the guest has departed. Here, once again, implementing recovery strategies quickly and effectively can change moods, build trust and create a long-lasting relationship between the hotel and the guest. What's even more impressive is the fact that not only will the hotel guests appreciate what the hotel did for them, but they will also show it in action: through positive word-of-mouth, by posting great reviews about the hotel property online, sharing their positive experience with friends, colleagues and relatives, as well as recommending the hotel to everyone, therefore generating more business.

2.9 Conclusions

The customer defines the value and the quality of the hospitality business's service, so if the tourism or hospitality business does not understand the customer's needs and wants, then service failure is guaranteed to happen. The customer sees, experiences and evaluates the service, so he/she is the most important source of authentic and constructive feedback to tourism hospitality businesses regarding areas for improvement or needing radical changes. Effective hospitality managers welcome customer complaints, embrace service failures, attend to them carefully and promptly, are not afraid to make operational changes to better serve their customers and make every effort to improve the quality of their services and value they provide to their customers. They are wise enough to know that service failures are golden opportunities to ensure repeat business, create better and stronger customer loyalty, and make their customers happy. They are also aware that the art of carefully selecting the appropriate recovery strategies and techniques can impress customers and create outstanding memorable guest experiences that will directly affect and reflect on the tourism or hospitality business's image and reputation.

Questions

1. Explain Ford *et al.*'s (2012) four types of service failures.
2. Give one example of a 'moment of truth' in a hospitality setting.
3. Why is service failure important to hospitality managers?
4. What are the most common mistakes when dealing with service failures in hospitality settings?
5. Describe the eight steps that hospitality managers should take when dealing with service recovery.

C.K. Dimitriou

Further Reading

Ford, R.C., Sturman, M.C. and Heaton, C.P. (2012) *Managing Quality Service in Hospitality: How Organizations Achieve Excellence in the Guest Experience*. Delmar, Cengage Learning, Clifton Park, New York.

Hoffman, K.D., Kelley, S.W. and Rotalsky, H.M. (1995) Tracking service failures and employee recovery efforts. *Journal of Services Marketing* 9, 49–61.

Michael, S., Bowen, D. and Johnston, R. (2009) Why service recovery fails: tensions among customer, employee, and process perspectives. *Journal of Service Management* 20, 253–273.

References

Bao, G., and Zhang, S. (2011) The impact of culture values on customer perceptions of service encounter and reactions to service failure and recovery. In *Artificial Intelligence, Management Science and Electronic Commerce (AIMSEC)*, 2nd International Conference on IEEE, pp. 768–771.

Bhandari, M.S. (2010) Impact of varying service recovery attributes on outcomes in process-based and outcome-based service failure: an empirical examination. Doctoral dissertation, Victoria University, Melbourne, Australia.

Craig, D.E. (2013) *Reviews, Ratings and Revenue: Managing Reputation in the Age of Social Media*. International Hotel, Motel & Restaurant Show (IHMRS), New York.

Ford, R.C., Sturman, M.C. and Heaton, C.P. (2012) *Managing Quality Service in Hospitality: How Organizations Achieve Excellence in the Guest Experience*. Delmar, Cengage Learning, Clifton Park, New York.

Guchait, P., Paşamehmetoğlu, A. and Dawson, M. (2014) Perceived supervisor and co-worker support for error management: impact on perceived psychological safety and service recovery performance. *International Journal of Hospitality Management* 41, 28–37.

Hoffman, K.D., Kelley, S.W. and Rotalsky, H.M. (1995) Tracking service failures and employee recovery efforts. *Journal of Services Marketing* 9, 49–61.

Koc, E. (2006) Total quality management and business excellence in services: the implications of all-inclusive pricing system on internal and external customer satisfaction in the Turkish tourism market. *Total Quality Management & Business Excellence* 17, 857–877.

Koc, E. (2010) Services and conflict management: cultural and European integration perspectives. *International Journal of Intercultural Relations* 34, 88–96.

Koc, E. (2013) Power distance and its implications for upward communication and empowerment: crisis management and recovery in hospitality services. *The International Journal of Human Resource Management* 24, 3681–3696.

Koc, E., Ulukoy, M., Kilic, R., Yumusak, S. and Bahar, R. (2017) The influence of customer participation on service failure perceptions. *Total Quality Management & Business Excellence* 28, 390–404.

Kotler, P., Armstrong, G., Harris, L.C. and Piercy, N. (2014) *Principles of Marketing*, 6th edn. Pearson Education, Harlow, UK.

Kotler, P., Bowen, J.T., Makens, J.C. and Baloglu, S. (2017) *Marketing for Hospitality and Tourism*, 7th edn. Prentice Hall, Boston, Massachusetts.

Lovelock, C. and Wright, L. (2002) *Principles of Service Marketing and Management*, 2nd edn. Prentice Hall, Upper Saddle River, New Jersey.

Michael, S., Bowen, D. and Johnston, R. (2009) Why service recovery fails: tensions among customer, employee, and process perspectives. *Journal of Service Management* 20, 253–273.

Miller, J.L., Craighead, C.W. and Karwan, K.R. (2000) Service recovery: a framework and empirical investigation. *Journal of Operations Management* 18, 387–400.

Park, J.J. and Park, J.W. (2016) Investigating the effects of service recovery quality elements on passengers' behavioral intention. *Journal of Air Transport Management* 53, 235–241.

Roschk, H. and Gelbrich, K. (2014) Identifying appropriate compensation types for service failures: a meta-analytic and experimental analysis. *Journal of Service Research* 17, 195–211.

Shoemaker, S., Lewis, R.C. and Yesawich, P.C. (2007) *Marketing Leadership in Hospitality and Tourism: Strategies and Tactics for Competitive Advantage*, 4th edn. Pearson Prentice Hall, Upper Saddle River, New Jersey.

Timm, P.R. (2001) *Customer Service: Career Success Through Customer Service*, 2nd edn. Prentice Hall, Upper Saddle River, New Jersey.

Van Vaerenbergh, Y., Larivière, B. and Vermeir, I. (2012) The impact of process recovery communication on customer satisfaction, repurchase intentions, and word-of-mouth intentions. *Journal of Service Research* 15, 262–279.

3 Service Failures and Recovery: Theories and Models

Melissa A. Baker

Learning Objectives

After reading this chapter, you should be able to:

- Understand and explain the expectancy disconfirmation paradigm.
- Explain justice theory in relation to the service recovery process.
- Explain the service recovery paradox.
- Understand and explain script theory and social learning theory to understand service failures and recovery processes.

3.1 Introduction

Service failures are inevitable in all service organizations, including hospitality and tourism. One of the major reasons is the labour-intensive nature of the hospitality industry (Mattila and Ro, 2008). As these failures will occur, it is critical to understand the theories and models associated with both service failure and service recovery. Therefore, this chapter presents and discusses the expectancy disconfirmation paradigm, justice theory, cultural models to service recovery, the service recovery paradox, script theory and social learning theory. By gaining a greater understanding of these models and theories, firms and managers will be able to better create and execute stronger recoveries to service failures in their hospitality and tourism business and interactions.

3.2 Expectancy Disconfirmation Paradigm

The dominant theoretical model with regards to satisfaction and dissatisfaction is the expectancy disconfirmation paradigm (Oliver, 1977). According to the expectancy disconfirmation paradigm, customer satisfaction is the consequence of an evaluation process in which the customer judges his or her expectations of how the service should be performed against the actual service experience (Oliver, 1993). Customer expectations are defined as internal standards or benchmarks against which customers judge or measure the quality of service they receive (McDougall and Levesque, 1998). As shown in Fig. 3.1, disconfirmation is defined as the gap between an individual's pre-purchase expectations and perceived actual performance of the product/service (Oliver, 1993). More specifically, consumers' expectations are confirmed when expectations equal the

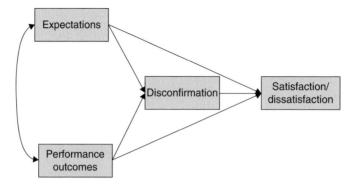

Fig. 3.1. Expectancy disconfirmation paradigm. (Based on Churchill and Surprenant, 1982; Oliver, 1997.)

actual performance. When the expectations are greater than the actual performance, customers' expectations are negatively disconfirmed and when actual performance is greater than the expectations, customer expectations are positively disconfirmed. It is important to note that the satisfaction related to the expectancy disconfirmation paradigm is related to, but distinct from, quality. For example, McDonald's has a lower quality of food products, while Ruth Chris' Steakhouse has a higher quality of food products. If a customer has very high expectations for a steak at Ruth Chris', yet the actual steak they receive falls below those expectations, they may be dissatisfied. Conversely, if a customer has very low expectations for a burger at McDonalds, but the actual burger received is above those expectations, they may be very satisfied with the experience. As such, it is important to consider how quality will affect expectations, but that quality is not the same as satisfaction.

One of the most controversial variables in the disconfirmation paradigm is the comparison standard (Wirtz and Mattila, 2001). More specifically, how do consumers develop the standard they use in the comparison process? Expectations are determined by factors such as external marketing efforts, advertising, brand messaging, and explicit and implicit promises (Baker and Magnini, 2016). Expectations are also determined by previous experience, personal needs and word-of-mouth (Parasuraman *et al.*, 1985). Two customers who experience the exact same meal at a restaurant may have very different levels of satisfaction based on their expectations. As such, it is important to consider that different customers have different expectations and that expectations will largely affect perceptions of the service experience.

3.3 Justice Theory

When there is a service failure and customers complain, these complaints stem from a perceived injustice. Justice theory and the three dimensions of distributive, procedural and interactional justice are widely accepted as the conceptual foundation for modelling customer assessments and responses to service recovery (Wirtz and McColl-Kennedy, 2010). Literature on service failure and recovery shows that consumers expect fair resolutions to product and service failures (Blodgett *et al.*, 1997).

3.3.1 Distributive justice

Distributive justice involves the perceived fairness of an actual outcome of a process (Palmer *et al.*, 2000). In reference to consumers, it may include the compensation afforded to the customer (Tax *et al.*, 1998). In hospitality and tourism, many firms offer such distributive justice outcomes as refunds, credits, discounts and compensation. These may involve deducting part of the bill, refunding the bill for a disliked food item or providing a free dessert in order to increase customer satisfaction after the service failure.

3.3.2 Procedural justice

Procedural justice addresses the perceived fairness of a process (Sparks and McColl-Kennedy, 2001), such as whether the procedures or criteria utilized in making the decision are perceived as being fair. This may include the policies and procedures used, the convenience of the process and the timeliness and responsiveness of the firm's recovery actions (Tax *et al.*, 1998; Smith *et al.*, 1999). In addition, procedural justice is primarily concerned with satisfaction on a moral and ethical level, and is only achieved when all the information surrounding a scenario is allocated proper attention and consideration (Palmer *et al.*, 2000). The speed with which service failures are corrected or complaints are handled is one of the major determinants of customer perceptions of procedural justice (Blodgett *et al.*, 1997).

3.3.3 Interactional justice

Interactional justice encompasses the manner in which an individual is treated through a process (Sparks and McColl-Kennedy, 2001). Interactional justice is demonstrated by interpersonal fairness, whereby individuals are treated with dignity and respect (Colquitt, 2001; Rupp and Spencer, 2006). It may refer to the interaction quality between the consumer and the employee, such as concern and friendliness exhibited by service staff during the recovery process (Tax *et al.*, 1998; Smith *et al.*, 1999), or the interaction quality between an employee and management. Interactional justice (Bies and Moag, 1986) also deals with the perceptions of how one is treated during decision-making or allocation processes, typically in terms of rudeness from others (Donovan *et al.*, 2004). For example, courtesy, empathy, politeness and concern have all been shown to influence consumer perceptions of justice.

Other scholars conceptualize interactional justice as two separate dimensions, interpersonal treatment and informational justice (Colquitt, 2001). Informational justice deals with the perceived adequacy and truthfulness of information explaining the causes for unfavourable outcomes (Colquitt, 2001). Information inadequacy increases customer frustration (Susskind, 2005). For example, when there is a delay for a flight, some of the first things the passengers want to know are: why is there a delay and when will we take off? When passengers don't receive adequate information about the delay, their frustration increases.

3.3.4 Third-party justice

Perceptions of how justly others are treated is called third-party justice perceptions (Spencer and Rupp, 2009). These perceptions focus on emotional reactions to perceived wrongdoing and reflect not the immediate self-interest of individuals but the inherited predisposition to react to injustice in general (Spencer and Rupp, 2009). Third-party justice research is a recent area of research and considers justice coming from the organization (Spencer and Rupp, 2009) in addition to first-party, such as the supervisor, co-worker or customer; sources of justice can stem from the organization as a whole–one's supervisor, co-workers, subordinates and customers (Rupp *et al.*, 2008). The observation of another customer being treated unfairly should result in a negative evaluation of fairness (Mattila *et al.*, 2014). The deontic perspective of fairness theory (Cropanzano *et al.*, 2003) suggests that people react to perceived wrongdoing not because of their own self-interest but due to an inherited predisposition to be sensitized to fair treatment (Mattila *et al.*, 2014).

Reactions to injustice are typically targeted back at the perpetrator of the injustice (Cropanzano *et al.*, 2011). However, the most immediate source of the injustice is not the only source. Third-party justice is also important in terms of who is responsible for a failure and recovery. People interpret behaviour and situations in terms of their causes and these interpretations play an important role in determining reactions to behaviours (Kelley and Michela, 1980). Interpreting who is ultimately attributed to an issue is a key area for justice and complaining research. Take, for example, service failure coming from another customer, such as loud, rude individuals seated near the focal customer on an airplane. Although the other customer is clearly at fault for causing the disturbance and service failure, the focal customer may still blame the firm, even though it is not their fault (Baker and Kim, 2016). This is an extension of third-party justice and greatly affects perceptions of service failure and recovery.

3.4   Cultural Models Approach to Service Recovery

Cultural models govern most daily interactions, including social, professional and personal dealings. Each thought community is identified by the specific interpretive strategy or cultural model that the individual applies to make sense of a particular issue. These are enabled and confined by the larger socio-cultural settings within which people exist and through which they traverse (Ringberg *et al.*, 2007). By understanding which models consumers apply to a service context, providers may be able to anticipate consumer recovery expectations. This in turn could provide managers a way to improve their recovery initiatives and customer recovery satisfaction (Hess *et al.*, 2003) and may be especially relevant for customer misbehaviour.

It is critical to encourage and track complaints through satisfaction surveys, direct customer feedback and online feedback in order to control the success of planned and actual interactional marketing efforts (Baker and Magnini, 2016). Cultural models have implications for research findings and managerial practice because they influence people's reactions to both situational and self-relevant breaches. Failing to control the influence of cultural models in practice may result in less successful recovery actions because there is not a one-size-fits-all model to recovery. This may be because customers are not homogenous as previously assumed, and that effectiveness of service recovery attempts may vary across customers based on their cultural models (Smith *et al.*, 1999). In other words, different customers place different levels of importance on recovery actions. Three main cultural models exist: the relational cultural model, oppositional cultural model and the utilitarian cultural model. Table 3.1 summarizes how to effectively manage cultural models during service recovery.

3.4.1 Relational cultural model

The relationship cultural model applies to people who express a strong desire to maintain emotional ties with the provider even in the face of adverse events (Ringberg *et al.*, 2007). They are accommodating and understanding in the event of a service failure. These people want to rectify and correct the emotional attachment (Ringberg *et al.*, 2007). When these customers experience a satisfactory recovery, their loyalty increases, which is consistent with the service recovery paradox (Smith and Bolton, 1998). Following a service failure, those with a relational cultural model will often seek a sincere apology and admission of wrongdoing. Interactional justice is of most importance in the relational cultural model. How they are treated, empathy and genuine care are the most critical ways they perceive the wrongdoing and recovery. They are also less likely

Table 3.1. Managing cultural models. (Adapted from Ringberg *et al.*, 2007.)

	Relational	Oppositional	Utilitarian
Key justice principle	Interactional justice	Distributive justice	Procedural justice
Response to failure	• Emotional • Anxious • Embarrassed • Willing to forgive • Looking for consolation	• Aggressive • Does not forgive easily • Emotional/angry • Sceptical/cynical	• Pragmatic • Shows irritation for time-related inconvenience • Does not want excuse, wants problem solved
How to identify	• Expresses hurt/vulnerability • Is helpful • May blame self • Shows understanding • Will work with provider • Understands limitations	• Is antagonistic • Blames provider • Is aggressive • Is overly demanding • Suggests excessive compensation	• Rational • Not emotional, but firm • Expects recovery for time/inconvenience
Expectations from recovery	• Sincere apology • Show interpersonal respect • Demonstrate genuine care • Provide explanation of why things went wrong • Assert the importance of the relationship	• Voices a range of recovery options • Desires to maintain control • Demands excessive compensation	• Compensate for time/energy • Offer exchange/refund • Make procedure easy • Solve problem quickly

to accept compensation and less likely to voice complaints. In hospitality contexts, making part of the meal complimentary or giving the person something for free may not be the most successful recovery strategy. For the relational cultural model, it is best to focus recovery efforts on interactional justice.

3.4.2 Utilitarian cultural model

The second cultural model is the utilitarian model, which embraces the idea of rationality and subjective utility theory. The success of a recovery situation depends on the provider's ability to act swiftly and offer compensation for the effort and time invested (Ringberg *et al.*, 2007). In the utilitarian cultural model, the person is very practical and possesses a matter-of-fact attitude. They are less likely to become emotional during a service failure and view failures as financial and time-related inconveniences. For example, if a utilitarian customer asked for the tomatoes on the side for a pasta dish, but the pasta arrived with tomatoes on it, they will assess the recovery in terms of benefits versus time-related inconvenience. If they perceive it will take too long to remake the pasta, they will not complain. In addition, the person in the utilitarian cultural model is not likely to return if there is an ineffective recovery. In other words, if the likelihood of recovery is slim, rather than investing additional time and energy, the person will leave and never return. The ease of the procedure and process is most important for this person. As such, in recovery efforts managers should focus on procedural justice when dealing with these people.

3.4.3 Oppositional cultural model

Next, the oppositional cultural model involves people with a consistently aggressive position toward providers in the wake of self-relevant goods or service failure. Oppositional consumers believe that service providers would not hesitate to take advantage of, coerce and control them, given the opportunity (Ringberg *et al.*, 2007). Oppositional customers may serve as an important component to the customer misbehaviour theory, and this has yet to be incorporated in the literature. The services literature is limited with regard to customer issues related to maintaining control and independence during consumer–provider interactions. With regard to oppositional customers, daily encounters and social norms often prevent outright antisocial behaviour. However, in the case of a service context, the maintenance of social norms cannot sustain the underlying disdain these consumers feel, and the customer is ready to explode at the moment of a self-relevant transgression (Ringberg *et al.*, 2007). A unique aspect of the oppositional cultural model is the notion of control and not wanting to be at the mercy of the provider. This customer's perspective is that all providers are cunning, and the consumer–provider interaction represents a temporary armistice in which both parties vie for control (Ringberg *et al.*, 2007). This cultural model resembles a deeply held ideology, which associates customer opposition with ideological predispositions that lead consumers to be less sympathetic and susceptible to developing and maintaining social ties (Holt, 2002). Oppositional customers remain affable and show no obvious signs of antagonism until the moment of a self-relevant transgression, which prompts more deep-seated cultural models. The oppositional cultural model embraced by oppositional customers flows from a larger current of consumer distrust and discontent with commercial providers (Holt, 2002). Oppositional customers are emotional and angry, not willing to forgive and the recovery paradox is unlikely (Ringberg *et al.*, 2007). With these customers, it is important to make them feel as though they are in control and to give them options during the recovery. More specifically, one useful tactic is to ask the oppositional customer what they would like for you to do to rectify the failure. This is called recovery voice (Karande *et al.*, 2007), whereby the customer is invited to provide input into how a service failure should be resolved. In these cases, however, it is important to resist satisfying all of these excessive demands regarding compensation.

CASE STUDY: SERVICE RECOVERY AND CULTURAL MODELS

During the course of dinner service at your upscale-casual restaurant, there are three separate service failures. In all three, the customer orders a steak medium-rare and in all three cases the steak is overcooked. The first customer says it is fine, understands the restaurant was very busy, that mistakes happen and will just eat the steak. The second customer calls you over very calmly and asks for another steak cooked properly. After another manager apologizes profusely for several minutes, the customer gets frustrated and cancels the order. The third customer is loud and aggressive, blames your untrained cook for not knowing how to cook a steak and demands you pay the entire table's bill.

Case study questions

1. What is each customer's cultural model, based on the clues in the scenario?
2. Which elements allowed you to identify each cultural model?
3. How could you have more effectively recovered from each failure, incorporating the justice principles into your recovery actions?

3.5   Service Recovery Paradox

The service recovery paradox is defined as the situation in which post-recovery satisfaction is greater than that prior to the service failure when customers receive high-recovery performance (Smith and Bolton, 1998). In other words, if there is a failure and then an excellent recovery, a service paradox occurs such that the post-failure satisfaction exceeds the pre-failure satisfaction. In this context, an effective service recovery may lead to higher satisfaction compared with the service that was correctly performed the first time (de Matos *et al.*, 2007). The paradox is related to a secondary satisfaction following a service failure in which customers compare their expectations for recovery to their perceptions of the service recovery performance. Most research finds that, following an effective recovery after a service failure, there is increased customer satisfaction, increased repurchase intention, positive word-of-mouth and increased brand image. Many firms have stories of how they have turned complaining customers into loyal ones following an effective service recovery. Walter Brosch,

Director of Operations of TMH Hotels Corporation, said: 'It is imperative that those of us in the hospitality industry through training and execution create a guest environment with minimal problems. However, it is not always the problem that causes disloyalty with our customers, but the matter in which the resolution is handled' (Magnini *et al.*, 2007, p. 214). There are also several important theoretical moderators that affect the service recovery paradox. Figure 3.2 shows the service recovery paradox model.

3.5.1 Failure severity

The first important theoretical moderator in the model is the severity of the failure. Service failures are inevitable in hospitality and tourism firms and these failures can range from mild to very severe. The higher the magnitude of the failure's severity, the more severe the consequences, such as decreased satisfaction (Hoffman *et al.*, 1995). For example, an apology and free beverage might create a paradoxical satisfaction for an additional 10-minute wait past dinner reservation at a restaurant, but would not if the diner was seated two hours past the reservation time. As such, the magnitude of the severity affects the service recovery paradox.

3.5.2 Prior failure experience

Satisfaction is a cumulative evaluation of all experiences with a firm (Cronin and Taylor, 1994), so previous failure experiences will affect the service recovery paradox. If a customer has a history of interactions with the firm, such as visiting their favourite coffee shop daily for their morning coffee, the satisfaction reflects the cumulative interactions. A customer with a history of positive experiences at the coffee shop may be more forgiving of a failure than a customer who has no experiences at this shop.

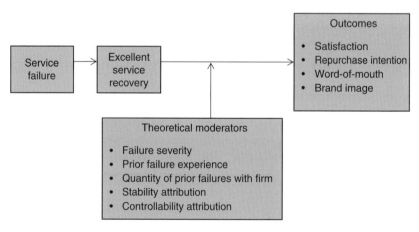

Fig. 3.2. Service recovery paradox model. (Adapted from Magnini *et al.*, 2007; de Matos *et al.*, 2007.)

M.A. Baker

3.5.3 Number of previous failures with the firm

Overall customer satisfaction is contingent on the customer's entire history with the firm, so a failure happening early in the customer–firm relationship will weigh more heavily on customer dissatisfaction because the customer has fewer successful service experiences to counterbalance the failure (Ganesan, 1994). The longer the history of satisfactory experiences, the greater the buffer when the inevitable service failure occurs (Magnini *et al.*, 2007). For example, if a customer has a long history of satisfactory experiences at a particular hotel brand, they will be more forgiving when a failure occurs at that particular brand.

3.5.4 Stability attribution

As previously discussed in this chapter, stability is the extent to which a cause is viewed as temporary or permanent (Hess *et al.*, 2003). For example, if a hotel room on the ground floor is unavailable because a pipe burst, this may be seen as a temporary occurrence. However, if the ground floor of that hotel is prone to frequent flooding in that city, this would be considered a more permanent cause. In other words, in the event of a service failure, a recovery paradox is more likely to occur if the customer perceives that the failure had an unstable cause rather than if the customer perceived the cause to be stable (Magnini *et al.*, 2007).

3.5.5 Controllability attribution

Customers are more forgiving if they perceive that the firm had little control over the occurrence of the failure (Maxham and Netemeyer, 2002). For example, if a flight is delayed because of bad weather, the airline has little control over that failure. However, if the flight is delayed because of poor employee scheduling, the airline has more control over scheduling and this customer may be more dissatisfied as they believe the service provider had control over the failure. In the event of a service failure, a recovery paradox is more likely to occur if the customer perceives that the firm had little control over the cause of the failure than if the customer perceived that the firm had more control over the failure (Magnini *et al.*, 2007).

3.6 Script Theory

Script theory and how hospitality and tourism management companies use scripts greatly affects service failure and recovery.

3.6.1 Role and script theory

Similarities in how customers and employees view service encounters are most likely when the two parties share common role expectations and the service script is well defined (Mohr and Bitner, 1991). The role is defined as the behaviour associated with a socially defined position (Solomon *et al.*, 1985) and the role expectations are the standards for the role behaviour (Biddle, 1986). Frontline service encounters are an integral part of everyday consumption in which people assume roles as customers or employees and follow established scripts in accordance with social exchange norms (Giebelhausen *et al.*, 2014). In most hospitality and tourism contexts, the roles of both the customer and the employee are well defined and the person in each role knows what to expect from the other. Many service encounters, such as checking into a hotel or being seated in a restaurant, occur frequently and thus have well-defined scripts. When service encounters have strong scripts, the employee and the customer are likely to share expectations about the events that will occur and the order of occurrence (Bitner *et al.*, 1994).

Script theory contends that knowledge about familiar, frequent situations is stored in one's mind as a coherent description of events expected to occur (Bateson, 2002). This means that customers and employees in routine, well-understood service encounters share similar beliefs regarding their roles and the expected sequence of events and behaviours (Bitner *et al.*, 1994). The degree to which the script is upheld is a critical determinant of evaluations of a service encounter and known to be an important determinant of frontline service assessments (Solomon *et al.*, 1985). Based on script theory, when customers experience a service failure, their sensitivities are heightened due to the incongruence between the anticipated and the actual (failed) script (Magnini *et al.*, 2007; Cheng *et al.*, 2015). This heightened attention and evaluation is particularly evident in failure scenarios that make the customer vulnerable, inconvenienced and/or uncomfortable (Magnini *et al.*, 2007). Due to this heightened sensitivity, satisfaction with the redress initiative is more important than initial attributes in influencing overall satisfaction (Bitner *et al.*, 1990). Therefore, service recovery efforts are usually very salient in the consumer's mind because of heightened attention and evaluation as a result of the service failure (Spreng *et al.*, 1995).

3.6.2 Service scripts

Service scripts are behavioural and verbal prescriptions used in most hospitality and tourism organizations as a way of standardizing employees' behaviours during their interactions with customers (Nguyen *et al.*, 2014). In most cases, service scripts specify what actions an employee needs to take during a service encounter and the general rules and procedures to follow during each step of the service process (Walsh *et al.*, 2012). Service scripts have a broader impact on the interactions and conversations between employees and customers by controlling what employees should say and do (Abelson, 1981). For example, McDonald's employees follow the 'Six steps of window service' and Ritz-Carlton employees used to be given a 20-item checklist of rules to follow when interacting with guests (Nguyen *et al.*, 2014). The use of service scripts can be an effective means to control employee behaviours because standardizing the service encounter allows firms to control and overcome differences in employees' skills, abilities and attitudes (Rafaeli *et al.*, 2008). However, service scripts may restrict employees' discretion to go beyond the pre-specified procedures in helping customers (Nguyen *et al.*, 2014).

Although service scripts are designed to deliberately shape the behaviours of employees, they can also affect how customers perceive, respond to and participate in the service encounter itself (Nguyen *et al.*, 2014). While the use of standardized scripts has merit, in order to maximize individual customer preferences hospitality firms should empower employees to be flexible with their approach to meet individual customer needs (Baker, 2016). Failing to read and respond effectively to individual customer expectations is likely to make a customer feel as if they are being treated as a number rather than a person (Rafaeli *et al.*, 2008). When a customer feels an employee is strictly following a script, they may become frustrated. This is especially relevant to service failures, as adherence to a script may make the customer feel as though the employee/firm is not listening to their specific failure and is using a scripted, inauthentic response.

3.7   Social Learning Theory

Social learning theory suggests that individuals learn from others by observing their behaviour (Bandura, 1977): individuals' social behaviour is learned primarily by observing and imitating the behaviours of others and is also affected when they are rewarded or punished for these behaviours (Tu, 2000). Individuals learn from the consequences of their behaviour and they are therefore more likely to adopt behaviours that result in positive consequences (Bandura, 1977).

3.7.1   Social learning theory and customer complaints

Social learning theory is important in service failure and recovery because, through social learning theory, customers learn how to complain. In other words, through word-of-mouth communication, positive reinforcements induced by financial and emotional rewards (Bennett, 1997) and accrued complaint successes (Andreassen, 1988), customers may learn to complain effectively. In addition, learning takes place vicariously by customers observing the actions of other customers (Baker *et al.*, 2012). So not only does learning take place when a customer complains, but learning also takes place when customers observe other customers successfully complain in the social servicescape. Therefore, it is critical to understand how social learning theory encourages customer complaints.

3.7.2   Social learning theory and opportunistic customers

Grounded in social learning theory, some customers may develop dysfunctional consumption and complaining habits. Based on the social learning theory, dysfunctional customer behaviour is argued to have a negative effect on some customers, who replicate such behaviour, and may come in the form of imitated complaints (Harris and Reynolds, 2003). When organizations allow the customer to always be right, allow ease in verbal behaviour and pacify the behaviour through financial compensation, the propensity to voice unjust complaints may increase (Baker *et al.*, 2012). Organizational practices and social learning theory encourage customers to complain and opportunistically complain. For example, many restaurants have liberal redress policies to do whatever it takes to satisfy the customer. When a customer knows that the restaurant is highly likely to make their meal complimentary if they complain about it, they learn that complaining equals free meal items. Taking it one step further, a customer may also learn that if they complain, even if satisfied, they can also get free items. This behaviour is opportunistic complaining, whereby individuals voice fictitious complaints to service providers with the goal of receiving compensation for their make-believe service failures (Baker *et al.*, 2012).

Furthermore, through the influence of the internet and word-of-mouth, customers may also learn how to complain successfully to specific companies to get free things. Illegitimate complaining can be contagious, such as via word-of-mouth of the benefits of making false complaints (Robertson and Shaw, 2009). The concept of emotional contagion is explained in Chapter 10 (this volume).

Various websites and blogs support customers to exploit companies and get certain product items free by making opportunistic claims. In many cases managers are unable to detect and control applications made by dysfunctional customers. Failure in detecting dysfunctional customers or the inability to take action against them encourages these customers. The problem is exacerbated as such behaviour becomes increasingly more socially acceptable (Reynolds and Harris, 2005). For example, as a result of abuse of the system, the retailer REI, which has had an unconditional guarantee and return policy for 75 years, now only takes back items within a year of their purchase (Grind, 2013).

3.8 Conclusion

Even in the most successful firms, service failures are inevitable. How a firm handles the failure is critical in whether customers develop positive or negative perceptions. This chapter provided an overview of the main theories and models regarding service failure and recovery: the expectancy disconfirmation paradigm, justice theory, cultural models to service recovery, the service recovery paradox script theory and social learning theory. With this foundational knowledge, the readers of this chapter should have a better understanding of the principles and theories behind service failure and recovery and be able to more effectively manage service failure and recovery in their hospitality and tourism businesses.

Questions

1. Why does the service recovery paradox occur? Is it possible for it to occur after each service recovery? (You are recommended to refer to Chapter 4, this volume).
2. Explain the three components of justice. Do people attach the same weighting to each of these dimensions?
3. Explain social learning theory in terms of the influence of other people. (You are recommended to refer to Chapters 9 and 10, this volume).

Further Reading

Bandura, A. (1977) *Social Learning Theory*. Prentice Hall, Englewood Cliffs, New Jersey.
Blodgett, J.G., Hill, D.J. and Tax, S.S. (1997) The effects of distributive, procedural, and interactional justice on post complaint behavior. *Journal of Retailing* 73, 185–210.

M.A. Baker

Maxham, J. III and Netemeyer, R. (2002) A longitudinal study of complaining customers' evaluations of multiple service failures and recovery efforts. *Journal of Marketing* 66, 57–71.

Ringberg, T., Odekerken-Schroder, G. and Christensen, G.L. (2007) A cultural models approach to service recovery. *Journal of Marketing* 71, 194–214.

Wirtz, J. and McColl-Kennedy, J. (2010) Opportunistic customer claiming during service recovery. *Journal of the Academy of Marketing Science* 38, 654–675.

References

Abelson, R.F. (1981) Psychological status of the script concept. *American Psychologist* 36, 715–729.

Andreassen, A.R. (1988) Consumer complaints and redress: what we know and what we don't know. In Maynes, S. (ed.) *The Frontier of Research in the Consumer Interest.* American Council on Consumer Interests, Tarpon Springs, Florida, pp. 675–722

Baker, M.A. (2016) Managing customer experiences in hotel chains. In: Ivanova, M., Ivanov, S. and Magnini, V.P. (eds) *The Routledge Handbook of Hotel Chain Management.* Routledge, Oxford, pp. 240–250.

Baker, M.A. and Kim, K. (2016) Other customer service failures: emotions, impacts, and attributions. *Journal of Hospitality and Tourism Research* DOI: 1096348016671394.

Baker, M.A. and Magnini, V.P. (2016) The evolution of services marketing, hospitality marketing and building the constituency model for hospitality marketing. *International Journal of Contemporary Hospitality Management* 28, 1510–1534.

Baker, M.A., Magnini, V.P. and Perdue, R.R. (2012) Opportunistic customer complaining: causes, consequences, and managerial alternatives. *International Journal of Hospitality Management* 31, 295–303.

Bandura, A. (1977) *Social Learning Theory*. Prentice Hall, Englewood Cliffs, New Jersey.

Bateson, J. (2002) Are your customers good enough for your service business? *Academy of Management Executive* 16, 110–120.

Bennett, R. (1997) Anger, catharsis and purchasing behavior following aggressive customer complaints. *Journal of Consumer Marketing* 14, 156–172.

Biddle, B.J. (1986) Recent developments in role theory. *Annual Review of Sociology* 12, 67–92.

Bies, R.J. and Moag, J.S. (1986) Interactional justice: communication criteria of fairness. *Research on Negotiation in Organizations* 1, 43–55.

Bitner, M.J., Booms, B.H. and Tetreault, S.M. (1990) The service encounter: diagnosing favorable and unfavorable incidents. *Journal of Marketing* 54, 71–84.

Bitner, M.J., Booms, B.H. and Mohr, L.A. (1994) Critical service encounters: the employee's viewpoint. *Journal of Marketing* 58, 95–106.

Blodgett, J.G., Hill, D.J. and Tax, S.S. (1997) The effects of distributive, procedural, and interactional justice on post complaint behavior. *Journal of Retailing* 73, 185–210.

Cheng, Y.H., Chang, C.J., Chuang, S.C. and Liao, Y.W. (2015) Guilt no longer a sin: the effect of guilt in the service recovery paradox. *Journal of Service Theory and Practice* 25, 836–853.

Colquitt, J.A. (2001) On the dimensionality of organizational justice: a construct validation of a measure. *Journal of Applied Psychology* 86, 386–400.

Cronin, J.J. Jr and Taylor, S.A. (1994) SERVPERF versus SERVQUAL: reconciling performance-based and perceptions-minus-expectations measurement of service quality. *The Journal of Marketing* 58, 125–131.

Cropanzano, R., Goldman, B. and Folger, R. (2003) Deontic justice: the role of moral principles in workplace fairness. *Journal of Organizational Behavior* 24, 1019–1024.

Cropanzano, R., Stein, J. and Nadisic, T. (2011) *Social Justice and the Experience of Emotion*. Routledge, New York.

de Matos, C.A., Henrique, J.L. and Rossi, C.A.V. (2007) Service recovery paradox: a meta-analysis. *Journal of Service Research* 10, 60–77.

Donovan, D., Brown, T.J. and Mowen, J.C. (2004) Internal benefits of service-worker-customer: job satisfaction, commitment, and organizational citizenship behaviors. *Journal of Marketing* 68, 128–146.

Ganesan, S. (1994) Determinants of long-term orientation in buyer-seller relationships. *Journal of Marketing* 58, 1–19.

Giebelhausen, M., Robinson, S.G., Sirianni, N.J. and Brady, M.K. (2014) Touch versus tech: when technology functions as a barrier or a benefit to service encounters. *Journal of Marketing* 78, 113–124.

Grind, K. (2013) Retailer REI ends era of many happy returns. *The Wall Street Journal* 15 September (http://www.wsj.com/articles/SB10001424127887324549004579068991226997928) Accessed 10 October 2016.

Harris, L. and Reynolds, K. (2003) The consequences of dysfunctional customer behavior. *Journal of Service Research* 6, 144–161.

Hess, R.L., Ganesan, S. and Klein, N.M. (2003) Service failure and recovery: the impact of relationship factors on customer satisfaction. *Journal of the Academy of Marketing Science* 31, 127–145.

Hoffman, D., Kelley, S. and Rotalsky, H. (1995) Tracking service failures and employee recovery efforts. *Journal of Services Marketing* 9, 49–61.

Holt, D. (2002) Why do brands cause trouble? A dialectical theory of consumer culture and branding. *Journal of Consumer Research* 29, 70–90.

Karande, K., Magnini, V.P. and Tam, L. (2007) Recovery voice and satisfaction after service failure: an experimental investigation of mediating and moderating factors. *Journal of Service Research* 10, 187–203.

Kelley, H.H. and Michela, J.L. (1980) Attribution theory and research. *Annual Review of Psychology* 31, 457–501.

Magnini, V.P., Ford, J.B., Markowski, E.P. and Honeycutt, E.D. Jr (2007) The service recovery paradox: justifiable theory or smoldering myth? *Journal of Services Marketing* 21, 213–225.

Mattila, A.S. and Ro, H. (2008) Customer satisfaction, service failure, and service recovery. In: Oh, H. and Pizam, A. (eds) *Handbook of Hospitality Marketing Management*. Butterworth-Heinemann, Oxford, pp. 297–323.

Mattila, A., Hanks, L. and Wang, C. (2014) Others service experiences: emotions, perceived justice, and behavior. *European Journal of Marketing* 48, 552–571.

Maxham, J. III and Netemeyer, R. (2002) A longitudinal study of complaining customers' evaluations of multiple service failures and recovery efforts. *Journal of Marketing* 66, 57–71.

McDougall, G.H. and Levesque, T.J. (1998) The effectiveness of recovery strategies after service failure: an experiment in the hospitality industry. *Journal of Hospitality and Leisure Marketing* 5, 27–49.

Mohr, L.A. and Bitner, M.J. (1991) Mutual understanding between customers and employees in service encounters. In: Holman, R.H. and Solomon, M.R. (eds) *Advances in Consumer Research*, Vol. 18. Association for Consumer Research, Provo, Utah, pp. 611–617.

Oliver, R.L. (1977) Effect of expectation and disconfirmation on post exposure product evaluations: an alternative interpretation. *Journal of Applied Psychology* 62, 480–486.

Oliver, R.L. (1993) Cognitive, affective, and attribute bases of the satisfaction response. *Journal of Consumer Research* 20, 418–430.

Nguyen, H., Groth, M., Walsh, G. and Hennig Thurau, T. (2014) The impact of service scripts on customer citizenship behavior and the moderating role of employee customer orientation. *Psychology and Marketing* 31, 1096–1109.

Palmer, A., Beggs, R. and Keown-McMullan, C. (2000) Equity and repurchase intention following service failure. *Journal of Services Marketing* 14, 513–526.

Parasuraman, A., Zeithaml, V. and Berry, L.L. (1985) A conceptual model of service quality and its implications for future research. *Journal of Marketing* 49, 41–50.

Rafaeli, A., Ziklik, L. and Douce, L. (2008) The impact of call center employees' customer orientation behaviors on service quality. *Journal of Service Research* 10, 239–255.

Reynolds, K. and Harris, L. (2005) When service failure is not service failure: an exploration of the forms and motives of opportunistic customer complaining. *Journal of Services Marketing* 19, 321–335.

Ringberg, T., Odekerken-Schroder, G. and Christensen, G.L. (2007) A cultural models approach to service recovery. *Journal of Marketing* 71, 194–214.

Robertson, N. and Shaw, R.N. (2009) Predicting the likelihood of voiced complaints in the self-service technology context. *Journal of Service Research* 12, 100–116.

Rupp, D.E. and Spencer, S. (2006) When customers lash out: the effects of customers' interactional injustice on emotional labor and the mediating role of discrete emotions. *Journal of Applied Psychology* 91, 971–978.

Rupp, D.E., McCance, A.S., Spencer, S. and Sonntag, K. (2008) Customer (in)justice and emotional labor: the role of perspective taking, anger, and emotional regulation. *Journal of Management* 34, 903–924.

Smith, A.K. and Bolton, R.N. (1998) An experimental investigation of customer reactions to service failure and recovery encounters: paradox or peril? *Journal of Service Research* 1, 65–81.

Smith, A., Bolton, R.N. and Wagner, J. (1999) A model of customer satisfaction with service encounters involving failure and recovery. *Journal of Marketing Research* 36, 356–372.

Solomon, M.R., Surprenant, C., Czepiel, J.A. and Guttmann, E.G. (1985) A role theory perspective on dyadic interactions: the service encounter. *Journal of Marketing* 49, 99–111.

Sparks, B. and McColl-Kennedy, J. (2001) Justice strategy options for increased customer satisfaction in a service recovery setting. *Journal of Business Research* 54, 209–218.

Spencer, S. and Rupp, D.E. (2009) Angry, guilty, and conflicted: injustice toward coworkers heightens emotional labor through cognitive and emotional mechanisms. *Journal of Applied Psychology* 94, 429–444.

Spreng, R.A., Harrell, G.D. and MacKoy, R.D. (1995) Service recovery. *Journal of Services Marketing* 9, 15–23.

Susskind, A. (2005) A content analysis of consumer complaints, remedies, and repatronage intentions regarding dissatisfying service experiences. *Journal of Hospitality and Tourism Research* 29, 150–169.

Tax, S.S., Brown, S.W. and Chandrashekaran, M. (1998) Customer evaluations of service complaint experiences: implications for relationship marketing. *Journal of Marketing* 62, 60–76.

Tu, C.H. (2000) On-line learning migration: from social learning theory to social presence theory in a CMC environment. *Journal of Network and Computer Applications* 23, 27–37.

Walsh, G., Gouthier, M., Gremler, D.D. and Brach, S. (2012) What the eye does not see, the mind cannot reject: can call center location explain differences in customer evaluations? *International Business Review* 21, 957–967.

Wirtz, J. and Mattila, A. (2001) Exploring the role of alternative perceived performance measures and needs-congruency in the consumer satisfaction process. *Journal of Consumer Psychology* 11, 181–192.

Wirtz, J. and McColl-Kennedy, J. (2010) Opportunistic customer claiming during service recovery. *Journal of the Academy of Marketing Science* 38, 654–675.

4 Emotions and Emotional Abilities in Service Failures and Recovery

ERDOGAN KOC, GULNIL AYDIN, AYBENIZ AKDENIZ AR
AND HAKAN BOZ

Learning Objectives

After reading this chapter, you should be able to:

- Understand basic emotions people have.
- Explain the relationship between emotions, service encounters, service failures and recovery.
- Explain the components of emotional intelligence in relation to service encounters.
- Understand the difference between surface acting and deep acting and their implications for the customer and for the individual service employee.
- Understand and explain how tourism and hospitality businesses may benefit from recruiting staff with emotional intelligence and emotional labour.

4.1 Introduction

Human beings are needs-driven. They have fundamental needs for subsistence, protection, affection, understanding, participation, leisure, creation, identity and freedom (Max-Neef *et al.*, 1991). Each of these needs can be categorized along the existential dimensions of being (qualities), having (things), doing (actions) and interacting (settings). When any of the above needs are not satisfied, human beings feel deprived and tense (Koc, 2016). Feelings are mental experiences of body states that signify a physiological need (i.e. they are mental experiences that accompany a change in body state such as hunger – or increasing level of hunger when a customer is kept waiting for his dinner), which arise as the brain interprets emotion (Damasio and Carvalho, 2013, p. 143). While in general it is believed that feelings are sparked by emotions, it may work other the way around, i.e. feelings may spark emotions too. For example, just thinking about a rude service employee can trigger an emotional response of anger.

From a consumption perspective, the main motivation behind purchasing and consumption is the satisfaction of needs to reduce tension and reach homeostasis, a state of physiological and psychological equilibrium. Service failures delay gratification and increase tensions people may have. For this reason, while customers engage in service encounters to satisfy their needs, service failures occurring during these service encounters work against reaching satisfaction and gratification.

As service encounters can be strongly emotion-laden and they take place in a social servicescape (Tombs and McColl-Kennedy, 2003), within which frequent and intense social interactions occur, service providers need to understand customers' emotions and be able to recruit staff with emotional abilities. Following an explanation of emotions, this chapter focuses on two emotional ability models: Emotional Intelligence (EI) and Emotional Labour (EL). Employees with high EI and EL scores can manage service encounters better and are more equipped to handle and deal with service failures.

4.2 Emotions

The number of signals coming from the limbic system (the emotional part of the human brain) to the frontal cortex (the rational part of the human brain) is ten times higher than signals heading the opposite way (Hawkins and Blakeslee, 2004). Hence, it could be argued that the human brain has a tendency to do more emotional processing than rational processing (Amaral *et al.*, 1992; McDonald, 1998; Baker *et al.*, 2006). This also means that, contrary to earlier belief, consumers in general go through a feel–think–do hierarchy, rather than a think–feel–do hierarchy (Koc, 2016). In other words, emotions can significantly influence customers' purchasing and consumption processes. Though largely ignored in the past (Stacey, 2003), the study of emotions is currently attracting a growing amount of attention, not only from academics but also from practitioners.

An emotion can be defined as an organized psychophysiological reaction to the appraisal of ongoing relationships with the environment (Scherer, 2003). According to the expectancy disconfirmation paradigm explained in Chapter 3 (this volume), customer satisfaction is the consequence of an evaluation process in which the customer judges how the service is performed against the expectations s/he has. When the expectancy is confirmed, the customer is satisfied and s/he develops positive emotions. On the other hand, when the expectancy is disconfirmed, the customer develops negative emotions.

Emotions can be caused by internal stimuli such as body states (e.g. pain or hunger) and external stimuli such as the feeling of disappointment or anger after a service failure. Service failures may act both as external stimuli or internal stimuli, e.g. as in the case of a tired customer having an unnecessarily long wait to check in. Chapter 12 (this volume) explains how people perceive different settings of waiting and develop emotions accordingly.

Moreover, emotions can be considered as either states or processes (Robinson, 2004). When considered as a state (such as being angry after a service failure), an emotion is a type of mental state interacting with other mental states and it causes certain outward behaviours. In the case of a service failure, an angry customer may shout at the service provider and make a complaint or just go quietly away and turn to another service provider. When considered as a process, an emotion can be viewed as having two phases. The early phase of the emotion is the period between the perception of the stimulus or an event and the triggering of the bodily response. The latter phase of the emotion is about the bodily response in the form of changes in the heart rate, blood pressure, facial expression, etc. Emotions can be classified along the positive–negative spectrum and activated and deactivated dimensions (Russell, 2003) (Table 4.1). In service encounters, while positive emotions (whether activated or deactivated) can be associated

---

Table 4.1. Types of emotions. (From Russell, 2003.)

Emotions	Positive	Negative
Activated	Joyful, happy, playful	Anxious, angry, tense
Deactivated	Relaxed, tranquil, serene	Sad, ashamed, grieving

with customer satisfaction, negative emotions can be associated with customer dissatisfaction occurring as a result of service failures or inefficient service recoveries.

Verduyn and Lavrijsen's (2015) study shows that people may place a greater significance on negative feelings. According to Verduyn and Lavrijsen (2015), the feeling of sadness is the longest-lasting feeling in the human mind. As Kahneman and Tversky's (1979) Prospect Theory suggests, people place a much greater significance on losing than winning. This may mean that a customer's feelings of frustration and unhappiness arising as a result of poor service are much stronger than the feelings of happiness and joy arising as a result of a satisfactory service. This is probably why customers tell an average of nine people about their good service experiences and sixteen people about their poor service experiences (TARP, 2007). Hence expectancy confirmation is not something tourism and hospitality businesses should strive to achieve. Tourism and hospitality businesses are recommended to aim for customer delightment, i.e. surprising a customer by exceeding her/his expectations, hence causing a positive emotional reaction. Customer delightment is related to the concept of service recovery paradox, explained in Chapter 3 (this volume). The main reason for the service recovery paradox is the lowering of expectations by the customer after a service failure. A service failure causes the individual customer to lower her/his expectations and creates a state similar to losing described in Kahneman and Tversky's (1979) Prospect Theory. Then, when the service is recovered eventually, the customer's expectations are significantly surpassed, causing a feeling of delight and joy.

4.3 Measurement of Emotions

Emotions are complex phenomena and hence difficult to understand. Scholars have developed several scales to measure emotions (e.g. Izard, 1971; Mehrabian and Russell, 1974; Plutchik, 1980; Edell and Burke, 1987; Batra and Holbrook, 1990). Table 4.2 demonstrates some of the scales used to measure emotions during service encounters (Schoefer and Diamantopoulos, 2008).

Although traditional data collection methods such as surveys, interviews and focus group studies have been used extensively to measure emotions over the past decades, there are strong criticisms of these methods because of their inherent weaknesses. Data collected through the accounts and evaluations of participants in several studies may not reflect the actual truth (Koc and Boz, 2014a) because of biased responses, analyses and interpretations. As a consequence, recommendations based on these responses, analyses and interpretations may mislead tourism and hospitality practitioners. A wide variety of factors may play a role in making data and outcomes unusable when collected through traditional data collection methods, but there are two clear reasons. First, participants in a study may have emotions and motives they themselves may not be aware

Table 4.2. Scales for measuring emotions in service encounters.

Scales	Main features	Related research
Differential Emotions Scale (DES/DES II)	Consists of both positive and negative dimensions, though concentrates more on negative emotions. DES II consists of 30 items. Developed mainly to understand and evaluate a situation in terms of its negativity or positivity.	Izard (1971)
Pleasure, Arousal, Dominance (PAD) Scale	Measures emotional reactions towards marketing stimuli (e.g. the service atmosphere).	Russell and Mehrabian (1977)
Positive Affect/ Negative Affect (PANAS) Scale	Takes negative affects (such as fear, scare, unhappiness, distress, stress, angriness, shame, guilt, hostility) and positive affects (eagerness, curiosity, determination, vividness, agility, activeness, strength, carefulness, excitement) into consideration.	Watson *et al.* (1988)
Consumption Emotions Set (CES)	Consists of emotions such as anger, dissatisfaction, anxiety and unhappiness based on consumption experiences.	Richins (1997)
Net Emotional Response Strength (NERS)	Provides a classification of negative and positive emotions.	Hansen *et al.* (2006)
Emotions During Service Recovery Encounters (ESRE)	Measures positive emotions of satisfaction and interest and negative emotions of dissatisfaction and anxiety.	Schoefer and Diamantopolous (2008)

of (Koc and Boz, 2014b) and people often find it difficult to describe their emotions (Simão *et al.*, 2008). Second, in many instances people may engage in impression management, a goal-directed conscious or unconscious effort to influence the perceptions of others through regulating and controlling information in social interaction (Goffman, 1959).

According to Braidot (2005), traditional data collection methods are not ideal ways to explore people's emotions because it is difficult to describe in exact words emotions and responses such as amusement, anger, contempt, contentment, disgust, distress, embarrassment, excitement, fear, guilt, pride, joy, relief, satisfaction, sensory pleasure and shame, which may be experienced by an individual customer. Braidot (2005) argues that researchers would be trying to ask the conscious mind about what the unconscious mind recorded to translate into language that accurately reflects the phenomenon. Several researchers (Kasser and Ryan, 1996; Tung and Ritchie, 2011; Gnoth and Matteucci, 2014) have demonstrated that there are serious problems of recall when people were asked how they thought and felt about the experiences they have had.

Koc and Boz (2014b) coined the term 'psychoneurobiochemistry' to refer to a group of psychophysiological factors relating to the disciplines of psychology, neurology, biology and chemistry which may be used to explore consumer behaviour and emotions. The above factors collectively influence consumers' intertwined physiological and psychological existence. Growing interest in psychoneurobiochemistry resulted in the extensive use of psychophysiological or neuromarketing research tools by scholars.

The use of psychophysiological tools, devices or measurements, such as EEG (electro-encephalogram), the eye tracker, fMRI (functional magnetic resonance imaging), heart rate, GSR (galvanic skin response) and various face recognition tools, can ensure objectivity and validity of data collected on customers' emotions. Additionally, the use of a combination of these tools may ensure data triangulation and would be expected to further strengthen the objectivity and validity of the findings (Koc and Boz, 2014a; Boz and Yılmaz, 2017). Figure 4.1 shows the process of measurement of customers' affective states by collecting data through the use of psychophysiological tools. By using various devices, researchers can collect data from the customer's face, hand, body, eye, voice and mouth. Based on the analysis and interpretation of data collected through psychophysiological tools, service businesses may be able to detect and understand the true feelings of customers and design their services in such a way as to reduce the frequency of service failures.

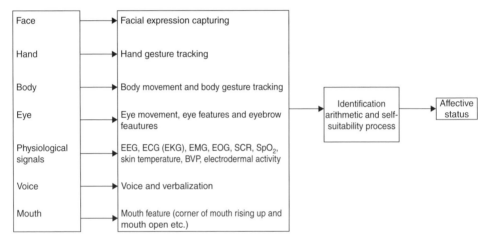

Fig. 4.1. Measurement of affective states. (From Wu *et al.*, 2015.)

4.4   Emotional Abilities: Emotional Intelligence and Emotional Labour

Measurement of customers' emotions is important, but not sufficient. Service personnel also need to have the necessary abilities to detect, understand, control and manage customers' emotions – and their own emotions (Koc, 2003). Two of the main groups of emotional abilities are Emotional Intelligence and Emotional Labour.

4.4.1   Emotional intelligence

Emotional intelligence is the ability or tendency to perceive, understand, regulate, control and manage emotions adaptively in the self and in others (Salovey and Mayer, 1990). Emotional intelligence reflects abilities to join intelligence, empathy and emotions to enhance thought and understanding of interpersonal dynamics (Mayer *et al.*, 2008). Mayer and Salovey's (1997) theory of emotional intelligence suggests that, unlike IQ, skills of emotional intelligence can be acquired and improved through learning and experience.

The skills of emotional intelligence, usually referred to as the five components of emotional intelligence, are self-awareness, self-regulation, motivation, empathy and social skill (Goleman, 2006). The skills can be explained from the perspective of service personnel, service encounters and service quality dimensions (Table 4.3).

The above explanations show that the skills of emotional intelligence can be instrumental not only in terms of service encounters, service failures and recovery, but also from a wide variety of perspectives relating to services marketing and management. For instance, almost all SERVQUAL dimensions, apart from tangibles, require service employees to have emotional intelligence. There are several research findings to suggest that employees' emotional intelligence can improve overall performance in a business. Studies show that approximately 60% of success in a wide variety of sectors can be attributed to emotional intelligence. A significant proportion of people (90%) who show outstanding success and performance tend to have a high level of emotional intelligence (Bradberry and Greaves, 2006, 2009). According to the World Economic Forum (2015), emotional intelligence is, and will continue be in the coming decade, among the top-ten skills for business success. Chernis (1999) found that sales staff with high emotional intelligence were capable of selling significantly more than sales staff with a lower level of emotional intelligence. Research also showed that employees with a high level of emotional intelligence coped with stress and burnout much better than employees who had low levels of emotional intelligence (Wiens, 2016).

Activity

Visit the websites below to measure your emotional intelligence. Make a personal evaluation based on the outcome. Identify your strengths and weaknesses in terms of your emotional intelligence. Search for ways to reduce your weaknesses and build on your strengths.
https://www.talentsmart.com/products/ei.php?ID=18
http://greatergood.berkeley.edu/ei_quiz/

Tourism and hospitality businesses are recommended to recruit staff with a high level of emotional intelligence and constantly train them to improve their emotional intelligence. Developed by Mayer *et al.* (2003), MSCEIT (Mayer Salovey Caruso Emotional Intelligence Test) is a 41-item scale designed particularly to measure the perceiving of emotions, using emotions to facilitate thought, understanding emotions and managing emotions. Another scale which may be used to measure emotional intelligence is the Emotional Intelligence Competence Model developed by Goleman. Goleman's (2000) model measures the above explained components of emotional intelligence (Table 4.3), i.e. self-awareness, self-regulation, motivation, empathy and social skills.

Table 4.3. Components of emotional ability. (Adapted from Goleman, 2006.)

Skill	Explanation	Characteristics	Relation to service personnel	Relation to SERVQUAL dimensions
Self-awareness	Having a deep understanding of one's emotions, strengths, weaknesses, needs and drives, as well as their effect on others.	Self-confidence, realistic self-assessment, self-deprecating sense of humour.	Ability to understand own role in service encounters. Ability to know own abilities, limits and weaknesses when making claims to solve problems.	Responsiveness Assurance Reliability Empathy
Self-regulation	Ability to control or redirect disruptive impulses and moods and the propensity to suspend judgement – thinking before acting.	Trustworthiness, integrity, comfort with ambiguity, openness to change.	Ability to understand and evaluate service failures. Ability to think and implement new approaches to deal with service failures.	Reliability Responsiveness Assurance Empathy
Motivation	A passion to work for reasons that go beyond money or status, with a propensity to pursue goals with energy and persistence.	Strong desire to achieve, optimism (even in the face of failure), organizational commitment.	Ability to cope with heavy demands of frequent and intense social interactions. Unyielding approach towards service failures. Commitment to service quality and maintaining a strong image of the service business.	Responsiveness Reliability Assurance Empathy

Empathy	Ability to understand the emotional makeup of other people, with skill in treating people according to their emotional reactions.	Provision of customer-oriented service, cross-cultural sensitivity, expertise in building and retaining talent.	Ability to understand the needs and expectations of customers – including customers from other cultures. Service orientation. Empathy towards the feelings of customers during service encounters. Handling complaints and conflicts. Handling difficult customers.	Empathy Responsiveness Assurance Reliability
Social skill	Proficiency in managing relationships and building networks, with an ability to find common ground and build rapport.	Managing relationships and building networks, with an ability to find common ground and build rapport.	Ability to manage social interactions effectively during service encounters. Ability to use help from networks of people from other departments to solve problems.	Responsiveness Assurance Reliability Empathy

4.4.2 Emotional labour

According to Hochschild (1983), emotion arises as a consequence of the physical coordination of the body, the mental planning of actions and the emotional inducement or suppression of feelings. However, emotional labour is the process of managing feelings and expressions to fulfil the emotional requirements of a job. For instance, a waitress in a restaurant or an employee working at the front desk of a hotel is expected to do emotional work, such as smiling, active listening, being responsive and expressing positive emotions to customers. This means that employees are expected to regulate and manage their emotions during their interactions not only with customers but also with peers and superiors as well (Koc, 2010, 2013). Emotional labour requires the expression of feelings which are appropriate and the suppression of feelings which are inappropriate (Hochschild, 1983). Emotional labour can be explained by the anonymous saying: 'There is no market for your emotions. So never advertise your feelings, just display your attitude'. A wide variety of factors may be influential on emotional labour (Table 4.4):

Table 4.4. Factors influential on emotional labour.

Factors	Explanations	Examples
Societal and cultural factors	People in different societies and cultures may perceive the demonstration of emotional labour skills differently.	McDonald's experts found that Russian customers were shocked by the smiling of McDonald's employees. The immediate reaction of Russian customers was 'What is wrong with this person?' (Hofstede et al., 2010).
Job-related factors	Front-stage employees need to have a higher level of emotional labour skills than back-stage employees.	While an unsmiling but talented cook may be tolerated at a hotel, an unsmiling but talented waitress may not be tolerated in the same hotel.
Business atmosphere and organizational factors	The level of customer orientation in the tourism and hospitality business, type and characteristics of the customers served and how busy the tourism and hospitality business is at a particular time.	In a busy restaurant, service employees' emotional labour skills are more often put to the test (Rafaeli and Sutton, 1989; Friedman, 1990; Grandey et al., 2005).
Personal and demographic factors	The ability of an individual service employee to use facial expressions, voice, gestures and body movements to transmit her/his emotions.	Men tend to smile less than women (Ellis and Das, 2011). The manifestation of aggression as a negative emotion occurs with greater intensity and frequency among people with low activity monoamine oxidase gene (MAOA) (McDermott et al., 2009). Thus, these people may be expected to be unable to hide their negative feelings and show positive feelings to customers.

Emotional labour skills become particularly important in instances of service fail-ures and in the ensuing recovery processes because service failures are negative occur-rences. As explained in Chapter 3 (this volume), customers place a significant amount of importance on interactional justice, i.e. how they have been treated and interacted with during the process of service recovery. The emotional labour skills of service employees may be conducive to increasing customers' perceptions of interactional justice during the service recovery processes.

Hochschild (1983) describes jobs involving emotional labour as jobs that:

- require face-to-face or voice-to-voice contact with the customers;
- require the employee to produce an emotional state in another person; and
- allow the employer, through training and supervision, to exercise a degree of control over the emotional activities of employees.

Based on the explanations above, it can be seen that most jobs in tourism and hos-pitality require emotional labour skills from service employees. While front-stage em-ployees, employees with constant and intense interaction with customers, are expected to have a high level of emotional labour skills, back-stage employees are expected to have at least a reasonable level of emotional labour skills.

The dimensions of emotional labour are surface acting and deep acting (Hochschild, 1983; Diefendorff et al., 2005). Surface acting can be explained as the act of service employees hiding their real feelings and exhibiting different emotions to others in the business. This implies that employees pretend to have certain emotions they do not have at a particular moment (Ashforth and Humphrey, 1993; Basim and Begenirbas, 2012). Employees use words, mimicry and body language to demonstrate the positive emotions they are expected to show.

However, when the service employee engages in deep acting s/he tries to feel the expected/required emotions and internalize the emotions because of the role expect-ations. In deep acting, emotions are actively encouraged, suppressed or shaped (Basim and Begenirbas, 2012). This means that the service employee tries to internalize and feel those particular behaviours, at the expense of empathy skills (Rupp et al., 2008). In other words, when deep acting the service employee puts herself/himself in the custom-er's place before exhibiting a behaviour, and acts on the basis of her/his expectation of the customer's reaction to her/his potential behaviour (Yilmaz et al., 2015).

According to Morris and Feldman (1996), while dissonance and emotional exhaustion are positively related, they are in contrast with effort. When a service em-ployee fakes her/his emotions (surface acting), s/he will eventually feel emotionally exhausted and this will reduce job satisfaction. Based on role conflict theory, it is assumed that there are two positive correlations between emotional dissonance, emotional exhaustion, emotional effort and job satisfaction. While service employees who display a fake emotion (surface acting) will experience a higher level of emo-tional exhaustion and lower level of job satisfaction, service employees who display genuine emotion (deep acting) will experience a lower level of emotional exhaustion and higher level of job satisfaction (Chu, 2002). As emotional intelligence can be instrumental in coping with stress and employee burnout (Wiens, 2016), it could help eliminate the side effects of emotional labour, i.e. when service employees en-gage in surface acting and deep acting.

Service failures and recovery processes can make employees feel nervous and stressed. In the event of service failures, service employees may feel stress for a number of reasons (Rafaeli and Sutton, 1989; Koc and Bozkurt, 2017). In the instance of a service failure, service personnel may be expected to show more effort, carry out additional tasks and carry out tasks they may be unfamiliar with. In the instance of service failure, the individual service employee may have to spend additional time to recover the service and hence lag behind in assigned tasks, deal with extended queues and cope with a backlog of work. As a consequence, s/he may have to forego breaks and meals and leave work late.

The emotional conflict or the contradiction in the process of surface acting has an impact on employees' gestures and actions (Ashforth and Humphrey, 1993; Pugliesi, 1999). The main source of this contradiction is the need to display positive behaviours while being under the influence of a negative mood and negative emotions. In a service failure situation when there are contradictions between his or her actual mood and emotions and the required emotions, service employees are expected to ignore the difference and display the required positive emotions (Theodosius, 2008). Even in the case of a service failure beyond her/his control, the service employee is expected to be calm, though s/he is angry, be relaxed, though s/he is tense and be enthusiastic and responsive, though s/he is reluctant to be so. This situation is like an actor playing his role for which he has to show the audience that he is a bad person, though he may not be a bad person at all, and vice versa (Brook, 2009).

5 Conclusion

This chapter has explained the emotions and emotional abilities of people from the perspective of service encounters, service failures and recovery. The explanations show that service employees who have a high level of emotional intelligence and emotional labour can outperform employees who do not. Explanations show that emotional intelligence may be instrumental for developing emotional labour skills, both from the perspective of surface acting and deep acting. Tourism and hospitality businesses are recommended not only to recruit staff with emotional intelligence and emotional labour skills, but also to constantly monitor and train them to improve their level of emotional intelligence and emotional labour.

Questions

1. What are the basic emotions people have? How do these emotions relate to service encounters, service failures and recovery?
2. How can emotions be measured?
3. What is emotional intelligence or emotional quotient? How does it differ from IQ?
4. What are the components of emotional intelligence? How do they relate to service encounters, service failures and recovery?
5. What is emotional labour? What is the difference between surface acting and deep acting?
6. Why is it important to recruit staff with emotional intelligence and emotional labour in tourism and hospitality businesses?

Further Reading

Bradberry, T. and Greaves, J. (2006) *The Emotional Intelligence Quick Book: Everything You Need to Know to Put Your EQ to Work*. Fireside, New York.
Goleman, D. (2006) *Emotional Intelligence*. Bantam, New York.
Hochschild, A. (1983) *The Managed Heart*. University of California Press, Berkeley, California.

References

Amaral, D.G., Price, J.L., Pitkanen, A. and Carmichael, T. (1992) Anatomical organization of the primate amygdaloid complex. In: Aggleton, J. (ed.) *The Amygdala: Neurobiological Aspects of Emotion, Memory, and Mental Dysfunction*. Wiley-Liss, New York, pp. 1–66.
Ashforth, B.E. and Humphrey, R.H. (1993) Emotional labor in service roles: the influence of identity. *The Academy of Management Review* 18, 88–115.
Baker, D., Greenberg, C. and Hemingway, C. (2006) *What Happy Companies Know*. Pearson Education, Upper Saddle River, New Jersey.
Basim, N. and Begenirbas, M. (2012) Çalısmayasamındaduygusalemek: Birölçekuyarlamacalısması [Emotional labor in work life: a study of scale adaptation]. *Yönetim ve Ekonomi* 19, 77–90.
Batra, R. and Holbrook, M.B. (1990) Developing a typology of affective responses to advertising. *Psychology & Marketing* 7, 11–25.
Boz, H. and Yılmaz, O. (2017) An eye tracker analysis of the influence of applicant attractiveness on employee recruitment process: a neuromarketing study. *Ecoforum Journal* 6, 354–361.
Bradberry, T. and Greaves, J. (2006) *The Emotional Intelligence Quick Book: Everything You Need to Know to Put Your EQ to Work*. Fireside, New York.
Bradberry, T. and Greaves, J. (2009) Emotional Intelligence 2.0. TalentSmart, San Diego, California.
Braidot, N. (2005) *Neuromarketing/Neuroeconomia y negocios.* E Puerto NORTE-SUR, Madrid.
Brook, P. (2009) In critical defence of 'emotional labour': refuting Bolton's critique of Hochschild's concept. *Work, Employment and Society* 23, 531–548.
Chernis, C. (1999) *The Business Case for Emotional Intelligence*. Consortium for Research on Emotional Intelligence in Organizations. Available at: http://www.eiconsortium.org/reports/business_case_for_ei.html (accessed 5 October 2016).
Chu, K.H.L. (2002) The effects of emotional labor on employee work outcomes. Doctoral dissertation, Virginia Polytechnic Institute and State University, Blacksburg, Virginia.
Damasio, A. and Carvalho, G.B. (2013) The nature of feelings: evolutionary and neurobiological origins. *Nature Reviews Neuroscience* 14, 143–152.
Diefendorff, J.M., Croyle, M.H. and Gosserand, R.H. (2005) The dimensionality and antecedents of emotional labor strategies. *Journal of Vocational Behavior* 66, 339–357.

Edell, J.A. and Burke, M.C. (1987) The power of feelings in understanding advertising effects. *Journal of Consumer Research* 14(3), 421–433.

Ellis, L. and Das, S. (2011) Sex differences in smiling and other photographed traits: a theoretical assessment. *Journal of Biosocial Science* 43, 345–351.

Friedman, J. (1990) Being in the world: globalization and localization. *Theory, Culture & Society* 7, 311–328.

Gnoth, J. and Matteucci, X. (2014) A phenomenological view of the behavioural tourism research literature. *International Journal of Culture, Tourism and Hospitality Research* 8, 3–21.

Goffman, E. (1959) The moral career of the mental patient. *Psychiatry* 22, 123–142.

Goleman, D. (2000) Leadership that gets results. *Harvard Business Review* 78, 4–17.

Goleman, D. (2006) *Emotional Intelligence*. Bantam, New York.

Grandey, A.A., Fisk, G.M., Mattila, A.S., Jansen, K.J. and Sideman, L.A. (2005) Is 'service with a smile' enough? Authenticity of positive displays during service encounters. *Organizational Behavior and Human Decision Processes* 96, 38–55.

Hansen, F., Percy, L. and Lundsteen, S. (2006) Outstanding brands "emotionally speaking". *European Advances in Consumer Research* 6, 511–515.

Hawkins, J. and Blakeslee, S. (2004) *On Intelligence*. Times Books, New York.

Hochschild, A. (1983) *The Managed Heart*. University of California Press, Berkeley, California.

Hofstede, G., Hofstede, G.J. and Minkov, M. (2010) *Cultures and Organizations: Software of the Mind*, rev. 3rd edn. McGraw-Hill, New York.

Izard, C.E. (1971) *The Face of Emotion*. Appleton-Century-Crofts, East Norwalk, Connecticut.

Kahneman, D. and Tversky, A. (1979) Prospect theory: an analysis of decision under risk. *Econometrica* XLVII, 263–291.

Kasser, T. and Ryan, R.M. (1996) Further examining the American dream: differential correlates of intrinsic and extrinsic goals. *Personality and Social Psychology Bulletin* 22, 280–287.

Koc, E. (2003) The role and potential of travel agency staff as a marketing communications tool. *Tourism Analysis* 8, 105–111.

Koc, E. (2010) Services and conflict management: cultural and European integration perspectives. *International Journal of Intercultural Relations* 34, 88–96.

Koc, E. (2013) Power distance and its implications for upward communication and empowerment: crisis management and recovery in hospitality services. *The International Journal of Human Resource Management* 24, 3681–3696.

Koc, E. (2016) *Tüketici Davranışı ve Pazarlama Stratejileri*, 7. Seçkin Yayıncılık, Ankara.

Koc, E. and Boz, H. (2014a) Triangulation in tourism research: a bibliometric study of top three tourism journals. *Tourism Management Perspectives* 12, 9–14.

Koc, E. and Boz, H. (2014b) Psychoneurobiochemistry of tourism marketing. *Tourism Management* 44, 140–148.

Koc, E. and Bozkurt, G.S. (2017) Hospitality employees' future expectations: dissatisfaction, stress and burnout. *International Journal of Hospitality and Tourism Administration* (Article in press).

Max-Neef, M.A., Elizalde, A. and Hopenhayn, M.M. (1991) *Human Scale Development: Conception, Application and Further Reflections*. Apex, New York.

Mayer, J.D. and Salovey, P. (1997) What is emotional intelligence? In: Salovey, P. and Sluyter, D. (eds) *Emotional Development and Emotional Intelligence: Implications for Educators*. Basic Books, New York, pp. 3–31.

Mayer, J.D., Salovey, P., Caruso, D.R. and Sitarenios, G. (2003) Measuring emotional intelligence with the MSCEIT V2.0. *Emotion* 3, 97–105.

Mayer, J.D., Roberts, R.D. and Barsade, S.G. (2008) Human abilities: emotional intelligence. *Annual Review of Psychology* 59, 507–536.

McDermott, R., Tingley, D., Cowden, J., Frazzetto, G. and Johnson, D.D.P. (2009) Monoamine oxidase A gene (MAOA) predicts behavioral aggression following provocation. *Proceedings of the National Academy of Sciences USA* 106, 2118–23.

McDonald, J.F. (1998) Transposable elements, gene silencing and macroevolution. *Trends in Ecology and Evolution* 13, 94–95.

Mehrabian, A. and Russell, J.A. (1974) *An Approach to Environmental Psychology*. The MIT Press, Cambridge, Massachusetts.

Morris, J.A. and Feldman, D.C. (1996) The dimensions, antecedents, and consequences of emotional labor. *Academy of Management Review* 21, 986–1010.

Plutchik, R. (1980) A general psychoevolutionary theory of emotion. *Theories of Emotion* 1, 3–31.

Pugliesi, K. (1999) The consequences of emotional labor: effects on work stress, job satisfaction, and well-being. *Motivation and Emotion* 23, 125–154.

Rafaeli, A. and Sutton, R.I. (1989) The expression of emotion in organizational life. *Research in Organizational Behavior* 11, 1–42.

Richins, M.L. (1997) Measuring emotions in the consumption experience. *Journal of Consumer Research* 24, 127–146.

Robinson, J.M. (2004) Emotion: biological fact or social construction. In: Robert, C.S. (ed.) *Thinking about Feeling: Contemporary Philosophers on Emotions*. Oxford University Press, Oxford, pp. 28–44.

Rupp, D.E., McCance, A.S., Spencer, S. and Sonntag, K. (2008) Customer (in)justice and emotional labor: the role of perspective taking, anger, and emotional regulation. *Journal of Management* 34, 903–924.

Russell, J.A. (2003) Core affect and the psychological construction of emotion. *Psychological Review* 110, 145–172.

Salovey, P. and Mayer, J.D. (1990) Emotional intelligence. *Imagination, Cognition and Personality* 9, 185–211.

Scherer, K.R. (2003) Vocal communication of emotion: a review of research paradigms. *Speech Communication* 40, 227–256.

Schoefer, K. and Diamantopoulos, A. (2008) The role of emotions in translating perceptions of (in) justice into post complaint behavioral responses. *Journal of Service Research* 11, 91–103.

Simão, C.P., Justo, M.G. and Martins, A.T. (2008) Recognizing facial expressions of social emotions: do males and females differ? *Psicologia* 22, 71–85.

Stacey, M. (2003) *The Sociology of Health and Healing: A Textbook*. Routledge, London.

TARP (Technical Assistance Research Programs Institute) (2007) *Consumer Complaint Handling in America: An Update Study*. White House Office of Consumer Affairs, Washington, DC.

Theodosius, C. (2008). *Emotional Labour in Health Care: The Unmanaged Heart of Nursing*. Routledge, London.

Tombs, A. and McColl-Kennedy, J.R. (2003) Social-servicescape conceptual model. *Marketing Theory* 3, 447–475.

Tung, V.W.S. and Ritchie, J.R.B. (2011) Exploring the essence of memorable tourism experiences. *Annals of Tourism Research* 38, 1367–1386.

Verduyn, P. and Lavrijsen, S. (2015) Which emotions last longest and why: the role of event importance and rumination. *Motivation and Emotion* 39, 119–127.

Watson, D., Clark, L.A. and Tellegen, A. (1988) Development and validation of brief measures of positive and negative affect: The PANAS Scales. *Journal of Personality and Social Psychology* 54, 1063–1070.

Wiens, K.J. (2016) Leading through burnout: the influence of emotional intelligence on the ability of executive level physician leaders to cope with occupational stress and burnout. Dissertation, University of Pennsylvania, Philadelphia, Pennsylvania.

World Economic Forum (2015) *World Economic Forum, Future of Jobs Report*. Available at: http://www3.weforum.org/docs/WEF_Future_of_Jobs.pdf (accessed 10 October 2016).

Wu, C.H., Huang, Y.M. and Hwang, J.P. (2015) Review of affective computing in education/ learning: trends and challenges. *British Journal of Educational Technology* 46(5), 1–20.

Yilmaz, K., Altinkurt, Y., Guner, M. and Sen, B. (2015) The relationship between teachers' emotional labor and burnout level. *Eurasian Journal of Educational Research* 59, 75–90.

---

5 Memorable Service Experiences: A Service Failure and Recovery Perspective

JONG-HYEONG KIM

Learning Objectives

After reading this chapter, you should be able to:

- Understand the memorable nature of service failure.
- Understand the influence of memory on consumer behaviour.
- Identify factors contributing to memorability of service failure.
- Understand the importance of provision of service recovery.
- Understand memory bias: fading affect bias.

5.1 Introduction

Service failures in the hospitality and tourism industry often occur because of the inconsistent nature of the service products, coupled with the inevitability of human errors (Kim and Jang, 2016; Kim, 2016). Researchers have noted that service failures lead to undesirable future consumer behaviour. For example, Kim and Chen (2010) found that dissatisfied customers who experienced service failures would engage in any one or a combination of the following actions: exit (i.e. never return), complaints and negative word-of-mouth. While the service failure literature covers diverse issues, such as consumer satisfaction (Sparks and Browning, 2010; Iglesias, 2009), complaint behaviours (Bodey and Grace, 2006; Ekiz and Au, 2011; Namkung *et al.*, 2011) and service recoveries (Kim *et al.*, 2009; Matos *et al.*, 2011; Kwon and Jang, 2012; Fu *et al.*, 2015), few studies have discussed the mechanism through which negative service experiences affect future behaviour. Therefore, this chapter aims to discuss the memorable nature of service failures that mediates consumer behaviour, with a focus on the working mechanisms of the human brain.

5.2 Memorable Nature of Service Failure

Researchers in the field of memory have noted that individuals are likely to remember emotional information vividly (Kensinger *et al.*, 2007). They have found that emotional events are more often associated with field memories in which the individual

© CAB International 2017. *Service Failures and Recovery in Tourism and Hospitality: A Practical Manual* (ed. E. Koc)

'sees' the event from his or her point of view and are less often associated with observer memories in which the individual engaged in the event as an observer. Neuroscientists have reasoned that the hippocampus and surrounding cortices are needed for the retrieval of both neutral and emotionally laden material, and memory performance is boosted by arousal because the amygdala becomes involved (Kilpatrick and Cahill, 2003). Furthermore, memory researchers have found that emotional stimuli are more strongly associated with increased amygdala activity than neutral stimuli (Davis and Whalen, 2001; Fredrikson and Furmark, 2003). Thus, memory can be enhanced by an emotional stimulus.

Regarding a specific valence of emotion (i.e. positive or negative) that leads to a strong memory, researchers have suggested that negative information receives more processing and contributes more strongly to the final impression than positive information (Baumeister *et al.*, 2001). In support of this notion, researchers have found that a negative valence leads to a stronger memory than a positive valence (Levine and Bluck, 2004; Kensinger *et al.*, 2007). Individuals who had a negative experience of an event remember it with more detail and accuracy than those who had a positive experience. Christianson (1992) suggested that negative emotional events are retained more vividly than ordinary events that occurred at the same time in the past. Based on the above discussion, service failures, which induce an individual's negative emotions, are likely to leave lasting impressions and affect the individual's consequent behaviour.

5.3   Significant Influence of Memory on Consumer Behaviour

Previous studies in various disciplines have investigated the effect of memory on consumer behaviour. For example, marketing researchers have noted that autobiographical memories mediate consumer behaviour (e.g. Ratnayake *et al.*, 2010). They reasoned that (i) individuals' level of motivation to purchase a product and their involvement with a product are high when information is drawn from their experiences and (ii) individuals perceive their recalled experiences as highly credible. Thus, individuals are likely to rely on their experiences during choice processing and decision-making about future consumer behaviours (Kerstetter and Cho, 2004). Numerous empirical studies have supported this notion (Kozak, 2001; Wirtz *et al.*, 2003; Kim and Jang, 2014; Adongo *et al.*, 2015). For example, examining the comparative influence of predicted, on-site and remembered experience of a vacation on future behavioural intention, Wirtz *et al.* (2003) reported that remembered experiences are the best predictor of this intention. Moreover, Adongo *et al.* (2015) reported that memorable local food experiences influence tourists' intentions to engage in word-of-mouth publicity.

5.4   Factors Contributing to Memorability of Service Failure

As discussed above, customers' memories of service experiences significantly affect future behaviour. Service failures that result in negative emotion are likely to be better remembered. Thus, the following sections discuss the characteristics of service failures that lead to a strong memory of the experience.

5.4.1 Intensity of negative emotion

Previous studies on arousal and memory have suggested that high levels of arousal facilitate memory formation and lead to long-term retention (e.g. Bradley, 1994; Dewhurst and Parry, 2000; Kensinger and Corkin, 2003). Researchers have found that emotionally arousing material is recalled more accurately than neutral material (Heuer and Reisberg, 1990; Christianson, 1992; Bradley, 1994). For example, traumatic events are remembered in more detail, involve more emotional content and are recollected more often than other emotional life experiences (e.g. Porter and Birt, 2001; Bohanek et al., 2005). Memory researchers have explained these results by focusing on the attention-grabbing nature of emotional stimuli at the encoding stage (Dolan and Vuilleumier, 2003; Wang et al., 2005). Kensinger et al. (2007) found that attention appears to be focused automatically and preferentially on emotionally arousing stimuli. Dolan and Vuilleumier (2003) found that emotionally arousing stimuli seem to be prioritized to facilitate processing, such that emotional stimuli can be processed even when attention is limited or divided. Besides this attentional explanation, some memory researchers have also noted that emotionally arousing stimuli benefit from effects at other stages of memory processing, such as consolidation and retrieval (e.g. Cahill, 2000; Cahill and McGaugh, 1998; Sharot and Phelps, 2004). For instance, intensely emotional events come to mind more often and are therefore rehearsed and may benefit from special neuronal consolidation processes (Cahill and McGaugh, 1998; Bohanek et al., 2005). A number of laboratory studies that utilized arousing pictures and words supported the above discussion, showing that the negatively arousing content of information enhances the richness associated with a memory (e.g. D'Argembeau and Van der Linden, 2004; MacKay and Ahmetzanov, 2005). For example, researchers have found that the vividness and specificity of autobiographical memory are consistently predicted by the emotional intensity of the events (Talarico et al., 2004).

In tourism and hospitality settings, different types of service failures may result in different levels of negative affect as well as perceived loss (e.g. Weun et al., 2004; Krishna et al., 2011; Piercy and Archer-Brown, 2014; Koc et al., 2017). Customers who experience a service failure are likely to be in emotional states ranging from neutral to extremely negative. Therefore, some researchers have noted that the severity of a service failure can be determined by the magnitude of resulting loss, damage or inconvenience (Blodgett et al., 1993; Krishna et al., 2011). Specifically, Krishna et al. (2011) suggested that the magnitude of a service failure in a restaurant can be calculated based on the magnitude of eight different losses: (i) health loss; (ii) emotional loss; (iii) respect loss; (iv) relationship loss; (v) time loss; (vi) money loss; (vii) comfort loss; and (viii) mental/physical energy loss. They further noted that the magnitude of a service failure decreases from loss (i) to loss (viii). Thus, based on the above discussion, a severe service failure that is accompanied by a greater magnitude of loss would result in a stronger arousal of negative affect and therefore lead to a better memory.

5.4.2 Frequency of occurrence

Memory researchers have reported that the effects of familiarity and frequency on memory consistently lead to strong memorability. For instance, Cox and Cox (1988) suggested that high-frequency stimuli positively affect stimuli evaluations. Thus, individuals' recall and attitude are generally favourable under familiar conditions. Researchers studying the memorability of advertisements corroborated this notion and found that memory retains well-known brand advertising longer than obscure brand advertising (Aravinadkshan and Naik, 2011). Jackson and Raymond (2008) identified the influence of face familiarity on memory. They presented participants with an array of familiar (famous) and unfamiliar faces and then measured the memory of these participants. They found enhanced visual memory for famous faces.

In a recent empirical study, Kim and Jang (2016) tested the influence of frequency on memory in situations of restaurant service failure. They found that a more frequently occurring service failure (i.e. slow service) was remembered better than a less frequently occurring one (i.e. delivery disorder). Researchers have reported common service failure cases in the hospitality setting. For example, Lewis and McCann (2004) identified the following most frequent failure cases in the hotel industry: slow restaurant service, slow check-in/out process, inefficient staff, unfriendly and unhelpful receptionists, low-quality food and beverage products, room not ready on time, having to keep waiting for a table at breakfast, items in the room not working (e.g. television and phone), limited food variety offered and staff not willing to offer help. Silber *et al.* (2009) identified the following most common service failures in a restaurant setting: defects in food (e.g. foreign objects in food), slow service, out-of-stock menu items, food/beverage served at incorrect temperature, wrong cooking method, servers' inappropriate behaviour, wrong order, billing error and food/beverage spillage. These incidents have been identified as frequently occurring service failures in the hospitality industry and are likely to be better remembered. Therefore, restauranteurs should pay more attention to preventing these common service failures.

5.5   Importance of Provision of Service Recovery

Researchers have discussed customers' responses to service failures, including switching behaviours and negative word-of-mouth publicity. Other consequences of service failure include customer dissatisfaction, declining customer confidence in the firm and customer defection (Kelley *et al.*, 1993; Bitner *et al.*, 1994; Boshoff, 1997). As the consequences of service failure impose major threats to the service provider, the topic of service recovery has received much attention over the past few years.

Service recovery is defined as actions taken by the service firm in an attempt to remedy a service failure (Andreassen, 2000). It includes all the actions taken by the management to turn customers' dissatisfaction into satisfaction. The benefits of recovery efforts have been well documented in the literature. For instance, service recoveries can either reinforce customer relationships or compound the failure (Hoffman *et al.*, 1995; Smith *et al.*, 1999). Effective recovery efforts increase customer satisfaction as well as future behavioural intentions, such as repurchase intentions and positive word-of-mouth (e.g. Bitner *et al.*, 1990; Susskind, 2005; Ha and Jang, 2009; Kim *et al.*, 2009; Kwon and Jang, 2012). Mack *et al.* (2000) noted that through successful recovery efforts, a business can regain a dissatisfied customer, gain referrals and save the costs associated with recruiting and retaining a new customer. On the other hand, poor service recovery efforts are viewed as a 'double deviation' or second failure, which can further aggravate the negative perceptions that the customer already has and can lead to considerably higher levels of switching and negative word-of-mouth (Hoffman and Kelley, 2000). Susskind (2005) stated that a low degree of correction coupled with negative service experiences leads to an unresolved service failure. Considering that unresolved customer dissatisfaction may result in negative future behaviours, such as switching and spreading negative word-of-mouth, recovery efforts are arguably the most important management strategy affecting future behaviour in the service sector, where service failures inevitably and frequently occur.

Acknowledging the importance of providing service recovery after a service failure, researchers have attempted to identify the most effective strategies to dissipate consumer anger and dissatisfaction after a service failure (e.g. Susskind, 2005; Kim et al., 2009). For example, employing justice theory, some researchers have focused on identifying appropriate recovery strategies that mitigate the negative effects of different types of failures. They suggested that businesses should ensure their recovery efforts provide benefits that customers believe make up equitably for their losses. The feeling of perceived fairness is intended to counterbalance the negative service experience. Some studies have found that satisfactory service recovery can even turn dissatisfied customers into satisfied and loyal customers via a phenomenon known as the recovery paradox (McCollough and Bharadwaj, 1992; Smith and Bolton, 1998; Tax et al., 1998; Mattila, 1999; Maxham and Netemeyer, 2002). The service recovery paradox refers to a peculiar effect where an excellent recovery can turn angry, frustrated customers into loyal ones. Some studies on recovery performance have found that superior recovery not only mitigates negative consequences from service failures but also increases overall satisfaction with the service (e.g. McCollough and Bharadwaj, 1992; Smith and Bolton, 1998; Maxham and Netemeyer, 2002). Therefore, the overall satisfaction of a customer who experienced a service failure can be even greater than that of a customer who did not experience any failures in the first place.

Researchers have explained this paradoxical increase in satisfaction using different theories such as the expectancy-disconfirmation paradigm (Oliver, 1997; McCollough et al., 2000), script theory (Bitner et al., 1990, 1994; Magnini et al., 2007) and commitment–trust theory in relationship marketing (Moorman et al., 1992; Magnini et al., 2007). According to the disconfirmation paradigm, the service recovery paradox is related to secondary satisfaction in a failure situation. If a customer receives an excellent service recovery that exceeds his or her expectations, positive disconfirmation will occur, resulting in a heightened state of post-satisfaction (Oliver, 1997; McCollough et al., 2000). Script theory suggests that there is a common sequence of acts in service delivery, with both employees and customers sharing similar beliefs regarding the expected order of events and their respective roles in the process (Bitner et al., 1994). Therefore, when a service failure occurs, it is a salient event in the predicted script that leads to increased sensitivity on behalf of the customer regarding the failure and the recovery process. As a result, satisfaction with recovery efforts becomes more important than satisfaction with the initial sequence of service events in influencing the overall level of contentment (Bitner et al., 1990; Magnini et al., 2007). The service recovery paradox can also be explained by the commitment–trust theory in relationship marketing (Morgan and Hunt, 1994). This theory proposes that providing a satisfying recovery to customers who experienced a service failure can enhance customers' trust because they will have confidence in a business that shows enough honesty and integrity to correct a problem. Morgan and Hunt (1994) noted that trust is an integral component in relationship marketing and that it exists when one party has confidence in the other's ability and integrity. As a result, if customers receive a superb recovery, then they will perceive the firm as more reliable (Ganesan, 1994).

Using a real-world example, this chapter presents a case study for a well-known Chinese online travel agency, Ctrip, to demonstrate the successful handling of service failures and its consequences.

Case Study: Ctrip

Event description

China's largest online provider of travel services, Ctrip, is embroiled in a row over flight tickets after it issued a ticket that was illegally exchanged for airline mileage to a Chinese passenger. The passenger, Fu Jingnan, was denied a boarding pass by the airline at Tokyo's Haneda Airport, leaving him in a panic. Fu, who posted about his ordeal online, said he was not allowed to board the flight because his ticket from Tokyo to Beijing – bought on Ctrip – was invalid. Fu, who claimed to be a gaming software engineer, said on his microblogging website that the airport police asked him to 'cooperate with the investigation' because his ticket was redeemed from another traveller's mileage.

Fu contacted Ctrip, which put him in touch with the agent who sold him the ticket. The Ctrip-approved agent got him a new ticket on another Japanese carrier, but as luck would have it, he was denied a boarding pass again – for the very same reason. 'I felt humiliated after being investigated for three hours at the Japanese airport and nearly detained,' Fu said. 'I want Ctrip to apologize and have the negative records removed by the airport and airlines.'

As it turned out, Ctrip sold him a ticket that was exchanged for the membership mileage of a Japanese traveller he did not know. The Shanghai-based Ctrip officials confirmed the incident had taken place and claimed one of the Ctrip ticketing agents had sold flight tickets that were exchanged for mileage without the knowledge of the travelling passenger. Ctrip officially apologized to the passenger and flew him back on a new ticket. It said it would offer triple compensation and a full refund to customers who encounter similar situations, and it promised to boost the supervision of its agents.

But apparently this was not a rare incident. A similar case involving a Chinese couple reportedly occurred in the same week. A traveller named Li Miao had booked two tickets on Ctrip for Air China for himself and his wife one month in advance, but the couple were refused travel in Beijing because the tickets were invalid. 'Air China said they could not find the ticket numbers on their system. That means they [the airline] did not sell the tickets,' Li said on his SNS account; his post was reposted and read over 100,000 times. The couple had to buy new tickets to get on the plane. This time, Ctrip claimed that 'a ticket agent had forgotten to issue tickets to the customers after receiving the payment.' But a travel agent from a rival website said that it could be another case of cheating.

Many airlines lure passengers with 'frequent flyer' deals, offering mileage that can be exchanged for gifts and even flight tickets. These deals are being misused by dubious travel agents. Almost all airlines prohibit the trade of mileage. China Southern Airlines, for instance, insists that 'all kinds of mileage trades are forbidden.' China Eastern Airlines stipulates that its members must apply with the airline if they want to exchange mileage with their family members, and this must be done almost two months in advance. Yet the illegal trade of mileage is not rare because of regulation loopholes.

Continued

Subsequent action

- In response, the public relations director of Ctrip publicly apologized for the trouble that the company had caused all the passengers whose trips had been affected by the 'fake' tickets: 'On behalf of Ctrip.com, I would like to express my deep sorrow for the inconvenience it has brought to all the passengers involved. We will offer triple compensation and a full refund to customers who have encountered similar situations. The refund and compensation will be sent to accounts of those passengers whose trips have been affected by the incidents. We will take every measure to make sure the rights of passengers would be protected.' The director added, 'Ctrip.com has been very strict with the travel agents on its platform. After this incident, Ctrip.com will strengthen its supervision, and harsher punishments will be imposed on those agents who violate relevant regulations (Gbtimes, 2016).'
- On January 11, Ctrip issued a statement saying that, at present, the probability of passengers being issued 'fake tickets' is less than one in a hundred and that Ctrip would strive to further reduce the probability of this incident occurring (Netease Technology, 2016a).
- Ctrip also announced the following commitments: (i) guests who purchased their tickets on Ctrip will be guaranteed unchanged prices; (ii) if the passenger's original flight has no available seats, Ctrip will try to provide a solution within 20 minutes; and (iii) if such an incident happens again due to vendor violations, Ctrip will compensate the passenger for three times the cost of the tickets (Netease Technology, 2016b).

Outcomes

- Ctrip's net revenue reached 4.2 billion Yuan (about US$648 million) in Q1, an increase of 80% compared with the same period in the previous year. Ctrip ticketing revenue increased by 106% (it.sohu.com, 2016).
- Ctrip's net revenue increased to 4.4 billion Yuan in Q2 and 5.6 billion Yuan in Q3, an increase of 75% from the previous year (PEdaily, 2016).
- In the online flight ticket market in China, Ctrip's market share was 33.6% in 2015 (Iresearch, 2016; see Fig. 5.1), up from 27.3% in 2014 (Iresearch, 2015; see Fig. 5.2).

Note

The Ctrip case study in this chapter demonstrates how the successful handling of service failures may benefit the company in the long run. While the company's success

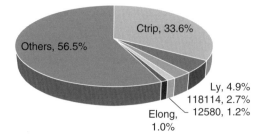

Fig. 5.1 Online ticket market share in China: 2015 (online travel agencies only). (From Iresearch, 2016.)

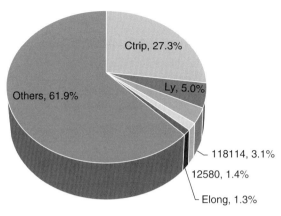

Fig. 5.2 Online ticket market share in China: 2014 (online travel agencies only). (From Iresearch, 2015.)

cannot be solely attributed to its service recovery strategies, many consider the company as reliable, trustworthy and the first choice when booking travel-related items online. The increase in Ctrip's market share and stock price also indicates consumers' confidence in the firm, possibly due to the company's fair handling of service failures.

5.6 Memory Bias: Fading Affect Bias

Research efforts have been made to develop appropriate recovery strategies that can help a business develop long-term customer relationships. Memory bias can provide an explanation for the long-lasting effect of service recovery. The remembered affect resulting from an autobiographical event typically decreases in intensity as time passes from the original event. However, the extent to which the intensity fades is not the same for positive and negative events. Memory researchers have compared the intensity of emotions that people feel when events occur and the intensity of emotions with later recollections of these events (e.g. Gibbons *et al.*, 2011). They reported that the intensity of the emotions felt when someone first retrieves a memory of a negative event tends to diminish faster than when the memory of a positive event is retrieved. This differential fading of affect over time is referred to as fading affect bias (Walker *et al.*, 2003b).

Drawing on Taylor's (1991) mobilization–minimization theory, researchers have explained the long-term suppression of negative affect as a healthy coping mechanism. When someone experiences a negative event, two sets of mechanisms are activated. The first mechanism involves the mobilization of resources. During the mobilization stage, the person draws on biological, psychological and social resources to regulate emotions produced by the negative event to help maintain a positive self-concept. In the second mechanism, which involves minimization, the person works to dampen the affect associated with the negative event to return to a state of homeostasis. Similar to mobilization, this involves drawing on biological, cognitive and social resources. These two mechanisms generally occur only in response to negative events to enable the individual to retain a hopeful outlook about the future (Walker *et al.*, 2003a). Such information can prove valuable for hospitality managers who are under pressure to prevent service failures.

Service failure research has reported many negative consequences of service failures, such as customer dissatisfaction (Kelley *et al.*, 1993), negative word-of-mouth publicity (Mattila, 2001), unwillingness to return (Brady *et al.*, 2002) and customer defection (Keaveney, 1995). If service firms utilize fading affect bias in service failure situations, then they will understand that the customer's negative feelings associated with the service failure will fade faster than the positive ones related to the satisfactory service recovery. Therefore, in the long run, customers who experienced service failures and received satisfying remedies may have a stronger recollection of their positive rather than negative feelings. Ultimately, the positive memories may overwrite the negative ones. Kim and Jang (2014) empirically supported fading affect bias in their experimental study. They found that when individuals re-evaluate service failure experiences in the recollection stage, satisfactory feelings following the service recovery overwrite the negative feelings. They also found that service recoveries were effective in decreasing the resulting negative behavioural intentions such as switching behaviours and negative word-of-mouth publicity.

5.7 Conclusions

Previous studies and industry reports have emphasized the importance of successful service failure recovery strategies. In the hospitality industry, service failures often occur because of the inconsistent nature of hospitality and restaurant services, coupled with the inevitability of human errors. Given that it is difficult to prevent service failures in the hospitality business, researchers and practitioners have been interested in effective ways of reacting to these failures. Service recovery is defined as the actions that a firm takes in response to the service failure (Grönroos, 1990). Appropriate levels of service recovery result in positive affect toward the recovery efforts and may balance negative affect in response to the service failures.

While the subject of service failure and recovery has received much attention in the literature, little research on the topic exists in relation to human memory. Therefore, this chapter provided examples and theories pertaining to the memorable nature of service failures and factors that mediate service failures and consumer behaviour in hospitality settings. This chapter also illustrated how service failures trigger negative emotions that lead to strong memorability and resulting consumer behaviours, with evidence from the literature on memory. Service firms should exert particular efforts to avoid those failures that would lead to a strong memory. Furthermore, appropriate service recoveries should be employed when service failures occur. Researchers have identified a number of recovery strategies, including apology, correction, empathy, compensation, follow-up, acknowledgement, explanation, exceptional treatment and managerial intervention (Lewis and McCann, 2004). However, the success of these strategies varies, based on the type of service, the type of failure and the speed of response (Boshoff, 1997; McDougall and Levesque, 1999; Mattila, 2001). More studies are needed in this area to develop guidelines to which service firms can refer when faced with service failure situations. Such guidelines can help hospitality operators develop their own service recovery strategies and realize the service recovery paradox.

Questions

1. Why is service failure observed more frequently by firms in the service industry than by firms in other industries?
2. What are some of the well-known consequences of service failure in service firms?
3. Think about an actual example of a service failure you experienced in a restaurant. Based on the magnitude of eight different losses suggested by Krishna *et al*. (2011), what was the impact of the service failure on your subsequent behaviour?
4. Why do individuals rely on their previous experiences during choice-processing and decision-making about future consumer behaviours, as presented in this chapter?
5. Do you agree with the statement 'Traumatic events are remembered in more detail, involve more emotional content and are recollected more often than other emotional life experiences?' Please support your answer with a discussion based on your own experiences.

Further Reading

Aravinadkshan, A. and Naik, P.A. (2011) How does awareness evolve when advertising stops? The role of memory. *Marketing Letters* 22, 315–326.

D'Argembeau, A. and Van der Linden, M. (2004) Influence of affective meaning on memory for contextual information. *Emotion* 4, 173–188.

Kim, J.H. (2016) Memorable tourism experiences: conceptual foundations and managerial implications for program design, delivery, and performance measurement. In: Sotiriadis, M. and Gursoy, D. (eds) *The Handbook of Managing and Marketing Tourism Experiences*. Emerald Group, Bingley, UK, pp. 431–450.

Kim, J.H. and Jang, S.C. (2016) Factors affecting memorability of service failures: a longitudinal analysis. *International Journal of Contemporary Hospitality Management* 28, 1676–1701.

References

Adongo, C.A., Anuga, S.W. and Dayour, F. (2015) Will they tell others to taste? International tourists' experience of Ghanaian cuisines. *Tourism Management Perspectives* 15, 57–64.

Andreassen, T.W. (2000) Antecedents to satisfaction with service recovery. *European Journal of Marketing* 34, 156–175.

Aravinadkshan, A. and Naik, P.A. (2011) How does awareness evolve when advertising stops? The role of memory. *Marketing Letters* 22, 315–326.

Baumeister, R.F., Bratslavsky, E., Finkenauer, C. and Vohs, K.D. (2001) Bad is stronger than good. *Review of General Psychology* 5, 323–370.

Bitner, M.J., Booms, B.H. and Tetreault, M.S. (1990) The service encounter: diagnosing favorable and unfavorable incidents. *Journal of Marketing* 54, 71–84.

Bitner, M.J., Booms, B.H. and Mohr, L.A. (1994) Critical service encounters: the employee's viewpoint. *The Journal of Marketing* 58, 95–106.

Blodgett, J.G., Granbois, D.H. and Walters, R.G. (1993) The effects of perceived justice on complainants' negative word-of-mouth behavior and repatronage intentions. *Journal of Retailing* 69, 399–428.

Bodey, K. and Grace, D. (2006) Segmenting service 'complainers' and 'non-complainers' on the basis of consumer characteristics. *Journal of Services Marketing* 20, 178–187.

Bohanek, J.G., Fivush, R. and Walker, E. (2005) Memories of positive and negative emotional events. *Applied Cognitive Psychology* 19, 51–66.

Boshoff, C. (1997) An experimental study of service recovery options. *International Journal of Service Industry Management* 8, 110–130.

Bradley, M.M. (1994) Emotional memory: a dimensional analysis. In: Van Goozen, S.H.M., Van De Poll, N. and Sergeant, J.A. (eds) *Emotions: Essays on Emotion Theory*. Lawrence Erlbaum Associates, Hillsdale, New Jersey, pp. 97–134.

Brady, M.K., Cronin, J.J. Jr and Brand, R.R. (2002). Performance-only measurement of service quality: A replication and extension. *Journal of Business Research* 55, 17–31.

Cahill, L. (2000) Modulation of long-term memory in humans by emotional arousal: adrenergic activation and the amygdala. In: Aggleton, J.P. (ed.) *The Amygdala*. Oxford University Press, New York, pp. 425–446.

Cahill, L. and McGaugh, J.L. (1998) Mechanisms of emotional arousal and lasting declarative memory. *Trends in Neurosciences* 21, 294–299.

Christianson, S.A. (1992) Emotional stress and eye-witness memory: a critical review. *Psychological Bulletin* 112, 284–309.

Cox, D. and Cox, A. (1988) What does familiarity breed? Complexity as a moderator of repetition effects in advertisement evaluation. *Journal of Consumer Research* 15, 111–116.

D'Argembeau, A. and Van der Linden, M. (2004) Influence of affective meaning on memory for contextual information. *Emotion* 4, 173–188.

Davis, M. and Whalen, P.J. (2001) The amygdala: vigilance and emotion. *Molecular Psychiatry* 6, 13–34.

Dewhurst, S.A. and Parry, L.A. (2000) Emotionality, distinctiveness, and recollective experience. *European Journal of Cognitive Psychology* 12, 541–551.

Dolan, R.J. and Vuilleumier, P. (2003) Amygdala automaticity in emotional processing. *Annals of the New York Academy of Sciences* 985, 348–355.

Ekiz, E.H. and Au, N. (2011) Comparing Chinese and American attitudes towards complaining. *International Journal of Contemporary Hospitality Management* 23, 327–343.

Fredrikson, M. and Furmark, T. (2003) Amygdaloid regional cerebral blood flow and subjective fear during symptom provocation in anxiety disorders. *Annals of the New York Academy of Sciences* 985, 341–347.

Fu, H., Wu, D.C., Huang, S., Song, H. and Gong, J. (2015) Monetary or nonmonetary compensation for service failure? A study of customer preferences under various loci of causality. *International Journal of Hospitality Management* 46, 55–64.

Ganesan, S. (1994) Determinants of long-term orientation in buyer–seller relationships. *Journal of Marketing* 58, 1–19.

Gbtimes (2016) Ctrip involved in fake flight tickets row. Available at: http://gbtimes.com/china/ctrip-involved-fake-flight-tickets-row (accessed 15 December 2016).

Gibbons, J.A., Lee, S.A. and Walker, W.R. (2011) The fading affect bias begins within 12 hours and persists for 3 months. *Applied Cognitive Psychology* 25, 663–672.

Grönroos, C. (1990) *Service Management and Marketing – Managing the Moments of Truth in Service Competition*. Lexington Books, Lexington, Massachusetts.

Ha, J. and Jang, S.S. (2009) Perceived justice in service recovery and behavioral intentions: the role of relationship quality. *International Journal of Hospitality Management* 28, 319–327.

Heuer, F. and Reisberg, D. (1990) Vivid memories of emotional events: the accuracy of remembered minutiae. *Memory and Cognition* 18, 496–506.

Hoffman, D.K. and Kelley, S.W. (2000) Perceived justice needs and recovery situation: a contingency approach. *European Journal of Marketing* 34, 418–432.

Hoffman, D.K., Kelley, S.W. and Rotalsky, H.M. (1995) Tracking service failures and employee recovery efforts. *Journal of Services Marketing* 9, 49–61.

Iglesias, V. (2009) The attribution of service failures: effects on consumer satisfaction. *The Service Industries Journal* 29, 127–141.

Iresearch (2015) 2015年中国在线旅游行业年度监测报告 [2015 Report on the survey of China on-line travel business]. Available at: http://wreport.iresearch.cn/uploadfiles/reports/635642833721562500.pdf (accessed 15 December 2016).

Iresearch (2016) 2016年中国在线旅游行业年度监测报告 [2016 Report on the survey of China on-line travel business]. Available at: http://wreport.iresearch.cn/uploadfiles/reports/636051305463620192.pdf (accessed 15 December 2016).

It.sohu.com (2016) 携程发布2016Q1财报净营收同比增长80%. Available at: http://it.sohu.com/20160616/n454651642.shtml (accessed 15 December 2016).

Jackson, M.C. and Raymond, J.E. (2008) Familiarity enhances visual working memory for faces. *Journal of Experimental Psychology* 34, 556–568.

Keaveney, S.M. (1995) Customer switching behavior in service industries: an exploratory study. *Journal of Marketing* 59, 71–82.

Kelley, S.W., Hoffman, K.D. and Davis, M.A. (1993) A typology of retail failures and recoveries. *Journal of Retailing* 69, 429–452.

Kensinger, E.A. and Corkin, S. (2003) Memory enhancement for emotional words: are emotional words more vividly remembered than neutral words? *Memory & Cognition* 31, 1169–1180.

Kensinger, E.A., Garoff-Eaton, R.J. and Schacter, D.L. (2007) How negative emotion enhances the visual specificity of a memory. *Journal of Cognitive Neuroscience* 19, 1872–1887.

Kerstetter, D. and Cho, M. (2004) Tourists' information search behavior: the role of prior knowledge and perceived credibility. *Annals of Tourism Research* 31, 961–985.

Kilpatrick, L. and Cahill, L. (2003) Amygdala modulation of parahippocampal and frontal regions during emotionally influenced memory storage. *Neuroimage* 20, 2091–2099.

Kim, J.H. (2016) Memorable tourism experiences: conceptual foundations and managerial implications for program design, delivery, and performance measurement. In: Sotiriadis, M. and Gursoy, D. (eds) *The Handbook of Managing and Marketing Tourism Experiences*. Emerald Group, Bingley, UK, pp. 431–450.

Kim, J.H. and Chen, J.S. (2010) The effects of situational and personal characteristics on consumer complaint behavior in restaurant services. *Journal of Travel & Tourism Marketing* 27, 96–112.

Kim, J.-H. and Jang, S.C. (2014) The fading affect bias: examining changes in affect and behavioral intentions in restaurant service failures and recoveries. *International Journal of Hospitality Management* 40, 109–119.

Kim, J.-H. and Jang, S.C. (2016) Factors affecting memorability of service failures: a longitudinal analysis. *International Journal of Contemporary Hospitality Management* 28, 1676–1701.

Kim, T., Kim, W.G. and Kim, H.-B. (2009) The effects of perceived justice on recovery satisfaction, trust, word-of-mouth, and revisit intention in upscale hotels. *Tourism Management* 30, 51–62.

Koc, E., Ulukoy, M., Kilic, R., Yumusak, S. and Bahar, R. (2017) The influence of customer participation on service failure perceptions. *Total Quality Management & Business Excellence* 28, 390–404.

Kozak, M. (2001) Repeaters' behavior at two distinct destinations. *Annals of Tourism Research* 28, 784–807.

Krishna, A., Dangayach, G.S. and Jain, R. (2011) A conceptual framework for the service recovery paradox. *The Marketing Review* 11, 41–56.

Kwon, S.Y. and Jang, S.C. (2012) Effects of compensation for service recovery: from the equity theory perspective. *International Journal of Hospitality Management* 31, 1235–1243.

Levine, L.J. and Bluck, S. (2004) Painting with broad strokes: happiness and the malleability of event memory. *Cognition & Emotion* 18, 559–574.

Lewis, B.R. and McCann, P. (2004) Service failure and recovery: evidence from the hotel industry. *International Journal of Contemporary Hospitality Management* 16, 6–17.

Mack, R., Mueller, R., Crotts, J. and Broderick, A. (2000) Perceptions, corrections and defections: implications for service recovery in the restaurant industry. *Managing Service Quality: An International Journal* 10, 339–346.

MacKay, D.G. and Ahmetzanov, M.V. (2005) Emotion, memory, and attention in the taboo Stroop paradigm. *Psychological Science* 16, 25–32.

Magnini, V.P., Ford, J.B., Markowski, E.P. and Honeycutt, E.D. (2007) The service recovery paradox: justifiable theory or smoldering myth? *Journal of Services Marketing* 21, 213–225.

Matos, C.A., Fernandes, D.V.H., Leis, R.P. and Trez, G. (2011) A cross-cultural investigation of customer reactions to service failure and recovery. *Journal of International Consumer Marketing* 23, 211–228.

Mattila, A.S. (1999) An examination of factors affecting service recovery in a restaurant setting. *Journal of Hospitality & Tourism Research* 23, 284–298.

Mattila, A.S. (2001) The effectiveness of service recovery in a multi-industry setting. *Journal of Services Marketing* 15, 583–596.

Maxham, J.G. III and Netemeyer, R.G. (2002) A longitudinal study of complaining customers' evaluations of multiple service failures and recovery efforts. *Journal of Marketing* 66, 57–71.

McCollough, M.A. and Bharadwaj, S.G. (1992) The recovery paradox: an examination of consumer satisfaction in relation to disconfirmation, service quality, and attribution based theories. In: Allen, C.T. (ed.) *Marketing Theory and Applications.* American Marketing Association, Chicago, Illinois.

McCollough, M.A., Berry, L.L. and Yadav, M.S. (2000) An empirical investigation of customer satisfaction after service failure and recovery. *Journal of Service Research* 3, 121–137.

McDougall, G.H. and Levesque, T.J. (1999) Waiting for service: the effectiveness of recovery strategies. *International Journal of Contemporary Hospitality Management* 11, 6–15.

Moorman, C., Zaltman, G. and Deshpande, R. (1992) Relationships between providers and users of market research: the dynamics of trust within and between organizations. *Journal of Marketing Research* 29, 314–339.

Morgan, R.M. and Hunt, S.D. (1994) The commitment-trust theory of relationship marketing. *The Journal of Marketing* 58, 20–38.

Namkung, Y., Jang, S.C. and Choi, S.K. (2011) Customer complaints in restaurants: do they differ by service stages and loyalty levels? *International Journal of Hospitality Management* 30, 495–502.

Netease Technology (2016a) How to avoid 'in Ctrip Invalid Tickets to the Airport?' Available at: http://www.hi3p.com/2016/01/11/how-to-avoid-in-ctrip-invalid-tickets-to-the-airport-38597.html (accessed 15 December 2016).

Netease Technology (2016b) Ctrip Fake tickets after the incident to push new measures: suppliers violation retreat one lose three. Available at: http://www.hi3p.com/2016/01/14/ctrip-fake-tickets-after-the-incident-to-push-new-measures-suppliers-violation-retreat-one-lose-three-38891.html (accessed 15 December 2016).

Oliver, R.L. (1997) *Satisfaction: A Behavioral Perspective on the Consumer.* McGraw-Hill, New York.

PEdaily (2016) 携程发布2016年Q2财报：受益中国经济长期潜力 业绩超华尔街预期 [Beneficial effects of long - term investment in China performance]. Available at: http://news.pedaily.cn/201609/20160901402618.shtml (accessed 15 December 2016).

Piercy, N. and Archer-Brown, C. (2014) Online service failure and propensity to suspend offline consumption. *The Service Industries Journal* 34, 659–676.

Porter, S. and Birt, A.R. (2001) Is traumatic memory special? A comparison of traumatic memory characteristics with memory for other emotional life experiences. *Applied Cognitive Psychology* 15, 101–117.

Ratnayake, B.N., Broderick, A.J. and Mitchell, L.R.C. (2010) A neurocognitive approach to brand memory. *Journal of Marketing Management* 26, 1295–1318.

Sharot, T. and Phelps, E.A. (2004) How arousal modulates memory: disentangling the effects of attention and retention. *Cognitive, Affective and Behavioral Neuroscience* 4, 294–306.

Silber, I., Israeli, A., Bustin, A. and Zvi, O.B. (2009) Recovery strategies for service failures: the case of restaurants. *Journal of Hospitality Marketing & Management* 18, 730–740.

Smith, A.K. and Bolton, R.N. (1998) An experimental investigation of service failure and recovery: paradox or peril? *Journal of Service Research* 1, 65–81.

Smith, A.K., Bolton, R.N. and Wagner, J. (1999) A model of customer satisfaction with service encounters involving failure and recovery. *Journal of Marketing Research* 36, 356–372.

Sparks, B.A. and Browning, V. (2010) Complaining in cyberspace: the motives and forms of hotel guests' complaints online. *Journal of Hospitality Marketing & Management* 19, 797–818.

Susskind, A.M. (2005) A content analysis of consumer complaints, remedies, and repatronage intentions regarding dissatisfying service experiences. *Journal of Hospitality & Tourism Research* 29, 150–169.

Talarico, J.M., LaBar, K.S. and Rubin, D.C. (2004) Emotional intensity predicts autobiographical memory experience. *Memory and Cognition* 32, 1118–1132.

Tax, S.S., Brown, S.W. and Chandrashekaran, M. (1998) Customer evaluations of service complaint experience: implications for relationship marketing. *Journal of Marketing* 62, 60–76.

Taylor, S.E. (1991) Asymmetrical effects of pleasant and unpleasant events: the mobilization-minimization hypothesis. *Psychological Bulletin* 110, 67–85.

Walker, W.R., Skowronski, J., Gibbons, J., Vogl, R. and Thompson, C. (2003a) On the emotions that accompany autobiographical memories: dysphoria disrupts the fading affect bias. *Cognition & Emotion* 17, 703–723.

Walker, W.R., Skowronski, J.J. and Thompson, C.P. (2003b) Life is pleasant and memory helps to keep it that way. *Review of General Psychology* 7, 203–210.

Wang, L., McCarthy, G., Song, A.W. and LaBar, K.S. (2005) Amygdala activation to sad pictures during high-field (4 tesla) functional magnetic resonance imaging. *Emotion* 5, 12–22.

Weun, S., Beatty, S.E. and Jones, M.A. (2004) The impact of service failure severity on service recovery evaluations and post-recovery relationships. *Journal of Services Marketing* 18, 133–146.

Wirtz, D., Kruger, J., Scollon, C.N. and Diener, E. (2003) What to do on spring break? The role of predicted, on-line, and remembered experience in future choice. *Psychological Science* 14, 520–524.

6 Customer Attribution in Service Failures and Recovery

POH THENG (BEATRICE) LOO AND HUEY CHERN BOO

Learning Objectives

After reading this chapter, you should be able to:

- Understand the underlying reasons why people make causal attributions.
- Understand the basic tenets of attribution theory.
- Understand the causal dimensions of customer attribution.
- Understand the influence of customer participation on customer service failure perceptions and attribution.
- Identify the factors influencing customer attribution.
- Discuss the outcomes of service failure and customer attribution.

6.1   Introduction

Clara and Mark were planning a dinner for their anniversary on Saturday. One of their close friends recommended a steakhouse in town. It had received many commendations on TripAdvisor.

On Saturday evening, Clara and Mark were impressed by the spectacular design and the serene ambience of the restaurant. They were greeted by a friendly host and were seated in an aesthetically pleasing part of the restaurant that allowed them to enjoy the décor.

When placing their orders, the service staff informed them that several of the items on the menu were not available. As it was their first visit, Clara and Mark asked the service staff to make a recommendation. When the food was served, it did not taste good. Furthermore, they found some of the items rather expensive.

If you were Clara or Mark, how would you have responded to the situation? Would you keep quiet, complain to the manager or decide not to patronize the restaurant again? If you were Clara or Mark, would you blame the staff for making a dishonest recommendation, or the chef for not cooking the food well or the manager for not holding enough stock? Or would you think you were responsible for listening to your friend's or the staff's recommendation? Or would you attribute the entire unpleasant incident to bad luck? Would it have been different if it had not been an anniversary dinner or if you had been to the restaurant several times before?

6.2 Attribution

Attribution refers to the effect of ascribing a particular source or cause (Jolibert and Peterson, 1976). When customers interpret the causes of service failures, these are attributions (Priluck and Wisenblit, 2009). Attribution theory was originally introduced by Fritz Heider (1958) in a book entitled *Psychology of Interpersonal Relations* (Weiner, 2000). This theory consists of a collection of different theories (including naïve psychology, self-perception theory, external attribution) on causal inferences and ways the interpreted inferences affect evaluation and customer behaviour (Swanson and Kelley, 2001). Heider (1958) proposes that some attribution elements fluctuate (e.g. luck and efforts), while others are fixed (e.g. capability). He found an internal–external dimension that comprises two different conditions: factors within a person or in the environment. Lastly, Heider highlights that attribution also relates to the controllability to credit and blame. In 1980, Weiner identified that the shifts of expectancies are affected by the stability of a cause; the internal–external dimension is called a locus of causality (Weiner, 1980a).

There are two antecedents of causal inferences: information and motivation (Kelley and Michela, 1980). The information antecedent is about knowing how customers utilize information to make causal inferences – these kinds of information are important to make an attribution. The consensus, consistency and distinctiveness of information influence attributions in customer behaviour. An example of consensus information (Folkes and Kotsos, 1986) is product failure: that encountered by most customers is called high consensus (e.g. the product is poorly made), whereas that experienced by a few customers is called low consensus (e.g. careless customers). Consistency is the individual customer's response over time and conditions. Distinction is the customer's response to a product as opposed to other products. Another attribution antecedent is motivation; the fundamental motivational bias is protecting one's esteem (Folkes, 1988). Attribution patterns that are relevant to motivational or esteem-related biases, such as internal or dispositional cause, include the tendency of customers to attribute good outcomes to one's self, but bad outcomes to external or situational causes. For instance, when customers have bad experiences of products, they tend to blame the company.

6.2.1 Causal dimensions of attribution

The most systematic categorization of attribution dimensions was introduced by Weiner in 1980 (Weiner, 1980b; Folkes, 1984), who classified the dimensions according to causal properties, including: (i) stability; (ii) locus of causality; and (iii) controllability. Stability is when the perceived cause of failure is attributed to the degree of permanence in time (likelihood of recurrence), whether it is temporary (fluctuates over time) or permanent (stable over time). For example, whether the hotel room was found to be poorly cleaned just once or consistently because of the carelessness of housekeeping staff. The second dimension is locus of causality, which describes whether the cause of failure is located in the customer her/himself or her/his decisions (internal attribution), or located in the company that offers services (external attribution), or located in unexpected environmental effects (situational attribution). In the case of an airline company's flight delay problem, passengers could attribute the cause of failure to their own decision to buy the plane ticket for the 'wrong' time, or poor management by the airline company, or bad weather. The third dimension, controllability, is the degree of subject alteration and when the outcome could have been different. In the case of a strand of hair found in a pasta dish, a complaining customer may think that the cause of failure was controllable by the restaurant through tight food quality control and the restaurant could have avoided it. A new dimension, called responsibility, is the combination of controllability and locus of causality (Tsiros *et al.*, 2004).

6.2.2 Factors affecting customer attribution in response to service failure

When service failures happen, customers may attribute the failures differently in three dimensions. However, the process of attribution could be affected by some factors that cause the customers to have different responses toward service failures. The factors include the severity of failures, customer participation, and cultural factors in online and off-line service failures.

Severity of failures

Severity of failures relates to the responsibility attribution (locus) as well as appropriateness of compensation for satisfaction of service recovery and is demonstrated in Table 6.1 (Bambauer-Sachse and Rabeson, 2015). This table is based on the scenario of restaurant customers having different reasons for going out for dinner (moderate involvement – going out for dinner on a normal evening instead of cooking at home; high involvement – celebrate a partner's birthday). Responsibility attribution is manipulated by: (i) waiting time for the table (restaurant's responsibility) and (ii) the customer being late and having to wait for another table (customer's responsibility). Different durations of waiting time were used to manipulate service failure severity. Regarding the

Table 6.1. Appropriateness of different types of tangible compensation. (Adapted from Bambauer-Sachse and Rabeson, 2015.)

Less severe failure		Highly severe failure	
Restaurant responsible	Customer responsible	Restaurant responsible	Customer responsible
Moderate involvement			
Gift	Gift	Gift	Credit
Discount	Discount	Discount	Refund
Credit	Credit	Credit	
Refund	Refund	Refund	
High involvement			
Discount	Gift	Credit	Credit
Credit	Discount	Refund	Refund
Refund	Credit		
	Refund		

compensation, gift refers to a cup of coffee or a dessert, credit for future consumption, discount for ordered items and refund for paid items. As can be seen in Table 6.1, for the case of highly severe failure, regardless of the responsible attribution, gifts and discounts are not appropriate, except with moderate involvement under the restaurant's responsibility. Surprisingly, for customers responsible for the failures, customers seem to have higher expectations of service recovery despite being responsible and the moderate involvement could be due to customers shifting the blame for service failure away from themselves.

Customer participation

Customers who participate (physical, emotional or mental participation) in the service are more likely to care less about the negative outcomes of a service failure (Koc *et al.*, 2017). Furthermore, when customers participate in service, they evaluate the attributions differently on the three attribution dimensions: they tend not to make external attributions blaming the service providers. Their participation only reduces customer dissatisfaction from service failure and does not eliminate it completely (Koc *et al.*, 2017). In fact, customer participation or co-production and co-creation enhances internal failure attribution due to customers having control over a situation and therefore they may feel guilty after co-created failures (Heidenreich *et al.*, 2014).

For restaurants, service employees should be trained to identify the customer who is responsible for choosing the restaurant and to check with this customer if everything is satisfactory: customers who have a higher level of participation in restaurant selection have significant influences on customer exit (McQuilken and Robertson, 2013). Customers who are responsible for choosing restaurants for group dining tend to feel the pressure to please everyone. When a service failure happens, an unconditional service guarantee would help reduce the negative impacts of failures because it could moderate negative word-of-mouth intentions of customers who are responsible for the restaurant choice (McQuilken and Robertson, 2013). Besides making restaurant choice, customer participation in decision-making during their dining experience helps to reduce any negative effect towards restaurants – for example, allowing customers to change their seats could reduce their perception of dissonance (Raajpoot and Sharma, 2006).

Customer citizenship behaviour is the extra-role behaviour that is extended to customers who participate in service delivery (Groth, 2005). Extra-role behaviour is the time and effort (support or assistance) contributed by customers beyond their required rules in service delivery which benefit the organization (Keh and Teo, 2001). There are three dimensions of customer citizenship behaviour, including provision of feedback to organizations, help offered to other customers and recommendations of business to others (Groth, 2005). Customers who participate in service delivery are partial employees (Bowen and Schneider, 2000). Their participation affects the overall success of an organization (Eisingerich *et al.*, 2014) and helps better satisfy customers (Vargo and Lusch, 2004).

In organizing a tour, for instance, selected tour members should be encouraged to participate to serve the needs of other tour members (such as any practice to forge a sense of togetherness and sociability during the tour), which would help to lighten the tour leader's workload (Liu and Tsaur, 2014). The co-creation interactions (citizenship behaviour) between the customers and other tour members in a shared service environment over a period of time, together with the interaction, has direct and indirect impacts on the tour members. Tour leaders can identify some of the tour members' characteristics from the beginning of the tour in order to select the right tour members. The right tour members, who could have substantial influences and are more likely to engage in citizenship behaviours, could have characteristics such as being empathetic and agreeable (Van Dyne *et al.*, 1995), good team-work spirit, positive emotions, good rapport with tour leaders and good communication skills (Liu and Tsaur, 2014). Thus, tour leaders themselves should set a good example to encourage tour members to reciprocate citizenship behaviours.

Nowadays, online services involve customer participation in service processes. Online customers are more likely to blame themselves for service failures (Harris *et al.*, 2006), and the more customers blame themselves for a service failure, the lower their expectations for companies' compensation.

Cultural factors

Culture has become one of the significant factors affecting customer attribution. Culture has a substantial influence on the perception of quality, perceived equity as well as problem attribution (Chang, 2008). Collectivists (e.g. the Chinese) are more likely than individualists (e.g. the Canadians) to attribute blame to the service provider because collectivists show stronger outgroups distrust (Au *et al.*, 2001). However, both groups are similar in the level of self-blame. Individual travel behaviour and personal values are strongly related to retention and service quality (Chang, 2008). Indeed, travellers retain their own cultural values while travelling (Warden *et al.*, 2003). Collectivist tour participants usually do not blame other tour members for failures because the Chinese culture emphasizes personal relationship (*kuan-hsi*) and personal face (*mien-tsu*) (Gilbert and Tsao, 2000).

6.3 Outcomes of Service Failure and Customer Attribution

The types of attribution customers engage in lead to different outcomes. The outcomes include service recovery actions, customer emotion and behavioural intentions as well as perceived quality and customer satisfaction. All these outcomes are critical to help service providers, managers and front-line employees know how to identify and manage service attributions better and enhance customer satisfaction, customer loyalty and company profits.

6.3.1 Service recovery actions

Customers tend to be more tolerant if the service or product failures are customer-related; they think of themselves as less deserving of any refunds or apologies compared to when there are company-related failures (Folkes, 1984). Furthermore, if the failure incidents happen due to unstable causes which are beyond the control of companies, customers are more willing to accept an exchange than if it was due to a stable cause (Folkes, 1984). For instance, in a restaurant, if electricity was unavailable during dining (unstable, uncontrolled by companies), customers are more likely to accept refunds or apologies compared with a situation when the food was unpalatable (stable, controlled by companies). Regardless of what or who is responsible for the failure, companies should apologize to customers (with or without any compensation) (Boshoff and Leong, 1998). Interestingly, sometimes, after acknowledging service failures, there is no re-covery attempt; even worse, in some cases it is followed with a blaming behaviour. In research studies, some Taiwan respondents classified service providers doing nothing as worse than blaming customers when considering bad service (Warden *et al.*, 2003).

6.3.2   Customer emotions and behavioural intentions

Depending on customer attributions, customers tend to respond differently in terms of their emotions and behavioural outcomes, such as repurchase intention and negative word-of-mouth (Harrison-Walker, 2012). If a failure resulted from incompetent em-ployees rather than an accident, customers are likely to experience greater negative emo-tions of frustration. Attribution for flight delays has affective consequences consistent with Weiner's (1980a) theory (Taylor, 1994). When passengers perceive the airline com-panies have more control over delays, or the cause of the delay is common, the delayed customers feel more anger. For example, flight delays due to fog are considered uncontrol-lable, therefore, in this case, airline companies should explain and justify that the failure is unavoidable and uncontrollable. In this case, airline companies should consider how to engage passengers and fill their time during the delay because passengers will then tend to pay less attention to the delay and there will be less anxiety, restlessness and boredom.

Nevertheless, customers experience strongest anger when they feel that the service failure is avoidable and is deliberate. Indeed, company-attributed service failures that make customers angry could have substantial negative effects, including lower service evaluations, poorer corporate image, lower satisfaction, more complaints, higher per-ceptions of injustice, increased likelihood of engaging in negative word-of-mouth and lower repurchase intentions (Kalamas *et al.*, 2008). Furthermore, response strategies and severity of failure affect customer attributions, which then have positive relation-ships with negative word-of-mouth and negative relationships with organizational reputation (Chang *et al.*, 2015). Thus, understanding customer behavioural outcomes or intentions based on customer attribution of service failures is critical in helping man-agers and companies to know how to promote greater positive word-of-mouth and repurchase intentions (Swanson and Davis, 2003).

Service providers who overpromise or provide insufficient clarity and details in their communications (locus and controllability) could disappoint customers (Harri-son-Walker, 2012). Furthermore, this could also lead to customer dissatisfaction and repurchase intention. Disappointed customers tend to engage in negative word-of-mouth to their friends and families as well as other potential customers. Hence, companies should review and assess service performance versus customer expectations to ensure promised service quality and products are delivered. Customers may feel regret when they make wrong decisions. It could be that companies attracted the 'wrong' customers

---

for the business. No service fits all customers; therefore, service providers should make great efforts to help customers make the right decisions so they have no regrets about their purchased services and products. When customers feel regret, this reduces their repurchase intentions. In fact, regret has a greater negative impact on repurchase intentions than disappointment (Harrison-Walker, 2012).

On top of that, attributions of controllable but intentional failures (such as rudeness of service employees) could trigger feelings of humiliation, especially when customers perceive that service providers broke a moral code of conduct. Intentionality attributions have impacts on customer switching behaviour, whereas humiliation mediates the relationship between intentionality attributions and switching behaviour (Varela-Neira et al., 2014). In other words, employee behaviour and attitude have impacts on customer attributions toward service failures. Service providers are recommended to avoid making promises they cannot fulfil, to carefully select employees with high service orientation and to train employees to know how to make customers feel important and be proactive in offering retrospective explanation about reasons for failures.

Emotions are considered partly as responses to dimensions of causality, whereby a clear mapping between causal thoughts and both positive and negative feelings is made (Weiner, 1980a). Weiner's study found the affect to be reactions to causal attributions: the affect reactions are related to success and failure. Table 6.2 demonstrates four causal attributions (including ability, long-term effort, others and luck). Each type of emotion is related to following success and failure. For success, the linkages are: ability–confidence, effort–relaxation, others–gratitude, luck–surprise. On the other hand, the linkages for failure are: ability–incompetence, effort–guilt, others–anger and luck–surprise. When a travel agent fails to handle a customer complaint effectively, complaining customers perceive it as the incompetence of the agent, whereas if the agent handles it effectively, customers perceive the agent as competent and have more confidence in the travel agency's services.

Table 6.3 shows locus of causality affects feelings in relation to success and failure. Internal attributions for success give rise to pride, confidence, competence and satisfaction; however, for failure it is guilt. Successes of external attribution magnify gratitude and thankfulness, whereas failures amplify anger and surprise. For example, on a rainy day, when a guest returns to the hotel and the staff in the hotel lobby offer him a towel to get warm and dry, the hotel guest would feel grateful for the thoughtful gesture. However, when a hotel guest's taxi to the airport was supposed to pick him up in 15 minutes but is more than 30 minutes late, the hotel guest could feel anger and surprise. Although the delay is beyond the hotel's control, the hotel guest would expect hotel staff to assist him to find out the reasons for the delay.

Table 6.2. Relations between causal attributions and feelings. (Adapted from Weiner, 1980b.)

Attribution	Success	Failure
Ability	Confidence	Incompetence
	Competence	
Effort	Relaxation	Guilt (shame)
Others	Gratitude	Anger
Luck	Surprise	Surprise

When customers attribute failure to different external parties such as service employees and company management, this affects their subsequent evaluation of service experiences (Swanson and Davis, 2003), as summarized in Table 6.4. When customers perceive that service employees have greater responsibilities for the service experiences, the outcome quality (what is delivered) influences customers' overall evaluations of service quality, satisfaction and behavioural intentions. On the other hand, when customers find that the management or manager is responsible, the process quality of how the service is delivered affects customers' subsequent evaluations. If the responsibilities are attributed equally between service employees and management, customer satisfaction towards their service experience would be affected by servicescape quality, which refers to the physical environment.

Perceived quality and customer satisfaction

Service attribution affects customer-perceived service quality (Chebat *et al.*, 1995; Iglesias, 2009). Service employees' empathy and assurance affect the attribution process; however, customers tend to be tolerant if the failure incidents are beyond the control or responsibilities of employees or the incidents tend not to recur. The role of employee–customer interactions could reduce the effects of customer attributions during service failures on customer satisfaction (Anderson *et al.*, 2009). Furthermore, the perceived service quality affects not only the customers who consumed the services but also other customers who may have observed the service processes (Chebat *et al.*, 1995).

Attribution also demonstrates direct effects on satisfaction (Iglesias, 2009). The research study conducted by Iglesias (2009) found that customers' satisfaction level was low when the failure was related to employee attitude. For airline companies, failures that are beyond the airline company's control (e.g. external factors such as bad weather

Table 6.3. Relations between locus of causality and feelings. (Adapted from Weiner, 1980b.)

Locus of causality	Success	Failure
Internal	Pride	Failure
	Confidence	Guilt
	Competence	
	Satisfaction	
External	Grateful	Anger
	Thankful	Surprise

Table 6.4. Relations between customer-attributed responsibilities and evaluation of service experiences. (From Swanson and Davis, 2003.)

Customer-attributed responsibilities	Evaluation of service experiences
Service employee	What is delivered (outcome quality)
Management/manager	How the service is delivered (process quality)
Service employee and manager (equally)	Physical environment (servicescape quality)

conditions) are perceived as less severe by customers than failures caused by internal factors (e.g. waiting in the queue because of the inefficiency of staff).

6.4 Discussion and Conclusions

Attribution theory has endured for many decades. One possible reason is that the theoretical model maps out the relationship between specific thoughts about service failure and specific courses of action by customers. In particular, attribution theory views people as rational information processors. People try to determine why a particular service failed and the inferred reason subsequently dictates how they respond (Folkes, 1984).

The causes of service failure can be categorized into three underlying causal properties or dimensions. First, the theory of attribution suggests that customers may make two types of locus of causality, namely internal and external attribution. When the cause of failure has something to do with the customer, internal attribution is made. On the other hand, an external attribution is made when the cause of failure lies in the production of a service (Weiner, 1980b). As a result, it is not surprising that co-creation has become a popular phenomenon in the hospitality industry. Hospitality operators increasingly involve customers in the production of services. For example, online ordering is an effective way of shifting the accountability to customers in the event of any error in the ordering. Similarly, getting customers to make their own dishes enables the restaurant operators to mitigate some of the responsibility for failure.

Although marketing research has often investigated whether the cause is located in the customer (internal) or in the service provider (external), causal attribution may also be categorized as dispositional or situational (Gilbert, 1995). Dispositional attribution is associated with internally caused outcomes, such as one's ability or efforts, while situational attribution is related to external factors, such as task complexity and luck (Oliver and DeSarbo, 1988). Customers who hold a collectivist perspective are more aware of the situational influences and are thus less likely to make dispositional attribution compared with those who are individualist (Newman, 1991; Mattila and Patterson, 2004).

The second causal dimension is stability, which means the causes of service failure may be temporary (unstable) or permanent (stable). When the causes of service failure are unstable, future outcomes are unpredictable. As customers do not expect the recurrence of such unpleasant incidents, they are more likely to patronize the hospitality establishments again or to accept an exchange rather than a refund. In contrast, if the cause of service failure is persistent, customers believe that poor service quality is highly likely to happen again in the future and are angry about the lack of preventive actions from the service providers (Folkes *et al.*, 1987). As a result, customers tend to avoid experiencing the dissatisfactory episodes and are more likely to request a refund instead of an exchange (Folkes, 1984). The stability dimension of attribution depends on the past experience of the customer (Cowley, 2005).

The third causal dimension is perceived controllability, which influences not only the locus of causality but also the intensity of emotion and aggressiveness of behaviour. Generally, negative outcomes trigger the attribution process. Specifically, customers examine whether the service failure is volitional or non-volitional. If the cause of failure is within the control of the service provider, the external attribution is much more damaging: customers feel angry and may seek revenge. However, the desire to hurt the company's business decreases when the failure is caused by factors beyond the company's control (Folkes, 1984; Weiner, 2000).

As noted above, the attribution process during failures influences customers' perceptions of current and future service quality, as well as their satisfaction level and expected recovery actions. Customers may regret their decisions when the causes are internally related. However, they are likely to be disappointed and angry when the cause of service failure is company-related.

The three causal dimensions can interact or may act alone in affecting the perception, emotion and behaviour of customers experiencing service failures. The importance of the event and the severity of the service failures are more likely to prompt the attribution process than an ordinary event and trivial problem. Previous research suggests that external or personal attribution may be mitigated directly through greater customer involvement in the service process, or indirectly by altering the controllability dimension, such as highlighting the operating constraints or situational factors.

Despite vigorous research in attribution theory, there are several avenues for future research in the area. First, the psychology literature has recently suggested intentionality as a possible dimension of attribution (Weiner, 2006; Struthers *et al.*, 2008). Specifically, customers may consider the cause of the service failure to be the outcome of the providers' intention of not wanting to meet the customers' needs. Second, the stability dimension may be further distinguished from globality (Coffee and Rees, 2008; Huang, 2008). The causes of service failures may not be associated with a particular hospitality establishment but common to the entire industry: hence, would that influence the customer's switching behaviour? Finally, more research efforts could be devoted to uncovering factors alleviating external attribution and the perceived controllability of cause.

Questions

1. Explain three types of attribution causal dimensions, with one example for each type relevant to the hospitality and tourism industry.
2. Severity of failure is one of the factors affecting customer attribution in response to service failures. Briefly explain.
3. Customer participation has substantial influences on customer attributions. Discuss these influences.
4. Customer emotions and behavioural intentions are the outcomes of service failure and customer attributions. Choose any two of the emotion types and explain the behavioural intentions in response to service failure and attributions.
5. Attribution also demonstrates direct effects on satisfaction. Discuss this statement with examples.

Further Reading

Chang, J.C. (2008) Tourists' satisfaction judgments: an investigation of emotion, equity, and attribution. *Journal of Hospitality & Tourism Research* 32, 108–134.
Folkes, V.S. (1988) Recent attribution research in consumer behavior: a review and new directions. *Journal of Consumer Research* 14, 548–565.

Koc, E., Ulukoy, M., Kilic, R., Yumusak, S. and Bahar, R. (2017) The influence of customer participation on service failure perceptions. *Total Quality Management & Business Excellence* 28, 390–404.

McQuilken, L. and Robertson, N. (2013) Who chose this restaurant anyway? The effect of responsibility for choice, guarantees, and failure stability on customer complaining. *Journal of Hospitality & Tourism Research* 37, 537–562.

References

Anderson, S.W., Baggett, L.S. and Widener, S.K. (2009) The impact of service operations failures on customer satisfaction: evidence on how failures and their source affect what matters to customers. *Manufacturing & Service Operations Management* 11, 52–69.

Au, K., Hui, M.K. and Kwok, L. (2001) Who should be responsible? Effects of voice and compensation on responsibility attribution, perceived justice, and post-complaint behaviors across cultures. *International Journal of Conflict Management* 12, 350–360.

Bambauer-Sachse, S. and Rabeson, L.E. (2015) Service recovery for moderate and high involvement services. *Journal of Services Marketing* 29, 331–343.

Boshoff, C. and Leong, J. (1998) Empowerment, attribution and apologising as dimensions of service recovery: an experimental study. *International Journal of Service Industry Management* 9, 24–47.

Bowen, D.E. and Schneider, B. (1985) Boundary spanning role employees and the service encounter: some guidelines for management and research. In: Czepiel, J.A., Solomon, M.R. and Surprenant, C. (eds) *The Service Encounter*. D.C. Heath, Lexington, Massachusetts, pp. 127–147.

Chang, H.H., Tsai, Y.-C., Wong, K.H., Wang, J.W. and Cho, F.J. (2015) The effects of response strategies and severity of failure on consumer attribution with regard to negative word-of-mouth. *Decision Support Systems* 71, 48–61.

Chang, J.C. (2008) Tourists' satisfaction judgments: an investigation of emotion, equity, and attribution. *Journal of Hospitality & Tourism Research* 32, 108–134.

Chebat, J.-C., Filiatrault, P., Gelinas-Chebat, C. and Vaninsky, A. (1995) Impact of waiting attribution and consumer's mood on perceived quality. *Journal of Business Research* 34, 191–196.

Coffee, P. and Rees, T. (2008) The CSGU: a measure of controllability, stability, globality, and universality attributions. *Journal of Sport and Exercise Psychology* 30, 611–641.

Cowley, E. (2005) Views from customers next in line: the fundamental attribution error in a service setting. *Journal of the Academy of Marketing Science* 33, 139–152.

Eisingerich, A.B., Auh, S. and Merlo, O. (2014) Acta non verba? The role of customer participation and word of mouth in the relationship between service firms' customer satisfaction and sales performance. *Journal of Service Research* 17, 40–53.

Folkes, V.S. (1984) Consumer reactions to product failure: an attributional approach. *Journal of Consumer Research* 10, 398–409.

Folkes, V.S. (1988) Recent attribution research in consumer behavior: a review and new directions. *Journal of Consumer Research* 14, 548–565.

Folkes, V.S. and Kotsos, B. (1986) Buyers' and sellers' explanations for product failure: who done it? *Journal of Marketing* 50, 74–80.

Folkes, V.S., Koletsky, S. and Graham, J. (1987) A field study of causal inferences and consumer reaction: the view from the airport. *Journal of Consumer Research* 13, 534–539.

Gilbert, D.T. (1995) Attribution and interpersonal perception. In: Tesser, A. (ed.) *Advanced Social Psychology*. McGraw-Hill, New York, pp. 98–147.

Gilbert, D. and Tsao, J. (2000) Exploring Chinese cultural influences and hospitality marketing relationships. *International Journal of Contemporary Hospitality Management* 12, 45–54.

Groth, M. (2005) Customers as good soldiers: examining citizenship behaviors in internet service deliveries. *Journal of Management* 31, 7–27.

Harris, K.E., Mohr, L.A. and Bernhardt, K.L. (2006) Online service failure, consumer attributions and expectations. *Journal of Services Marketing* 20, 453–458.

Harrison-Walker, L.J. (2012) The role of cause and affect in service failure. *Journal of Services Marketing* 26, 115–123.

Heidenreich, S., Wittkowski, K., Handrich, M. and Falk, T. (2014) The dark side of customer co-creation: exploring the consequences of failed co-created services. *Journal of the Academy of Marketing Science* 43, 279–296.

Heider, F. (1958) *Psychology of Interpersonal Relations*. Lawrence Erlbaum Associate, Hillsdale, New Jersey.

Huang, W.H. (2008) The impact of other-customer failure on service satisfaction. *International Journal of Service Industry Management* 19, 521–536.

Iglesias, V. (2009) The attribution of service failures: effects on consumer satisfaction. *The Service Industries Journal* 29, 127–141.

Jolibert, A.J.P. and Peterson, R.A. (1976) Causal attributions of product failure: an exploratory investigation. *Journal of the Academy of Marketing Science* 4, 446–455.

Kalamas, M., Laroche, M. and Makdessian, L. (2008) Reaching the boiling point: consumers' negative affective reactions to firm-attributed service failures. *Journal of Business Research* 61, 813–824.

Keh, H.T. and Teo, C.W. (2001) Retail customers as partial employees in service provision: a conceptual framework. *International Journal of Retail & Distribution Management* 29, 370–378.

Kelley, H.H. and Michela, J.L. (1980) Attribution theory and research. *Annual Review of Psychology* 31, 457–501.

Koc, E., Ulukoy, M., Kilic, R., Yumusak, S. and Bahar, R. (2017) The influence of customer participation on service failure perceptions. *Total Quality Management & Business Excellence* 28, 390–404.

Liu, J.S. and Tsaur, S.H. (2014) We are in the same boat: tourist citizenship behaviors. *Tourism Management* 42, 88–100.

Mattila, A.S. and Patterson, P.G. (2004) The impact of culture on consumers' perceptions of service recovery effort. *Journal of Retailing* 80, 196–206.

McQuilken, L. and Robertson, N. (2013) Who chose this restaurant anyway? The effect of responsibility for choice, guarantees, and failure stability on customer complaining. *Journal of Hospitality & Tourism Research* 37, 537–562.

Newman, L.S. (1991) Why are traits inferred spontaneously? A developmental approach. *Social Cognition* 9, 221–253.

Oliver, R.L. and DeSarbo, W.S. (1988) Response determinants in satisfaction judgments. *Journal of Consumer Research* 14, 495–507.

Priluck, R. and Wisenblit, J. (2009) The impact of exchange lineage on customers' responses to service debacles and subsequent recovery. *Services Marketing Quarterly* 30, 365–376.

Raajpoot, N.A. and Sharma, A. (2006) Perceptions of incompatibility in customer-to-customer interactions: examining individual level differences. *Journal of Services Marketing* 20, 324–332.

Struthers, C.W., Eaton, J., Santelli, A.G., Uchiyama, M. and Shirvani, N. (2008) The effects of attributions of intent and apology on forgiveness: when saying sorry may not help the story. *Journal of Experimental Social Psychology* 44, 983–992.

Swanson, S.R. and Davis, J.C. (2003) The relationship of differential loci with perceived quality and behavioral intentions. *Journal of Services Marketing* 17, 202–219.

Swanson, S.R. and Kelley, S.W. (2001) Attributions and outcomes of the service recovery process. *Journal of Marketing Theory & Practice* 9, 50–65.

Taylor, S. (1994) Waiting for service: the relationship between delays and evaluations of service. *Journal of Marketing* 58, 56–69.

Tsiros, M., Mittal, V. and Ross, W.T. (2004) The role of attributions in customer satisfaction: a re-examination. *Journal of Consumer Research* 31, 476–483.

Van Dyne, L., Cummings, L.L. and Parks, J.M. (1995) Extra-role behaviors: in pursuit of construct and definitional clarity (a bridge over muddied waters). In: Cummings, L.L. and Staw, B.M. (eds) *Research in Organizational Behavior* (Vol. 17). JAI Press, Greenwich, Connecticut, pp. 215–285.

Varela-Neira, C., Vázquez-Casielles, R. and Iglesias, V. (2014) Intentionality attributions and humiliation: the impact on customer behavior. *European Journal of Marketing* 48, 901–923.

Vargo, S.L. and Lusch, R.F. (2004) Evolving to a new dominant logic for marketing. *Journal of Marketing* 68, 1–17.

Warden, C.A., Liu, T.-C., Huang, C.-T. and Lee, C.-H. (2003) Service failures away from home: benefits in intercultural service encounters. *International Journal of Service Industry Management* 14, 436–456.

Weiner, B. (1980a) The role of affect in rational (attributional) approaches to human motivation. *Educational Researcher* 9, 4–11.

Weiner, B. (1980b) *Human Motivation*. Holt, Rinehart & Winston, New York.

Weiner, B. (2000) Attributional thoughts about consumer behavior. *Journal of Consumer Research* 27, 382–387.

Weiner, B. (2006) *Social Motivation, Justice, and the Moral Emotions. An Attribution Approach*. Lawrence Erlbaum Associates, Mahwah, NJ.

7 Technology, Customer Satisfaction and Service Excellence

Minwoo Lee and Melissa A. Baker

Learning Objectives

After reading this chapter, you should be able to:

- Understand and explain the role played by technology in tourism and hospitality.
- Explain hotel technology adoption.
- Explain how technology enables both employees and customers to enhance satisfaction in service encounters.
- Explain customer relationships in terms of brand image, online reviews, information search and (dis)satisfaction in social media and technology.
- Understand how tourism and hospitality businesses can manage service recovery in social media.
- Understand the influence of technology on service personnel.
- Understand the newly emerging issues in technology.

7.1 Introduction

The proliferation and spread of a variety of rapidly advancing technologies is dramatically altering the essence of service encounters and affecting all aspects of service provision and consumption. Hospitality service experiences occur between the firm and the target customer segments (external marketing), the firm and frontline employees (internal marketing) and the frontline employees and target market segments (interactional marketing) (Baker and Magnini, 2016). While traditional service encounters have been facilitated by interpersonal contact based on the dyadic relationship between employees and customers, the changing landscape of service encounters is based on the dynamic relationship between employees, customers and technology (Parasuraman, 1996; Bitner *et al.*, 2000), as shown in Fig. 7.1.

Technology is one of the three most important research priorities in service research (Ostrom *et al.*, 2015). Increasingly, service firms are establishing more efficient and customer-focused technologies (e.g. smartphones, tablets, wearable devices, virtual reality and cloud computing) through multiple modes (personal/face-to-face, self-service, automated and social media) (Fellah, 2014; Rauch, 2014; Ostrom *et al.*, 2015). For instance, Accor, a leading global hotel group with a portfolio of 20 hospitality brands

Fig. 7.1. The service marketing pyramid. (Adapted from Bitner *et al.*, 2000.)

in 95 countries, spent 22 million euros (US$25 million) to enhance customer experience through digital technology (REUTERS, 2015). With the widespread use of technology, the internet and social media, firms need to consider technology in terms of customer interactions and satisfaction (Baker and Magnini, 2016).

Therefore, this chapter aims to provide a better understanding of how technology plays a role in the hospitality and tourism industry in terms of interactive marketing, external marketing and internal marketing. We discuss technology adoption and then review the importance of technology in services and customers' satisfaction and dissatisfaction regarding technology use in service encounters. Technology in relation to managing customers' satisfaction and dissatisfaction in social media and managing service recovery in social media are also discussed. We briefly review the impact of technology use on service employees. Lastly, this chapter introduces and discusses newly emerging technologies in services to enhance customer satisfaction and deliver service excellence.

7.2 Technology Adoption

Service technology interfaces can include point-of-sale terminals, smartphones, tablets and kiosks. These firm-deployed technologies are frequently used during the employee–customer exchange and provide customers with ubiquitous, always on, always connected, smart and seamless service experiences. However, customer reactions to technology-infused service exchanges depend on the valence of employee–customer interactions (Giebelhausen *et al.*, 2014) and customer adoption and satisfaction of technology in service encounters (Meuter *et al.*, 2000; Makarem *et al.*, 2009; Lin and Hsieh, 2011; Oh *et al.*, 2016).

The technology acceptance model investigates customers' perceptions of usefulness and ease of use, intention to use and usage behaviour (Venkatesh and Davis, 2000). For hospitality and tourism organizations, technology adoption, not just technology acceptance, is one of the most critical factors. Hotel technology enables hotels to drive their service objectives better by reducing complexity, increasing system availability and managing properties more efficiently (Amadeus, 2011). In other words, as service technology is becoming an increasingly essential part of many service operations, customers' technology adoption and use is one of the major issues in the hospitality and tourism industry (Law *et al.*, 2013, 2014; Werthner *et al.*, 2015). This is because

M. Lee and M.A. Baker

technology adoption and use significantly influence experience satisfaction with technology in service encounters (Meuter *et al.*, 2003; Liu, 2012), behavioural intentions such as service co-creation and mobile payments (Morosan, 2015; Morosan and DeFranco, 2016) and destination visit intentions (Huang *et al.*, 2013). Demographic factors such as gender, age and level of education all affect customer use of technology. In hospitality settings, technology adoption and use is influenced by situational determinants (i.e. waiting in line and service complexity) and attitudinal determinants (i.e. technology trust and technology anxiety) (Oh *et al.*, 2016). It is also important to consider the effectiveness and integration of technologies in the adoption and use of technology such as smartphones, tablets and other handheld devices in hospitality and tourism settings (Law *et al.*, 2014). These technologies are often used to assist in trip planning and finding trip information.

7.3 Technology and Satisfaction

Technology can play an important role in enabling both employees and customers to enhance their service encounter satisfaction (Bitner *et al.*, 2000; Melián-González and Bulchand-Gidumal, 2016). Satisfaction refers to a customer's evaluation of the pre- and post-purchase experience in relation to their expectations (Oliver, 2010) and satisfaction significantly influences customer behaviours. For instance, effective use of technology may enhance the customer's total experience and service encounter satisfaction by (i) customizing service offerings; (ii) recovering from service failure; and (iii) spontaneously delighting customers (Bitner *et al.*, 2000). In addition, recent research demonstrates that technology can improve organizational performance (Melián-González and Bulchand-Gidumal, 2016) and employees' performance and satisfaction (Jeong *et al.*, 2016) in hospitality firms. Prior research suggests that technology in services results in positive outcomes, including firm performance (Makarem *et al.*, 2009; Melián-González and Bulchand-Gidumal, 2016; Ryu and Lee, 2016), behavioural intentions (Meuter *et al.*, 2000; Morosan, 2015; Morosan and DeFranco, 2016) and customer retention (Scherer *et al.*, 2015). In these relationships, satisfaction plays a pivotal role in enhancing customer behavioural intentions and firm performance (Makarem *et al.*, 2009). A study of Makarem *et al.* (2009) examines technology-related factors enhancing customer satisfaction. They find that service convenience, technology service process, touch service process and service outcome are positively associated with customer satisfaction, resulting in behavioural intentions (i.e. word-of-mouth and future business).

While positive perceptions of technology use leads to positive behavioural outcomes (Huang *et al.*, 2013; Morosan, 2015; Morosan and DeFranco, 2016), forced use of technology may increase technology anxiety, in turn leading to customer dissatisfaction (Liu, 2012). Therefore, service firms need to design and implement technology-infused service encounters very carefully in order to enhance customers' technology use. For example, Meuter *et al.* (2000) demonstrate that customers are satisfied with technology use when technology can solve intensified needs or find the improvements or additional benefits provided by using technology. However, when technology failure occurs, the technology interface is poorly designed or the design of service experience related to technology is not user-friendly, customers may be dissatisfied. Such customer (dis)satisfaction can result in different customer reactions, such as customer complaining and future behaviours (e.g. word-of-mouth and repurchase intentions) (Meuter *et al.*, 2000). Furthermore, malfunctions or failures of service technology due to technical or human error may lead to dissatisfaction and switching behaviours (Zhu *et al.*, 2013). When customers are forced to use service technology, their technology anxiety can increase and technology trust can decrease, leading to a decrease in satisfaction with technology (Liu, 2012). It is also suggested that customers with technology anxiety are less satisfied with the service experience, and are unlikely to engage in positive word-of-mouth or reuse such technology in the future (Meuter *et al.*, 2003). Therefore, technology infusion in service encounters can be a double-edged sword and technology should be designed, implemented and managed very carefully for service excellence.

Recent studies suggest that the presence of employee rapport and customer-recovery expectancy can influence customer reactions to technology-infused service exchanges (Zhu *et al.*, 2013; Giebelhausen *et al.*, 2014). According to the findings of Giebelhausen *et al.* (2014), when employee rapport is present during the service exchange, the use of technology is considered an interpersonal barrier preventing the customer from responding in kind to employee rapport-building efforts, thereby decreasing service encounter evaluations. However, when employees do not engage in rapport-building, technology functions as an interpersonal barrier, enabling customers to retreat from the relatively unpleasant service interaction, in turn increasing service encounter evaluations. In other words, the infusion of technology and employee rapport-building behaviours are fundamentally incompatible in service encounters. In addition, when service technology failure occurs, customers tend to engage in recovery or switching behaviours (Zhu *et al.*, 2013). This study demonstrates that customer-recovery expectancy plays a significant role in the customer-recovery process and therefore firms need to design appropriate strategies and technologies to minimize service failures and encourage customers to repair service failure on their own. In sum, technology in service encounters plays a pivotal role in affecting customers' service satisfaction and evaluations (Bitner *et al.*, 2000; Giebelhausen *et al.*, 2014).

7.4   Customer Relationships in Social Media and Technology

Social media and Web 2.0 are evolving and becoming essential tools, leading to pervasive changes in business-to-business communication, business-to-customer communication and customer-to-customer communication (Kaplan and Haenlein, 2010; Weinberg and Pehlivan, 2011; Leung *et al.*, 2013; Weinberg *et al.*, 2013). Branded hotel properties have an average of 3.7 social media accounts, including Facebook, Instagram, Twitter and Pinterest. A significant proportion of the followers (33%) of these companies follow these companies using these social media accounts (HospitalityNet, 2016). Social media has changed the dynamics of communication between service providers and customers, transforming the way customers communicate with companies (Balaji *et al.*, 2015). Traditionally, customer relationship management focuses on firms using supporting information from technology to manage customer relationships more effectively. What is critical to consider in today's environment is the role played by social media and how it facilitates the three-way interaction between customers, other customers and the firm (Baker, 2017). Social media customer relationship management is a philosophy and business strategy that is supported by technology and designed to engage the customer in a collaborative interaction, providing mutually beneficial value (Greenberg, 2012). How to manage online customer relationships in order to achieve satisfaction and loyalty is a new form of customer relationship management that many firms are attempting to navigate.

7.4.1 Brand image through social media and technology

Hospitality firms such as hotels are actively participating in creating and maintaining their brand pages on various social media platforms. Through this ubiquitous and interactive medium, individuals can be in one community, sharing their daily lives with anyone online, reading others' service experiences and witnessing the hotel's managerial responses to customers' postings. A recent Harvard Business School case study by Avery *et al.* (2015) suggests that a hotel's digital marketing can enhance brand image by exploring new technologies through a new distribution channel and developing the online marketing space for travel reservations. As such, service firms recognize that maintaining ongoing relationships with their customers is beneficial (Oh, 2002). In particular, building a desirable customer–brand relationship through interactive social media channels has become critical (Hudson and Thal, 2013; Hudson *et al.*, 2015). Such a relationship focusing on personalized services can enhance customer satisfaction, trust and commitment (Kim *et al.*, 2006). In the social media context, service firms' continuous and effective efforts can provide more valuable information and create more opportunities to frequently interact with current and potential customers, leading to customer satisfaction (Sashi, 2012; Wei *et al.*, 2013). For example, a potential customer joins a hotel's Facebook brand page to establish an initial relationship (i.e. connection). Once connected, he or she can interact with the hotel and also other members through hotel-initiated contents and/or user contents (i.e. interaction). If such interactions are satisfactory to a focal customer, he or she will stay connected and will continue to interact with the hotel's Facebook brand page and other members there (i.e. satisfaction). Customer satisfaction with a hotel's social media interactions can lead to customer engagement and positive behavioural outcomes such as customer retention, commitment and advocacy (Sashi, 2012).

7.4.2 Posting experiences and searching for information

Online reviews are a very clear indicator of customer satisfaction or dissatisfaction. People posting comments can rate a product or service from one to five stars, lower star rankings showing lower levels of satisfaction. Third-party websites, such as TripAdvisor and Yelp, as well as social media channels such as Facebook, Twitter and Instagram, aim to facilitate and enrich online purchases and enable customers to share experiences and opinions with other customers (Mauri and Minazzi, 2013). Customers search for opinions and experiences of peer customers before purchasing a product or service (Xie *et al.*, 2014). This is especially relevant for hospitality and tourism industries for which dedicated websites such as TripAdvisor review hotels and tourism services and Yelp reviews restaurants. These reviews are posted by a customer, read by other customers and often involve responses from businesses. Frequent ways of measuring these reviews include valence (positive and negative), intensity (quality of the comments), speed (number of contacts in a period of time), persistence (length of time), importance (role of comments in the customer decision-making process) and credibility (assurance and confidence of the poster and posted message) (Mauri and Minazzi, 2013). However, with the proliferation of online postings and information sources, customers can struggle to find reliable and appropriate sources (Law *et al.*, 2014).

7.4.3 Social media satisfaction and dissatisfaction

Social media is considered one of the major channels for customer satisfaction and customer relationship management (Baker, 2017). It can play an important role in managing both employee–customer interactions (i.e. interactive marketing) and company–customer interactions (i.e. external marketing and service recovery) (Hennig-Thurau *et al.*, 2010; Gensler *et al.*, 2013; Malthouse *et al.*, 2013; Baker and Magnini, 2016). The unique nature of social media (i.e. scale, interactivity, speed and real time) enables people to express and share opinions. For instance, if your Facebook friend posts his or her bad experience on a hotel's Facebook brand page, many people can see the service provider's responses to such a complaint and other follow-ups. Thus, social media plays a critical role in spreading customer complaints (Clerck, 2015) and their negative impact on others can often be magnified (Sparks and Bradley, 2014; Sparks *et al.*, 2016). Therefore, managing customers' (dis)satisfaction in social media plays a pivotal role in not only building positive customer relationships, but also enhancing customer satisfaction.

7.5 Managing Service Recoveries in Social Media

Managing online reviews in social media to deal with customer (dis)satisfaction is one of the major roles of enhancing a service provider's reputation and enhancing customer satisfaction (Xiang and Gretzel, 2010; Gu and Ye, 2014; Sparks and Bradley, 2014; Sparks *et al.*, 2016). This is because an individual's service experience and opinions (e.g. online reviews) can significantly affect other customers' information search and decision-making behaviours in hospitality and tourism industries (Xiang and Gretzel, 2010; Sparks and Browning, 2011). When service firms interact with reviewers on third-party websites or customers on their Facebook brand pages by responding to their complaints, such managerial actions can help them to address issues and recover from service failures (Kim *et al.*, 2011; Xie *et al.*, 2014). Accordingly, managing customers' (dis)satisfaction in social media leads to positive outcomes such as other customers' satisfaction (Gu and Ye, 2014), future purchase intentions (Xie *et al.*, 2014), positive impressions (Sparks *et al.*, 2016) and firm performance (Kim *et al.*, 2015). In other words, service firms can meet customers' needs and enhance customer satisfaction by investing their financial and human resources in social media (Anderson, 2012; Kim *et al.*, 2015).

Interestingly, how a firm, such as a hotel, responds or does not respond affects how others perceive the hotel brand and influences their willingness to book a reservation (Baker, 2017). The firm's reaction to the customer review can often have a greater influence on perceptions of the firm than the original post itself. It is suggested that service firms, such as hotels and restaurants, need to constantly update their activities and respond to customers' requests and opinions on social media platforms, because Web 2.0 has transformed how customers develop relationships with service providers (Gensler *et al.*, 2013). Accordingly, recent studies demonstrate that responding to customers' negative reviews or service recovery efforts in social media significantly affects customers' behavioural intentions (Sparks and Bradley, 2014; Azemi and Ozuem, 2016; Manika *et al.*, 2016; Schaefers and Schamari, 2016). In particular, service failure apologies toward the complainant on social media result in his/her positive behavioural intentions (Manika *et al.*, 2016) and virtual presence (Schaefers and Schamari, 2016).

7.6 Impact of Technology Use on Service Employees

While prior research mainly focuses on the customer side of technology use (i.e. external customer), few studies examine the impact of technology use on service employees (i.e. internal customer) (Cheng and Cho, 2011; Hsieh *et al.*, 2013; Jeong *et al.*, 2016; Ryu and Lee, 2016). For instance, a study by Hsieh *et al.* (2013) showed that employee satisfaction with technology plays a major role in influencing the relationship between internal IT service quality and employees' service quality to external customers. They emphasize that managers should understand service employees' different levels of expectations of internal IT service and the differential performance impact of those levels. Similarly, employees' perceptions of using mobile devices in their workplaces positively affect their perceived job performance and satisfaction and employee retention (Jeong *et al.*, 2016). Employees' perceived job performance using mobile devices is positively associated with job retention through their job satisfaction. Furthermore, the findings of Ryu and Lee (2016) suggest that highly qualified employees, customer interaction and technology are essential for improving financial performance. While many firms are focusing on customer adoption, it is also critical for these firms to consider employee use and adoption of the technology.

7.7 Newly Emerging Issues in Technology

Technology is the most dramatic change that is transforming the service field (Ostrom *et al.*, 2015). Based on survey participants' comments, respondents anticipate, in the emergence of a new technology-dominated service context, a ubiquitous, always on, always connected, smart and global world. As shown in Fig. 7.2, future service research centres on technology. There are several current and future technical developments and issues, such as technology-enabled wearable devices, cars, internet of things (IoT), smart tourism, data analytics and collective intelligence (e.g. crowdsourcing).

7.7.1 New technology examples

Virtual reality or augmented reality is considered a new approach to promoting tourism sites, service products and mobile games (Huang *et al.*, 2013, 2016). 3D-based virtual reality enables destination marketing organizations to communicate with targeted markets by offering a rich and entertaining environment for potential visitors. Positive perceptions toward 3D virtual worlds positively influence customers' behavioural intentions and destination brand awareness by enhancing the experiences of 3D tourism sites. Facebook started new services based on virtual reality and presented

Fig. 7.2. Most dramatic change in the future of the service field: Word cloud based on survey comments. (Adapted from Ostrom *et al.*, 2015.)

Fig. 7.3. Virtual reality headset.

M. Lee and M.A. Baker

new platforms, social games and other services that can be played through the virtual reality headset at the company's own developer conference (Sag, 2016).

Recent studies also suggest that mobile technology and applications are instrumental in the development of intentions to engage in co-creation behaviours and use of mobile payments in hotels (Morosan, 2015; Morosan and DeFranco, 2016). Mobile technology (e.g. Smartphone and tablet PC, as shown in Fig. 7.4) has shaken up the travel and hospitality industries and their use is higher among global travellers than in other groups (INTELITY, 2016). Uber (e.g. UberEats) and Amazon (e.g. Amazon Go) recently launched smartphone-based delivery services that also allow customers to make, track and change orders (Wirth, 2016). Through mobile payments such as Apple Pay and Google Wallet, customers can easily pay as well. In addition, e-menus are perceived as an effective way of imparting information about food and enhancing satisfaction in recipients (Hartwell *et al.*, 2016). Wearable technology is another new technology influencing customers' service encounter evaluations and revisit intentions (Wu *et al.*, 2015). Hotels recognize wearable technology as an integral part of guest service in the future (Nerger, 2015). For example, a guest's message requesting additional towels or ordering room services could be easily sent, received and acknowledged by an employee wearing a smart watch (see Fig. 7.5). Domino's also allows customers to order pizza via an Apple Watch.

Restaurants rapidly adopt new technologies for customer ordering, payment and delivery to enhance customer satisfaction and service innovation (Wirth, 2017). Such high-tech advances, including robots, virtual reality and artificial intelligence, have

Fig. 7.4. Mobile technology (tablet PC).

substantially changed the restaurant industry. For instance, S'baggers in Germany and Dalu robot restaurant in Japan provide fully automated services based on robotics. Taco Bell's Tacobot and Wingstop's automated ordering systems are good examples of automated interaction between the restaurant and customers (Wirth, 2016). Wingstop allows social media users to order, interact and ask questions solely with technology. Robots (e.g. drones, as shown in Fig. 7.6) and autonomous cars can be used for food delivery. We believe there is ample room for continued expansion and diverse services based on these new technologies.

Fig. 7.5. Wearable technology.

Fig. 7.6. Drone delivery service.

M. Lee and M.A. Baker

7.7.2   Smart tourism and internet of things

The availability and popularity of mobile technology is rapidly changing the way travellers search and share information, make decisions, communicate and socialize. In addition, the service-dominant logic has received much attention lately as the alternative view of the goods-dominant logic. The service-dominant logic highlights customer-defined and co-created value, a focus on the process of serving and two-way communication, and the long-term relational exchange (Vargo and Lusch, 2008; Ng *et al.*, 2012; Wang *et al.*, 2013). Therefore, mobile technology and the service-dominant logic can make tourism destinations more accessible and enjoyable for visitors, leading to the advent of 'smart tourism'. Smart tourism is the ubiquitous tour information service received by tourists during a touring process (Li *et al.*, 2017, p. 297). It provides real-time and context-based information services intelligently to the tourists, agents, destinations and industries through various communication types and destination data. In addition, smart tourism enhances tourists' experience, improves the effectiveness of resource management, maximizes both destination competitiveness and economic impacts, and demonstrates sustainability (Boes *et al.*, 2015; Buhalis and Amaranggana, 2015; Gretzel *et al.*, 2015). Effective implementation of smart tourism requires three main components: cloud computing, internet of things (IoT) and end-user internet service systems (EUISS) (Buhalis and Amaranggana, 2014). Cloud computing offers convenient and scalable access to applications, software and data through centralized systems and web browsers, while IoT (e.g. RFID tags, QR-codes, sensors, smartphones) enables interaction and cooperation with its neighbours to reach common goals such as information and analysis, automation and control, personalized services, and real-time and societal interactions. EUISS are the applications and equipment support of cloud computing and IoT at various levels of end-users. Thus, through public wireless connections, tourism service providers and government organizations can provide web or mobile portal services and connections to cloud computing services, or tourists can interact with the IoT to obtain various travel services through EUISS.

7.7.3   Intercultural Issues with Technology

An understanding of culture is also important to information technology research because culture can influence successful technology implementation and adoption at various levels, including national, organizational and group (Leidner and Kayworth, 2006). For instance, a study by Truong (2013) demonstrates that culture (national-level) significantly influences consumer attitudes to technological service innovation. In a similar vein, other research suggests that international hotel chains need to consider the diversity of national cultures when they implement self-service technology because undifferentiated use of technology may negatively affect customer service and organizational performance (Fisher and Beatson, 2002). Furthermore, cultural differences (i.e. individualistic culture and collectivistic culture) can lead to different mobile technology adoption patterns by customers (Lee *et al.*, 2013). Therefore, we believe that comprehensive research that examines the impact of culture on new technology adoption and use in hospitality and tourism contexts can help provide a better understanding and more complete perspective on the relationship of new technology and customer satisfaction in the hospitality and tourism literature.

7.8 Conclusion

The proliferation and spread of rapidly advancing technologies has attracted much attention from both industry and academia, and has fundamentally changed the way customers and service firms communicate and interact. To understand the significant roles and effects of technologies in hospitality and tourism, this chapter discusses (i) the importance of technology and customers' (dis)satisfaction regarding technology use in service encounters; (ii) technology as effective tools managing customers' (dis)satisfaction and building customer relationships; (iii) the impact of technology use on service employees as the internal marketing perspective; and (iv) newly emerging technologies in services.

Service firms have devoted considerable efforts to better understand, use and manage technologies to enhance customer satisfaction. However, there are still challenges and opportunities that both industry and academia should tackle to move the hospitality and tourism field forward in terms of understanding the implications of technology use in services for both customers and employees, social media, and the dynamic relationship between employees, customers, firms and technology.

CASE STUDY: NEW TECHNOLOGIES AND CUSTOMER BENEFITS

Accor Launches App for Apple Watch

March 11, 2015

From the end of April, Accor will offer guests an Accorhotels iOS app for Apple Watch™, which is to be released soon. By launching this Accorhotels application for Apple Watch™, Accor is hoping to establish itself as an audacious digital hospitality player.

The policy is part of the group's digital plan, which aims to accompany the changeover to new mobile practices. Accor is embracing the era of connected wearables and adopting an ongoing improvement approach to this market trend so it can provide guests with a value-added service before, during and after their stay.

The Accorhotels app for Apple Watch™ is available in 10 languages and works in connection with the smartphone app.

It notably promotes top hotels and destinations and allows users to manage current bookings on Accorhotels.

Accorhotels customers will:

- Receive alerts telling them the online check-in service is open;
- Access information about their bookings: arrival date, number of nights, number of guests;
- Receive information about the hotel's services (free Wi-Fi, car park, spa, swimming pool, etc.);
- Access the interactive map, the itinerary to find the hotel and the local weather forecast;
- Access their Le Club Accorhotels loyalty card details, with their status and loyalty points.

Continued

M. Lee and M.A. Baker

Questions

1. How does technology play a role in the hospitality and tourism industry?
2. What is hotel technology adoption?
3. How does technology enable both employees and customers to enhance their service encounter satisfaction?
4. What are customer relationships in terms of brand image, online reviews, information search and (dis)satisfaction in social media and technology?
5. How do hospitality firms manage service recovery in social media?
6. How does technology influence service employees?
7. What are the newly emerging issues in technology?

Further Reading

Amadeus (2011) The future of hotels: how technology can move us forward. Available at: http://www.amadeus.com/hotels/newsrepository/articles/future-hotels-how-technology-can-move-us-forward (accessed 3 January 2017).

Huang, Y.-C., Backman, S.J., Backman, K.F. and Moore, D. (2013) Exploring user acceptance of 3D virtual worlds in travel and tourism marketing. *Tourism Management* 36, 490–501.

Kim, W.G., Lim, H. and Brymer, R.A. (2015) The effectiveness of managing social media on hotel performance. *International Journal of Hospitality Management* 44, 165–171.

Liu, S. (2012) The impact of forced use on customer adoption of self-service technologies. *Computers in Human Behavior* 28, 1194–1201.

Zhu, Z., Nakata, C., Sivakumar, K. and Grewal, D. (2013) Fix it or leave it? Customer recovery from self-service technology failures. *Journal of Retailing* 89, 15–29.

References

Amadeus (2011) The future of hotels: how technology can move us forward. Available at: http://www.amadeus.com/hotels/newsrepository/articles/future-hotels-how-technology-can-move-us-forward (accessed 3 January 2017).

Anderson, C. (2012) The impact of social media on lodging performance. *Cornell Hospitality Report* 12, 6–11.

Avery, J., Dev, C.S. and O'Connor, P. (2015) Accor: strengthening the brand with digital marketing. *Harvard Business School Case* 9-315-138.

Azemi, Y. and Ozuem, W. (2016) Online service failure and recovery strategy: the mediating role of social media. In: Bowen, G. and Ozuem, W. (eds) *Competitive Social Media Marketing Strategies*. IGI Global, Hershey, Pennsylvania, pp. 112–135.

Baker, M.A. (2017) Electronic customer relationship management and customer satisfaction. In: Dixit, S.K. (ed.) *The Routledge Handbook of Consumer Behaviour in Hospitality and Tourism*. Taylor & Francis, Abingdon, UK.

Baker, M.A. and Magnini, V.P. (2016) The evolution of services marketing, hospitality marketing and building the constituency model for hospitality marketing. *International Journal of Contemporary Hospitality Management* 28, 1510–1534.

Balaji, M.S., Jha, S. and Royne, M.B. (2015) Customer e-complaining behaviours using social media. *The Service Industries Journal* 35, 633–654.

Bitner, M.J., Brown, S.W. and Meuter, M.L. (2000) Technology infusion in service encounters. *Journal of the Academy of Marketing Science* 28, 138–149.

Boes, K., Buhalis, D. and Inversini, A. (2015) Conceptualising smart tourism destination dimensions. In: Tussyadiah, I. and Inversini, A. (eds) *Information and Communication Technologies in Tourism 2015*. Proceedings of the International Conference in Lugano, Switzerland, 3–6 February. Springer International, Cham, Switzerland, pp. 391–403.

Buhalis, D. and Amaranggana, A. (2014) *Smart Tourism Destinations in Information and Communication Technologies in Tourism 2014*. Springer International, Cham, Switzerland, pp. 553–564.

Buhalis, D. and Amaranggana, A. (2015) Smart tourism destinations enhancing tourism experience through personalization of services. In: Tussyadiah, I. and Inversini, A. (eds) *Information and Communication Technologies in Tourism 2015*. Proceedings of the International Conference in Lugano, Switzerland, 3–6 February. Springer International, Cham, Switzerland, pp. 377–389.

Cheng, S. and Cho, V. (2011) An integrated model of employees' behavioral intention toward innovative information and communication technologies in travel agencies. *Journal of Hospitality & Tourism Research* 35, 488–510.

Clerck, J.-P. De (2015) Understanding word-of-mouth in the digital age. Available at: http://www.i-scoop.eu/understanding-word-mouth-social-media-age/ (accessed 15 January 2016).

Fellah, A. (2014) Hotel chain focuses on guest experience through digital strategy. Available at: https://www.linkedin.com/pulse/20141104144529-570537-hotel-chain-focuses-on-guest-experience-through-digital-strategy (accessed 1 January 2015).

Fisher, G. and Beatson, A. (2002) The impact of culture on self-service on technology adoption in the hotel industry. *International Journal of Hospitality & Tourism Administration* 3, 59–77.

Gensler, S., Völckner, F., Liu-Thompkins, Y. and Wiertz, C. (2013) Managing brands in the social media environment. *Journal of Interactive Marketing* 27, 242–256.

Giebelhausen, M., Robinson, S.G., Sirianni, N.J. and Brady, M.K. (2014) Touch versus tech: when technology functions as a barrier or a benefit to service encounters. *Journal of Marketing* 78, 113–124.

Greenberg, J. (2012) *Managing Behavior in Organizations*. Pearson Higher Education, Upper Saddle River, New Jersey.

Gretzel, U., Werthner, H., Koo, C. and Lamsfus, C. (2015) Conceptual foundations for understanding smart tourism ecosystems. *Computers in Human Behavior* 50, 558–563.

Gu, B. and Ye, Q. (2014) First step in social media: measuring the influence of online management responses on customer satisfaction. *Production and Operations Management* 23, 570–582.

Hartwell, H., Johns, N. and Edwards, J.S.A. (2016) E-menus –managing choice options in hospital foodservice. *International Journal of Hospitality Management* 53, 12–16.

Hennig-Thurau, T., Malthouse, E.C., Friege, C., Gensler, S., Lobschat, L., Rangaswamy, A. and Skiera, B. (2010) The impact of new media on customer relationships. *Journal of Service Research* 13, 311–330.

HospitalityNet (2016) 12 Luxury hotel brands: a social media presence overview. Available at: http://www.hospitalitynet.org/news/4078765.html (accessed 3 January 2017).

Hsieh, J.J.P.A., Sharma, P., Rai, A. and Parasuraman, A. (2013) Exploring the zone of tolerance for internal customers in IT-enabled call centers. *Journal of Service Research* 16, 277–294.

Huang, Y.-C., Backman, S.J., Backman, K.F. and Moore, D. (2013) Exploring user acceptance of 3D virtual worlds in travel and tourism marketing. *Tourism Management* 36, 490–501.

Huang, Y.C., Backman, K.F., Backman, S.J. and Chang, L.L. (2016) Exploring the implications of virtual reality technology in tourism marketing: an integrated research framework. *International Journal of Tourism Research* 18, 116–128.

Hudson, S. and Thal, K. (2013) The impact of social media on the consumer decision process: implications for tourism marketing. *Journal of Travel & Tourism Marketing* 30, 156–160.

Hudson, S., Roth, M.S., Madden, T.J. and Hudson, R. (2015) The effects of social media on emotions, brand relationship quality, and word of mouth: an empirical study of music festival attendees. *Tourism Management* 47, 68–76.

INTELITY (2016) A brief look at the history of hotel technology. Available at: http://intelitycorp.com/main/brief-look-history-hotel-technology (accessed 3 January 2017).

Jeong, M., Lee, M. and Nagesvaran, B. (2016) Employees' use of mobile devices and their perceived outcomes in the workplace: a case of luxury hotel. *International Journal of Hospitality Management* 57, 40–51.

Kaplan, A.M. and Haenlein, M. (2010) Users of the world, unite! The challenges and opportunities of social media. *Business Horizons* 53, 59–68.

Kim, E.E.K., Mattila, A.S. and Baloglu, S. (2011) Effects of gender and expertise on consumers' motivation to read online hotel reviews. *Cornell Hospitality Quarterly* 52, 399–406.

Kim, W.G., Lee, Y.-K. and Yoo, Y.-J. (2006) Predictors of relationship quality and relationship outcomes in luxury restaurants. *Journal of Hospitality & Tourism Research* 30, 143–169.

Kim, W.G., Lim, H. and Brymer, R.A. (2015) The effectiveness of managing social media on hotel performance. *International Journal of Hospitality Management* 44, 165–171.

Law, R., Leung, D., Au, N. and Lee, H.A. (2013) Progress and development of information technology in the hospitality industry: evidence from Cornell Hospitality Quarterly. *Cornell Hospitality Quarterly* 54, 10–24.

Law, R., Buhalis, D. and Cobanoglu, C. (2014) Progress on information and communication technologies in hospitality and tourism. *International Journal of Contemporary Hospitality Management* 26, 727–750.

Lee, S.-G., Trimi, S. and Kim, C. (2013) The impact of cultural differences on technology adoption. *Journal of World Business* 48, 20–29.

Leidner, D.E. and Kayworth, T. (2006) Review: a review of culture in information systems research: toward a theory of information technology culture conflict. *MIS Quarterly* 30, 357–399.

Leung, D., Law, R., van Hoof, H. and Buhalis, D. (2013) Social media in tourism and hospitality: a literature review. *Journal of Travel & Tourism Marketing* 30, 3–22.

Li, Y., Hu, C., Huang, C. and Duan, L. (2017) The concept of smart tourism in the context of tourism information services. *Tourism Management* 58, 293–300.

Lin, J.-S.C. and Hsieh, P.-L. (2011) Assessing the self-service technology encounters: development and validation of SSTQUAL scale. *Journal of Retailing* 87, 194–206.

Liu, S. (2012) The impact of forced use on customer adoption of self-service technologies. *Computers in Human Behavior* 28, 1194–1201.

Makarem, S.C., Mudambi, S.M. and Podoshen, J.S. (2009) Satisfaction in technology-enabled service encounters. *Journal of Services Marketing* 23, 134–143.

Malthouse, E.C., Haenlein, M., Skiera, B., Wege, E. and Zhang, M. (2013) Managing customer relationships in the social media era: introducing the social CRM house. *Journal of Interactive Marketing* 27, 270–280.

Manika, D., Papagiannidis, S. and Bourlakis, M. (2016) Understanding the effects of a social media service failure apology: a comparative study of customers vs. potential customers. *International Journal of Information Management* 37, 214–228.

Mauri, A.G. and Minazzi, R. (2013) Web reviews influence on expectations and purchasing intentions of hotel potential customers. *International Journal of Hospitality Management* 34, 99–107.

Melián-González, S. and Bulchand-Gidumal, J. (2016) A model that connects information technology and hotel performance. *Tourism Management* 53, 30–37.

Meuter, M.L., Ostrom, A.L., Roundtree, R.I. and Bitner, M.J. (2000) Self-service technologies: understanding customer satisfaction with technology-based service encounters. *Journal of Marketing* 64, 50–64.

Meuter, M.L., Ostrom, A.L., Bitner, M.J. and Roundtree, R. (2003) The influence of technology anxiety on consumer use and experiences with self-service technologies. *Journal of Business Research* 56, 899–906.

Morosan, C. (2015) An empirical analysis of intentions to co-create value in hotels using mobile devices. *Journal of Hospitality & Tourism Research* doi.org/10.1177/1096348015597034.

Morosan, C. and DeFranco, A. (2016) It's about time: revisiting UTAUT2 to examine consumers' intentions to use NFC mobile payments in hotels. *International Journal of Hospitality Management* 53, 17–29.

Nerger, M. (2015) Wearables to play an integral role in guest service. CIOReview. Available at: http://travel-hospitality.cioreview.com/cioviewpoint/wearables-to-play-an-integral-role-in-guest-service-nid-5309-cid-40.html (accessed 3 January 2017).

Ng, I., Parry, G., Smith, L., Maull, R. and Briscoe, G. (2012) Transitioning from a goods dominant to a service dominant logic. *Journal of Service Management* 23, 416–439.

Oh, H. (2002) Transaction evaluations and relationship intentions. *Journal of Hospitality & Tourism Research* 26, 278–305.

Oh, H., Jeong, M., Lee, S.A. and Warnick, R. (2016) Attitudinal and situational determinants of self-service technology use. *Journal of Hospitality & Tourism Research* 40, 236–265.

Oliver, R.L. (2010) *Satisfaction: A Behavioral Perspective on the Consumer*. M.E. Sharpe, Armonk, New York.

Ostrom, A.L., Parasuraman, A., Bowen, D.E., Patrício, L. and Voss, C.A. (2015) Service research priorities in a rapidly changing context. *Journal of Service Research* 18, 127–159.

Parasuraman, A. (1996) Understanding and leveraging the role of customer service in external, interactive and internal marketing. In: *Frontiers in Services Conference*, Nashville, Tennessee.

Rauch, R. (2014) Top 10 hospitality industry trends in 2015. Hotel-Online. Available at: http://hotel-online.com/press_releases/release/top-10-hospitality-industry-trends-in-2015 (accessed 3 January 2017).

REUTERS (2015) Accor steps up digital push and changes name. Available at: http://www.reuters.com/article/us-accor-digital-idUSKBN0OJ0CW20150603 (accessed 3 January 2017).

Ryu, H.-S. and Lee, J.-N. (2016) Innovation patterns and their effects on firm performance. *Service Industries Journal* 36, 81–101.

Sag, A. (2016) Facebook's Oculus Connect 3 and the Future of Virtual Reality. *Forbes* 14 October.

Sashi, C.M. (2012) Customer engagement, buyer–seller relationships, and social media. *Management Decision* 50, 253–272.

Schaefers, T. and Schamari, J. (2016) Service recovery via social media: the social influence effects of virtual presence. *Journal of Service Research* 19, 192–208.

Scherer, A., Wünderlich, N.V. and von Wangenheim, F. (2015) The value of self-service: long-term effects of technology-based self-service usage on customer retention. *MIS Quarterly* 39, 177–200.

Sparks, B.A. and Bradley, G.L. (2014) A 'Triple A' typology of responding to negative consumer-generated online reviews. *Journal of Hospitality & Tourism Research* doi.org/10.1177/1096348014538052.

Sparks, B.A. and Browning, V. (2011) The impact of online reviews on hotel booking intentions and perception of trust. *Tourism Management* 32, 1310–1323.

Sparks, B.A., So, K.K.F. and Bradley, G.L. (2016) Responding to negative online reviews: the effects of hotel responses on customer inferences of trust and concern. *Tourism Management* 53, 74–85.

Truong, Y. (2013) A cross-country study of consumer innovativeness and technological service innovation. *Journal of Retailing and Consumer Services* 20, 130–137.

Vargo, S.L. and Lusch, R.F. (2008) Service-dominant logic: continuing the evolution. *Journal of the Academy of Marketing Science* 36, 1–10.

Venkatesh, V. and Davis, F.D. (2000) A theoretical extension of the technology acceptance model: four longitudinal field studies. *Management Science* 46, 186–204.

Wang, D., Li, X.R. and Li, Y. (2013) China's 'smart tourism destination' initiative: a taste of the service-dominant logic. *Journal of Destination Marketing & Management* 2, 59–61.

Wei, W., Miao, L. and Huang, Z.W. (2013) Customer engagement behaviors and hotel responses. *International Journal of Hospitality Management* 33, 316–330.

Weinberg, B.D. and Pehlivan, E. (2011) Social spending: managing the social media mix. *Business Horizons* 54, 275–282.

Weinberg, B.D., de Ruyter, K., Dellarocas, C., Buck, M. and Keeling, D.I. (2013) Destination social business: exploring an organization's journey with social media, collaborative community and expressive individuality. *Journal of Interactive Marketing* 27, 299–310.

Werthner, H., Alzua-Sorzabal, A., Cantoni, L., Dickinger, A., Gretzel, U., Jannach, D., Neidhardt, J., Pröll, B., Ricci, F., Scaglione, M., Stangl, B., Stock, O. and Zanker, M. (2015) Future research issues in IT and tourism. *Information Technology & Tourism* 15, 1–15.

Wirth, S.R. (2016) The 7 most important tech developments of 2016. *Restaurant Business*. Available at: http://www.restaurantbusinessonline.com/operations/technology/7-most-important-tech-developments-2016#page=0 (accessed 3 January 2017).

Wirth, S.R. (2017) What's the next big thing in restaurant tech? *Restaurant Business*. Available at: http://www.restaurantbusinessonline.com/operations/technology/what-s-next-big-thing-restaurant-tech#page=1 (accessed 3 January 2017).

Wu, L., Fan, A.A. and Mattila, A.S. (2015) Wearable technology in service delivery processes: the gender-moderated technology objectification effect. *International Journal of Hospitality Management* 51, 1–7.

Xiang, Z. and Gretzel, U. (2010) Role of social media in online travel information search. *Tourism Management* 31, 179–188.

Xie, K.L., Zhang, Z. and Zhang, Z. (2014) The business value of online consumer reviews and management response to hotel performance. *International Journal of Hospitality Management* 43, 1–12.

Zhu, Z., Nakata, C., Sivakumar, K. and Grewal, D. (2013) Fix it or leave it? Customer recovery from self-service technology failures. *Journal of Retailing* 89, 15–29.

8

Self-Service Technologies: Service Failures and Recovery

Petranka Kelly, Jennifer Lawlor and Michael Mulvey

Learning Objectives

After reading this chapter, you should be able to:

- Understand self-service technologies in tourism (definition and classifications).
- Understand the benefits/drawbacks of self-service technologies.
- Explain self-service technology failures (definition and types).
- Understand self-service technology recovery strategies.
- Understand customer participation in self-service technology recovery.
- Evaluate the effectiveness of self-service technology recovery activities.

8.1   Introduction

The technological revolution has facilitated increased implementation of various technological interfaces by the tourism sector, thus enabling customers to deliver services independent of direct employee involvement (Meuter *et al.*, 2000; Oh *et al.*, 2013). This self-service technology usage requires the active involvement of the customer in the delivery of the core service offering, which may have both positive and negative implications for their experience (Hilton *et al.*, 2013). Self-service technology usage may empower customers by providing them with more control over the service they obtain, but it may also force them into unwanted 'work' and responsibilities (Kelly *et al.*, 2017). The leveraged role of tourism customers as producers of the service poses questions regarding the readiness of customers to undertake their active role as 'quasi-employees' and deliver positive tourism experiences (Lawlor, 2010). With the ever-increasing amount of technology being utilized in the tourism sector, it is essential that research does not recognize technology only as enhancing the tourism experience, but also explores how it may possibly destroy this experience and lead to service failures (Neuhofer, 2016). With the increasing importance placed on technology in the tourism experience (e.g. Gretzel and Jamal, 2009; Neuhofer *et al.*, 2013) and the critical influence of self-service technology failures on customer satisfaction (Meuter *et al.*, 2000), the effective recovery from self-service technology failures becomes necessary to ensure that customers receive superior tourism experiences. Therefore, the focus of this chapter is the customer perspective on the impact of self-service technology failure and recovery on their service experiences in the tourism sector. The chapter begins with a review of definitions and classifications of self-service technologies in the tourism sector, followed by a review of the research literature on service failure and recovery in self-service technologies. This review provides a synthesis of current knowledge and identifies areas for further research in the concluding section.

8.2 Self-Service Technologies in a Tourism Context

The advance of information and communication technologies in the tourism sector (Gretzel and Jamal, 2009; Neuhofer *et al.*, 2013) has facilitated the implementation of self-service technologies. Self-service technologies are not new to customer service and they allow customers to get actively involved in co-producing the core service offering with the service provider, thus shifting the role of customers to 'partial employees' (Graf, 2007). The banking industry has been a leader in the adoption of self-service technologies with the introduction of the ATM in 1967 by Barclays Bank in London (Abdelaziz *et al.*, 2010). Self-service technologies have since been adopted in industries such as retail, education, health care, government services, insurance, financial services, transport and tourism. Popular self-service technologies include interfaces such as self-checkouts in supermarkets (Dabholkar *et al.*, 2003; Wang *et al.*, 2012), e-commerce websites (Forbes *et al.*, 2005; Connolly and Bannister, 2008), train ticketing kiosks (Reinders *et al.*, 2008), internet banking (Walker and Johnson, 2006; Yousafzai *et al.*, 2009), touch screens for ordering at fast-food restaurants (Dabholkar and Bagozzi, 2002) and m-commerce (Ondrus and Pigneur, 2006; Lu and Su, 2009).

Self-service technologies have been infusing the tourism industry with growing speed and are changing the roles of customers and companies in providing tourism services (Lawlor, 2010). Ticketing counters at train stations are being replaced by self-service kiosks and automatic scanning facilities (Reinders *et al.*, 2015). Air travel is the most forward-thinking transport sector in terms of technology implementation. In the airline industry, traditional customer check-in is in the process of being totally replaced by onsite kiosks, online check-in and mobile check-in facilities (Abdelaziz *et al.*, 2010). The concept of a 'smart airport', where self-service technology is introduced at every stage of the customer journey, is already being implemented at Hamad International Airport, Qatar (Future Travel Experience, 2016). Airports worldwide are taking steps towards automating the air passenger journey. Dublin International Airport was the first to implement one of the latest airport technological innovations, i.e. express self-service bag-drop facilities (Gittens, 2016). This €2 million investment was made in order to streamline and improve the passenger journey (Gittens, 2016). Geneva Airport is currently running a test project to implement a self-service bag-drop robot that checks in the luggage outside the airport and transports it straight to the airplane (SITA, 2016).

Traditional hotel services are being transformed by technologies such as automated check-in and check-out facilities, automated room-service ordering systems, automated messaging services and automated house-keeping services (Beatson *et al.*, 2007; Oh *et al.*, 2013). Hospitality technology innovation, which was pioneered by brands like Omena Hotels, Premier Inn and CitizenM, is now becoming the norm in the modern hospitality industry. According to the Lodging Technology Study 2016, 56% of surveyed hotels are going to invest more in technology across their hotel service (Terry, 2016). Omena Hotels offer full self-service technology facilities in the Netherlands and

Denmark, providing attractively priced accommodation in city centres (Egger and Buhalis, 2008; Castro *et al.*, 2010). Omena Hotel rooms are booked online, the check-in process is performed online, the room key is a code received at check-in and the onsite reception desk is replaced by a 24-hour hotline which connects guests to a central customer service desk and security operation (Egger and Buhalis, 2008). Similarly, hotel chains like Premier Inn and CitizenM have embraced the mobile and on-site kiosk check-in in their operations (www.premierinn.com; www.citizenm.com). Furthering the evolution, in July 2015, the first robot-staffed hotel Hen-na opened in Japan (Rajesh, 2015). The hotel has introduced robot front-desk check-in and concierges who utilize speech recognition in a few languages to assist customers (Rajesh, 2015). Although the introduction of robots was driven by cost savings, the hotel has become an attraction in itself with people looking to experience a different hotel stay.

In the restaurant industry, the UK-based Inamo restaurants offer innovative self-service technologies where customers order their meal from interactive technology table tops (Neuhofer *et al.*, 2013). The table top provides a variety of other services, such as entertainment and taxi ordering. Self-service technologies have been implemented by the fast-food chain McDonald's to fuel their customers' creativity and increase customization with the 'Create your taste' campaign (www.yesmcd.com). Customers can choose from a variety of ingredients and create a custom-made burger at the McDonald's website or the on-site kiosks at selected McDonald's restaurants. It is the crafty implementation of technology that helped the pizza delivery chain Domino's gain a competitive edge and overcome its falling sales back in 2008 (Maze, 2016). Domino's pizza can be ordered via computer, mobile or a smart watch, while customers' data are carefully analysed by data scientists to deliver a superior experience (Maze, 2016).

The attractions sector is also embracing technology with large museums, such as the British Museum and the Brooklyn Museum, offering interactive augmented reality and beacon technology applications (Shu, 2015). These applications guide visitors through the museum and allow users to gain additional information about exhibits. The Louvre Museum in France has partnered with Nintendo to use the 3DS XL technology for its interactive guides (www.louvreguide.nintendo.com).

The concept of self-service technologies is further examined in the following sections, in terms of their definition, classifications and the benefits and drawbacks of implementing them.

8.2.1 Definition of self-service technologies

Self-service technologies are a distinctive form of information and communication technology (ICT) in that they not only allow for co-creation of experiences, but also for co-production of a core service offering with the customer (Hilton and Hughes, 2013). As identified above, self-service technologies are a form of ICT that enable companies to deliver a self-service independently of direct service employee involvement (Meuter *et al.*, 2000). The permeation of technology in customer self-service started attracting research attention in the 1980s, with Bateson (1985) identifying automated teller machines (ATMs) and pay-at-the-pump automated self-service facilities in his research on customer usage of self-service options. A 'technology-based self-service' was the first term introduced by Dabholkar (1994) to reflect this self-service customer–technology interaction. Dabholkar and Bagozzi provide the following definition of technology-based self-service as including 'on-site' and 'off-site' elements:

> Technology-based self-service includes 'on-site' options such as touch screens in department stores, information kiosks at hotels, and self-screening in grocery stores and libraries; it also includes 'off-site' options such as telephone and on-line banking and shopping on the Internet. (2002, p. 184)

Self-service technologies and technology-based self-service are used interchangeably in the research literature, although Reinders *et al.* (2008) argue that technology-based self-service is a more accurate term because it accentuates the self-service process rather than the technology. Studies into technology-based self-service (see, for example, Reinders *et al.*, 2008; Kinard *et al.*, 2009; Dabholkar and Spaid, 2012) and self-service technologies (see, for example, Curran and Meuter, 2007; Dean, 2008; Wang *et al.*, 2012) provide important contributions to our knowledge regarding the challenges associated with the successful implementation of self-service technologies. Recent studies have displayed a preference for the term self-service technologies (see for example, Leung and Matanda, 2013; Rosenbaum and Wong, 2015). Therefore, the term that will be used throughout this chapter is self-service technologies, in order to comply with the prevailing trend and avoid ambiguity. Since self-service technologies are a diverse group, the effective management of service failures requires understanding of the various classifications of self-service technologies.

8.2.2 Classifications of self-service technologies

This section provides a discussion of the various classifications of self-service technologies in the literature to date. These classifications have been introduced with the purpose of providing a conceptual foundation for self-service technology research (Meuter *et al.*, 2000) and for facilitating research into specific self-service technology issues (e.g. Forbes *et al.*, 2005). One of the first classifications of self-service technologies was proposed by Dabholkar (1994). She suggested a classification of technology-based services consisting of three dimensions: by whom, where and how the service is delivered. The first dimension relating to 'who' delivers the service seeks to differentiate between the customer and the employee using the technology to deliver the service (Dabholkar, 1994). This dimension does not specifically relate to self-service technologies as employee usage of technology is not self-service (Anselmsson, 2001). The second dimension relating to 'where' the service is delivered divides technology-based services into those delivered at the service site and those delivered from the customer's home or work place (Dabholkar, 1994). For example, an ATM or an airport check-in kiosk would be classified as self-service technologies at the service site, while internet shopping and distance learning would be at the customer's site (Anselmsson, 2001). The third dimension, relating to 'how' the service is delivered, includes the options of direct interaction with the technology or indirect contact (Dabholkar, 1994). The self-service technology service may be direct when the customer directly interacts with the technology, such as self-scanning, or indirect when the customer is not in direct interaction with the technology, such as automated time schedules (Anselmsson, 2001).

A popular typology of self-service technologies is proposed by Meuter *et al.* (2000), who categorize self-service technologies according to the dimensions of interface (for example, telephone/interactive voice response, online/internet, interactive kiosks and video/CD) and purpose (for example, customer service, transactions and self-help). The interface dimension reflects the types of technological interfaces that customers interact with, and the dimension of purpose reflects the tasks that customers can achieve by using the self-service technology. It is noticeable from later reviews of self-service technology interfaces (see, for example, Castro *et al.*, 2010) that the video/CD interface is not as prominent and that other interfaces such as smart phones and mobile devices are discussed. Mobile devices are not present in Meuter *et al.*'s (2000) classification, because of the lack of availability of smart phones and mobile internet access in consumer markets at the time. Smart phones are currently used for commercial and financial transactions, online reservations, airline check-in and boarding and mobile banking (Castro *et al.*, 2010).

The specific characteristics of a self-service technology and the context of where and how a self-service technology is used are associated with the types of failures and corresponding recovery strategies (Forbes, 2008). Forbes *et al.* (2005) and Forbes (2008) refer to self-service technology service failure and recovery strategies under two broad groups: internet self-service technologies (e-commerce websites) and non-internet self-service technologies (such as kiosks and telephone selection menus). Furthermore, Schumann *et al.* (2012) propose that self-service technologies can be classified based on the provision of the technological interface by the service provider (provider-based self-services) or by the customer (customer-based self-services). The ownership of the technology will have an effect on the level of responsibility for the management of technological breakdowns (Schumann *et al.*, 2012).

Gelbrich and Sattler (2014) and Collier *et al.* (2014) introduce a public/private dimension to differentiate the social context of self-service technology delivery. The location of the self-service technology may also be connected to the public/private dimension (Collier *et al.*, 2014). Public self-service technologies are generally used at the service site where interaction between patrons may take place (Collier *et al.*, 2014). Private self-service technologies allow for encounters to take place without interactions with others, such as internet and interactive phone systems (Collier *et al.*, 2014). Dabholkar and Spaid (2012) suggest that the crowdedness of the area where service recovery takes place had an effect on customer perceptions of the recovery outcome.

A summary of self-service technology classifications and specific examples is presented in Table 8.1. This table has been developed by the authors, and it represents a synthesized illustration of the diversity of self-service technologies and the myriad dimensions applicable to their classification.

8.2.3 Benefits and drawbacks of self-service technologies

There are benefits to be gained from implementing self-service technologies, both for the customer and the service provider (Lawlor, 2010). According to Anitsal and Schumann (2007), both the service provider and the customer need to perceive gains from using self-service technologies in order to ensure their successful implementation. Since customer adoption of self-service technologies is central to their successful implementation,

Table 8.1. SST classification dimensions. (From Kelly *et al.*)

Authors	Dimension	Examples
Dabholkar (1994) Anselmsson (2001)	Where is the service delivered? (at service site, at customer's home or work)	At service site – library checkouts, ATMs, tourist information At customer's site – internet shopping, financial transactions, distance learning
	How is the service delivered? (direct, indirect)	Direct – self-scanning at retail, online information Indirect – telephone banking, automated time schedules
Meuter *et al.* (2000)	Purpose (customer service, transactions, self-help)	Customer service – order status, account information, ATMs Transactions – financial transactions, pay at the pump Self-help – internet information search, tourist information
	Interface (telephone/interactive voice response, online/internet, interactive kiosk, video/CD)	Telephone – telephone banking, information telephone lines Online – retail purchasing, distance learning, order tracking Kiosk – ATMs, hotel checkouts, blood pressure machines Video/CD – tax preparation software, CD-based training
Forbes (2008), Forbes *et al.* (2005)	Internet medium (internet, non-internet)	Internet – e-commerce Non-internet – kiosks
Castro *et al.* (2010)	Interface (electronic kiosks, internet applications, mobile devices, telephone applications)	Electronic kiosks – photo printing kiosks, postal kiosks, electronic voting, food ordering kiosks, airport kiosks Internet applications – online banking, e-learning, e-commerce, ticketing and reservation Mobile devices – smart phones, mobile payments, smart cards Telephone applications – dual tone multi-frequency, interactive voice response
Schumann *et al.* (2012)	Ownership of the technology (provider-based, customer-based)	Provider-based – ATMs Customer-based – online banking
Collier *et al.* (2014); Gelbrich and Sattler (2014)	Presence of other customers (private, public)	Private – online shopping, online banking, interactive phone systems Public – ATM, self-checkout

service providers need to be familiar with what might encourage or discourage customers from using self-service technologies (Bitner *et al.*, 2002). Self-service technologies may be accompanied by some limitations and disadvantages for the service provider, which also need to be considered and weighed against the potential rewards (Lee and Allaway, 2002).

Self-service technologies may reduce the number of employees necessary for a service operation, which represents a major operational cost savings advantage for companies (Lawlor, 2010). Customers benefit from greater control over the service, convenience, and price and time savings (Meuter *et al.*, 2003). Researchers suggest that by actively participating in the service delivery, the customer feels in control, thereby contributing to the service quality and thus being in charge of their own satisfaction (Bitner *et al.*, 2000; Dabholkar *et al.*, 2003; Lawlor, 2006). Putting customers in greater control provides for better customization and hence satisfaction with the service (Neuhofer *et al.*, 2013).

On the negative side, self-service technology implementation may be perceived as depriving customers of personal contact and resulting in a reduction in the quality of the service (Gerrard *et al.*, 2006). Self-service technology usage may result in negative psychological outcomes for the customer, such as technological anxiety (Meuter *et al.*, 2003) or social embarrassment in situations when customers do not possess the necessary technological skills to operate the self-service technology (Forbes, 2008). Furthermore, there are perceptions among customers of financial, privacy and security threats when using self-service technologies (McKnight *et al.*, 2002). Self-service technologies may also be associated with job losses and may be perceived by the public as a socio-economic threat (Castro *et al.*, 2010; Schumann *et al.*, 2012).

Although self-service technologies may create new markets and opportunities, the immediate job losses may affect the image of the business if the transition is not communicated in a positive manner by governments and businesses (Castro *et al.*, 2010). Self-service technology implementation may represent a disruptive organizational and social change that requires informed and professional leadership and management (Lee and Allaway, 2002; Castro *et al.*, 2010).

Similarly to traditional personal service, self-service technology failures will reduce customers' perceptions of benefits from self-service technology usage and enhance the drawbacks (Anitsal and Schumann, 2007). Service failure is defined as the situation when customers' perceived quality of a service does not match their expectations (Dabholkar and Spaid, 2012).

Since service failures can have severe negative impacts on customer satisfaction with self-service technologies and their continued usage, research has explored the efficiency of various service recovery strategies to mitigate negative perceptions (e.g. Dabholkar and Spaid, 2012; Castillo-Manzano and López-Valpuesta, 2013). Self-service technology recovery research suggests that recovery strategies in traditional personal services may not be fully effective in self-service technologies because of the technological environment, reduced employee contact and the role of the customer in the delivery of the service (Forbes, 2008; Mattila *et al.*, 2011). The following sections provide an overview of the theoretical background of self-service technology failure and recovery research and the challenges in this field of study.

8.3 Self-Service Technology Failure

Service failure is the situation when customers' perceived quality expectations of a service do not match the actual service quality delivered (Castillo-Manzano and López-Valpuesta 2013). Similarly to offline services, self-service technology failure occurs when customer service evaluations fall below their expectations, thus resulting in service dissatisfaction (Tan *et al.*, 2016). The aim of service provision is to achieve customer satisfaction and profit for businesses (Fisk *et al.*, 1993). Customer satisfaction is a central concept of the expectation-disconfirmation paradigm in service (Westbrook and Oliver, 1991). Customer satisfaction is present when customer expectations of the quality of a service coincide with the actual level of service quality achieved (Dabholkar and Spaid, 2012). Alternatively, service quality may exceed customer expectations (positive disconfirmation) or fail to meet customer expectations (negative disconfirmation) (Etzel and Silverman, 1981). Following on from service failure, service recovery constitutes actions undertaken to restore service satisfaction (Xu *et al.*, 2016). Although research into total quality management has focused on designing service processes which provide 'zero defect' strategies, 'zero defect' is an unattainable and often undesirable strategy in services (Hart *et al.*, 1990).

Services in their essence cannot be managed as a rigid manufacturing process because of their interactive nature and dependency on human and contextual factors (Vargo and Lusch, 2004). Aiming to satisfy every customer of a company and recover any negative disconfirmation may ultimately stimulate over-complaining in customers who take advantage of the company and affect its profitability (Etzel and Silverman, 1981; Fisk *et al.*, 2010). The unattainability of a 100% customer satisfaction strategy is further intensified by the specific characteristics of the tourism context (Kim *et al.*, 2009). First, most tourism services, such as a visit to a museum or a fine dining experience, represent intangible experiences that are interpreted subjectively by the customer. Second, some tourism services are purchased before experience, which increases the risk of not meeting customer expectations. Third, there could be variations in performance because of dependence on situational variables like weather, performance of the different components of the package and other tourists. And lastly, tourism services are perishable, so service quality is largely dependent on fluctuations in demand (Kim *et al.*, 2009).

There are two main characteristics of self-service technology environments that make self-service technology failures different from personal service failures, namely less customer–employee contact and active delivery of the core service offering by the self-service technology user. Although higher levels of co-creation in service delivery generate more customer satisfaction, higher co-creation amplifies the negative disconfirmation in service failures (Heidenreich *et al.*, 2015). Self-service technology users may internalize guilt for the service failure and feel obliged to participate in service recovery (Zhu *et al.*, 2013; Heidenreich *et al.*, 2015). These specific characteristics of the self-service technology environment pose a challenge when adapting existing traditional service recovery strategies to a self-service technology context (Zhu *et al.*, 2013).

The nature of self-service technology encounters does not typically include much employee intervention, which makes it hard to monitor service failures and initiate timely and efficient service recovery efforts (Forbes, 2008; Mattila *et al.*, 2011; Dabholkar and Spaid, 2012). This raises the question of what happens when the technology fails. In many cases, customers may have to contact a service representative to solve their problem, which defeats the purpose of self-service (Bitner *et al.*, 2002). Current research has not provided sufficient understanding of self-service technology failures on customer usage behaviour and how such failures could be managed (Dabholkar and Spaid, 2012). The following section examines different types of self-service technology failures.

8.3.1 Self-service technology failure types

Self-service technology failures may be evidenced when users' expectations of the service are not achieved or a service breakdown occurs. When using self-service technologies, customers expect to achieve benefits, such as control, convenience, lower price, independence, enjoyment and efficiency (Meuter *et al.*, 2003; Kelly *et al.*, 2013). These benefits are not always achieved in self-service technology usage, leading to negative customer evaluations of self-service technologies and thus failure of the service (Hilton *et al.*, 2013; Kelly *et al.*, 2013). Customer expectations of e-service have been conceptualized by Zeithaml *et al.* (2000) in a scale called e-SERVQUAL. The e-SERVQUAL scale provides a starting point for understanding what aspects of self-service technology usage may lead to service failure from a customer perspective. The four dimensions of e-SERVQUAL comprise efficiency, reliability, fulfilment and privacy (Zeithaml *et al.*, 2000). These dimensions are further sub-divided into access, ease of navigation, efficiency, flexibility, reliability, customization/personalization, security/privacy, responsiveness, assurance/trust, site aesthetics and price knowledge (Zeithaml *et al.*, 2000). Therefore, service failure in self-service technologies may be present when any of the defined quality dimensions is not fulfilled in the service process. Wolfinbarger and Gilly (2003) have similarly conducted a study with the aim of producing a scale for measuring electronic, retail service quality, called eTailQ. eTailQ encompasses the whole service experience in four main dimensions that echo those of Zeithaml *et al.* (2000), namely fulfilment/reliability, website design, privacy/security and customer service.

Self-service technology users may also evaluate the level of responsibility and effort they have to provide towards self-service technology usage (Anitsal and Schumann, 2007; Kelly *et al.*, 2017). Negative service evaluations may occur when customers perceive that they had been given unfair responsibilities by self-service technology providers (Hilton *et al.*, 2013; Kelly *et al.*, 2017). Although self-service technology users express views that they do have a certain level of responsibility in their self-service technology usage, such as cooperating in entering information and learning how to use the interface, they expect to share the responsibility for the outcome with the service provider (Kelly *et al.*, 2017). Customers may perceive that they are overburdened with responsibility when they are held fully accountable for any customer mistakes through oversight or misunderstanding the information on the self-service technology interface (Kelly *et al.*, 2017).

Customer expectations of self-service technologies may not be achieved because of specific problems in the service process. From a customer perspective, self-service technology failures represent 'technology failure', 'process failure', 'poor design' and 'customer-driven failure' (Meuter *et al.*, 2000, p. 56). Technology failure relates to a breakdown of the self-service technology while the customer is interacting with it. Process failures refer to incidents when the technology may have performed, but the customer never received goods that they ordered or the transaction was processed wrongly (Meuter *et al.*, 2000). The design may be evaluated as poor when the technology was not efficient or the service process caused inconvenience for the customer. Users may even admit to failures that were caused by their own actions when using the self-service technology (Meuter *et al.*, 2000).

Forbes (2008) suggests that internet and non-internet self-service technologies should be researched separately in terms of service failures because of their differences, e.g. location, communication medium and security. Some of the most common internet self-service technology problems experienced by customers comprise delivery problems, website design and payment problems (Holloway and Beatty, 2003), and packaging and special orders (Forbes *et al.*, 2005). Tan *et al.* (2016) identify four groups of e-service failures: information, functional, system and non-technological failures. Information failures relate to inaccurate, incomplete, irrelevant and untimely information during the self-service technology transaction. Information failures can significantly affect the outcome expectancy from e-services (Tan *et al.*, 2016), suggesting the importance of a clear interface design and frequent or automatic updating of the content.

Functional failures ensue from an interface that is not conducive for customers to efficiently identify their needs, choose and evaluate alternatives, acquire the service and deal with any post-purchase problems (Tan *et al.*, 2016). The third group of e-service failures is system failure, which relates to the quality of technological processes, i.e. inaccessibility, non-adaptability, non-navigability, delay and insecurity of processes (Tan *et al.*, 2016). Self-service technologies may be inaccessible to some customer segments because of certain characteristics, such as technology readiness (Meuter *et al.*, 2003; Lin and Chang, 2011) and age, gender, education and income (Dean, 2008). Online security and privacy are a sensitive customer concern that may significantly affect their trust in the service provider (Connolly and Bannister, 2008; Yousafzai *et al.*, 2009). The final group of e-service failures is non-technological failures, which include faults such as mischarging, product delivery problems and lack of response to customer enquiries (Tan *et al.*, 2016).

Non-internet self-service technologies include options such as banking ATMs, ticketing machines, vending machines, supermarket check-outs and library kiosks (Forbes, 2008). The failures associated with these self-service technologies are presented in three groups: failure of the self-service technology system, failure to respond to customer needs and requests, and unsolicited activities (Forbes, 2008). The first two groups of failures are not radically different from failures in internet self-service technologies, such as technology failure, pricing and packaging errors, inefficient information, customer mistakes and special order failures (Forbes, 2008). In the third group of failures, unsure response and embarrassment are not identified in internet self-service technology failures (e.g. Forbes *et al.*, 2005) and are specific to non-internet self-service technologies. The largest magnitude of failures in non-internet self-service technologies is attributed to system failure, customer mistakes, embarrassment and unsure responses (Forbes, 2008). Self-service technology processes often suffer from malfunctions and technical and human errors (Zhu *et al.*, 2013).

The discussion of self-service technology failure types suggests that there are numerous aspects of the self-service technology process that may cause customer dissatisfaction, such as the self-service technology interface design and responsiveness, customer mistakes and delivery problems. Furthermore, the finding that service recovery after self-service technology failures is often ineffective has attracted research into strategies for service recovery and alleviation of customer negative attributions to the service (e.g. Holloway and Beatty, 2003; Mattila *et al.*, 2011; Dabholkar and Spaid, 2012). The following section reviews research on strategies for recovery of self-service technology failures and evaluates their effectiveness.

8.4   Self-Service Technology Recovery

Service failure episodes are generally regarded as negative events requiring customer and provider activities towards restoring customer satisfaction (Zhu *et al.*, 2013).

The effectiveness of customer and company recovery efforts has been measured by their ability to reduce negative experiences (see, for example, Forbes *et al.*, 2005; Forbes, 2008; Mattila *et al.*, 2011). Recovery efforts may reduce negative attributions to the technology, company and employees (Dabholkar and Spaid, 2012) and improve customer service fairness perceptions (Mattila *et al.*, 2011), satisfaction (Forbes, 2008; Lin *et al.*, 2011; Dabholkar and Spaid, 2012; Yeoh *et al.*, 2014) and intentions for re-patronage of the service company (Holloway and Beatty, 2003; Forbes *et al.*, 2005).

When a self-service technology failure occurs, the company and the customers may engage in a number of activities towards restoring the service, or may choose to undertake no action (Forbes, 2008). First, the self-service technology failure needs to be identified by either the company or the customer, depending on the nature of the self-service technology process. Following the establishment of a service failure, a recovery may be executed by the company, jointly between the customers and the company, or by the customer (Dong *et al.*, 2008). The various self-service technology recovery activities identified in the literature are now examined.

A starting point in self-service technology recovery is the detection and establishment of a self-service technology failure. The reduced number of employees in self-service technology encounters and the direct customer–technology interaction may often lead to self-service technology failure situations where the customer has difficulty in accessing employee assistance (Forbes, 2008). For on-site self-service technology kiosks, such as in supermarkets or public service institutions, employees may be assigned to monitor customer usage and assist when needed (Mattila *et al.*, 2011). Where monitoring the self-service technology usage process is difficult, Kinard *et al.* (2009) recommend regular technical checks of the technology in order to prevent failures. Even so, this strategy of routine technological maintenance does not eliminate customer mistakes that are part of self-service technology failures. Therefore, in many self-service technology contexts, the establishment of self-service technology failure is reliant on customers making a complaint and reporting failures (Robertson, 2012). Customer complaint behaviour is discussed later in the section on customer participation in self-service technology recovery. When self-service technology failures occur, both the company and the customer may respond in an attempt to recover the service (Lin *et al.*, 2011). The effectiveness of these responses depends on the self-service technology usage context, i.e. online or offline, and on-site self-service technologies (Forbes, 2008).

Internet self-service technologies recovery strategies may include a refund, an apology, product replacement either in the original channel or at an offline store, and pursuing a strategy of doing nothing (Forbes *et al.*, 2005). The strategies which appear most effective in terms of customer satisfaction and continued patronage of the service provider prove to be product replacement and refund (Forbes *et al.*, 2005; Lin *et al.*, 2011; Yeoh *et al.*, 2014). In an online catering order context, Mattila *et al.* (2011) have examined how the recovery strategies of apology and compensation offered in person or via e-mail affect customer fairness perceptions. The research finds that when a failure occurred during an online self-service technology encounter, compensation or an apology offered in the same delivery channel is more effective than when offered by a contact-employee. However, when the self-service technology failure was very severe, an employee apology is necessary to restore the relationship with the customer (Mattila *et al.*, 2011).

Therefore, customer evaluations of the service recovery are influenced not only by the quality of the recovery itself, but also by situational factors, including the customer–company relationship (Yeoh *et al.*, 2014). Customers who have a strong relationship with the provider, i.e. relational-style customers, will want that relationship to continue and their prior positive experiences will mitigate the negative emotional consequences from the self-service technology failure (Yeoh *et al.*, 2014). Customers who evaluate the costs and benefits of taking a certain action in self-service technology failures, i.e. utilitarian-style customers, will restore their loyalty to the provider when favourable compensation is provided following a service failure (Yeoh *et al.*, 2014).

In the case of non-internet self-service technologies, service failure is often unresolved by the service provider, leading to negative implications for customer satisfaction (Forbes, 2008). Customers either do not receive the service or they re-purchase and cover the financial loss for the service failure (Forbes, 2008). Both of these strategies are rated as least favourable in terms of customer satisfaction and repeat purchase intentions (Forbes, 2008). The strategy that is rated highest in terms of customer satisfaction emerges as being managerial intervention unprompted by the customer, where the issue is resolved or the customer receives a discount (Forbes, 2008). The on-site kiosk failure strategies of immediate problem resolution and employee assistance have been examined by Dabholkar and Spaid (2012). When an immediate problem resolution was provided during the service encounter, rather than afterwards, the customer was more satisfied and had less negative attributions to the company (Dabholkar and Spaid, 2012). For on-site self-service technology options, a less crowded environment around the technology was found to contribute towards better evaluations of the service recovery by the customer (Dabholkar and Spaid, 2012).

Since self-service technologies empower customers to actively participate in the delivery of the service, it is logical that this active role continue in terms of their participation in service recovery (Dong *et al.*, 2008). Therefore, the following section explores the research regarding customer participation in self-service technology recovery.

8.4.1 Customer participation in self-service technology recovery

With the infusion of technologies in service, the traditional approach of researching customer responses to service failure and their effects on customer perceptions has been suggested as being insufficient to fully capture service failure and recovery (Xu *et al.*, 2016; Koc *et al.*, 2017). The increased customer role in service delivery, enabled through technology, has started to gain recognition in the context of service recovery from the perspective of the Service-Dominant (S-D) Logic in marketing (e.g. Dong *et al.*, 2008; Koc *et al.*, 2017). Within the framework of the S-D Logic (Vargo and Lusch, 2004), the customer is no longer only a passive consumer of service, but also an active resource integrator in the co-creation of the service experience and an active participant in service recovery (Dong *et al.*, 2008; Zhu *et al.*, 2013). The self-service technology context introduces another mode of service failure, that of customer failure to complete the service successfully (Meuter *et al.*, 2000; Robertson, 2012). Hence, self-service technology recovery research has recognized the need to draw on the theoretical foundations of the S-D Logic in addition to the traditional expectation-disconfirmation framework (e.g. Dong *et al.*, 2008; Zhu *et al.*, 2013; Xu *et al.*, 2016; Koc *et al.*, 2017).

Forbes (2008) suggests that the reduced employee–customer contact during self-service technology encounters creates problems in timely company responses to self-service technology failures. The key customer activities relating to self-service technology service recovery are where customers provide inputs towards filing complaints (Robertson and Shaw, 2009), joint service recovery with the service provider (Dong *et al.*, 2008) and self-recovery (Zhu *et al.*, 2013). In the self-service technology context, customers may often complain via e-mail, telephone or face-to-face (Holloway and Beatty, 2003; Robertson, 2012). E-mail is preferred because it is convenient and easy, but often the SST failure situation may require more investigation, thus rendering the telephone and personal channels more effective in successful recovery (Robertson, 2012). The difficulty of monitoring self-service technology processes highlights the importance of customer complaints in successful service recovery (Holloway and Beatty, 2003).

Robertson and Shaw (2009) have addressed the likelihood of consumers voicing complaints in a self-service technology context, namely 'likelihood of voice'. They define six variables and have tested how they influence the likelihood of voice: (i) likelihood of voice success; (ii) ease of voice; (iii) causal locus; (iv) self-service technology self-efficacy; (v) self-service technology powerlessness; and (vi) need to vent. They found ease of voice to be the strongest predictor of consumers' likelihood of voicing their complaints. As previous research has shown that customers tend to complain more in a self-service technology environment (Meuter *et al.*, 2000; Holloway and Beatty, 2003; Forbes *et al.*, 2005; Forbes, 2008), the problem of illegitimate complaints can be further facilitated if complaining procedures are made extremely easy (Holloway and Beatty, 2003).

The second form of customer participation in self-service technology recovery is joint service recovery. This involves the customer providing information about the service failure and then following instructions by the service provider in terms of how to fix the problem (Dong *et al.*, 2008). In joint service recovery, customers act as 'partial employees' who undertake some recovery functions specified by the company, e.g. instructions over the phone via a call centre (Dong *et al.*, 2008). The third form of customer participation is self-recovery, when self-service technology customers may also be able to recover service failures themselves and avoid contacting an employee (Dong *et al.*, 2008). Zhu *et al.* (2013, p. 16) classify customer responses to self-service technology failures into three types: modifying the effort level (e.g. try harder or repeat the transaction), altering their recovery strategy (e.g. try an alternative route to solve the problem) and seeking service staff assistance. Customers are found to be more likely to attempt self-recovery if they expect to be able to recover the service (Zhu *et al.*, 2013). Customers are also more likely to attempt self-recovery when they assume the blame for the failure, perceive they have control over the self-service technology and hold positive perceptions of the self-service technology interactivity (Zhu *et al.*, 2013).

The user's perspective on their self-service technology participation role may affect their actions during a service failure and the perceptions of the experiences created (Dong *et al.*, 2008). Kelly *et al.* (2017) refine self-service technology user perceptions of their roles in a self-service technology context. The roles identified by Kelly *et al.* (2017) may provide a basis for understanding the customer perspective on self-service technology usage and how it may affect their responses to self-service technology service failures. The roles of convenience seeker, motivated worker and enthusiastic assistance provider are associated with positive, value-creating self-service technology experiences, while the roles of un-skilled worker, enforced worker and reluctant assistant provider pre-empt negative, value-destroying experiences. The six roles are interpreted and adapted by the authors in this chapter in terms of self-service technology failure episodes. These roles may be undertaken both in the form of reporting complaints, joint or self-recovery of self-service technology failures. These insights provide understanding of the customer perspective on self-service technology failure situations, which may be utilized by service providers in crafting self-service technology recovery strategies. Each role is discussed in turn.

1. Convenience seeker. A self-service technology user undertakes a convenience-seeker role when they perceive that service recovery is prompt and effortless. Customers do not mind taking part in self-service technology service recovery because it is perceived as convenient and easy. For example, the self-service technology process is designed so that failures may easily be reported and rectified by the company or the users.

2. Motivated employee. The motivated employee role is also evident in self-service technology failure episodes when customers willingly provide inputs towards service recovery. A common response to technology failures involves the customer trying to solve the problem there and then before contacting the service company for help. The role of the motivated worker during service failures is differentiated from that of the convenience seeker by the perception that they extend considerable effort towards recovering the service. The customer may view themselves as partly responsible for the failure, which motivates their extended attempts towards self-recovery.

3. Unskilled employee. In some cases, the expertise to recover the failure is exclusive to the self-service technology provider; therefore, the customer does not have the competence or the authority to participate in service recovery. At times when customers are unsure of how to act during a service failure episode, they find themselves in an unskilled worker role and undertake no action. A customer in an unskilled worker role may also seek assistance from fellow customers or family/friends during a service failure.

4. Enforced employee. The enforced employee role is also evident during self-service technology failure episodes in which the customer has had no choice but to participate in service recovery. This perception is intensified when customers have chosen to use self-service technologies for time savings and convenience. A self-service technology user may undertake an enforced worker role because if they do not attempt service re-covery, they may have to forgo the opportunity of obtaining a service.

5. Enthusiastic assistance provider. One aspect of the assistance provider role is the enthusiastic assistance provider, i.e. positively disposed towards helping others with self-service technology failures because it is deemed a nice thing to do. This role is undertaken when a self-service technology user is clearly experiencing a failure and is demonstrating a need for help.

6. Reluctant assistance provider. Self-service technology users are not always enthusi-astic about undertaking an assistance provider role and assisting other users during self-service technology failures, i.e. they are reluctant assistant providers. These users do not believe that recovering self-service technology failures should be the responsibility of technology-adept customers.

The above classification of customer roles that may be undertaken in self-service technology failure and recovery episodes provides a managerial tool for crafting specific customer-centric self-service technology recovery strategies. For example, in service designs where customer mistakes may lead to service failures, self-service technology providers may introduce options for recovery of these mistakes (i.e. facilitate a motivated worker role). Alternatively, where a self-service technology user may be completely powerless to recover a technological failure, self-service technology providers should offer timely intervention and prevent customers from having to undertake an unskilled or enforced worker role.

Although the customer plays an active production role during self-service technology encounters (Meuter *et al.*, 2000), this production role during service failure episodes has received limited attention (Dong *et al.*, 2008; Zhu *et al.*, 2013). When self-service technology customers are able to contribute to resolving self-service technology failures and avoid contacting an employee, this increases their satisfaction and future usage intentions (Dong *et al.*, 2008). Empirical evidence from Dong *et al.*'s (2008) scenario-based research confirms that customer participation in service recovery has a positive effect on behavioural intentions and on customer role clarity for subsequent service encounters. The following section evaluates how the various customer and company responses to self-service technology failures affect positively or negatively the recovery of the service.

8.4.2 Effectiveness of self-service technology recovery

The preceding discussion of customer and provider responses to self-service technology failures provides a backdrop for an evaluation of their effectiveness in terms of service recovery. The customer and service provider responses and strategies to self-service technology failure are summarized in Table 8.2 below, based on whether they influence the self-service technology service recovery positively or negatively.

Research suggests that one of the most successful company responses to self-service technology failure for both online and offline self-service technology failures is the refund, replacement or compensation strategy (Forbes *et al.*, 2005; Lin *et al.*, 2011; Mattila *et al.*, 2011). Therefore, it is of primary importance for self-service technology users that service failures do not cause financial losses for them. Where a self-service technology failure may lead to a financial loss for the customer, fast failure detection should be initiated by both the customer and the service provider. For example, a ticketing kiosk may fail to print a ticket, but take the customer's money. If the machine cannot self-identify the failure, the self-service technology interface needs to incorporate a clear indication for the customer on how to call for assistance or 'self-recover' the failure. Furthermore, in addition to incurring financial losses, customers may have to expend time and effort to recover the service. Customers do not like to engage in a lengthy recovery process and so the strategy of providing timely self-service technology recovery by an employee is rated very highly by customers (Dabholkar and Spaid, 2012; Yeoh *et al.*, 2014).

The proactive approach described above in terms of quickly compensating the customer and fixing the service is similar to strategies for recovering traditional personal services, but there are also recovery strategies specific to self-service technology services

Table 8.2. SST customer/provider responses to SST failure and influence on SST recovery. (From Kelly *et al.*)

Positive influence on SST recovery	Negative influence on SST recovery
Customer responses	*Customer responses*
Joint and self-recovery (Dong *et al.*, 2008)	Re-purchase (Forbes, 2008)
Repeat a transaction (Zhu *et al.*, 2013)	Do nothing (Forbes *et al.*, 2005)
Try an alternative route to solve the problem (Zhu *et al.*, 2013)	Leave the company (Yeoh *et al.*, 2014)
Convenience seeker, motivated worker, enthusiastic assistance provider (Kelly *et al.*, 2017)	Unskilled worker, enforced worker and reluctant assistance provider (Kelly *et al.*, 2017).
Provider responses	*Provider responses*
Refund (Mattila *et al.*, 2011; Forbes *et al.*, 2005)	Do nothing (Forbes, 2008; Forbes *et al.*, 2005)
Apology (Mattila *et al.*, 2011; Forbes *et al.*, 2005)	
Replacement (Forbes *et al.*, 2005)	
Immediate problem resolution by an employee (Dabholkar and Spaid, 2012)	
Less crowded environment (Dabholkar and Spaid, 2012)	
Match the level of co-creation in service delivery (Heidenreich *et al.*, 2015)	
Compensation, apology, fast recovery (Lin *et al.*, 2011)	
Match recovery with cultural style (i.e. prior positive experiences affect relational customers, and offer a refund to utilitarian customers) (Yeoh *et al.*, 2014)	

(Forbes, 2008; Mattila *et al.*, 2011). Since self-service technology delivery is of a co-creation nature, matching the level of customer participation in the delivery stage with the level of participation in service recovery proves an effective strategy in self-service technology recovery (Heidenreich *et al.*, 2015). Indeed, self-recovery is associated with more positive post-recovery outcomes than joint recovery with the self-service technology provider (Dong *et al.*, 2008). Another self-service technology recovery strategy is the recovery of the service in the same self-service technology service channel (Mattila *et al.*, 2011). For example, if a customer experiences a service failure online, recovering this service via email is more effective than via a personal channel (Mattila *et al.*, 2011). The strategy of offering a personal apology may prove effective where the failure is very severe and it is important to preserve the company–customer relationship (Mattila *et al.*, 2011).

In both internet and non-internet self-service technologies, when the company undertakes no actions to recover a self-service technology failure, this results in negative customer evaluations (Forbes *et al.*, 2005; Forbes, 2008). The lack of response from the company may be due to the self-service technology environment where 'no one is around' and the failure may not get reported by the customer because they do not have the time or do not believe the service provider will respond effectively (Forbes, 2008). In such situations, company recovery efforts may be aided by stimulating more effective voicing of complaints by customers (Robertson and Shaw, 2009).

In addition to company responses to self-service technology failures, the self-service technology context favours customer involvement in self-service technology recovery

(Zhu *et al.*, 2013). Customer self-recovery in self-service technologies increases customer satisfaction and re-patronage intentions, and improves skills to operate self-service technologies in the future (Dong *et al.*, 2008). Self-service technology users should be facilitated to participate in self-service technology recovery by making recovery easy (i.e. facilitating a convenience-seeker role), providing facilities for customers to recover any mistakes they make in the delivery stage (i.e. motivated worker role) or encourage customer-to-customer recovery when this is suitable (i.e. assistance provider role). Customer-to-customer recovery may be face-to-face, but it may also take place on online forums and platforms (Xu *et al.*, 2016). Indeed, some customers may undertake the role of 'key replier' and actively assist other customers online with service failures (Xu *et al.*, 2016, p. 434). These active and knowledgeable users may be contacted by the company and 'recruited' as an online 'help-desk' (Xu *et al.*, 2016).

Self-service technology user responses that may contribute negatively to self-service technology recovery evaluation include re-purchase (Forbes, 2008), doing nothing (Forbes *et al.*, 2005) or even leaving the company (Yeoh *et al.*, 2014). Although self-service technology users may re-purchase a service, this activity is not evaluated positively by customers (Forbes, 2008; Kelly *et al.*, 2017). Effectively, the customer is re-purchasing because they cannot get a refund or replacement, and they will not obtain any service if they abandon the self-service technology. Alternatively, the customer may be invited by the provider to contribute to service recovery, but they may be unwilling to cooperate, thus undertaking an enforced worker role in service recovery (Kelly *et al.*, 2017). Hence, in situations where customers are unwilling to participate in service recovery, they should be provided with a choice of other options. The customer may leave the company after a self-service technology failure, which is a severely negative outcome for both the company and the customer (Yeoh *et al.*, 2014).

8.5 Conclusions and Directions for Further Research

This chapter reviewed the current areas of research into customers' perspectives on self-service technology failure and recovery. Self-service technologies are a diverse group, which may be affected by technological, informational and customer failures (Tan *et al.*, 2016). These failures may be recovered by interventions from the user, the service provider or other users (Kelly *et al.*, 2017). The most effective strategy for self-service technology recovery represents a quick customer self-recovery, thus avoiding having to contact the service company for assistance (Dong *et al.*, 2008; Mattila *et al.*, 2011). Further research is required to understand the factors affecting customer willingness to participate in self-recovery (Zhu *et al.*, 2013). Furthermore, self-service technology failures may be recovered via customer-to-customer interactions in terms of providing assistance and instructing other customers (Kelly *et al.*, 2017). Research may explore the nature of such social assistance, including interactions such as pointing out the right button to use and explaining tips for better usage of the self-service technology (Kelly *et al.*, 2017). Therefore, encouraging effective customer participation in self-service technology recovery represents a fruitful avenue for further research.

In a self-service technology context, service failures may be hard to monitor and rectify by the company (Zhu *et al.*, 2013). Therefore, encouraging effective complaining by users is essential (Robertson, 2012). The voicing of complaints by the customer in a self-service technology context may be lessened by the service provider applying service guarantees (Robertson *et al.*, 2012). These may include fixing the problem, providing a choice of compensation, providing a personal response, reimbursing the customer if the problem cannot be fixed and providing an easy means for guarantee invocation (Robertson *et al.*, 2012). Further research could explore how each of these guarantees affects customer complaining behaviours.

Self-service technology recovery evaluation by customers is influenced by factors such as the crowdedness of the self-service technology site (Dabholkar and Spaid, 2012), the self-service technology channel (Mattila *et al.*, 2011), the customer–company relationship (Yeoh *et al.*, 2014) and the extent of service failure severity (Robertson *et al.*, 2012). Therefore, further research may be necessary to explore contextual influences that may affect customers' evaluations of self-service technology recovery (Robertson *et al.*, 2012). The understanding of contextual influences also requires the development of self-service technology recovery strategies that best match the specific self-service technology failure types (Forbes, 2008).

This chapter reviewed the state of self-service technology service failure and recovery research, and its theoretical underpinnings. Self-service technology failures may occur when customer expectations of the service are not achieved, or when there is an obvious technological or process breakdown. Previous research has established conceptual foundations by identifying self-service technology failure types for internet and non-internet self-service technologies (e.g. Forbes, 2008; Tan *et al.*, 2016) and corresponding self-service technology recovery responses by companies and customers (e.g. Forbes *et al.*, 2005; Dong *et al.*, 2008; Zhu *et al.*, 2013). In addition to traditional service recovery strategies, the self-service technology context introduces specific failure situations that require unique recovery activities (Mattila *et al.*, 2011). For example, it is more effective to recover an online service failure in the online channel than in a personal channel (Mattila *et al.*, 2011). Furthermore, self-service technology recovery is more effective when the level of co-creation that the customer engages in during the delivery stage is matched to the level of co-creation in recovery (Heidenreich *et al.*, 2015). Self-service technology service recovery requires a re-thinking of traditional personal service recovery strategies and an awareness of the positive and constructive involvement of the customer in joint service recovery and self-recovery of self-service technology failures.

Questions

1. What are self-service technologies?
2. Identify and explain one classification of self-service technologies.
3. What are the benefits of self-service technologies to the customer and service provider?
4. What are the drawbacks of self-service technologies to the customer and service provider?
5. Define self-service technology service failure and recovery.
6. How are self-service technology failures different from traditional personal service failures?
7. What are the three types of self-service technology failures?
8. Who recovers the service?
9. How can failure in a self-service technology service be recovered?
10. How can customers participate in self-service technology recovery?
11. What are the most effective self-service technology recovery strategies?

Further Reading

Beatson, A., Lee, N. and Coote, L. (2007) Self-service technology and the service encounter. *The Service Industries Journal* 27, 75–89.

Collier, J., Sherrell, D., Babakus, E. and Horky, A. (2014) Understanding the differences of public and private self-service technology. *Journal of Services Marketing* 28, 60–70.

Dabholkar, P. and Spaid, B. (2012) Service failure and recovery in using technology-based self-service: effects on user attributions and satisfaction. *The Service Industries Journal* 32, 1415–1432.

Kelly, P., Lawlor, J. and Mulvey, M. (2017) Customer roles in self-service technology encounters in a tourism context. *Journal of Travel & Tourism Marketing* 34, 222–238.

References

Abdelaziz, S., Hegazy, A. and Elabbassy, A. (2010) Study of airport self-service technology within experimental research of check-in techniques. *International Journal of Computer Science* 7, 17–26.

Anitsal, I. and Schumann, D. (2007) Toward a conceptualization of customer productivity: the customer's perspective on transforming customer labour into customer outcomes using technology-based self-service options. *Journal of Marketing Theory and Practice* 15, 349–363.

Anselmsson, J. (2001) Customer-perceived service quality and technology-based self-service. Doctoral dissertation, Institute of Economic Research, Lund University, Lund, Sweden.

Bateson, J. (1985) Self-service consumer: an exploratory study. *Journal of Retailing* 61, 49–76.

Beatson, A., Lee, N. and Coote, L. (2007) Self-service technology and the service encounter. *The Service Industries Journal* 27, 75–89.

Bitner, M., Brown, S. and Meuter, M. (2000) Technology infusion in service encounters. *Journal of the Academy of Marketing Science* 28, 138–149.

Bitner, M., Ostrom, A. and Meuter, M. (2002) Implementing successful self-service technologies. *Academy of Management Executive* 16, 96–108.

Castillo-Manzano, J. and López-Valpuesta, L. (2013) Check-in services and passenger behaviour: self-service technologies in airport systems. *Computers in Human Behavior* 29, 2431–2437.

Castro, D., Atkinson, R. and Ezell, S. (2010) *Embracing the self-service economy*. The Information Technology and Innovation Foundation, Washington, DC.

Collier, J., Sherrell, D., Babakus, E. and Horky, A. (2014) Understanding the differences of public and private self-service technology. *Journal of Services Marketing* 28, 60–70.

Connolly, R. and Bannister, F. (2008) Factors influencing Irish consumers' trust in internet shopping. *Management Research News* 31, 339–358.

Curran, J. and Meuter, M. (2007) Encouraging existing customers to switch to self-service technologies: put a little fun in their lives. *Journal of Marketing Theory and Practice* 15, 238–298.

Dabholkar, P. (1994) Technology-based service delivery: a classification scheme for developing marketing strategies. In: Swartz, T., Bowen, D. and Brown, S. (eds) *Advances in Services Marketing and Management*, Vol. 3. JAI, Greenwich, Connecticut, pp. 241–271.

Dabholkar, P. and Bagozzi, R. (2002) An attitudinal model of technology-based self-service moderating effects of consumer traits and situational factors. *Journal of the Academy of Marketing Science* 30, 184–201.

Dabholkar, P. and Spaid, B. (2012) Service failure and recovery in using technology-based self-service: effects on user attributions and satisfaction. *The Service Industries Journal* 32, 1415–1432.

Dabholkar, P., Bobbitt, L. and Lee, E. (2003) Understanding consumer motivation and behavior related to self-scanning in retailing. *International Journal of Service Industry Management* 14, 59–95.

Dean, D. (2008) Shopper age and the use of self-service technologies. *Managing Service Quality* 18, 225–238.

Dong, B., Evans, K. and Zou, S. (2008) The effects of customer participation in co-created service recovery. *Journal of the Academy of Marketing Science* 36, 123–137.

Egger, R. and Buhalis, D. (2008) *Etourism Case Studies*. Butterworth Heinemann, Oxford.

Etzel, M. and Silverman, B. (1981) A managerial perspective on directions for retail customer dissatisfaction research. *Journal of Retailing* 57, 124–136.

Fisk, R., Brown, S. and Bitner, M. (1993) Tracking the evolution of the services marketing literature. *Journal of Retailing* 69, 61–103.

Fisk, R., Grove, S., Harris, L., Keeffe, D., Daunt, K., Russell-Bennett, R. and Wirtz, J. (2010) Customers behaving badly: a state of the art review, research agenda and implications for practitioners. *Journal of Services Marketing* 24, 417–429.

Forbes, L. (2008) When something goes wrong and no one is around: non-internet self-service technology failure and recovery. *Journal of Services Marketing* 22, 316–327.

Forbes, L., Kelley, S. and Hoffman, D. (2005) Typologies of e-commerce retail failures and recovery strategies. *Journal of Services Marketing* 19, 280–292.

Future Travel Experience (2016) Hamad international airport outlines ambitious 'smart airport' vision. Available at: http://www.futuretravelexperience.com/2016/04/hamad-international-airport-outlines-smart-airport-vision (accessed 23 July 2016).

Gelbrich, K. and Sattler, B. (2014) Anxiety, crowding, and time pressure in public self-service technology acceptance. *Journal of Services Marketing* 28, 82–94.

Gerrard, P., Cunningham, B. and Devlin, J. (2006) Why consumers are not using internet banking: a qualitative study. *Journal of Services Marketing* 20, 160–168.

Gittens, G. (2016) Dublin airport becomes first in the world to introduce touchless self-service bag drop. *The Independent*, 6 July 2016.

Graf, A. (2007) Changing roles of customers: consequences for HRM. *International Journal of Services Industry Management* 18, 491–509.

Gretzel, U. and Jamal, T. (2009) Conceptualising the creative tourist class: technology, mobility, and tourism experiences. *Tourism Analysis* 14, 471–481.

Hart, C., Heskett, J. and Sasser, E. (1990) The profitable art of service recovery. *Harvard Business Review* July–August, 148–156.

Heidenreich, S., Wittkiwski, K., Handrich, M. and Falk, T. (2015) The dark side of customer co-creation: exploring the consequences of failed co-created service. *Journal of the Academy of Marketing Science* 43, 279–296.

Hilton, T. and Hughes, T. (2013) Co-production and self-service: the application of service-dominant logic. *Journal of Marketing Management* 29, 861–881.

Hilton, T., Hughes, T., Little, E. and Marandi, E. (2013) Adopting self-service technology to do more with less. *Journal of Services Marketing* 27, 3–12.

Holloway, B. and Beatty, S. (2003) Service failure in online retailing: a recovery opportunity. *Journal of Service Research* 6, 92–105.

Kelly, P., Lawlor, J. and Mulvey, M. (2013) Customer decision-making processes and motives for self-service technology usage in multichannel hospitality environments. *International Journal of Electronic Customer Relationship Management* 7, 98–116.

Kelly, P., Lawlor, J. and Mulvey, M. (2017) Customer roles in self-service technology encounters in a tourism context. *Journal of Travel & Tourism Marketing* 34, 222–238.

Kim, L., Qu, H. and Kim, D. (2009) A study of perceived risk and risk reduction of purchasing air-tickets online. *Journal of Travel and Tourism Marketing* 26, 302–324.

Kinard, B., Capella, M. and Kinard, J. (2009) The impact of social presence on technology based self-service use: the role of familiarity. *Services Marketing Quarterly* 30, 303–314.

Koc, E., Ulukoy, M., Kilic, R., Yumusak, S. and Bahar, R. (2017) The influence of customer participation on service failure perceptions. *Total Quality Management & Business Excellence* 28, 390–404.

Lawlor, J. (2006) Trends and developments in the hospitality industry. In: Connolly, P. and McGing, G. (eds) *Hospitality Management in Ireland: Theory and Practice.* Blackhall, Dublin, pp. 325–341.

Lawlor, J. (2010) The role of the customer as a quasi-employee in service organizations: research agenda. In: Gorham, G. and Mottiar, Z. (eds) *Contemporary Issues in Irish and Global Tourism and Hospitality.* Dublin Institute of Technology, Dublin, pp. 179–187.

Lee, J. and Allaway, A. (2002) Effects of personal control on adoption of self-service technology innovations. *Journal of Services Marketing* 16, 553–573.

Leung, L. and Matanda, M. (2013) The impact of basic human needs on the use of retailing self-service technologies: a study of self-determination theory. *Journal of Retailing and Consumer Services* 20, 549–559.

Lin, J. and Chang, H. (2011) The role of technology readiness in self-service technology acceptance. *Managing Service Quality* 21, 424–444.

Lin, H., Wang, Y. and Chang, L. (2011) Customer responses to online retailer's service recovery after a service failure. *Managing Service Quality* 21, 511–543.

Lu, H. and Su, Y. (2009) Factors affecting purchase intention on mobile shopping web sites. *Internet Research* 19, 442–458.

Mattila, A., Cho, W. and Ro, H. (2011) The role of self-service technologies in restoring justice. *Journal of Business Research* 64, 348–355.

Maze, J. (2016) How Domino's became a tech company. *Nation's Restaurant News.* Available at: http://nrn.com/technology/how-domino-s-became-tech-company?page=1 (accessed 23 July 2016).

McKnight, D., Choudhury, V. and Kacmar, C. (2002) Developing and validating trust measures for e-commerce: an integrative typology. *Information Systems Research* 13, 334–359.

Meuter, M., Ostrom, A., Roundtree, R. and Bitner, M. (2000) Self-service technologies: understanding customer satisfaction with technology-based service encounters. *Journal of Marketing* 64, 50–64.

Meuter, M., Ostrom, A., Bitner, M. and Roundtree, R. (2003) The influence of technology anxiety on consumer use and experiences with self-service technologies. *Journal of Business Research* 56, 899–906.

Neuhofer, B. (2016) Value co-creation and co-destruction in connected tourist experiences. In: Inversini, A. and Schegy, R. (eds) *Information and Communication Technologies in Tourism 2016.* Proceedings of the International Conference in Bilbao, Spain. Springer, Berlin, pp. 779–792.

Neuhofer, B., Buhalis, D. and Ladkin, A. (2013) High tech for high touch experiences: a case study from the hospitality industry. In: Cantoni, L. and Xiang, Z. (eds) *Information and Communication Technologies in Tourism 2013* (Proceedings of the International Conference in Innsbruck, Austria). Springer, Berlin, pp. 290–301.

Oh, H., Jeong, M. and Baloglu, S. (2013) Tourists' adoption of self-service technologies at resort hotels. *Journal of Business Research* 66, 692–699.

Ondrus, J. and Pigneur, Y. (2006) Towards a holistic analysis of mobile payments: a multiple perspectives approach. *Electronic Commerce Research and Applications* 5, 246–257.

Rajesh, M. (2015) Inside Japan's first robot-staffed hotel. *The Guardian,* 14 August 2015.

Reinders, M., Dabholkar, P. and Frambach, R. (2008) Consequences of forcing consumers to use technology-based self-service. *Journal of Service Research* 11, 107–123.

Reinders, M., Frambach, R. and Kleijnen, M. (2015) Mandatory use of technology-based self-service: does expertise help or hurt? *European Journal of Marketing* 49, 190–211.

Robertson, N. (2012) Self-service technology complaint channel choice: exploring consumers' motives. *Managing Service Quality* 22, 145–164.

Robertson, N. and Shaw, R. (2009) Predicting the likelihood of voiced complaints in the self-service technology context. *Journal of Service Research* 12, 100–116.

Robertson, N., McQuilken, L. and Kandampully, J. (2012) Consumer complaints and recovery through guaranteeing self-service technology. *Journal of Consumer Behaviour* 11, 21–30.

Rosenbaum, M. and Wong, I. (2015) If you install it, will they use it? Understanding why hospitality customers take 'technological pauses' from self-service technology. *Journal of Business Research* 68, 1862–1868.

Schumann, J., Wünderlich, N. and Wangenheim, F. (2012) Technology mediation in service delivery: a new typology and an agenda for managers and academics. *Technovation* 32, 133–143.

Shu, L. (2015) Van Gogh vs. Candy Crush: how museums are fighting tech with tech to win your eyes. *Digital Trends*, 1 May 2015. Available at: http://www.digitaltrends.com/cool-tech/how-museums-are-using-technology (accessed 23 July 2016).

SITA (2016) Leo, SITA's baggage robot. Available at: https://www.sita.aero/innovation/sita-lab/leo-sitas-baggage-robot (accessed 23 July 2016).

Tan, C., Benbasat, I. and Confetelli, R. (2016) An exploratory study of the formation and impact of electronic service failures. *MIS Quarterly* 40, 1–29.

Terry, L. (2016) 6 mega-trends in hotel technology. *Hospitality Technology Magazine.* Available at: http://hospitalitytechnology.edgl.com/news/6-Mega-Trends-in-Hotel-Technology105033 (accessed 23 July 2016).

Vargo, S. and Lusch, R. (2004) Evolving to a new dominant logic for marketing. *Journal of Marketing* 68, 1–17.

Walker, R. and Johnson, L. (2006) Why consumers use and do not use technology-enabled services. *Journal of Services Marketing* 20, 125–135.

Wang, C., Harris, J. and Patterson, P. (2012) Customer choice of self-service technology: the role of situational influences and past experience. *Journal of Service Management* 23, 54–78.

Westbrook, R. and Oliver, R. (1991) The dimensionality of consumption emotion patterns and consumer satisfaction. *Journal of Consumer Research* 18, 84–91.

Wolfinbarger, M. and Gilly, M. (2003) ETailQ: dimensionalizing, measuring and predicting etail quality. *Journal of Retailing* 79, 183–198.

Xu, Y., Yap, S. and Hyde, K. (2016) Who is talking, who is listening? Service recovery through online customer-to-customer interactions. *Marketing Intelligence and Planning* 34, 421–443.

Yeoh, P., Eshghi, A., Woolford, S. and Butaney, G. (2014) Customer response to service recovery in online shopping. *Journal of Services Research* 14, 33–56.

Yousafzai, S., Pallister, J. and Foxhall, G. (2009) Multi-dimensional role of trust in internet banking adoption. *The Service Industries Journal* 29, 591–605.

Zeithaml, V., Parasuraman, A. and Malhotra, A. (2000) E-service quality: definition, dimensions and conceptual model. Working Paper, Marketing Science Institute, Cambridge, Massachusetts.

Zhu, Z., Nakata, C., Sivakumar, K. and Grewal, D. (2013) Fix it or leave it? Customer recovery from self-service technology failures. *Journal of Retailing* 89, 15–29.

9 The Influence of Other Customers in Service Failure and Recovery

Kawon Kim and Melissa A. Baker

Learning Objectives

After reading this chapter, you should be able to:

- Understand the influence of other customers in service encounters in tourism and hospitality.
- Explain the main components of social servicescape.
- Understand the consequences of service failures caused by other customers.
- Explain the components of emotional intelligence in relation to service.
- Explain how service failures caused by other customers could be recovered.

9.1 Introduction

Social influence plays an important role in the consumption process (Bearden and Etzel, 1982). This is especially true in the hospitality industry, which often involves sharing the physical environment with others, such as fellow customers. As many services are performed in the presence of other customers, customers naturally affect each other during the service experience, both directly and indirectly. Martin (1996) suggests that customers affect one another in the service context directly through interpersonal encounters or indirectly by being part of the environment. Often, the presence and behaviours of other customers have a stronger impact on influencing an individual's perception of service quality than the contact with service personnel (Lehtinen and Lehtinen, 1991). Consequently, the other customers' behaviour creates a part of the atmosphere that becomes an environmental stimulus. Tombs and McColl-Kennedy (2003) suggest that other customers influence the focal customer's affective and cognitive responses by being a part of the service experience environment. As such, other customers can either directly or indirectly affect one's service experience.

Due to the inseparability and heterogeneity of service, service failures are unavoidable in service encounters (Maxham and Netemeyer, 2002). Since most hospitality environments represent shared territory and space for customers, service failure that originates from the misbehaviour of other customers is also inevitable in hospitality and tourism contexts (Huang and Wang, 2014). Many people may have encountered children screaming in a restaurant or a customer in the hotel room next door being extremely loud and obnoxious during the night. It is hard to ignore that service failures can be caused by other customers and affect the observing customers' attitudes and behaviours. Therefore, this chapter will discuss: (i) other customers in service settings; (ii) other customer service failure; (iii) characteristics of other customers; (iv) attribution of other customer service failure; (v) recovery strategies from other customers; and (vi) observing service recovery aimed at other customers.

9.2   Other Customers in Service Settings

Customers not only purchase services, but are also frequently involved in the production, design, delivery and consumption of services (Huang, 2008; Nicholls, 2010). Stated differently, service experiences are co-created and co-produced through customer-to-customer interactions (McColl-Kennedy *et al.*, 2014), where the emphasis is on how the service is uniquely and contextually interpreted and experienced by an individual. In fact, customer-to-customer interactions often outnumber consumer–provider interactions (Martin, 1996). Consequently, an emerging view is to consider the service experience not only from the firm to customer, but also in a more dynamic way by incorporating how individuals influence other individuals, who then influence others in a progressive system (McColl-Kennedy *et al.*, 2014).

Starting from the 1970s, service management theory began accommodating the reality that a customer's perception of a service can be affected by the behaviour of other customers. Belk (1975), in defining his framework of situational influences affecting consumer's behaviour, suggested other customers constitute part of the social surrounding. In the servuction model of the service experience (participation of customers in the production of services; Bateson, 1985), the components of the model that are visible to a customer (Customer A) comprise contact personnel, the inanimate environment and Customer B, i.e. other customers in the system. In the 1980s, the 7Ps of services marketing, one of the major services marketing frameworks, introduced the theme of 'participants' as service providers and other customers. In addition, the servicescape literature has taken other customers into account. Baker (1986) first incorporated other customers and employees as social cues as a part of the service's physical environment in the servicescape framework. Bitner's (1992) framework, the seminal work of the servicescape literature, focuses only on the man-made physical aspects of the environment without considering the social aspects such as employees and customers. Therefore, Tombs and McColl-Kennedy (2003) developed a more integrative view of servicescapes based on Bitner's servicescape model, social facility theory (Zajonc, 1965), behaviour setting theory (Barker, 1968) and affective events theory (Weiss and Cropanzano, 1996) (Fig. 9.1). They propose that the purchase occasion influences the reaction to and acceptance of social density and the expressed emotions of the other customers, which in turn influence the customer's affective responses and customer cognitive responses (repurchase intentions). The basic assumption of their framework is that the contextual component of the environment, whether private or public (behaviour setting theory; within a specific place or occasion, certain behaviours are expected regardless of the individual's personality or recent experiences), will dictate the desired density and displayed emotions of others to operate differently.

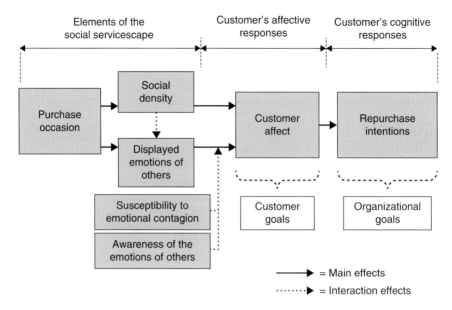

Elements of the social servicescape | Customer's affective responses | Customer's cognitive responses

Fig. 9.1. The social servicescape conceptual model. (From Tombs and McColl-Kennedy, 2003.)

9.3 Other Customer Service Failure

Customers are co-creators, implying that they do not merely have an influence on their own experience, but also have an impact on the experience of other customers (Huang, 2008). When other customers are analysed as part of the service environment, their influence is manifested through an individual customer's perceptions (Brocato *et al.*, 2012). Negative customer-to-customer experiences are quite common across service contexts (Zhang *et al.*, 2010). As such, when any action by another customer has a negative impact on one's service experience, it leads to service failure (Huang, 2008). In other words, other customer service failure is where another customer directly causes a service failure that disrupts the service environment (Baker and Kim, 2016).

9.3.1 Other customer service failure types of incidents

During the past few decades, a number of terms have been suggested by various researchers to describe customers' misbehaviour in service settings, such as Bitner *et al.'s* (1994) 'problem customer', Lovelock's (1994) 'jay customers' and Harris and Reynolds' (2004) 'dysfunctional customer behaviour'. Zemke and Anderson (1990) present a typology of 'customers from hell', such as abusive egocentrics, insulting whiners, hysterical shouters, dictators and free-loaders. Bitner *et al.* (1994) identify four problematic customer behaviours from the employees' perspective, including drunkenness, verbal and physical abuse, breaking company policies and uncooperative customers. Martin (1996) investigates customers' dissatisfaction with other customers in public business environments and shows that respondents were generally displeased with violent or inappropriate behaviours. Similarly, Harris and Reynolds (2004) note eight main types of jay customer behaviour in the hospitality industry, including: compensation letter writers; undesirable customers; property abusers; service workers; vindictive customers; verbal abusers; physical abusers and sexual predators. Zhang *et al.* (2010) identify negative customer-to-customer interactions in a service setting, such as fighting, loudness and rudeness. Most recently, Baker and Kim (2016) find that the most common types of incidents include other customers being rude or loud and misbehaving children. They also find that proximity and closeness to other customers plays a significant role in the focal customer's perceptions. In hospitality contexts, this is incredibly important because the social, spatial and proximity elements are important to consider and manage with regards to restaurant tables, airplane seating and waiting in queues (Baker and Kim, 2016).

9.3.2   Other customer service failure contexts

Other customer service failure can happen in any place where social interaction can occur either directly or indirectly. This is especially true in the hospitality industry, which has a high possibility of other customer service failure because sharing the service environment with other customers is often an intrinsic part of the hospitality and tourism experience (Miao and Mattila, 2013). Baker and Kim (2016) find that hospitality and tourism settings, including restaurants, airplanes and hotels, involve the most frequent forms of other customer service failure. In a hotel setting, noise from other customers is the major complaint among hotel guests and accordingly it negatively influences the hotel because 86% of people are less likely to recommend a hotel if they had a bad noise-related experience (Leizer, 2016). There was one case during a flight when two intoxicated women played loud music from a boom box: after they refused to turn it down, a fight broke out (Rocha, 2016). Restaurants are not an exception to other customer service failure. Customers can find other customers sitting next to them very obnoxious and using increasingly inappropriate language (Bauer, 2013). In addition, children misbehaving, such as screaming and running around the service setting, often happens in a restaurant setting. As such, social and spatial factors are critical to consider in hospitality and tourism settings because other customers can easily affect each other in the same servicescape.

9.3.3   Consequences of other customer service failure

Other customer service failure is an important aspect of the service encounter because it has negative consequences not only for other customers, but also for the employee and firm as well (Harris and Reynolds, 2004). First, it directly influences the focal customer's overall service experience. For example, Harris and Reynolds (2004) show that dysfunctional customer behaviour diminishes customer satisfaction as well as loyalty with the service firm. Similarly, Huang (2010) reveals that service failure occurring from other customers lessens the focal customer's satisfaction and repurchase intention, and increases negative word-of-mouth. Second, it has a negative impact on customer-contact employees who need to deal with such dysfunctional customer be-haviour (Harris and Reynolds, 2004). For instance, employees experience emotional and psychological stress caused by rude, disruptive or intoxicated customer behaviour (Baker *et al.*, 2012). Moreover, from a long-term perspective, such extreme dys-functional customer behaviour increases employees' likelihood of low motivation and decreases their psychological well-being (Harris and Reynolds, 2004; Baker *et al.*, 2012). Finally, the effect of other customer service failure can influence the firm's finan-cial performance and market position. Dysfunctional customer behaviour increases the likelihood of financial costs to the firm because dissatisfied customers are less likely to revisit (Harris and Reynolds, 2004). Research shows that failing to consider the negative influence of other customers may reduce customer intentions to revisit a firm by as much as 30% (Brocato *et al.*, 2012). Stated differently, other customer service failure negatively influences customers' global evaluations of the service firm, which negatively influences their market position.

9.4 Characteristics of Other Customers

The extent to which other customers may influence the focal customer's service experi-ence and behaviour depends on the context of the service encounter and the character-istics of other customers. For example, a customer may expect other customers in a sports bar to be loud and rowdy when watching a football game. However, customers may want a quieter, peaceful environment when having a date at a fine dining res-taurant. Furthermore, within the same environment, depending on whether it is a family gathering or a business meeting, the influence of co-consumption others may vary. Simply stated, the influence of other customers may be specific to the context or the characteristics of a company.

In hospitality services, such as restaurants, cruises, theme parks and airplanes, the presence of co-consumption others is an indispensable part of the consumption ex-perience (Wei *et al.*, 2012). In a service failure and recovery context, the influence of co-consumption others on focal customer behaviour can be explained by impression management. People have a tendency to conform to the positive expectations of their reference group by adopting the referent's opinions to determine appropriate behav-iour, especially when their behaviour is identifiable (Deutsch and Gerard, 1955). This is because they want to give a good impression to others by managing their behaviour. Along with that, research shows that customers utilize different complaining strat-egies depending on the characteristics of co-consumption others. For example, Huang *et al.* (2014) reveal that when with a close companion of the same sex, customers tend to disclose more about their emotions, which leads to a higher likelihood of com-plaining. Similarly, Fan *et al.* (2015) examine the impact of social distance between the focal customer and other customers on complaint intentions in a cross-cultural context and find that Americans are more likely to complain when dining out with family than the Chinese, while in the presence of strangers complaints are uniformly high for both cultures. This can be explained by the fact that individuals' evaluations of their interactions with other customers significantly depends on their perceived compatibility with them (Grove and Fisk, 1997). Individuals feel more comfortable being with other people who have similar attributes such as age, behaviour, gender and culture (Martin and Pranter, 1989), which leads to a higher likelihood of complaining.

In general, customers feel anger and frustration when other customers behave inappropriately. However, in situations of co-consumption, when encountering inappropriate behaviour by other customers, a focal customer, with a high level of need for self-monitoring, may be more likely to regulate her/his own behaviour for the purpose of impression management (Miao, 2014). In other words, in this case the customer may prefer to refrain from expressing her/his negative emotions towards the other customer/s who behave inappropriately. The main motivation behind this behaviour would be to maintain the earlier positive impression that the focal customer believes s/he developed.

9.5 Attributions of Other Customer Service Failure

Attribution theory provides important insight into the behaviour of focal customers when other customer service failure occurs. As discussed in Chapter 6 (this volume), according to attribution theory (Kelley, 1967), when faced with unexpected or negative events, consumers search for meaningful explanations for the cause and make attributions based on the cause and blame. Especially when a service failure occurs, consumers attempt to determine the cause and make attributions according to information received, which then influences subsequent emotions, attitudes and future actions (Weiner, 1985). Weiner (1985) identifies three common dimensions of causal attributions: (i) locus of causality; (ii) controllability; and (iii) stability.

First, locus of causality refers to customers' perceptions of where or with whom the responsibility for the failure rests (Weiner, 1985). When the service failure is caused by the firm or service provider, customers can easily assign causality of the failure to the internal source: the firm. However, when service failure occurs due to other customers, the judgement of locus of causality gets more complicated. Logically speaking, customers should blame the other customer, not the firm, when service failures occur due to the misbehaviour of other customers. However, previous research shows that although customers attribute responsibility for the service failure to the other customers, they still form negative perceptions and behaviours toward the firm (Baker and Kim, 2016). This is because consumers perceive the firm is responsible for the service recovery and when the firm does not deal with the situation appropriately, they develop a negative perception toward the firm. In other words, it is highly related to the controllability attribute.

Controllability is the degree to which the cause is perceived to be under the service firm's control (Weiner, 1985). Previous research has demonstrated that the greater a firm's perceived control over the cause of the service failure, the more negative the emotional and behavioural reactions toward the firm (Bitner, 1990; Huang, 2010). Stated differently, when other customer service failure happens, and focal customers perceive it to be within the control of the firm, the focal customers are more likely to blame the service firm rather than the dysfunctional customers. Huang *et al.* (2010) show that when customers consider the cause of other customer failure to be controllable by the firm, they engage in negative word-of-mouth and are less likely to repurchase.

Finally, stability refers to whether the failure is relatively temporary or permanent (Weiner, 1985). The perception that a cause of the service failure is stable leads customers to expect a similar outcome to recur in the future, which then leads to negative behavioural responses (Folkes, 1984). In the case of other customer service failure, when customers perceive other customer failure to be a stable cause, they tend to show lower levels of dissatisfaction, negative word-of-mouth and unfavourable future purchase intentions toward the firm (Huang *et al.*, 2010).

In summary, people assign accountability for the offence to whomever they determine is to blame for the failure, based on various causal attributions (Collie *et al.*, 2000). This is critical since emotional and behavioural responses vary depending on how consumers attribute blame (Machleit and Mantel, 2001). Therefore, service firms should take corrective actions to reduce the blame for failure directed towards them.

9.6 Recovery Strategies

Customers' dissatisfactory service experiences are likely to happen when the service provider fails to address issues caused by the misbehaviour of other customers (Bitner, 1990). Since customers who have negative interactions with other customers often form negative feelings toward the service providers and firms, service firms cannot simply ignore failure caused by other customers but instead must have a proactive service recovery strategy (Baker and Kim, 2016). More importantly, although firms might view the misbehaviour of other customers as uncontrollable, customers still consider management of other customer misbehaviour to be an important component of the service process, and this affects their overall service evaluation (Huang, 2010; Baker and Kim, 2016). Previous studies suggest recovery strategies for other customer service failure include: (i) compatibility management; (ii) recovery by communication with other customers; and (iii) recovery by communicating with focal customer.

9.6.1 Compatibility management

Service firms can prevent negative customer-to-customer interactions by being proactive. Some researchers argue that customers' satisfaction with service encounters depends on customers' compatibility with other customers. Martin and Pranter (1989) suggest that service firms should actively engage in 'customer compatibility management', which is the process of attracting a homogeneous clientele to the service environment, then actively managing both the physical environment and customer interactions, to minimize the frequency of dissatisfying customer-to-customer encounters. The logic behind this is that there is less possibility of negative customer-to-customer interactions when customers are more compatible with each other in the service setting. Service organizations should therefore engage in compatibility management to increase the likelihood of appropriate customer mix and positive customer-to-customer interaction, which then reduces the likelihood of other customer service failure. The cruise industry is adopting customer compatibility management by segmenting customers by age and lifestyle. For example, Carnival Cruises targets younger people who like to have a fun nightlife and a party atmosphere, while Princess Cruises provides a calmer

ration is the act of
of things to work

*ic **integration***
ed to bring

nmigrants into
has become much
i in the past.

Integration

(*uncountable*) **Inte**

combining a numbe

together.

European econon
was widely expec
enormous benefit
Integration *of i*
American society
more difficult tha

and elegant servicescape for an older demographic. This kind of segmentation prevents conflict among customers who have different lifestyles and expectations. A college-aged student would not have a satisfactory cruise based on the other customers present on a Princess Cruise and vice versa. In addition, given that proximity is one of the factors affecting negative customer-to-customer interaction, service firms should carefully consider seating arrangements (Zhang *et al.*, 2010).

9.6.2 Recovery by communication with other customer

If a customer complains excessively loudly and diners at the next table are disrupted, does the restaurant have an obligation to manage it? This is always a very sensitive area, but it is important to manage this issue appropriately. If ignored, it can easily turn into a lose/lose situation. Previous research shows consensus that service firms should actively engage in service recovery when other customer service failure occurs. Customers expect the service employees to keep the disruptive customer from disturbing others (Huang, 2010). Stated differently, customers evaluate the service not only based on the misbehaviours of other customers, but more importantly based on the active reaction from the firm and service providers. If customers are being disruptive, management should speak to them to try to minimize the disruption. When customers believe that the employees have done everything possible to solve an other customer failure problem, they feel more highly satisfied, are more willing to come back and are less willing to engage in negative word-of-mouth (Huang, 2010). Baker and Kim (2016) show customers expect the firm to actively try to control other customers' misbehaviour, regardless of the results. As such, it is critical that managers do not simply ignore the effects of other customers, but manage them properly. To do so, service firms should develop protocols for dealing with other customer service failure to provide a proactive service recovery strategy as well as training programmes to immediately react to disruptive other customer behaviour with appropriate problem-solving skills.

9.6.3 Recovery by communicating with focal customer

Service firms should also pay attention to mitigating the negative emotions of victim customers by actively engaging in service recovery for them. Although the service provider corrected the core problem of other customers, they still need to take care of the victim customers who suffered from the other customer failure. Baker and Kim (2016) show that customers expect an apology, an attentive attitude to the situation from the service provider and even reimbursement from the firm for service recovery when other customer service failure occurs. It is important for a firm to acknowledge the situation because many customers still think the firm is responsible for the service recovery (Baker and Kim, 2016). Along with that, an explanation about the situation and a sincere apology should follow. When customers do not know exactly what happened, they are more likely to blame the service firm, not the occasion of service failure caused by other customers. Liao (2007) shows that an apology, courteous behaviour and an explanation positively influence customer satisfaction and customer repurchase intentions. Therefore, service providers should explain to customers what caused the service failure and politely apologize. Providing compensation for affected customers is another option. Davidow and Leigh (1998) reveal that compensation has a positive effect on repurchase intentions. In summary, an active problem-solving recovery strategy is important to rectify other customer service failure and prevent negative consequences to the service firm.

9.7 Observing Service Recovery Aimed at Other Customers

As service failure is inevitable in service encounters, customers can often witness other customers experiencing service failure and how the firm recovers the failure. This is an important issue because people not only perceive fairness from the treatment they experience but also from observing the treatment of others (Cropanzano *et al.*, 2003). Consequently, the service recovery aimed at other customers indirectly influences the focal customer's service experience. Spencer and Rupp (2009) suggest the concept of third-party justice, which refers to perceptions of how fairly others are treated, and argue that the observation of third-party justice has an impact on behaviours and attitudes of the observers. People perceive that each individual should be equally treated in similar situations; the observation of others being treated unfairly results in a negative evaluation of fairness (Mattila *et al.*, 2014). This is explained by deontic justice theory (Cropanzano *et al.*, 2003), which suggests that observation of another customer being treated unfairly results in a negative evaluation of fairness and anger by third parties. People respond to unfairness not because of their own self-interest but due to an inherited tendency to be sensitized to unfair treatment (Cropanzano *et al.*, 2003). People judge fairness based on their a priori standards, regardless of their involvement with the parties affected. Accordingly, observing other customers being treated unfairly negatively affects perceived fairness, emotions, behaviours and attitudes toward wrongdoers (Mattila *et al.*, 2014). This is critical for service firms in terms of the service recovery aimed at other customers because it not only directly influences the focal customers, but also indirectly influences other customers who observe the service recovery process. In a hospitality and tourism setting, Mattila *et al.* (2012) show that when service recovery for the other customer is bad, observing customers have negative emotional and behavioural responses to the firm regardless of their own experience. It emphasizes that service providers should pay attention not only to victim customers but also to surrounding customers who can observe and listen to the treatment of the victim customers.

CASE STUDY

You and your friend visit a restaurant in your town to have dinner. You sit at one of the tables next to a group of customers. Throughout your stay, you receive good and attentive service from your server.

However, during your meal you overhear the other customers next to you yelling loudly and aggressively at the server, complaining that their food tasted terrible. They are loud, rude and ruin your dining experience.

Continued

K. Kim and M.A. Baker

Questions

1. What opinions might you and other customers form, based on observing the service failure that occurred toward and from the other customers?
2. Within the given case, what are the service failures and who is to blame for the service failures: the other customers or the firm?
3. What should the firm or managers do to make the situation better regarding this other customer service failure?

9.8 Conclusion

Even when they do not directly interact, customers affect one another in service settings. Although co-creation and the effect of third parties are increasingly prevalent, the influence of other customers in a service setting has received considerably less attention both in academia and industry because it is not considered easy for firms to control or manage. However, given that customers share the same service environment, they often either directly or indirectly affect other customers' emotions, attitudes and behaviours, which then strongly affects their overall evaluation of the service and the service firm. As such, service firms should actively manage customer encounters to ensure that all their customers' behaviour is appropriate and if other customer service failure happens, they need to react immediately to recover from the service failure, rather than accepting negative customer-to-customer interactions as inevitable phenomena.

Questions

1. Explain the concept of social servicescape and its influence on service failures from the perspective of tourism and hospitality businesses.
2. What are the main types of service failures caused by other customers?
3. What sort of action can be taken to recover service failures caused by other customers?

Further Reading

Baker, M.A. and Kim, K. (2016) Other customer service failures: emotions, impacts, and attributions. *Journal of Hospitality & Tourism Research* doi: 10.1177/1096348016671394.
Bitner, M.J. (1992) Servicescapes: the impact of physical surroundings on customers and employees. *The Journal of Marketing* 56, 57–71.
Brocato, E.D., Voorhees, C.M. and Baker, J. (2012) Understanding the influence of cues from other customers in the service experience: a scale development and validation. *Journal of Retailing* 88, 384–398.

Grove, S.J. and Fisk, R.P. (1997) The impact of other customers on service experiences: a critical incident examination of 'getting along'. *Journal of Retailing* 73, 63–85.

Huang, W.H. (2008) The impact of other-customer failure on service satisfaction. *International Journal of Service Industry Management* 19, 521–536.

References

Baker, J. (1986) The role of the environment in marketing services: the consumer perspective. *The Services Challenge: Integrating for Competitive Advantage* 1, 79–84.

Baker, M.A. and Kim, K. (2016) Other customer service failures: emotions, impacts, and attributions. *Journal of Hospitality & Tourism Research*. doi: 10.1177/1096348016671394.

Baker, M.A., Magnini, V.P. and Perdue, R.R. (2012) Opportunistic customer complaining: causes, consequences, and managerial alternatives. *International Journal of Hospitality Management* 31, 295–303.

Barker, R.G. (1968) *Ecological Psychology: Concepts and Methods for Studying the Environment of Human Behaviour.* Stanford University Press, Stanford, California.

Bateson, J.E.G. (1985) Self-service consumer: an exploratory study. *Journal of Retailing* 61, 49–76.

Bauer, M. (2013) How do restaurants deal with loud, obnoxious guests? Available at: http://insidescoopsf.sfgate.com/blog/2013/07/10/how-do-restaurants-deal-with-loud-obnoxious-guests (accessed 19 December 2016).

Bearden, W.O. and Etzel, M.J. (1982) Reference group influence on product and brand purchase decisions. *Journal of Consumer Research* 9, 183–194.

Belk, R.W. (1975) Situational variables and consumer behavior. *Journal of Consumer Research* 2, 157–164.

Bitner, M.J. (1990) Evaluating service encounters: the effects of physical surroundings and employee responses. *Journal of Marketing* 4, 69–82.

Bitner, M.J. (1992) Servicescapes: the impact of physical surroundings on customers and employees. *The Journal of Marketing* 56, 57–71.

Bitner, M.J., Booms, B.H. and Mohr, L.A. (1994) Critical service encounters: the employee's viewpoint. *The Journal of Marketing* 58, 95–106.

Brocato, E.D., Voorhees, C.M. and Baker, J. (2012) Understanding the influence of cues from other customers in the service experience: a scale development and validation. *Journal of Retailing* 88, 384–398.

Collie, T.A., Sparks, B. and Bradley, G. (2000) Investing in interactional justice: a study of the fair process effect within a hospitality failure context. *Journal of Hospitality & Tourism Research* 24, 448–472.

Cropanzano, R., Goldman, B. and Folger, R. (2003) Deontic justice: the role of moral principles in workplace fairness. *Journal of Organizational Behavior* 24, 1019–1024.

Davidow, M. and Leigh, J. (1998) The effects of organizational complaint responses on consumer satisfaction, word of mouth activity and repurchase intentions. *Journal of Consumer Satisfaction, Dissatisfaction & Complaining Behavior* 11, 91–102.

Deutsch, M. and Gerard, H.B. (1955) A study of normative and informational social influences upon individual judgment. *The Journal of Abnormal and Social Psychology* 51, 629–636.

Fan, A., Mattila, A.S. and Zhao, X. (2015) How does social distance impact customers' complaint intentions? A cross-cultural examination. *International Journal of Hospitality Management* 47, 35–42.

Folkes, V.S. (1984) Consumer reactions to product failure: an attributional approach. *Journal of Consumer Research* 10, 398–409.

K. Kim and M.A. Baker

Grove, S.J. and Fisk, R.P. (1997) The impact of other customers on service experiences: a critical incident examination of 'getting along'. *Journal of Retailing* 73, 63–85.

Harris, L.C. and Reynolds, K.L. (2004) The consequences of dysfunctional customer behaviour. *Journal of Service Research* 6, 144–161.

Huang, M.C.J., Wu, H.C., Chuang, S.-C. and Lin, W.H. (2014) Who gets to decide your complaint intentions? The influence of other companions on reaction to service failures. *International Journal of Hospitality Management* 37, 180–189.

Huang, W.H. (2008) The impact of other-customer failure on service satisfaction. *International Journal of Service Industry Management* 19, 521–536.

Huang, W.H. (2010) Other-customer failure: effects of perceived employee effort and compensation on complainer and non-complainer service evaluations. *Journal of Service Management* 21, 191–211.

Huang, W.H. and Wang, Y.C. (2014) Situational influences on the evaluation of other-customer failure. *International Journal of Hospitality Management* 36, 110–119.

Huang, W.H., Lin, Y.C. and Wen, Y.C. (2010) Attributions and outcomes of customer misbehavior. *Journal of Business and Psychology* 25, 151–161.

Kelley, H.H. (1967) Attribution theory in social psychology. In: *Nebraska Symposium on Motivation*. University of Nebraska Press, Lincoln, Nebraska.

Lehtinen, U. and Lehtinen, J.R. (1991) Two approaches to service quality dimensions. *Service Industries Journal* 11, 287–303.

Leizer, L. (2016) Why hotels should take noise complaints seriously. Available at: https://www.quiethotelroom.org/why-hotels-should-take-noise-complaints-seriously (accessed 19 December 2016).

Liao, H. (2007) Do it right this time: the role of employee service recovery performance in customer-perceived justice and customer loyalty after service failures. *Journal of Applied Psychology* 92, 475–489.

Lovelock, C. H. (1994) *Product Plus: How Product and Service Equals Competitive Advantage*. McGraw-Hill, New York.

Machleit, K.A. and Mantel, S.P. (2001) Emotional response and shopping satisfaction moderating effects of shopper attributions. *Journal of Business Research* 54, 97–106.

Martin, C.L. (1996) Consumer-to-consumer relationships: satisfaction with other consumers' public behavior. *Journal of Consumer Affairs* 30, 146–169.

Martin, C.L. and Pranter, C.A. (1989) Compatibility management: customer-to-customer relationships in service environments. *Journal of Services Marketing* 3, 5–15.

Mattila, A., Hanks, L. and Wang, C. (2014) Others service experiences: emotions, perceived justice, and behavior. *European Journal of Marketing* 48, 552–571.

Mattila, O., Toppinen, A., Tervo, M. and Berghäll, S. (2012) Non-industrial private forestry service markets in a flux: results from a qualitative analysis on Finland. *Small-scale Forestry* 12, 559–578.

Maxham, J.G. III and Netemeyer, R.G. (2002) A longitudinal study of complaining customers' evaluations of multiple service failures and recovery efforts. *Journal of Marketing* 66, 57–71.

McColl-Kennedy, J., Cheung, L. and Ferrier, E. (2014) Co-creating service experience practices. *Journal of Service Management* 26, 249–275.

Miao, L. (2014) Self-regulation and 'other consumers' at service encounters: a sociometer perspective. *International Journal of Hospitality Management* 39, 122–129.

Miao, L. and Mattila, A.S. (2013) The impact of other customers on customer experiences: a psychological distance perspective. *Journal of Hospitality & Tourism Research* 37, 77–99.

Nicholls, R. (2010) New directions for customer-to-customer interaction research. *Journal of Services Marketing* 24, 87–97.

Rocha, V. (2016) Complaint over loud 'boom box' music leads to 5-woman brawl on Spirit Airlines flight. Available at: http://www.latimes.com/local/lanow/la-me-ln-five-women-fight-spirit-airlines-boombox-20160309-story.html (accessed 18 December 2016).

Spencer, S. and Rupp, D.E. (2009) Angry, guilty, and conflicted: injustice toward coworkers heightens emotional labor through cognitive and emotional mechanisms. *Journal of Applied Psychology* 94, 429–444.

Tombs, A. and McColl-Kennedy, J.R. (2003) Social-servicescape conceptual model. *Marketing Theory* 3, 447–475.

Wei, W., Miao, L., Cai, L.A. and Adler, H. (2012) The influence of self-construal and co-consumption others on consumer complaining behavior. *International Journal of Hospitality Management* 31, 764–771.

Weiner, B. (1985) An attributional theory of achievement motivation and emotion. *Psychological Review* 92, 548–573.

Weiss, H.M. and Cropanzano, R. (1996) Affective events theory: a theoretical discussion of the structures, causes and consequences of affective experiences at work. *Research in Organizational Behavior* 18, 1–74.

Zajonc, R.B. (1965) *Social Facilitation*. Research Center for Group Dynamics, Institute for Social Research, University of Michigan, Michigan.

Zemke, R. and Anderson, K. (1990) Customers from hell. *Training* 26, 25–33.

Zhang, J., Beatty, S.E. and Mothersbaugh, D. (2010) A CIT investigation of other customers' influence in services. *Journal of Services Marketing* 24, 389–399.

10 Emotional Contagion and the Influence of Groups on Service Failures and Recovery

A. Celil Cakici and Ozan Guler

Learning Objectives

After reading this chapter, you should be able to:

- Understand the role and potential of group consumption in tourism and hospitality.
- Explain the group service interaction process.
- Understand the contexts in which group service failures take place.
- Understand and explain the concept of emotional contagion and its influence on service failures and recovery processes.

10.1   Introduction

Service is a concept based on a complex and subjective evaluation (Gronroos, 1988, p. 10). Until the 1980s, advances in goods and commodity marketing were not capable of solving the problems in service marketing, which caused marketers to emphasize services (Mucuk, 1999, p. 322). Marketers have come to attach great importance to customers' perceptions, attitudes and behaviours regarding service experience as well as customer satisfaction and loyalty (Yüksel and Yüksel, 2003, p. 53). Characteristics that distinguish services from goods (intangibility, non-standardization, inseparability of production and consumption, and perishability) have obliged businesses to consider different dimensions of service in their strategies (Parasuraman et al., 1985, p. 42; Kotler et al., 2010, p. 35). Co-consumption and service interaction are at the forefront when the characteristics of service are considered, and most particularly the inseparability of production and consumption. The relationships between buyers and sellers, or businesses and customers, are essential to achieve desirable results from service marketing efforts (Solomon et al., 1985, p. 99; Susskind, 2004, p. 22). Customers carry out an evaluation process about a business and its services throughout the whole consumption period (before, during and after), considering interactions with employees and businesses (Shamdasani and Balakrishnan, 2000, p. 399).

In the tourism and hospitality industry, one of the biggest service industries, service interaction is crucial (Koc and Boz, 2014, p. 144). This interaction occurs mostly with group customers, as customers engage with restaurants, hotel accommodation, tours, etc. mainly with their families, friends and co-workers (Huang et al., 2014, p. 181). For example, studies reveal that children between the ages of 13 and 21 influence more than two-thirds of family holiday decisions (Kotler and Keller, 2012, p. 176). One of the primary objectives of the tourism and hospitality industry is to ensure absolute customer satisfaction. Customer satisfaction has well-known positive effects on business profitability and sustainability (Bearden and Teel, 1983, p. 21). However, it is almost impossible and unrealistic for service businesses to target 100% satisfaction among all customers at the same time (Bearden and Teel, 1983, p. 21; Maxham, 2001, p. 11; McColl-Kennedy *et al.*, 2003, p. 66; McQuilken and Robertson, 2011, p. 953). Because service interaction is evident and intense in group consumption, individuals' attitudes, beliefs and behaviours could be easily transformed. Thus, group service interaction could lead to common impulsive and emotional reactions (Du *et al.*, 2014, pp. 326–327).

While some of these reactions may be specific to a group, some may be related to individuals and be spontaneous. Thus, different from individual service failure, group service failure indicates affective disorders during consumers' experience with a business. From this point of view, emotions and emotional contagion have become a significant influence throughout the service encounter for tourism and hospitality businesses. Group buying behaviours differ notably from individual buying behaviours. Buying decisions taken in common by groups lead marketing managers to use different approaches in determining marketing components (Koc, 2016, p. 447). Accordingly, customers' emotional responses and the inclination of group members' emotional contagion are key concepts for the service industry, particularly the tourism and hospitality industry. According to the 2015 *US Family Travel Survey* of the US Family Travel Association, families greatly value the emotional benefits of travel. This finding shows that group buying and consumption have more than monetary value. In this chapter, emotional responses and emotional contagion among group members after group service failures have been addressed in the context of the tourism and hospitality industry. The conceptual and theoretic background of the topic has been enriched with examples, cases and discussion points, and implications have been asserted for theoreticians and practitioners.

Discussion point 1. Group consumption

Many people working in tourism companies are aware of how difficult serving groups of customers can be. For example, imagine that you are working as a hotel receptionist: A group of 100 Italian customers with a reservation for 40 rooms checks in to the hotel. Only 20 rooms are ready for the arriving group because some customers that you expected to check out at 12 a.m. did not check out from their rooms before 2:00 p.m. How will you divide up the clean rooms? Customers are grumbling, babies are crying and kids are running around the crowded lobby! Do you think these customers remember the cheaper group price of their rooms? What can be done to prevent customers from having negative reactions when they travel in groups? Please split up into small groups and discuss with your friends the dos and don'ts of serving groups.

10.2 Development of Group Consumption in Tourism and Hospitality Industry

The tourism and hospitality industry mostly promotes group, rather than individual, consumption through such methods as early bookings, package tours, online group buying and coupons. Opportunities for group buying encourage consumers (tourists) to travel together. According to the number of tourists by purpose of visit, 53% of all tourist arrivals (632 million) were intended for leisure, recreation and holidays, and these mostly travelled in different sized groups (UNWTO, 2016, pp. 4–5). Another 27% (320 million) travelled for other reasons such as visiting friends and relatives, religious reasons and pilgrimages, health treatment, etc. When these numbers are examined considering with whom people go on holiday, it stands out that tourists go on holiday in groups year after year. According to the 2014 *Consumer Holiday Trends Report* by the Association of British Travel Agents, while it is most common for people to holiday with their partner (50%) or immediate family (35%), one in five consumers (20%) went on holiday with a group of adult friends.

Families travelling with children represent one of the largest and most constant markets for the tourism and leisure industry. Family tourism is one of the most important market segments around the world, accounting for approximately 30% of the leisure travel market (Schanzel *et al.*, 2012). Tourism and hospitality purchases involve various unknowns and risks because of their service-based characteristics, such as intangibility and inseparability. These characteristics make collective decisions inevitable. In family group buying behaviour, importance and risk perception of the services involved in collective decision-making differ from those associated with individual buying behaviour. According to the 2015 *US Family Travel Survey* of the US Family Travel Association, 93% of 2614 respondents are either 'very likely' or 'likely' to travel with their children in the next two years. The report revealed that 77% of the respondents took holidays to see friends and relatives, and 89% of this group is likely to take the same holidays with the same purpose again. Furthermore, the report shows that 19% of the travellers went on holiday with their extended family (family members from outside the household), more than double the number in the previous 12 months (7%). As is clearly seen, group size is not limited to family members but expands to include relatives and friends. Hence, group consumption has become highly significant for the whole service industry. Figure 10.1 shows how family buying differs from individual buying.

The internet, which has changed and transformed many industries' ways of doing business (Wen, 2009, p. 752), is the most significant factor increasing group consumption (Tsai *et al.*, 2011, p. 1091) and travellers' travel decisions (Tanford and Montgomery, 2015, p. 596). The number of group-buying customers in China was approximately 19 million at the end of 2010, and the market's worth reached US$3.64 billion at the end of 2011 (Zhou *et al.*, 2013, p. 1146). Discounted consumption opportunities encourage group consumption via 'online group buying' internet platforms, such as Groupon.com and Livingsocial.com (Shiau and Luo, 2012, p. 2431; Zhang *et al.*, 2013, p. 237; Kim *et al.*, 2014, p. 380). As an indication of this growth, the revenue earned by the daily deal site Groupon increased by 32% year on year, to US$568.6 million in the third quarter of 2012, compared with US$430.2 million in the third quarter of 2011 (Zhang *et al.*, 2013, p. 237). In Canada, local companies offer their services at a discount of between 30% and 90% for group sales (Shiau and Luo, 2012, p. 2431).

Group buying is regarded as purchase volume-focused discounted product sale by businesses selling online (Tsai *et al.*, 2011, p. 1091; Shiau and Luo, 2012, p. 2431; Kim *et al.*, 2014, p. 380); however, it is also a means of satisfying groups' expectations of the businesses where the consumption will be made. Group buying platforms such as Groupon.com and Livingsocial.com are the platforms where not only products such as

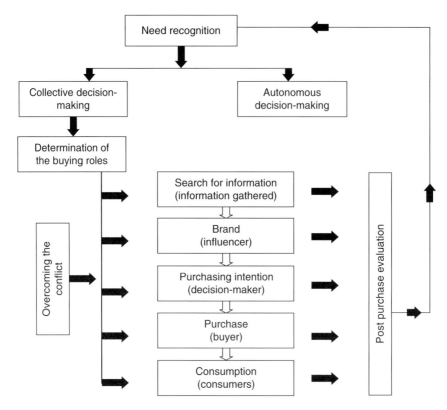

Fig. 10.1. Family buying model. (From Koc, 2016, p. 448.)

clothes, electronics and cosmetics but also many service-oriented products such as hotels, restaurants, tour services, transportation, entertainment and activities can be bought. As an example, there were approximately 108,000 daily deal offers for restaurants in one month, with a value of approximately US$148 million and accounting for 44.1% of the total turnover, and the number of restaurant coupons sold for an offer always far exceeds the minimum group size required before the deadline (Zhang *et al.*, 2013, p. 237).

Online coupons are being quickly and widely adopted by the tourism industry. Design and sale of coupons have become more widespread and attractive for tourism services thanks to websites specializing in tourism such as weecation.com and deals. touristorama.com, in addition to major players such as Groupon.com and Expedia. com (Sigala, 2013, p. 165). According to Rezdy.com, approximately 96.8 million adult tourists identified as 'coupon hunters' are expected to have used online coupons in 2013. Online coupons promise substantial savings, often 50% or more for tourism products (Sigala, 2013, p. 165; Kim *et al.*, 2014, p. 380). People are expected to inform each other about discounted tourism opportunities and make plans together. Group sales opportunities are in abundance, such as revenue management and differential pricing strategies for restaurants, hotels, package tours, spa services, museums, etc. (Sigala, 2013, p. 165); however, the group service process could turn out to be challenging and speculative, while individual service quality/satisfaction assessment might be lower.

10.3 Group Service Interaction

The transformation of consumer behaviours from a rational physiological phenomenon into a psychological and emotional phenomenon lies behind the increasing interest in understanding consumer behaviour in the 21st century (Koc, 2016, p. 39). Companies become aware of their products' emotional value in the eyes of consumers and emphasize emotional themes in marketing communication tools. For instance, treating emotional themes such as 'holiday of your dreams' and 'romanticism' and cognitive elements such as the number of days at the hotel, hotel star rating and type of accommodation in a package tour holiday influence consumer attitudes and behaviours (Koc, 2016, p. 306). Consumers regard the products that they have or consume as a communication tool. Products have become a source of information about the consumer's personality, mentality, attitudes and characteristics. People do not wear clothes only to protect themselves from the cold or as a covering, and they do not eat only to fill their stomachs. People try to fulfil the desires, wishes, dreams and imaginations that they cannot clearly express and prove that they are different from others (Koc, 2016, p. 37).

Undoubtedly, when consumption is made in a group, emotions become more evident and lead customers to show different attitudes and behaviours than they would individually (Du *et al.*, 2014, p. 327; Huang *et al.*, 2014, p. 182). Significance level and risk perception of the products categorized by joint decision-making will be different compared with individual purchase behaviour because of the need to satisfy more people (Koc, 2016, p. 447). McQuilken and Robertson (2013) revealed that group service failure and negative experiences at a restaurant mostly affect the revisit intention of the person responsible for choosing the restaurant. The authors report that the intention to complain about negative experiences occurs most in cases where the person with the negative experience chose the restaurant himself; however, joint decisions by individuals and groups lower the intention to complain about negative experiences. Huang *et al.* (2014) searched the effect of co-consumption on customer complaint intention and found that restaurant customers' complaint intention is significantly higher when they are with their friends than when they are alone.

While some parts of our daily consumption can be made individually, some are made in groups, such as families, relatives, school mates, colleagues, etc. Customers' service quality perception and satisfaction are affected significantly by other customers' behaviours as well as the customers' own expectations and employees' attitudes and behaviours (Patterson *et al.*, 2006, p. 263). As consumers, we watch and observe the consumption behaviours of the people around us and learn how to behave and solve problems regarding the consumption. What we learn affects our consumption decisions and behaviours. This process is called socialization of consumers (Odabaşı and Barış, 2015, p. 227).

Groups that play a significant role in the socialization of consumers are a valuable market segment for service marketers. According to Odabaşı and Barış (2015, p. 228), the group is a community in which people have relationships, expectations and pleasures, and where relationships have continuity. Families, relatives, friends, voluntary groups, school mates, business environment, associations/foundations relations, prisons, army and long-term treatment centres (for coping with alcohol, drugs or losing weight) are examples of groups. Seven primary groups that influence consumers' buying and consumption behaviours are shown in Fig. 10.2 (Odabaşı and Barış, 2015, p. 234). Kotler and Keller (2012, p. 175) note two additional groups: the aspirational group, in

Fig. 10.2. Types of consumption groups. (From the authors.)

which we are not included but we wish to be, and the dissociative group, in which we avoid being included.

10.3.1   Group service failure

Service failure is a mishap and/or problem that occurs during a consumer's service experience with a business (Richins, 1982, p. 502; Maxham, 2001, p. 11). Service failure is a negative result of economic and social interactions between customers and businesses (Smith *et al.*, 1999, p. 357). Service failures may cause a fracture in the relationship between firms and their customers and lead to negative consumer behavioural intention in the future (Ha and Jang, 2009, p. 319). Negative behaviours may be noticeable, in that previously loyal customers give up frequenting the business, or unnoticeable, in that there is a decrease in new customers visiting the business because of unhappy customers' negative word-of-mouth (Koc *et al.*, 2017, p. 392).

Satisfying group customers is as important as satisfying individual customers for tourism and hospitality companies. Tourism companies now face a critical dilemma: how can an employee provide a distinctive and unique service for group members and at the same time keep service standardized (Solomon *et al.*, 1985, p. 107; Surprenant and Solomon, 1987, p. 86)? This dilemma represents a vital problem for the tourism and hospitality industry. Regardless of the precautions proposed to ensure proper service delivery, even companies that generally display exceptional service are vulnerable to some extent to service failure because of the characteristics of the service sector (Richins, 1982, p. 502; Miller *et al.*, 2000, p. 387; Palmer *et al.*, 2000, p. 517; Shamdasani and Balakrishnan, 2000, p. 400; Maxham, 2001, p. 11; Namkung and Jang, 2009, p. 397; Kotler *et al.*, 2010, p. 42).

Another element that makes service failures more pronounced for tourism and hospitality companies is their group-oriented structure. Interaction and emotion-sharing are quite high in groups; however, during service failures, interaction and emotion-sharing dramatically rise. The customers who perceive service failure make the other group members aware of the unfair treatment they are exposed to, and they exchange ideas about what should be done. Consequently, service failure causes a common negative emotion within the group (Du *et al.*, 2014, p. 327). When people are included in a group, they are exposed to intensity and contagion of emotions conveyed by other group members (Barsade, 2002, p. 647). Based on group and service failure conceptualizations, group service failure is defined as 'service which cannot meet all or most of the customers' expectations in a group' (Du *et al.*, 2014, p. 327). Group service failure can also be stated as problems customers experience in 'co-consumption with other people' (Wei *et al.*, 2012, p. 764).

Group service failures may have major negative effects on companies' reputations and financial situations. As a true example, 300 tourists made a deal with a tour agency to visit the Three Gorges Dam in 2006. When the guides only allowed the tourists to view the dam from far away instead of close up, the tourists felt cheated and sought their rights by taking legal action in a local tourist office. The tourist office ordered the tour agency to pay each tourist compensation of US\$60, US\$18,000 in total. This case was publicized by the leading media organizations in China (Du *et al.*, 2014, p. 326). The compensation paid may not be evaluated as a considerable amount from the perspective of big businesses; however, negative word-of-mouth has greater potential for harm than paid compensation. Another example of group service failure shows that the adjudged compensation can reach huge amounts. Ten aircraft belonging to Jet Blue Airlines had to fly for 6–10 hours longer than expected because of bad weather conditions. The customers stranded in the planes collectively sued Jet Blue Airlines because of blocked toilets, smelly cabin air, insufficient food and water, etc. The court ordered the airline company to pay plaintiffs approximately US\$30 million in total (Brennan and Morgan, 2013, cited by Du *et al.*, 2014, p. 326).

10.3.2 Factors affecting perception of group service failure

Researchers studying organizational psychology research group processes consider variables such as group size, group familiarity (group structure and group homogeneity), group potential, collective productivity, group efficiency, group mood and group beliefs (Mason and Griffin, 2005, p. 272). The variables that receive the most emphasis are group familiarity and group size (Du *et al.*, 2014, pp. 327–328; Odabaşı and Barış, 2015, p. 232).

Group familiarity expresses the closeness of relationships among the customers and can also be called 'relational distance' (Zhou *et al.*, 2014, p. 2481). Consumers' group familiarities can be split into primary and secondary groups (Koc, 2016, p. 436). Primary groups include families and groups of close friends that have a small number of members, high frequencies of interaction and communication and great effect on the concerned individuals. Secondary groups include groups of friends, shopping groups, business/work groups, virtual groups, product club groups (Volkswagen Club, Honda Team, etc.), consumer groups, professional organization groups, religious groups and fan groups that have many members and relatively low frequencies of interaction and communication. These groups have less potential to affect an individual's consumption behaviours (Kotler and Keller, 2012, p. 175). The difference between the two groups distinguishes customers' responses to service failures. In other words, the levels of interaction and communication among group members are the significant factors that can determine the level and type of reaction against any service failure.

Huang *et al.* (2014) researched whether there was a difference in terms of the complaint behaviour intention between family and friend groups after a perceived service failure. They found that complaint intention is higher among customers who are with their friends than with their families. While individuals pay attention to the size of service compensation offered after service failures in the groups in which group familiarity is low, they are more concerned about the procedural or interactional compensation in groups in which relational distance is close (Zhou *et al.*, 2014, p. 2481). Wei *et al.* (2012) investigated the effect of the level of group familiarity on intention to complain and exit the business in the context of dependent or independent customer self-construal. The authors revealed that customers whose level of group familiarity is low have a considerably higher intention to complain and exit from the business after service failure compared with customers with high familiarity. Similarly, Yang and Mattila (2012) revealed that customers whose group familiarity is low have a higher intention to complain about negative experiences stemming from service failure than customers with high familiarity. Huang *et al.* (2014) found that even the gender of other customers is a factor influencing their complaint tendency. The authors stated that tolerance for failures is lower when people are with friends of the same gender.

It is stated that the greater the cognitive and emotional similarities among the group members, the greater their adaptation in ideas and attitudes (Koriat *et al.*, 2016, p. 176). Accordingly, the success of group members in infecting the negative or positive emotions of other group members could affect group interaction and achievement of the objectives (Anderson *et al.*, 2003, p. 1055). Zhou *et al.* (2014) investigated perceived service recovery within the context of relational distance in a group. The authors revealed that group members who have close relationships with each other become happier when their economic compensation is public and their social compensation is private. However, they found that group members whose relational distances are great are more pleased when both economic and social recoveries are carried out publicly. Du *et al.* (2014) researched the relationship between emotional contagion resulting from group service failure and complaint intention in the context of hotel and restaurant service failure. When the effect of perceived emotional contagion on individual anger is compared, it is understood that groups with high familiarity showed a higher level of anger resulting from negative emotional contagion than groups with low familiarity.

Group size is another element that influences perception of group service failure. Group size expresses the number of people affected by group service failure (Zhou *et al.*, 2014, p. 2481). Groups of up to seven people are considered small groups, between eight and eleven medium-sized groups and twelve or more large groups (Du *et al.*, 2014, p. 331). Small groups generally express primary (in which face-to-face relationships and familiarity are high) and informal (no certain rules are required to come together) groups. Large groups generally express secondary (vocational groups, unions and political party members) and formal (school environment, co-workers and sport centres) groups (Odabaşı and Barış, 2015, p. 232).

The effect of group size on customers' common expectations is a controversial subject in the literature. However, the crowd of people sharing a common emotion is generally expected to cause emotional reaction and emotional contagion at a high level (Du *et al.*, 2014, p. 329). Du *et al.* (2014) carried out a study on hotel and restaurant service failure and found that the effect of group emotional contagion on members' individual anger is higher in large groups than in small groups. Group size is an important agent in customers obtaining not only common service expectations but also expected service recovery outputs (Zhou *et al.*, 2014). Huang *et al.* (2014) considered group size in a study investigating the effective recovery types for restaurant service failures. They reported that big groups (50 people) would be happier to receive economic recoveries offered publicly and social recoveries privately after service failure. On the contrary, small groups (five people) express no preference between obtaining economic recoveries privately or publicly.

10.4 Emotional Contagion in Group Service

10.4.1 Role of emotions in consumption

The study of moods and emotions has become an important field of research and theory within psychology and has been a focus of evolutionary theory since Darwin's early publications (Spoor and Kelly, 2004, p. 400). Many studies have revealed that emotions are an indispensable part of consumers' consumption behaviours (Richins, 1997, p. 127). The first of these studies investigated consumers' emotional reactions to advertisements (Richins, 1997, p. 127) and advanced to researching emotions' behavioural and cognitive results (Chang, 2008, p. 113). Emotions can be expressed as 'a special and neurological phenomenon shaped with natural selections and motivating and organizing creatures' psychological, cognitive and behavioural structures enabling them to give harmonizing reactions to surrounding events' (Izard, 1992, p. 561). In simpler words, emotions can be defined as 'people's reflection of their moods spontaneously as a result of scientific evaluation of an event or their own thoughts' (Bagozzi *et al.*, 1999, pp. 184–185). However, mood and emotion are separate concepts. Emotions are experienced in shorter time periods and more intensely, and their cause can be identified more easily and clearly than moods (Spoor and Kelly, 2004, p. 400).

CASE STUDY 1. USE OF EMOTIONAL FACTORS INCREASED THE NUMBER OF AMERICAN TOURISTS VISITING TURKEY BY 30%

The number of American tourists visiting Turkey in the first four months of 2011 increased by 30% compared with the first four months of 2010, from 100,000 to 130,000. Mr Yücel, coordinator of the advertising campaign, says that the ads were designed to resemble a Hollywood movie poster. Yücel claims that attracting tourists to Turkey is not best done by taking photographs of the Maiden's Tower, Ephesus or Fethiye-Ölüdeniz and placing them in the middle of Times Square and in the *New York Times*. Yücel indicates that he benefited from his accumulated experience and knowledge of the cinema industry when designing the promotional campaign for Turkey. He filled the adverts with emotions and conducted a human-oriented campaign. After Yücel discussed the details of the promotional campaign, he added that, while preparing posters of destinations such as the Maiden's Tower, Nemrut, Ölüdeniz, Kapadokya (Cappadocia) and Side, he added key characters that would appeal to potential American visitors' emotions and connect with something in their lives. For example, American children seeing the poster will feel that the characters are heroes in the movies *Gladiator* or *Troy*. Mothers who see their children's excitement could then make the decision to take their holiday in Turkey.

Source: Koc (2016, p. 304).

Considering the decisions we take, the behaviours we exhibit and the ideas we present in the flow of life, could we claim that individual emotions have sole responsibility? How much do other people's emotions affect us (Parkinson and Simons, 2009, p. 1071; Becker *et al.*, 2011, p. 1587)? For instance, when you get advice about a restaurant you have not visited before, don't your friend's non-verbal types of communication, such as body language and gestures, also affect your decision as well as words and tone of voice? Emotional reactions are important resources that can provide useful information about customers' opinions on service interactions and a business (Mattila and Enz, 2002, pp. 270–271). Emotions and moods help to coordinate an individual's behaviour and responses (Spoor and Kelly, 2004, p. 401), in addition to affecting individuals' thoughts, judgements and other subsequent behaviours (Boshoff, 2012, p. 401). Moreover, emotions are sensed in the body physically through indicators such as increase in blood pressure, paleness of skin or trembling of hands and voice (Koc, 2016, p. 304).

Richins (1997, pp. 144–145) developed a set of 'Consumption Emotions' consisting of 47 emotional responses classified under the 16 basic consumption emotion clusters following six-staged verification. These 16 positive or negative emotion clusters are: anger, discontent, worry, sadness, fear, shame, envy, loneliness, excitement, romantic love, love, peacefulness, contentment, optimism, joy and surprise (see Table 10.1).

Unlike the cognitive responses consisting of an objective perspective, emotional responses embody positive (happiness, joy, admiration and satisfaction) or negative feelings (e.g. regret, anger, boredom and fear) (Koc, 2016, p. 303). Intensity of emotional responses may differ in accordance with three criteria: (i) personal purpose of consumption event; (ii) personal importance of consumption event; and (iii) degree of admissibility of service failure (McColl-Kennedy and Sparks, 2003, p. 254). Positive or negative emotional responses could cause a variety of customer behaviours (Bagozzi and Dholakia, 2006, p. 50). A generally accepted approach claims that negative emotions appear and dissatisfaction increases when the perceived performance of products or service is inferior to consumers' expectations (Chang, 2008,

Table 10.1. Consumption emotion set. (From Richins, 1997.)

Cluster	Descriptor	Cluster	Descriptor
Anger	Frustrated, angry, irritated	Loneliness	Lonely, homesick
Discontent	Unfulfilled, discontented	Romantic love	Sexy, romantic, passionate
Worry	Nervous, worried, tense	Love	Loving, sentimental, warm hearted
Sadness	Depressed, sad, miserable	Peacefulness	Calm, peaceful
Fear	Scared, afraid, panicky	Contentment	Contented, fulfilled
Shame	Embarrassed, ashamed, humiliated	Optimism	Optimistic, encouraged, hopeful
Envy	Envious, jealous	Joy	Happy, pleased, joyful
Excitement	Excited, thrilled, enthusiastic	Surprise	Surprised, amazed, astonished
Others	Guilty, proud, eager, relieved		

p. 113; Han and Back, 2008, p. 467); however, positive emotions emerge and satisfaction increases in the opposite case (Chang, 2008, p. 113; Mattila and Ro, 2008, p. 90). Accordingly, emotional responses indicate signs about customers' perceived quality, satisfaction and behavioural intentions in the future (Mattila and Enz, 2002, p. 270; McColl-Kennedy and Sparks, 2003, p. 252; Mattila and Ro, 2008, p. 90; Gustafsson, 2009, p. 1221).

Smith and Bolton (2002) conducted a study on the most frequently experienced negative emotions in restaurants and hotels. These researchers observed that while the most frequently experienced negative emotions in restaurants were dissatisfaction (34.4%) and disappointment (19.4%), in hotels they were dissatisfaction (30.6%) and anger (5.5%). The authors indicate that more negative emotions emerged in restaurants (59%) than in hotels (40%). Grace (2007) investigated customers' negative emotions and psychological responses remaining from previous service failures. According to 166 consumer stories, the most recalled negative emotional responses were anger (35%) and humiliation (15%). Similarly, Choraria (2013) carried out a study of 968 customers' stories of failure that had occurred in the last 12 months. Reactions of anger, nervousness, unhappiness, disappointment and depression were expressed as the most common negative emotional responses.

10.4.2 Emotional contagion

People probably exhibit various behaviours because they are impressed by other people's emotional reactions. Although people's emotions are individual, emotions are shaped mostly through interpersonal or group-focused interaction (Bagozzi *et al.*, 1999, p. 202), particularly in the service experience. In other words, others' emotional behaviours could be spread quickly from person to person (Wild *et al.*, 2001, p. 110). The concept of emotional contagion is based on the Latin word 'contagio', which means 'through touching'. It was introduced in the field of psychology (Vijayalakshmi and Bhattacharyya, 2012, p. 364), but it is a common concept discussed in a wide range of disciplines such as philosophy, economy, social psychology, cultural psychology, history, biology, anthropology, primatology and neurology (Hatfield *et al.*, 1993, p. 96; von Scheve and Ismer, 2013, p. 407; Hatfield *et al.*, 2014, p. 159). Emotional contagion can be expressed as 'influencing a person or a group consciously or unconsciously by a person or group's emotions and behaviours' (Schoenewolf, 1990, p. 50) or 'the processes whereby the moods and emotions of one individual are transferred to nearby individuals' (Spoor and Kelly, 2004, p. 402). Through emotional contagion, people feel themselves to be in the same emotional landscape (Hatfield *et al.*, 1993, p. 96).

Emotional contagion can be described as 'a person or people's tendency to automatically (consciously or unconsciously) and synchronically imitate facial expressions, voice tone, movements, behaviours exhibited by a person or people and to show similar reactions and the case of emotional conveyance' (Hatfield *et al.*, 1993, p. 96; Hatfield *et al.*, 1994, p. 5; Barsade, 2002, p. 647). Mimicking involves imitating and emulating others' non-verbal methods of communication or exhibiting similar behaviours, and it plays an important role in conveying emotions (Hess and Blairy, 2001, p. 129). One of the most important elements that distinguishes contagion of cognitive attitudes from contagion of emotions is non-verbal communication (Barsade, 2002, p. 645). Even though verbal communication is effective in constituting and conveying emotions, non-verbal communication has a key function in conveying emotions (Barsade, 2002, p. 645). Facial expressions of people involved in interactions are quite effective in triggering others' facial muscles and unintentional reactions (mimicking). This also triggers individuals' tendency to establish social communication and show empathy (McHugo et al., 1991, p. 20).

Emotional contagion is regarded as a multi-stage phenomenon because one person's emotional expressions are reciprocated by the other person (Vijayalakshmi and Bhattacharyya, 2012, p. 364). 'It fosters behavioural synchrony and the moment-to-moment tracking of other people's feelings even when individuals are not explicitly attending to this information' (Hatfield et al., 1993, p. 96). Level of emotional contagion may vary from person to person (Doherty, 1997, pp. 133–134), but it could be said that each person is more or less inclined to convey or transmit his/her emotions (Anderson et al., 2003, p. 1055). While some individuals are exposed to emotional contagion more easily, others can show a stricter attitude. Genetic codes, gender, whether the individual has experienced similar experiences and personal characteristics are the primary factors affecting tendency for emotional contagion (Doherty, 1997, pp. 133–134). Factors affecting people's levels of emotional contagion are in abundance. Individuals (i) who take close interest in other people and love to read others' emotional expressions, (ii) who regard their self-construal dependent on a group, (iii) who tend to imitate others' facial, vocal and behavioural expressions and (iv) whose conscious emotional experiences are easily affected by feedback they receive are more inclined to emotional contagion (Doherty, 1997, pp. 133–134). In addition to these factors, (v) cultural differences or similarities among the individuals, (vi) intentions to show emotions as a way of stimulating others, (vii) degree of familiarity with those present, (viii) the presence of a dominant person in sending or receiving messages and (ix) the expected aim of interpersonal emotional interaction are the other key factors determining individuals' inclination for emotional contagion (Hatfield et al., 2014, pp. 165–166).

Emotional contagion is an important variable in the fields of management and organizational behaviour (Barsade, 2002, p. 647; Becker et al., 2011, p. 1587, Vijayalakshmi and Bhattacharyya, 2012, p. 364; Elfenbein, 2014, p. 327). Organizational success depends on teamwork and not superior talents, and so emotional contagion becomes a vital agent for organizations (Vijayalakshmi and Bhattacharyya, 2012, p. 364). Colleagues infect each other with positive and negative emotions, which directly influences the quality of their collaborative work (Elfenbein, 2014, p. 327). Emotional contagion contributes to regulating interpersonal thoughts, movements, consistencies, purposes and interactions (Hatfield et al., 1994, p. 5). Emotional contagion not only positively affects the long-term durability and happiness of interpersonal relationships (Anderson et al., 2003, p. 1055), but also helps employees in a business become informed and manage their emotional awareness (Vijayalakshmi and Bhattacharyya, 2012, p. 364). If positive emotional contagion occurred in a group, there would be a movement towards positivity and a concurrent decrease in negativity, which would be related to a decrease in internal group conflict (McHugo et al., 1991, p. 22; Barsade, 2002, pp. 650–651; Becker et al., 2011, pp. 1588–1589).

A.C. Cakici and O. Guler

Barsade (2002) carried out a study on the effect of emotional contagion on individual and group behaviours and found that positive emotional contagion among employees develops relationships, decreases conflicts and enhances the perceived sense of mission.

According to emotional contagion theory, an individual's emotion infects group members in three stages. Group emotional interaction launches with the individuals being affected by facial expressions, vocal tones, movements and/or behaviours of others with whom they interact and unconsciously showing similar behaviours. In the second stage, they get feedback by receiving similar emotional reactions from the people around them. Getting feedback provides the interpersonal, synchronized and harmonious emotional experiences that are part of conscious contagion. In the third and final stage, the process results in individuals capturing each other's emotions and infecting each other. As a result of this multi-level phenomenon of interrelated stages, the emotional transformation process is completed (Hatfield *et al.*, 1993, pp. 96–99; Wild *et al.*, 2001, p. 110; Barsade, 2002, pp. 647–648).

To summarize, emotional contagion theory explains a process in which people are collectively influenced by psycho-physical, cognitive, behavioural and social decision-making processes. People act in harmony with others and finally are changed emotionally by showing emotional reactions compatible with and complementing others' reactions (Doherty, 1997, p. 134; Hatfield *et al.*, 2014, p. 159). Variables such as number of members in the group, level of familiarity among the members, group loyalty and self-construal are important variables affecting the intensity and manner of individuals' emotional contagion (Wei *et al.*, 2012, p. 764; Boshoff, 2012, p. 403; Huang *et al.*, 2014, p. 182).

Group members' emotional responses are shaped by means of a common emotional atmosphere in the group (negative or positive) and its prevalence and energy (Barsade, 2002, pp. 650–651) (see Fig. 10.3). Individuals who pay attention to others' emotions compare group members' emotions with their own. As a result of this comparison, contagion that turns an individual's mood positive is called positive emotional contagion, and contagion that turns their mood negative is called negative contagion (Barsade, 2002, pp. 650–651).

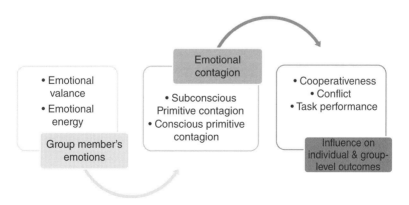

Fig. 10.3. Group emotional contagion model. (From Barsade, 2002.)

10.4.3 Role of emotional contagion in group service failure

Customers' emotional reactions are shaped by not only their own perception but also perceptions of people around them during the service experience, and this 'infection' could shape their entire service experience (McColl-Kennedy and Sparks, 2003, p. 252; Chebat and Slusarczyk, 2005, p. 665). Customers' behaviours are quite open to being affected by others' emotions in the service sector environment, where interpersonal social interaction and co-consumption intention are high (Wei *et al.*, 2012, pp. 765–766).

Emotional contagion is an important variable that can be related to numerous variables for service marketing. Academic studies have discussed emotional contagion in the context of interaction between (i) employees and customers (Pugh, 2001; Barger and

Grandey, 2006; Thurau *et al.*, 2006; Du *et al.*, 2011; Groth and Grandey, 2012; Wieseke *et al.*, 2012) and (ii) group members (Du *et al.*, 2014; Huang *et al.*, 2014; López-López *et al.*, 2014; Maher and Sobh, 2014). General opinion indicates that negative or positive emotional contagion is an important variable affecting customers' emotional reactions, perceived service quality, complaint behaviour, service satisfaction and purchase intentions.

10.4.4 Employee to customer emotional contagion

Absence of key elements during service interactions could lead to negative emotions, contagion of emotions and consequently dissatisfaction (Wieseke *et al.*, 2012, p. 316). Service interactions provide suitable conditions for positive or negative emotional responses between employees and customers (Grace, 2007, p. 271). During service failure, the way customers express their dissatisfaction and anger may cause similar undesired reactions among the service staff (Dallimore *et al.*, 2007, p. 80). However, positive consumer responses even in service failure may ensure more positive employee reactions. Criteria such as common kindness, politeness and understanding could produce satisfying service outputs in businesses such as restaurants, hotels, consulting services or rental services where individualized service is important (Wieseke *et al.*, 2012, p. 316).

Discussion point 2. Is everything all right?

An increasingly popular practice in recent years, in addition to the waiter or waitress responsible for each table, the head waiter, manager, chef, cook or owner visits tables and asks customers if they have any complaints or extra requests. Do you think this practice could be a way to prevent negative emotional reactions that could spread to other customers?

Customers' and employees' 'feeling of empathy' is a crucial element in service interaction and emotional contagion. Levenson (1996, p. 187) stated that the breaking point, or the red line of individuals' emotional contagion, is the feeling of empathy with others. Individuals' inclination towards empathizing enables them to understand what others feel and give empathetic responses to their emotions. Wieseke *et al.* (2012) studied the effect of customer and employee empathy on customers' satisfaction and loyalty among travel agency employees and customers. The results showed that employees' emotional contagion tendencies were higher than those of customers. Moreover, it was revealed that the interaction of employee empathy and customer empathy showed a positive and significant moderation effect on customer satisfaction.

Service interaction is a process of exchange of aspects, including mutual expectations between employees and customers and comparisons of available outputs (Susskind, 2004, p. 21). Service interaction problems usually refer to problems stemming from: (i) employee response to service delivery system failures; (ii) employee response to customer needs and requests; (iii) unprompted and unsolicited employee actions; and (iv) problematic customer behaviours (Bitner *et al.*, 1990, 1994). Firm managers and customers consider that the firm's basic responsibility following failures requires only the employee's contact with customers. Of course, the employee is of vital importance because he/she represents the business's image at the first stage (Maxham and Netemeyer, 2003, p. 46). However, it must be emphasized that service interaction is not a simple process that can be attributed to only a single employee (Groth and Grandey, 2012, p. 209). Problems may not always stem from the employee. The customers defined as dysfunctional or illegitimate in the literature may cause problems for the business, employees or even other customers. Dysfunctional customer behaviour refers to interpersonal customer behaviours perceived as illegitimate by employees in that the service business and employees are not responsible for the behaviours and failures (Gong *et al.*, 2014, p. 102).

It is notable that the employee puts himself in the customer's position by feeling empathy (Dallimore *et al.*, 2007, p. 78); however, employees need manager intervention as well (Gong *et al.*, 2014, p. 102). Gong *et al.* (2014) carried out research on 133 call centre employees working in the telecommunication industry in South Korea and reported remarkable findings; managers' use of intervening mechanisms such as social support, empowerment and reward affect employees' justice perceptions positively and significantly. Most particularly, employees' reward perception creates the most positive effect on their justice perception; however, managers' attitude of participation in decision-making does not have a significant effect on employees' justice perception. It seems that employees think they can deal with problematic customers without managers' direct intervention. Additionally, the researchers reported that employees' satisfaction of managerial intervention has a positive and significant effect on the employees' satisfaction and loyalty. Barger and Grandey (2006) investigated the effect of emotional contagion between customers and employees on customers' service quality perceptions and satisfaction. The data gathered from 173 restaurant and cafeteria customers revealed that employees' sincere smiles affect customers' smiles and their service quality and satisfaction positively and significantly.

Söderlund and Rosengren (2010) carried out a study aiming to determine the effect of happy and good-humoured service on customer satisfaction among airline customers. As expected, the happier and more good-humoured service was perceived to be, the higher the customer satisfaction. Du *et al.* (2011) investigated the multiple and consecutive emotional contagion between employees and customers during service failure. The researchers manipulated employee and customer interaction through service failure scenarios as if customers were in a casual à la carte restaurant. Their results reveal that the waiter's low and high tendency of negative emotional contagion has a significant effect on customers' negative emotional responses. Similarly, it was reported that the restaurant manager's intervention and the manager's low and high tendency of emotional contagion make a significant difference to customers' positive emotional responses.

10.4.5 Customer-to-customer emotional contagion

Thoughts and behaviours are shaped in the emotional contagion process in accordance with a social appraisal sequence; namely, by considering a second or third person's emotions (Parkinson and Simons, 2009, p. 1072). Individuals' conscious emotional evaluations about others' emotional responses involve those with similar emotions. In the 'emotional comparison process' (Barsade, 2002, p. 647), people compare their emotions with others' emotions and start using their emotions as a social communication tool (Thurau *et al.*, 2006, p. 59). Another person's sadness may cause an individual to recall similar previous experience(s), and these emotions may be spread among individuals (Hsee *et al.*, 1990, p. 328).

When individuals consume in a group, they are quite inclined to share their thoughts, personal values and experiences with the group members (Vijayalakshmi and

Bhattacharyya, 2012, p. 364). Accordingly, individuals in the group are exposed consciously or unconsciously to others' emotional responses and experience a similar alteration in their own emotional responses (Pugh, 2001, p. 1020; Du *et al.*, 2014, p. 328). At this point, group familiarity and group size are the crucial agents that influence the perception of emotional contagion among group members.

Du *et al.* (2014) researched the relationship between emotional contagion and complaint intention resulting from service failure experienced in the group. It was revealed that customers are positively and significantly affected by their friends' anger, and accordingly, the anger of individuals in the group is significantly higher than that of customers on their own. Similarly, Huang *et al.* (2014) investigated the effect of co-consumption on complaint intention during restaurant service failure. When individuals are with their friends, their tendency to complain is significantly higher than when they are alone. It was also reported that their intention to revisit the business is significantly higher when they are with their friends.

López-López *et al.* (2014) searched for the relationship between negative emotional responses and service satisfaction in the context of sharing emotions with a stranger or a friend. Data were gathered through scenarios consisting of various service failures stemming from hotel and destination choice. The researchers reported that individuals' sharing the emotion of 'anger' with strangers creates higher satisfaction than their sharing the same emotion with their friends. On the contrary, they found that individuals' sharing the emotion of 'regret' with their friends creates higher satisfaction than their sharing the same emotion with strangers.

Discussion point 3. Group service failure and emotional contagion

Tonight, you and your six close friends go to a casual à la carte restaurant to refresh yourselves after a tiring week. After 15 minutes of sitting at the table, your friend Datome notices that no one has taken your order yet. He shouts for the waiter but can barely make himself heard, even with a second call. The orders are two steaks, one well done and the other rare; two pizzas, one thick crust; one pasta dish; and a hamburger for yourself. After the waiter finally writes down your orders, you politely ask him to serve all the orders at the same time. While the waiter is busy checking the orders, he nods his head without looking at you, which you think means he has confirmed your request.

After 30 minutes have passed, you remind the waiter about your order because no one has informed you what is going on. The waiter tells you that the food will be done in two minutes, but he gets back to your table 10 minutes later only with the steaks and hamburger. One of your friends asks about their food, and the waiter tells him that the remaining three orders will be ready in two minutes. Your friends tell you, 'Please start eating. Do not let them get cold.' The waiter brings the other meals 10 minutes later. Vessely's steak looks well-done instead of rare, and Udoh's pizza does not look as thick as he wanted. You turn to the waiter nervously and say, 'We wanted to start eating together, but you could not organize that. Now, some of us have nothing to eat!'

Discussion: What would you guess are the group's emotions in this situation? Do you think the important thing is being together, or are the things that you are experiencing ruining the entire evening? What should the restaurant do to recover from this service failure? Please discuss which recovery strategies could turn your group's anger and disappointment into happiness and satisfaction.

10.5 Conclusions

Today, physiological satisfaction may be the lowest level of expectation from goods or services. Businesses aiming to be unique and distinctive need to offer value for customers' psychological/emotional satisfaction in addition to their physiological needs (Koc, 2016, p. 43). Could a meal's flavour solely explain the reason why customers pay 20 times more than regular market price? (Koc, 2016, p. 38). Probably not! Then, is it possible to say that a customer is satisfied simply by the guarantee of service quality and cost efficiency? Imagine a famous hotel that is known to be top quality and whose prices are remarkably high: A customer who booked a summer vacation at this hotel would probably expect everything to go perfectly. Nevertheless, tourism companies should not forget that the service industry is an industry where failures occur frequently, despite it being crucial for a service business to avoid such failures.

No matter how hard companies try, even in the best businesses they cannot prevent occasional service failures stemming from products, employees (e.g. rude and ignorant behaviours, slow service and reservation mistakes) and customers (Hart *et al.*, 1990, p. 148; Palmer *et al.*, 2000, p. 517; Kotler *et al.*, 2010, p. 42; Yang and Mattila, 2012, p. 399). Kotler *et al.* state that companies' basic purpose should be to 'reset the number of consumers leaving from the companies with negative emotions' (2010, p. 41). There is nothing better for a business than satisfying its customers without any service failure; however, there is nothing worse for a business than not identifying the reasons for dissatisfied customers (Halstead *et al.*, 1996, p. 107).

In many cases, the consumer (tourist) makes a huge effort to experience his/her aim, which can lead to impaired psychological health, lack of energy, memory lapses and depressed moods (Koc and Boz, 2014, p. 143). This situation may decrease their tolerance towards service failures, and it may cause them to be affected by others' emotional reactions. Imagine that you are a tourist having travelled long hours. When you arrive at the hotel, you learn that the room expected to be available is not ready yet. Won't you speak more loudly with the support you get from accompanying people? If you pay attention to groups, you can notice that once someone makes an utterance, others in the group do too. When one person dares to complain, others speak up immediately. The most distinct examples for this case are flight delays.

Unlike individual service failures, service failure likely to be experienced within the group refers to customers' cognitive reactions and multiple emotional reactions that are difficult for the businesses to cope with. From this point of view, hospitality and tourism companies should consider emotional contagion as an important variable throughout the entire service interaction. Studies reveal that emotional contagion differs according to factors such as service failure type, place and activity, group size and group familiarity. Thus, recovery expectations may have to be differentiated as well. McDougall and Levesque (1998) showed in a study on restaurant service failure that customers pay attention to distributive compensation regardless of whether the related service failure is a special activity or an ordinary meeting, but offering solely distributive recovery to customers in a special activity will not benefit customer satisfaction, recommendation and revisit intention.

Ha and Jang (2009) carried out a study on the food cooking problem of a customer who goes out for meal with a group of friends. They found that perception of distributive justice in recovery is the variable that has the highest effect on people's revisit intention and intention to express positive experiences, followed by the perception of interactional recovery justice and finally procedural recovery justice. Fu *et al.* (2015) investigated the efficiency of monetary and non-monetary service recovery practices. They showed that while monetary recovery justice creates the highest effect on recovery satisfaction, perception of non-monetary and interactive recovery justice has a lower but significant effect on customers' recovery satisfaction. Differing from these findings, Barakat *et al.* (2015), who worked in the context of airline service failure, revealed that the only significant recovery perception that decreases the effect of service failure on recovery satisfaction was the perception of interactional service recovery.

The efficiency of recovery strategies may change in accordance with service failure type, type of tourism and hospitality firm and customer segment. What is important is that the businesses should be aware of which recovery type could yield the desired results according to the customer segment. Tourism companies should take lessons from previous service failures and recovery processes. The recovery expectations of groups having a problem should be considered by businesses in accordance with groups' socio-economic and cultural class and characteristics.

Relating to emotional disorders, managers of hospitality businesses are recommended to design their service offerings and servicescapes in such a way as to create positive emotions and moods for their customers. Additionally, mood-enhancing foods and beverages, the physical design of the facilities of the hospitality establishments and calming music could create positive emotions and overcome negative emotions (Koc and Boz, 2014, p. 145). Facilities in the hospitality industry such as restaurants could re-construct their menus with a view to adding serotonin-rich foods and beverages to provide happiness (Koc and Boz, 2014, p. 142) rather than negative emotions that could infect other customers.

Customers' emotional responses and methods to cope with negative emotions should be known not only to operation managers but also by marketing and human resources managers (McColl-Kennedy and Sparks, 2003, pp. 251–252). Marketing departments should get preliminary information about the characteristics of the group to be served and if possible determine who is the group leader or opinion leader. If it is not possible to get this information, the manager should assign employees with experience and emotional intelligence to observe who in the group is influential in taking joint decisions throughout service provision. Sometimes this person could be a three-year-old child, a grandfather or the host. You may often have heard a mother or father say, 'bring the child's meal first, we can wait for ours'. In fact, the parent gives the message that 'my baby is hungry; if baby is hungry, he/she becomes grumpy and if he/she is grumpy, I become unhappy as well. Please prevent my child's unhappiness'.

CASE STUDY 3. SMALL DETAILS, GREAT HAPPINESS...

Did you know that Italians tend to prefer to prepare their salads themselves? This may seem to be a small detail, but it is a culturally significant one. A cucumber, tomato, green pepper and plenty of olive oil and vinegar could make them much happier than a ready-to-eat salad prepared by the cook. In a similar vein, some Australians do not consider themselves to have had breakfast without the food spread Vegemite. Maybe little surprises such as these could cause customers to ignore or forgive some failures encountered during their holiday experiences.

Success cannot be reached in tourism and hospitality businesses just by meeting customers' needs because of the industry's human-oriented structure. Employees' needs should not be neglected. Human resources departments could help prevent group service failures by applying tests measuring potential employees' emotional intelligence during recruitment. Furthermore, training opportunities should be developed for employees regarding emotional intelligence techniques, complaint management and communication techniques, empathy, etc.

Of course, tourism and hospitality companies could recover current group service failures in the most pleasing ways. However, it is more important that employees understand customers' moods and emotions, by their gestures, tone and body language, and intervene before negative emotions are spread to group members. For this reason, tourism companies should give authority, responsibility and initiative to the employees who have direct contact with customers to meet and care about the customers' expectations. Managers should strengthen, train and support their employees (Hart *et al.*, 1990, p. 154; Shamdasani and Balakrishnan, 2000, p. 401; Maxham and Netemeyer, 2003, p. 46). An effective method should include training in behaviours that can meet customers' satisfaction, and motivating and rewarding employees appropriately for the complexity of their work and expertise (Bitner *et al.*, 1990, p. 71; Kandampully, 1998, p. 433).

As we said at the start of this chapter, tourism and hospitality companies are unique because of their service and human-oriented structure. To summarize, when customers enter a tourism and hospitality business, they feel themselves to be the most important and unique person in the world. Hence, emotions are everything, and similar to a double-edged sword, they can help or harm tourism and hospitality companies. This depends heavily on customer retention, given that it costs five to ten times as much to recruit new customers than it does to keep current customers happy (Hart *et al.*, 1990, p. 153; Blodgett *et al.*, 1995, p. 31; Han and Back, 2008, p. 467).

Questions

1. Why is group consumption important in tourism and hospitality?
2. What is the role of emotions in tourism and hospitality service consumption?
3. What is emotional contagion?
4. How does emotional contagion occur during service failures in tourism and hospitality?
5. How does emotional contagion influence service recovery processes?

Further Reading

Bolton, L.E. and Mattila, A.S. (2015) How does corporate social responsibility affect consumer response to service failure in buyer–seller relationships? *Journal of Retailing* 91, 140–153.

Brennan, J. and Morgan, F. (2013) In jet blue: high-flying airline melts down in ice storm. In: Zeithaml, V.A., Bitner, J. and Gremler, D. (eds) *Service Marketing: Integrating Customer Focus across the Firm*, 6th edn. McGraw-Hill, New York, pp. 591–606.

Doherty, R.W. (1997) The emotional contagion scale: a measure of individual differences. *Journal of Nonverbal Behavior* 21, 131–154.

A.C. Cakici and O. Guler

Janis, I.L. (1982) *Groupthink: Psychological Studies of Policy Decisions and Fiascoes*, Vol. 349. Houghton Mifflin, Boston, Massachusetts.

Ok, C., Back, K.J. and Shanklin, C.W. (2006) Service recovery paradox: implications from an experimental study in a restaurant setting. *Journal of Hospitality & Leisure Marketing* 14, 17–33.

References

Anderson, C., Keltner, D. and John, O.P. (2003) Emotional convergence between people over time. *Journal of Personality and Social Psychology* 84, 1054–1068.

Association of British Travel Agents (ABTA) *The Consumer Holiday Trends Report*. Consumer Survey 2014. Available at: https://abta.com/resource-zone/publication/the-consumer-holiday-trends-report-2014 (accessed 1 October 2016).

Bagozzi, R.P. and Dholakia, U.M. (2006) Antecedents and purchase consequences of customer participation in small group brand communities. *International Journal of Research in Marketing* 23, 45–61.

Bagozzi, R.P., Gopinath, M. and Nyer, P.U. (1999) The role of emotions in marketing. *Journal of the Academy of Marketing Science* 27, 184–206.

Barakat, L.L., Ramsey, J.R., Lorenz, M.P. and Gosling, M. (2015) Severe service failure recovery revisited: evidence of its determinants in an emerging market context. *International Journal of Research in Marketing* 32, 113–116.

Barger, P.B. and Grandey, A.A. (2006) Service with a smile and encounter satisfaction: emotional contagion and appraisal mechanisms. *Academy of Management Journal* 49, 1229–1238.

Barsade, S.G. (2002) The ripple effect: emotional contagion and its influence on group behavior. *Administrative Science Quarterly* 47, 644–675.

Bearden, O.W. and Teel, J.E. (1983) Selected determinants of consumer satisfaction and complaint reports. *Journal of Marketing Research* 20, 21–28.

Becker, J.C., Tausch, N. and Wagner, U. (2011) Emotional consequences of collective action participation differentiating self-directed and outgroup-directed emotions. *Personality and Social Psychology Bulletin* 37, 1587–1598.

Bitner, M.J., Booms, B.H. and Tetreault, M.S. (1990) The service encounter: diagnosing favorable and unfavorable incidents. *The Journal of Marketing* 54, 71–84.

Bitner, M.J., Booms, B.H. and Mohr, L.A. (1994) Critical service encounters: the employee's viewpoint. *The Journal of Marketing* 58, 95–106.

Blodgett, J.G., Wakefield, K.L. and Barnes, J.H. (1995) The effects of customer service on consumer complaining behavior. *Journal of Services Marketing* 9, 31–42.

Boshoff, C. (2012) A neurophysiological assessment of consumers' emotional responses to service recovery behaviors: the impact of ethnic group and gender similarity. *Journal of Service Research* 15, 401–413.

Chang, J.C. (2008) Tourists' satisfaction judgments: an investigation of emotion, equity, and attribution. *Journal of Hospitality & Tourism Research* 32, 108–134.

Chebat, J.C. and Slusarczyk, W. (2005) How emotions mediate the effect of perceived justice on loyalty in service recovery situations: an empirical study. *Journal of Business Research* 58, 664–73.

Choraria, S. (2013) Exploring the role of negative emotions on customer's intention to complain. *The Journal of Business Perspective* 17, 201–211.

Dallimore, K.S., Sparks, B.A. and Butcher, K. (2007) The influence of angry customer outbursts on service providers' facial displays and affective states. *Journal of Service Research* 10, 78–92.

Doherty, R.W. (1997) The emotional contagion scale: a measure of individual differences. *Journal of Nonverbal Behavior* 21, 131–154.

Du, J., Fan, X. and Feng, T. (2011) Multiple emotional contagions in service encounters. *Journal of the Academy of Marketing Science* 39, 449–466.

Du, J., Fan, X. and Feng, T. (2014) Group emotional contagion and complaint intentions in group service failure: the role of group size and group familiarity. *Journal of Service Research* 17, 326–338.

Elfenbein, H.A. (2014) The many faces of emotional contagion: an affective process theory of affective linkage. *Organizational Psychology Review* 4, 326–362.

Fu, H., Wu, D.C., Huang, S.S., Song, H. and Gong, J. (2015) Monetary or nonmonetary compensation for service failure? A study of customer preferences under various loci of causality. *International Journal of Hospitality Management* 46, 55–64.

Gong, T., Yi, Y. and Choi, J.N. (2014) Helping employees deal with dysfunctional customers: the underlying employee perceived justice mechanism. *Journal of Service Research* 17, 102–116.

Grace, D. (2007) How embarrassing! An exploratory study of critical incidents including affective reactions. *Journal of Service Research* 9, 271–284.

Gronroos, C. (1988) Service quality: the six criteria of good perceived service. *Review of Business* 9, 10–13.

Groth, M. and Grandey, A. (2012) From bad to worse: negative exchange spirals in employee–customer service interactions. *Organizational Psychology Review* 2, 208–233.

Gustafsson, A. (2009) Customer satisfaction with service recovery. *Journal of Business Research* 62, 1220–1222.

Ha, J. and Jang, S.S. (2009) Perceived justice in service recovery and behavioral intentions: the role of relationship quality. *International Journal of Hospitality Management* 28, 319–327.

Halstead, D., Morash, E.A. and Ozment, J. (1996) Comparing objective service failures and subjective complaints: an investigation of domino and halo effects. *Journal of Business Research* 36, 107–115.

Han, H. and Back, K.J. (2008) Relationships among image congruence, consumption emotions, and customer loyalty in the lodging industry. *Journal of Hospitality & Tourism Research* 32, 467–490.

Hart, C.W., Heskett, J.L. and Sasser, W.E. Jr (1990) The profitable art of service recovery. *Harvard Business Review* 68, 148–156.

Hatfield, E., Cacicoppo, T.J. and Rapson, R.L. (1993) Emotional contagion. *Current Directions in Psychological Sciences* 2, 93–99.

Hatfield, E., Cacicoppo, T.J. and Rapson, R.L. (1994) *Emotional Contagion*. Cambridge University Press, New York.

Hatfield, E., Bensman, L., Thornton, P.D. and Rapson, R.L. (2014) New perspectives on emotional contagion: a review of classic and recent research on facial mimicry and contagion. *Interpersona* 8, 159–179.

Hess, U. and Blairy, S. (2001) Facial mimicry and emotional contagion to dynamic emotional facial expressions and their influence on decoding accuracy. *International Journal of Psychophysiology* 40, 129–141.

Hsee, C.K., Hatfield, E., Carlson, J.G. and Chemtob, C. (1990) The effect of power on susceptibility to emotional contagion. *Cognition and Emotion* 4, 327–340.

Huang, M.C.J., Wu, H.C., Chuang, S.C. and Lin, W.H. (2014) Who gets to decide your complaint intentions? The influence of other companions on reaction to service failures. *International Journal of Hospitality Management* 37, 180–189.

Izard, C.E. (1992) Basic emotions, relations among emotions, and emotion–cognition relations. *Psychological Review* 99, 561–565.

Kandampully, J. (1998) Service quality to service loyalty: a relationship which goes beyond customer services. *Total Quality Management* 9, 431–443.

A.C. Cakici and O. Guler

Kim, M.J., Lee, C.K., Chung, N. and Kim, W.G. (2014) Factors affecting online tourism group buying and the moderating role of loyalty. *Journal of Travel Research* 53, 380–394.

Koc, E. (2016) *Tüketici Davranışı ve Pazarlama Stratejileri: Global ve Yerel Yaklaşım*. Seçkin Yayıncılık, Ankara.

Koc, E. and Boz, H. (2014) Psychoneurobiochemistry of tourism marketing. *Tourism Management* 44, 140–148.

Koc, E., Ulukoy, M., Kilic, R., Yumusak, S. and Bahar, R. (2017) The influence of customer participation on service failure perceptions. *Total Quality Management & Business Excellence* 28, 390–404.

Koriat, A., Adiv, S. and Schwarz, N. (2016) Views that are shared with others are expressed with greater confidence and greater fluency independent of any social influence. *Personality and Social Psychology Review* 20, 176–193.

Kotler, P. and Keller, K.L. (2012) *Marketing Management Global Edition*, 14th edn. Pearson Education, New York.

Kotler, P., Bowen, J.T. and Makens, J.C. (2010) *Marketing for Hospitality and Tourism*, 5th edn. Pearson Education, Harlow, UK.

Levenson, R.W. (1996) Biological substrates of empathy and facial modulation of emotion: two facets of the scientific legacy of John Lanzetta. *Motivation and Emotion* 20, 185–204.

López-López, I., Ruiz-de-Maya, S. and Warlop, L. (2014) When sharing consumption emotions with strangers is more satisfying than sharing them with friends. *Journal of Service Research* 17, 475–488.

Maher, A. and Sobh, R. (2014) The role of collective angst during and after a service failure. *Journal of Services Marketing* 28, 223–232.

Mason, C.M. and Griffin, M.A. (2005) Group task satisfaction. Applying the construct of job satisfaction to groups. *Small Group Research* 33, 271–312.

Mattila, A.S. and Enz, C.A. (2002) The role of emotions in service encounters. *Journal of Service Research* 4, 268–277.

Mattila, A.S. and Ro, H. (2008) Discrete negative emotions and customer dissatisfaction responses in a casual restaurant setting. *Journal of Hospitality & Tourism Research* 32, 89–107.

Maxham, J.G. III (2001) Service recovery's influence on consumer satisfaction, positive word-of-mouth, and purchase intentions. *Journal of Business Research* 54, 11–24.

Maxham, J.G. III and Netemeyer, R.G. (2003) Firms reap what they sow: the effects of shared values and perceived organizational justice on customers' evaluations of complaint handling. *Journal of Marketing* 67, 46–62.

McColl-Kennedy, J.R. and Sparks, B.A. (2003) Application of fairness theory to service failures and service recovery. *Journal of Service Research* 5, 251–266.

McColl-Kennedy, J.R., Daus, C.S. and Sparks, B.A. (2003) The role of gender in reactions to service failure and recovery. *Journal of Service Research* 6, 66–82.

McDougall, G. and Levesque, T. (1998) The effectiveness of recovery strategies after service failure: an experiment in the hospitality industry. *Journal of Hospitality & Leisure Marketing* 5, 27–49.

McHugo, G.J., Lanzetta, J.T. and Bush, L.K. (1991) The effect of attitudes on emotional reactions to expressive displays of political leaders. *Journal of Nonverbal Behavior* 15, 19–41.

McQuilken, L. and Robertson, N. (2011) The influence of guarantees, active requests to voice and failure severity on customer complaint behavior. *International Journal of Hospitality Management* 30, 953–962.

McQuilken, L. and Robertson, N. (2013) Who chose this restaurant anyway? The effect of responsibility for choice, guarantees, and failure stability on customer complaining. *Journal of Hospitality & Tourism Research* 37, 537–562.

Miller, J.L., Craighead, C.W. and Karwan, K.R. (2000) Service recovery: a framework and empirical investigation. *Journal of Operations Management* 18, 387–400.

Mucuk, İ. (1999) *Pazarlama İlkeleri*. 11 Baskı. Türkmen Kitapevi, Istanbul.

Namkung, Y. and Jang, S.S. (2009) The effects of interactional fairness on satisfaction and behavioral intentions: mature versus non-mature customers. *International Journal of Hospitality Management* 28, 397–405.

Odabaşı, Y. and Barış, G. (2015) *Tüketici Davranışı*. MediaCat Akademi, Istanbul.

Palmer, A., Beggs, R. and Keown-McMullan, C. (2000) Equity and repurchase intention following service failure. *Journal of Services Marketing* 14, 513–528.

Parasuraman, A., Zeithaml, V.A. and Berry, L.L. (1985) A conceptual model of service quality and its implications for future research. *The Journal of Marketing* 49, 41–50.

Parkinson, B. and Simons, G. (2009) Affecting others: social appraisal and emotion contagion in everyday decision making. *Personality and Social Psychology Bulletin* 35, 1071–1084.

Patterson, P.G., Cowley, E. and Prasongsukarn, K. (2006) Service failure recovery: the moderating impact of individual-level cultural value orientation on perceptions of justice. *International Journal of Research in Marketing* 23, 263–277.

Pugh, S.D. (2001) Service with a smile: emotional contagion in the service encounter. *Academy of Management Journal* 44, 1018–1027.

Rezdy.com (n.a.) A compilation of statistics for the Tours & Activities Sector. Available at: https://www.rezdy.com/resource/travel-statistics-for-tour-operators (accessed 1 October 2016).

Richins, M.L. (1982) An investigation of consumers' attitudes toward complaining. *Advances in Consumer Research* 9, 502–506.

Richins, M.L. (1997) Measuring emotions in the consumption experience. *Journal of Consumer Research* 24, 127–146.

Schanzel, H.A., Yeoman, I. and Backer, E. (eds) (2012) *Family Tourism: Multidisciplinary Perspectives*. Channel View, Bristol, UK.

Schoenewolf, G. (1990) Emotional contagion: behavioral induction in individuals and groups. *Modern Psychoanalysis* 15, 49–61.

Shamdasani, P.N. and Balakrishnan, A.A. (2000) Determinants of relationship quality and loyalty in personalized services. *Asia Pacific Journal of Management* 17, 399–422.

Shiau, W.L. and Luo, M.M. (2012) Factors affecting online group buying intention and satisfaction: a social exchange theory perspective. *Computers in Human Behavior* 28, 2431–2444.

Sigala, M. (2013) A framework for designing and implementing effective online coupons in tourism and hospitality. *Journal of Vacation Marketing* 19, 165–180.

Smith, A.K. and Bolton, R.N. (2002) The effect of customers' emotional responses to service failures on their recovery effort evaluations and satisfaction judgments. *Journal of the Academy of Marketing Science* 30, 5–23.

Smith, A.K., Bolton, R.N. and Wagner, J. (1999) A model of customer satisfaction with service encounters involving failure and recovery. *Journal of Marketing Research* 36, 356–372.

Söderlund, M. and Rosengren, S. (2010) The happy versus unhappy service worker in the service encounter: assessing the impact on customer satisfaction. *Journal of Retailing and Consumer Services* 17, 161–169.

Solomon, M.R., Surprenant, C., Czepiel, J.A. and Gutman, E.G. (1985) A role theory perspective on dyadic interactions: the service encounter. *The Journal of Marketing* 49, 99–111.

Spoor, J.R. and Kelly, J.R. (2004) The evolutionary significance of affect in groups: communication and group bonding. *Group Processes & Intergroup Relations* 7, 398–412.

Surprenant, C.F. and Solomon, M.R. (1987) Predictability and personalization in the service encounter. *The Journal of Marketing* 51, 86–96.

Susskind, A.M. (2004) Consumer frustration in the customer-server exchange: the role of attitudes toward complaining and information inadequacy related to service failures. *Journal of Hospitality & Tourism Research* 28, 21–43.

Tanford, S. and Montgomery, R. (2015) The effects of social influence and cognitive dissonance on travel purchase decisions. *Journal of Travel Research* 54, 596–610.

A.C. Cakici and O. Guler

Thurau, H.T., Groth, M., Paul, M. and Gremler, D.D. (2006) Are all smiles created equal? How emotional contagion and emotional labor affect service relationships. *Journal of Marketing* 70, 58–73.

Tsai, M.T., Cheng, N.C. and Chen, K.S. (2011) Understanding online group buying intention: the roles of sense of virtual community and technology acceptance factors. *Total Quality Management & Business Excellence* 22, 1091–1104.

UNWTO (2016) *Tourism Highlights*. UNTWO, Madrid.

U.S. Family Travel Association (2015) *US Family Travel Survey 2015*. Available at: http://www.sps.nyu.edu/content/dam/scps/pdf/2015_FTA_Family_Travel_Survey.pdf (accessed 1 October 2016).

Vijayalakshmi, V. and Bhattacharyya, S. (2012) Emotional contagion and its relevance to individual behavior and organizational processes: a position paper. *Journal of Business and Psychology* 27, 363–374.

von Scheve, C. and Ismer, S. (2013) Towards a theory of collective emotions. *Emotion Review* 5, 406–413.

Wei, W., Miao, L., Cai, L.A. and Adler, H. (2012) The influence of self-construal and co-consumption others on consumer complaining behavior. *International Journal of Hospitality Management* 31, 764–771.

Wen, I. (2009) Factors affecting the online travel buying decision: a review. *International Journal of Contemporary Hospitality Management* 21, 752–765.

Wieseke, J., Geigenmüller, A. and Kraus, F. (2012) On the role of empathy in customer–employee interactions. *Journal of Service Research* 15, 316–331.

Wild, B., Erb, M. and Bartels, M. (2001) Are emotions contagious? Evoked emotions while viewing emotionally expressive faces: quality, quantity, time course and gender differences. *Psychiatry Research* 102, 109–124.

Yang, W. and Mattila, A.S. (2012) The role of tie strength on consumer dissatisfaction responses. *International Journal of Hospitality Management* 31, 399–404.

Yüksel, A. and Yüksel, F. (2003) Measurement of tourist satisfaction with restaurant services: a segment-based approach. *Journal of Vacation Marketing* 9, 52–68.

Zhang, Z., Zhang, Z., Wang, F., Law, R. and Li, D. (2013) Factors influencing the effectiveness of online group buying in the restaurant industry. *International Journal of Hospitality Management* 35, 237–245.

Zhou, Y., Huang, M., Tsang, A.S. and Zhou, N. (2013) Recovery strategy for group service failures: the interaction effects between recovery modes and recovery dimensions. *European Journal of Marketing* 47, 1133–1156.

Zhou, Y., Tsang, A.S., Huang, M. and Zhou, N. (2014) Group service recovery strategies effectiveness: the moderating effects of group size and relational distance. *Journal of Business Research* 67, 2480–2485.

11 Staff Training for Service Failures and Recovery

ISIL ARIKAN SALTIK, UGUR CALISKAN AND UMUT AVCI

Learning Objectives

After reading this chapter, you should be able to:

- Define staff training, service failure and service recovery.
- Explain the importance of staff training in service failure and recovery.
- Offer training recommendations to overcome service failure and manage the service recovery.

11.1 Introduction

As previously explained, tourism and hospitality bear all the general service characteristics of intangibility, heterogeneity, inseparability and perishability (McLaughlin, 1996). As the tourism and hospitality industry is labour intensive, employees may be considered the most important resource of a tourism and hospitality business. Employees can help establish a competitive advantage and strongly influence the success of the business. As staff training improves the knowledge, skills and abilities of personnel (Cannon, 2008), training of employees can make a significant contribution to the sustainability and success of the business (Hayes and Ninemeier, 2009). Hence, staff training can be considered a strategic tool for tourism and hospitality businesses.

When training service employees, special attention should be paid to developing self-confidence in service employees. When service employees have self-confidence, they can make efficient, effective and timely decisions to deliver high-quality services (Ro and Chen, 2011). Service training not only improves frontline employees' ability to cope with various issues, but also develops employees' knowledge, ability and skills that are instrumental in meeting and surpassing customers' overall demands (Bamford and Xystouri, 2005).

11.2 Importance of Trained Staff for Efficient Service Recovery

Service failures occur during service encounters in which employee performance does not meet customer expectations (Hoffman and Bateson, 1997). Hence, service failures pose a major challenge for service businesses (Berry and Parasuraman, 1992). Irritated customers can be transformed into loyal customers by effective service recoveries. Businesses must not rely on incidental service recovery by one individual and should ensure that everyone in the organization has the required skills, motivation and authority to provide service recovery at any stage in the service process (Hart *et al.*, 1990).

Training and development, employee involvement and employee relations are the key human resource practices for organizations committed to providing quality customer service. Training should be both skills-based and attitude-based. Operational and interpersonal skills are needed to encourage the development of 'service orientations', as well as attitude-based training that promotes coaching and includes practices to facilitate leadership (Redman and Matthews, 1998). Employees can gain knowledge, skills and experience only through formal training and education (Forrester, 2000). A formal training process generally contains five phases: analysis, design, development, implementation and evaluation. It also provides the knowledge, skills and attitudes to develop employees' competency (Fig. 11.1).

Employee behaviour has a significant influence on service recovery because of the critical importance of service encounters (Krishna *et al.*, 2011). The literature on the relationship between employee and service recovery examines issues such as the role of employee, adaptability (Boshoff and Leong, 1998), proactiveness requirements (Iacobucci, 1998) and the importance of self-managing teams (Jong and de Ruyter, 2004). Service providers can learn how to respond to a variety of service failures, even if they cannot know every potential failure beforehand (Lin *et al.*, 2011). However, employee empowerment is not enough. Management should also consider training employees to display behaviours that meet minimum standards in line with the mission and vision of the management. Training programmes should mainly focus on:

- General organizational policies, values and strategies (Tax and Brown, 1998).
- Service standards, job descriptions and employee expectations.
- Analysis of potential problems (Lorenzoni and Lewis, 2004).
- Customer analysis.
- Emotional intelligence and listening skills to calm irritated, frustrated and sometimes abusive customers (Tax and Brown, 1998).
- Understanding and explaining difficult situations (Lorenzoni and Lewis, 2004), swiftly finding proper solutions and considering alternatives (Tax and Brown, 1998).

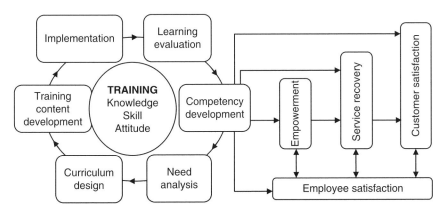

Fig. 11.1. Training process and service recovery. (Adapted from Dick *et al.*, 2001.)

- Respecting all customers, including those with special needs (Lorenzoni and Lewis, 2004).
- Importance of reporting service failures and transferring data to management.
- Importance of involving customers in the service process.
- Importance of encouraging customers to make a complaint first and then join recovery.

In the absence of formal training, employees may lack the competence to meet the customers' or managers' expectations (Dobbs, 1993). As mentioned by Boella and Goss-Turner (2005), an employee needs to have the proper knowledge, skills and attitude to perform well. Knowledge, skills and attitude can all be improved or developed through different training techniques. For example, learning about the check-in process for hotel receptionists can be provided through lectures or direct talks, but any skills requiring improvement, such as using the reservation software, need to be practised by employees. The most efficient strategy is when the supervisor/manager controls the training and allows the employee to practice.

Employee attitudes are the hardest to address. Techniques such as role play and case studies may be more relatable and can teach human behaviour, developing technical and communication skills to increase self-confidence. Training is a necessity not only to have fewer service failures, but also to solve the service failures (Ro and Chen, 2011). In addition, training prevents poor recovery attempts that deepen customers' dissatisfaction.

11.3 Training Practices for Effective Service Recovery

Training practices can minimize failures by developing service recovery processes. Activities can be diversified, from managing the customer's perception of the service failure to equipping employees with the service recovery skills, and developing motivated employees eager to recover. In the following sections, service failure and recovery processes are discussed from different approaches and examples of training practices are given.

11.4 Training Practices to Influence Customer Attribution

Service failure is more about the customer's reaction to service than about what the management believes (Ennew and Schoefer, 2003). As per customer attribution, service failure is classified in three dimensions: controllability, stability and locus (Weiner, 2000). Koc *et al.* (2015) revealed in their empirical study that respecting these dimensions is important for the service recovery process since they may also affect the customer's perception. More precisely, considering a matter from the attribution perspective may cause customers to blame the employees and organization less for service failures in the tourism sector. It is recommended that management take the required measures in such a way that the customer perception related to service failure is in favour of the business (see Fig. 11.2).

The customer's perception of how much the service failure depends on the control or will of the management is called controllability. In other words, the customer perceives whether or not the employees of an organization make an effort in the prevention

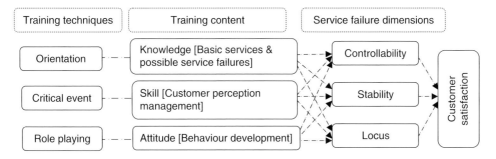

Fig. 11.2. Training practices, customer attribution of service failure. (From the authors.)

or rectification of a service failure (Koc, 2015). As service failure frequency increases, customers' negative evaluation and customer loss increases (Smith *et al.*, 1999). Front-line employees, to whom customers react first about the organization, have to be trained in reacting to positively affect the customer's perception. For example, in the case of not being able to provide the requested room to a customer who is respecting the check-in hours, role-play training for the receptionists as frontline employees will ensure that they display appropriate behaviours while dealing with an angry customer. The training not only prevents a negative reaction from the customer, but creates employee awareness regarding the responsibilities of being on the front line. As a part of their job, frontline employees contend with negative customer reactions and must manage them to promote a good corporate image, even when they are not responsible for the failure.

An important point to acknowledge is when an undesirable result has occurred despite all measures being taken to prevent any failure. For example, a waiter who receives a complaint about a delay in a meal's service should start the recovery process by explaining that, even though all orders at the table should be served at the same time, an unfortunate failure has occurred. The customer will perceive the management makes all efforts to prevent such a failure, but a singular event has occurred and the possibility of recurrence is low, so the negative effects of the service failure can be decreased.

The stability dimension is about whether the failure is temporary or permanent. If it is thought that the reason for the failure is permanent, it will increase the expectation that it will recur in the future (Koc, 2015). Service recovery can be effective after a solitary service failure, but not after even one repetition of a failure to the same customer (Maxham and Netemeyer, 2003). Thus, in order for employees to be able to manage the service recovery process, they should be trained to craft the customer's perception that the failure has occurred momentarily and not due to chronic failure. In the example given for the control dimension, a perception must be created that the service failure is not recurring by politely stating that the service is not typical, rather that such a problem has occurred only on that day due to a transaction/person that is not routinely involved in the process.

Locus is the dimension concentrating on who is responsible for the failure (Koc, 2015). In the tourism industry, this dimension comes to the foreground and it involves the customer's perception of whether the responsibility for the service failure has arisen from the employees or from other factors, such as other customers. Some claim that the reason for customer dissatisfaction is other customers (Bitner *et al.*, 1994;

Grove *et al.*, 1998), so the ability to manage the customer's perception so they do not regard the business as responsible for the service failure becomes important. For example, when the current customer staying in a room does not leave the room on time and thus another customer cannot check in, a service failure has occurred. In this case, the service failure could be perceived as the management's fault or, with an effective recovery process, it could be perceived as the failure of another customer, independent from the management. As another example, dissatisfaction could occur in a customer who cannot use the pool as he/she likes because of the weather. In the event of service failures occurring because of factors beyond the control of the business, the customers need to be informed accordingly, otherwise they may develop negative perceptions about their service encounter experience. However, the staff informing the customers need to be trained so that they can handle these situations efficiently and effectively. Service personnel can be informed about the types of service failure that may occur that are beyond the control of the service business and managers can analyse previous service failures in line with their various service processes (e.g. failures because of other customers, weather conditions, suppliers, business partners, etc.) (Hayes and Ninemeier, 2009).

11.4.1 Justice perception and service failure types

Another classification that is made according to the customer perception is the assessment of service failure under two different groups: outcome failures and process failures (Parasuraman *et al.*, 1988). Generally, outcome failures are recovered by material compensation and process failures are recovered by moral compensation (Smith *et al.*, 1999; Miller *et al.*, 2000; Chuang *et al.*, 2012). However, there are several studies arguing that culture affects the compensation expectations of the customer. For example, while Asian customers place more importance on a respectable and polite serving style, western customers are more affected by compensation (Mattila, 1999). In the tourism sector, where intercultural interaction is intensive, employees should be trained about the customer profile and cultural attributes to decrease service failures. In other research, Warden *et al.* (2008) state that culture affects the perception of product type (peripheral or core product), which is a determinant factor for evaluating both service failure and recovery expectations (see Fig. 11.3).

Outcome failures are tangible (Kim and Jang, 2014) and occur when the business cannot provide the service promised to the customer. Thus, tangible recovery efforts try to compensate customers' real and perceived losses. Discounts, replacement of the service/product with a new one, correction of the service/product without any charge, refund of money paid by the customer or a voucher for future purchases may be examples of compensation, either singly or in combination (Tax and Brown, 1998; Krishna *et al.*, 2011; Chuang *et al.*, 2012). Mattila (1999) expresses that outcome failures are connected with the reliability of the company and tend to be less forgivable (Kim and Jang, 2014). While solving the problem is possible, a more comprehensive recovery strategy is required for outcome failures since an immediate solution is not possible (Shapiro and Nieman-Gonder, 2006). Room upgrade, price discount, refund or a combination of any of these are noted as the most common forms of material compensation to recover service failures in hospitality management (Lovelock *et al.*, 2004).

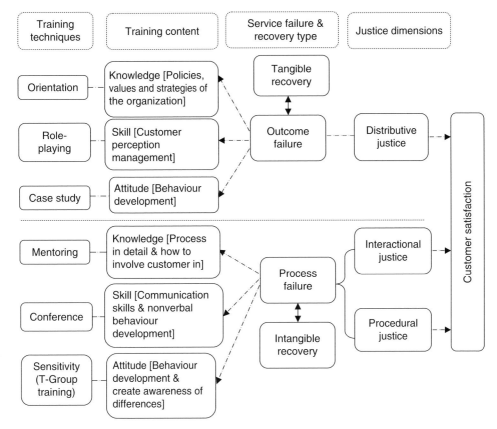

Fig. 11.3. Training practices, service failure and recovery types, justice dimensions. (From the authors.)

The subject of outcome failure is also related to the distributive (sometimes called outcome) justice perception of the customer. As explained in detail in other chapters, service recovery literature utilizes the theories of psychology, particularly justice theory, which is based on how individuals perceive the fairness of performance, behaviours, decisions or situations (Wirtz and Mattila, 2004; Prasongsukarn and Patterson, 2012). Researchers say that service recovery systems should be developed on the three dimensions of justice equity: distributive justice, procedural justice and interactional justice. Distributive justice is related to how individuals perceive they were treated and compensated for their losses (Grönroos, 1990; Huang, 2011; Chen *et al.*, 2014). As Maxham (2001) states, individuals compare what they sacrifice (financially or non-financially) and what they gain in outcome. Therefore, employees need to be trained comprehensively about their authority when an outcome failure occurs. One of the easiest methods is giving standard information during orientation programmes for newly hired employees. In addition to a general outline of the limitations of recovery activities, training programmes should include examples of both efficient and redundant recoveries to avoid unacceptable responses from employees.

Service failures occur when the business provides a service to the customer in a manner that they do not like. This may occur because of any factors causing customer dissatisfaction during the business/customer interaction. In outcome failure, the issue is the lack of service; in process failure, it is about providing a service that does not match the expectations of the customer. Sensitivity (T-Group) training, which allows employees to learn based on their experiences, is a good practice (Seashore, 1968). Employees have an opportunity to examine not only feelings and perceptions but also reactions and behaviours after participating. It is possible to train and develop skilled employees in accordance with all the perspectives of the organization, group and individual.

Two of the above-mentioned three dimensions of justice equity – namely interactional justice and procedural justice – are related to process failure. The skills and training of employees are critical in this view, because interactional justice also involves how the service recovery is implemented and the results presented (Hoffman and Kelly, 2000). There are two process failures: interpersonal and procedural. While interpersonal failures consist of intangible factors that could arise from interpersonal interactions, procedural failures are systemic (extremely slow or wrong order delivery, etc.) during the provision of a main product or service (Kim and Jang, 2014). Smith et al. (1999) express that process failures are considered more important by customers. As stated by Nguyen et al. (2012), when a process failure occurs, the service provider has an opportunity to discuss it and to determine if the expectation of the customer is to get interactional or relational recovery. For example, one customer might want to bargain for an alternative flight, another might prefer relational recovery and would expect higher category services and/or preferential treatment. In both cases, non-verbal behaviour and attitude training for employees to show empathy, compassion, honesty and politeness will help solve the problem. When customers feel the management and employees care about their distress, they feel less aggravated (Koc, 2015).

Another action that can be taken is to involve the customer in the process to prevent all responsibility from falling on the company. Even though there is a service failure, customers ascribe less importance to the problem if they perceive that they are involved in the production process or service encounter (Koc et al., 2014). Bitner et al. (1997) say there are three different ways of involving the customer in the process: as a production resource; as a contributor to the quality and degree of satisfaction; or as a competitor to the service business. For example, if a private tour is planned according to a customer's special request, the customer also becomes the travel service's resource. In the case where a customer prefers a comfortable travel option with no overnight accommodation to allow him to visit more cities, then the customer becomes a contributor to the service business. If the customer prefers to travel without a tour guide, then the customer competes with the service business in some way. The customer would become a part of the process as a consequence of using any of these methods described by Bitner et al. (1997), hence their perception of service failure could decrease. A process flow to support customer participation in the decision-making and experimental service production should be planned and employees should be trained. Features that differentiate the organization should be used in the most effective manner to involve the customer and employees should make customers feel that they are decision-makers and are responsible for the service themselves.

11.5 Training Practices for Service Recovery Process

Service recovery includes three pillars: customer recovery (regaining the customer by fixing the failure), process recovery (learning from failures and improving processes) and employee recovery (training the employees) (Michel *et al.*, 2009). The process of supporting employees to overcome the challenges they face while dealing with complaining customers, which is termed internal service recovery (Bowen and Johnston, 1999) or employee recovery (Michel *et al.*, 2009), should not be neglected in the service recovery process (Johnston and Michel, 2008).

Michel *et al.* (2006) make further recommendations for efficient service recoveries. According to researchers, not only frontline employees but also other employees – even those not interacting with customers directly – should be trained and developed. Additionally, performance evaluation and reward systems should be designed to include service recovery performance. For example, excellent service recovery performance should be rewarded instead of low customer complaint rates. Also, the possibility of service sabotage should be considered and employees should be supported to eliminate this possibility. Efficient service recovery requires organizational desire and motivation for long-term investment into customer relations, which requires an important long-term employee training investment to ensure they are able to cope with unexpected, real-time cases and situations of service failure (Michel *et al.*, 2009).

11.5.1 Training practices for employee recovery

In this section, the focus is on training practices for employee recovery in three dimensions of the recovery process. To avoid duplication, employee recovery is examined through the taxonomy of Bitner (1990), which is based on the critical incident technique. Employees' reaction to service failure is investigated and then the employees' behaviour in relation to customer needs and requirements is examined. This section ends with an evaluation of unexpected employee behaviour and problematic customer behaviour, respectively (see Fig. 11.4).

Employee response to service delivery failure

When it comes to service failure, customers' reactions or behavioural features may create huge differences. For that reason, management should not only try to employ staff possessing the features most preferred and important to their customers – caring attitude, politeness, empathy, emotional intelligence, etc. – but should also train their current employees to display those behaviours (Krishna *et al.*, 2011). In this context, Du *et al.* (2010) suggest that employees should be trained to act as sincerely as possible to create positive feelings in customers.

Employees' communication abilities, knowledge, manner, behaviours and technical skills are important to prevent service failures or to recover from them effectively (Lucas, 2005). Bitner (1990) states that almost half of dissatisfactory service encounters derive from the reluctance or lack of skill of the employees in responding. Employees should be trained in what to do and also in what not to do. As Lucas (2005) indicates, not listening,

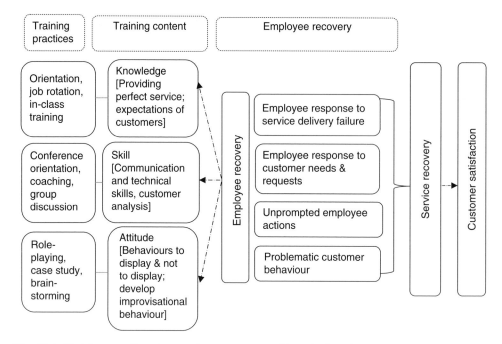

Fig. 11.4. Training practices for employee recovery. (From Authors.)

lack of respect, poor or inadequate communication, inadequate or outdated materials or equipment and work conflict are some important obstacles to service recovery. Another important point is that helping a customer faced with a service failure creates satisfaction and loyalty, not only for the customer but for the employee too (Krishna *et al.*, 2011). The employee's ability to cope actively with customer problems is closely associated with their loyalty and commitment (Schlesinger and Heskett, 1991). Frontline employees in particular may work under high stress and find themselves caught between reasonable complaints from customers and uncompromising management, or unchangeable organizational policies and procedures (Johnston and Michel, 2008). Therefore, training will not only be useful in decreasing stress and developing relationships among workers, but also in making the employees feel valued in the company by rescuing them from that feeling of being stuck (Hayes and Ninemeier, 2009).

Employee response to customer needs and requests

Service failures occur when expectations are not met, and employees must be aware of the general expectations of customers (Kelley and Davis, 1994). Pioneer service businesses ascribe great importance to investing in people and invest mostly in interpersonal and problem-solving ability training. By doing so, they are able to increase the capacity of employees to meet customers' complicated service demands (Lytle *et al.*, 1988; Schlesinger and Heskett, 1991).

Customers' expectations of services are considered in the literature in two groups: 'will' and 'should' expectations. 'Will' expectations are what the customer believes will happen in the process of a service and 'should' expectations are broadly 'what should be', characterized as the normative standard within the scope of the rules (Boulding *et al.*, 1993). To train on this subject, information about the company's general service standards should be given, and then differentiate the 'will' expectations and how to provide them, focusing on the company's strength factors. As a result, employees will have a general idea of what customers expect. Training programmes should focus on creating competence, which is required for efficient service recovery (Michel *et al.*, 2009) and should guide and develop employees with the aim of providing perfect service (Ro and Chen, 2011). In cases where the training is only to develop employee behaviour, it is more important for management to employ those who have a willingness to help customers and who always show positive reactions (Prasongsukarn and Patterson, 2012).

Unprompted employee actions

The service recovery process is considered to have a greater effect on employees and process improvement than on customers (Johnston and Michel, 2008). As Tax and Brown (1998) indicate, it is possible to support behaviour development and prevent sudden behaviours from being displayed through training. They suggest intensive training programmes, such as on written and oral communication, listening skills, problem analysis, organizing and following through, resilience and stress management, before starting to work and additional ongoing training programmes, particularly for frontline employees.

Through improvisation training, it is possible to train flexible, capable and self-confident employees to improvise. While organizing an improvisational recovery training programme, it may be worth separating pre-designed recovery strategies and those happening completely without warning. Employees should give the impression that they are aware of the urgency and importance of the problem, meanwhile trying to understand and manage the problem. Training in improvisational behaviours seems paradoxical, but reinforcing with case studies will contribute ideas and establish guidelines for employees on how to act in specific situations. Employees should not only be trained to improvise, but also to encourage customers to improvise, thereby making them a part of the process and making them feel they have some control (Vera and Crossan, 2004).

It must be taken into consideration that employees make extensive emotional efforts to recover process failures successfully. Within this context, employees must be trained not only in what to do, but also in how to display honesty and emotional support, decreasing their superficial behaviours and emotional conflict levels and protecting themselves emotionally. Michel *et al.* (2009) recommend management practices oriented towards removing the negative feelings of employees that could occur to increase their job satisfaction. Training is also oriented to increase job satisfaction and may prevent employees from experiencing such negative feelings. Such training should prevent employees from acting in a negative manner towards the customer (treating the customer unfairly, service sabotage, etc.) and help to prevent negative feelings and thoughts, such as job alienation or a decrease in organizational commitment as a result of the idea that management should not put employees into difficult positions with customers (Michel *et al.*, 2009). Human resources management must provide training to prevent any negative effects of service failure on employees within the process. Training methods such as role play, case study and brainstorming in particular may ensure that employees participate in training more actively and benefit more from the training (Hayes and Ninemeier, 2009).

Problematic customer behaviour

Employees may feel uncomfortable when they encounter a customer who is in the wrong if they are trained in the idea that 'the customer is always right' (Stauss and Seidel, 2005). For that reason, employees should know, beginning with the orientation training, that in some rare conditions the reverse may be true. They should also be trained in what to do, how to act and with whom they will manage the process in such a situation. In particular, it should be noted that the only thing to be respected in this situation is that it is not the customer who is in trouble, or who is the problem. In tourism businesses, it should be underlined that many services are provided to different customers simultaneously or in a short period of time. Thus it is easily possible to be faced with problematic customer behaviour which will be witnessed by other customers. Accordingly, it should be emphasized in service recovery training that the process needs to be managed to prevent misunderstanding on the part of the other customers, who have no idea about the problem and who may misconstrue the organization's approach towards service recovery.

Customer complaints are very important, not only for detecting service failures and service recovery but also for taking measures to find the reasons. However, it is not correct to focus only on the service failure: the person who makes the complaint should also be assessed. To examine the person who makes the complaint is important for two reasons: first, to prevent repeat of the failure; and second, to detect the 'wrong customer'. A customer who complains frequently or is never satisfied may be the 'wrong customer'. These customers may be in search of services that are not provided by the organization, or services that cost more than they earn, or they may be 'criminals'. Criminal customers know the importance of efficient service recovery for the organization and look for any kind of service failure they can then benefit from. In order to solve this problem, it may be possible not to offer service to those customers or to suggest other businesses to them in accordance with their demands, as done by Hampton Inn (Tax and Brown, 1998).

Customers who do not or cannot use the information given by the business may also be perceived as service failures (Lucas, 2005). They are often rare/spontaneous/one-time problematic customers. For instance, despite detailed information given by the receptionist, a customer who could not unlock the door and had to go back to reception tends to blame the employee for that problem. The very first response of the employee is vital in preventing further complaints. Training in communication techniques would be beneficial so they can learn to focus on the immediate solution by relaxing the customer without blaming them, using appropriate words and offering them correct alternatives. Examining the example situation, the receptionist should check the card and then send the bellboy or housekeeper with the customer to open the door. This makes the customer feel comfortable, neither hinting nor blaming them for

I.A. Saltik *et al.*

not being able to open the door. Off-the-job training, such as case studies or role playing, can develop employees' ways of thinking, acting and serving.

11.5.2   Training practices for process recovery

When customers have a problem, they want it to be fixed not only for themselves but also for other customers (Johnston and Michel, 2008) and they want to see the improvement. In other words, service recovery is not only fixing the problem that occurred in the service moment, but also improvement in all such service processes (Bell and Ridge, 1992). To achieve this, there are four elements: (i) determining the standards of performance; (ii) understanding the importance of service recovery; (iii) simplifying the complaints mechanism; and (iv) utilizing call centre and technological support (Tax and Brown, 1998). These four elements are explained below.

Determination of performance standards

The determination of performance standards is suggested in order to eliminate the uncomfortable, obscure situation that happens when the customer does not know exactly what he will or will not receive. In this context, the organization establishes the basic quality standards of the service it provides by first determining the minimum standards for its employees (Bitner *et al.*, 1997). There are many examples of where service time is determined as a standard in restaurants (lunch service within 15 minutes of ordering, complimentary food or beverage to compensate for errors or delays in service) (Tax and Brown, 1998) and in receptions or sales offices (responding to any call within three rings). Setting such standards aims to give the organization a chance to recover the failure in case of a complaint by a customer.

In this context, employees should first be allowed to decide on and/or be trained in the criteria used to determine the standards to make them more self-confident and efficient. Then, considering the organization's conditions and work analysis, employees should learn the key steps to accomplish these standards to ensure they understand the necessary points for a successful service. Another point to be remembered here is that a service failure can still occur and, in that case, it is necessary to empower the employees with the appropriate authority and responsibility. Internal service quality standards should be discussed and should make sense to all members of the organization to give management self-reliant employees (Lytle *et al.*, 1988; Yoon *et al.*, 2007). In addition, service recovery performance should absolutely be included in human resource management practices. The fact that the employees' role in service recovery affects customers' evaluation of fairness directly should be taken into account when determining and improving the criteria for recruitment and training programmes (Schlesinger and Heskett, 1991).

Understanding the importance of service recovery

Management demonstrates the importance of understanding responsibility and solving problems to prevent service failure to employees through symbols (the Ritz-Carlton

---

Basics card), slogans ('the customer is always right') and values (ECHO – every contact has opportunity). This helps employees to listen to customers more closely, to explore customers' concerns and to perform service recovery more efficiently (Tax and Brown, 1998).

Continuous training is one of the most important tools to internalize this perception, allowing for the consolidation of ideas and reflection on behaviours by employees. Most service failure cannot be identified and hence cannot be recovered due to the fact that employees are often reluctant to inform management about the situation and sometimes even tend to accuse customers (Krishna *et al.*, 2011). However, employees should report any kind of service failure to a nominated person immediately. By doing so, it will be possible to categorize service failures and to accelerate service recovery (Tax and Brown, 1998). Creating employee awareness about both service failures and the importance of reporting them is an indispensable part of training.

Simplifying the complaints mechanism

The complaints process should be designed to be as fast, simple and problem-free as possible for the customers. To do this, toll-free call centres, customer feedback cards, communication with customers during the provision of the service, getting customers' opinions after service delivery via surveys and software solutions may be used (Stauss and Seidel, 2005).

Utilizing call centre and technological support

The most common method of technological support is toll-free call centres. Call centres may act as catalysts in service recovery by reason of being easy to access, requiring little effort and being more comfortable for the customers than a face-to-face talk or written communication. As frontline employees who interact directly with customers even without seeing them, employees at the call centre should be trained as a key component of the service recovery process.

11.5.3   Training practices for customer recovery

The lack of complaints by customers is the biggest obstacle to effective service recovery. There are four possible reasons for this: (i) customers thinking that the company may not reply; (ii) customers not wishing to feel blamed for the failure; (iii) customers not having accurate information about their rights and the responsibilities of the company; and (iv) the customer being unable to afford the material and moral cost (time, effort) of complaining (Tax and Brown, 1998). Management should encourage customers to complain, while eliminating the above-mentioned issues. Organizations are recommended to provide customers with information about their rights, performance standards and the recovery process of the organization. As a result of the knowledge gained about their concerns, customers will tend to report their problems about any service failures and the organization will have a chance to change unsatisfied customers to satisfied ones.

Customer training is as important as employee training for decreasing service failure. Koc *et al.* (2014) recommend that hospitality management trains customers to participate in the service delivery process at different levels, which will make customers perceive any failure as less important. In addition, customers need to be trained in how, when and to whom to complain so that management can be made aware of a problem and recover it. The essential issues that must be established before training the customer are to determine the service standards and to inform them about the service that is deserved for the money paid. Only then, when the service provided is below the promised standards, should an easy complaints system be presented as an indication that any service failure is also undesirable for management and that they are also an advocate for the customer's rights. For this reason, policies, procedures and management systems should be customer-friendly and supportive of customer satisfaction (Krishna *et al.*, 2011).

A complaints system should be operated with a win-win principle; more clearly, it should be considered as a channel both for the customers to seek his/her rights and for the employees to get involved in the service recovery process, meanwhile allowing management to be aware of the situation. Therefore, this channel should be designed to be as simple, fast and accessible to both sides as possible. An information system should give the customer confidence in the organization's position in relation to complaints without creating the perception that there are a lot of complaints to the company. The design of the system should be as direct, stepless and results-oriented as possible, and the customer should be trained and informed by emphasizing this care directly and indirectly within the company.

The employee who will operate the system is an important factor in a simple, fast and customer-friendly complaint system, so they must be trained to operate it efficiently and be aware of customer expectations. In such training, use of feedback that explains the reasons for recovery expectations at higher levels or reasons for not being satisfied with the current service recovery or information gathered via complaint surveys will provide an invaluable contribution to service recovery (Prasongsukarn and Patterson, 2012). Training that includes learning how to develop interpersonal communication skills and giving detailed information about the organization's complaints system supports fair recovery plans (Tax and Brown, 1998). Otherwise, when the organization's complaints system is inadequate or ambiguous, the service recovery process causes feelings of inadequacy and confusion in employees (Krishna *et al.*, 2011). Thus, training the customer and building up an easy complaints system will also help employees to act more clearly and self-confidently.

11.6 Conclusions

Increasing service quality and ensuring customer satisfaction are crucial for tourism organizations. Employees have critical roles in providing service quality and customer satisfaction. As the service economies and the competition increases in the tourism sector, researchers have focused on service failures and service recovery.

Service providers should have trained teams to respond and ensure the promise given to the customer is kept and to provide a recovery to deliver on those promises (Lucas, 2005).

Empowerment is crucial in service recovery and empowered employees consider themselves as decision-makers and try to do their best (Lorenzoni and Lewis, 2004). It affects self-efficacy, adaptability and commitment to the organization (Ro and Chen, 2011; Smith *et al.*, 2012), but it should be kept in mind that empowerment should be accompanied with training (Ro and Chen, 2011), from improvising communication skills to developing creative thinking in order to deal with an irate customer. The principal point of service recovery training should be helping employees to make their own decisions and thus stand on their own feet, developing an awareness of customer concerns (Hart *et al.*, 1990).

Tourism businesses should indicate expectations and emphasize employees' need to be sensitive to service failure and service recovery. Employees should be informed about the importance of their role in solving the service failures. Communicating with employees encourages them to identify and solve problems.

Simulation training can be applied for newly hired employees to provide realistic foresight about work and an understanding of the organization as a whole. The most direct way to give employees this point of view is job rotation. Creating a team that is both rule-bound and capable of conscious effort is at the heart of the ability of service recovery (Hart *et al.*, 1990). Rotation training enables employees to expand their workplaces by shifting them between different departments or different units of the same department to increase their work experience and skills, to awaken their working spirit and to improve interpersonal relationships (Ho *et al.*, 2009).

Michel *et al.* (2009) stated that employee recovery is one of the three essentials of effective service recovery. Managers should have a realistic perspective while managing a 'no failure' target and remember the danger that aiming for no failure may cause employees to deny problems. They may become desperate and unmotivated, and may sometimes tend to ignore the service failure or even put the blame on customers. Thus, instead of aiming for zero defects, it is recommended that effective service recovery consciousness should be integrated in the organizational culture to motivate employees to put more effort into the service recovery process.

Training should focus on complaint systems and developing interpersonal communication skills to support implementation of fair recovery plans (Tax and Brown, 1998). Both on- and off-the-job training programmes can be arranged, depending on the required learning outcomes. However, on-the-job training becomes more important, particularly for newly hired employees, when it focuses on providing experience of how to interact and deal with customers (Boella and Goss-Turner, 2005). The service personnel need to receive continuous training, starting with the orientation training given on their first day of work.

Achieving quality service and customer satisfaction require services provided without any failure. However, service failures are inevitable and cause customer loss. Frontline employees are generally blamed, creating role stress. Empowerment alone is not sufficient, and without skills can increase the role stress. Therefore, tourism businesses should train the employees to gain competency for efficient service recovery and provide services and tools to help develop employees.

Case Studies

CASE STUDY 1: TYPE OF SERVICE AND TRAINING TECHNIQUES

ABC Hotel located in Bodrum, Turkey set up a database of service failures based on customer complaints. Customer complaints to reception or the customer relationship department were collected between 24 April and 30 May 2015. Service failures were classified according to their content and grouped, such as technical issues, structural issues and people-driven issues.

There were two restaurants in the hotel. One was the main restaurant, which provided services as part of the all-inclusive system (without any extra payment), the other was an à la carte restaurant where the customers needed to pay extra. The most common service failures were examined for both restaurants. The report demonstrated that the top four service failures related to employees of the main restaurant were: 'rude behaviours of employees', 'unwillingness of employees to meet customers' requests', 'careless and rushing service' and 'employees ignoring customers'. In the à la carte restaurant, the most common customer complaints related to employees were: 'employees' insufficient knowledge about the menu', 'food served at an incorrect temperature', 'wrong order service' and 'slow service'.

Accordingly, hotel management decided to train employees to prevent these service failures and found an external training programme by Ace Training & Consultancy Firm. The Department of Human Resource Management (HRM) of ABC Hotel determined the subjects of training. Employees participated in a training programme consisting of communication techniques, customer relationship, complaint management, time management and problem-solving techniques between 5 and 15 June 2015 (15 hours in total). Sixty days after the training, HRM investigated the customer complaints and customers' satisfaction surveys to evaluate the outcome of training.

The findings indicated that while the customer complaints from the main restaurant decreased by more than 60%, customer complaints related to the à la carte restaurant decreased by just 17%. The results of a customers' satisfaction survey of the à la carte restaurant were not significantly different from the results of surveys before the training.

HRM discussed the contents of customer complaints with Ace Training & Consultancy Firm and gave them detailed information about the working system of the à la carte restaurant. After analysing all the complaints, Ace Training & Consultancy Firm indicated that customers were paying too much at the à la carte restaurant. Additionally, they asserted that preventing service failures was not sufficient and that efficient service recovery was needed to prevent customers' complaints. In accordance with this, they suggest the à la carte restaurant's employees should be given special training and also be provided autonomy by the management. Thus a new training programme was given to the à la carte restaurant's staff, consisting of customer psychology, emotional intelligence, understanding people and motivation, empathy, dealing with difficult people and service recovery techniques. In this training programme, which lasted 10 days, training techniques such as role playing and case study were applied. The data related to customer complaints and satisfaction were gathered and examined 45 days after the second training. As a result, customer complaints about the à la carte restaurant decreased by 86% and customers' satisfaction increased by 17%.

Continued

Discussion questions

1. What was the problem?
2. How did the hotel respond to this problem?
3. Were training programmes effective?
4. What was the outcome?

CASE STUDY 2: THE ROLE OF LEARNING BY EXPERIMENTAL TRAINING

ABC Hotel mainly serves Turkish guests (approximately 70%) and an overnight stay costs above the average price in the sector. ABC Hotel managers ascertained that employees' responses to complaints and requests from customers were unsatisfactory. The most common customer complaints, particularly negative comments in social media forums and blogs, were:

- uncompensated losses;
- unsolved problems;
- not being able to contact any managers;
- employees not understanding customer requests; and
- a feeling that employees were unwilling to comprehend the problem.

The assistant general manager and HRM of the hotel discussed what could be done about these complaints. They decided to train guest relations department staff to develop employees for efficient service recovery. Accordingly, a training programme consisting of 'problem-solving techniques', 'conflict management', 'dealing with angry and difficult customers', 'personality analysis', 'stress management', 'importance of feedback to customers and applicable techniques' was applied by an external training and consultancy firm.

Customer complaints significantly decreased after the training. However, the level of customer complaints was much higher than expected. Even though mainly dealing with domestic tourists, guest relations department staff were unable to develop empathy. Therefore an off-the-job training programme lasting a week was planned for them. Each employee was individually sent to Z Hotel, which was rated as successful in customer complaints management. In this training, role-play was used so that trainees acted as customers of Z Hotel who had to communicate with the hotel's guest relations department staff. After completing this training, which was also a kind of vacation, considerable performance improvement was achieved in the short-term, and a reduction in customer complaints in social media was recorded long-term.

Questions

1. What were the main complaints?
2. How did the company resolve the problem?
3. Can the hotel company resolve this problem through a different approach?

Questions

1. How do we define service failure and recovery?
2. Why is training important for service recovery?
3. What are the main reasons for service failures?
4. What is the relationship between staff training and service recovery success?
5. How can the service recovery process be managed?

Further Reading

Bell, C. and Ridge, K. (1992) Service recovery for trainers. *Training and Development* 46, 58–62.

Cannon, D. (2008) Contributing to employee development through training and education. In: Tesone, D.V. (ed.) *Handbook of Hospitality Human Resources Management*. Routledge, New York, pp. 373–390.

Hart, C.W.L., Heskett, J.L. and Sasser, W.E.J. (1990) The profitable art of service recovery. *Harvard Business Review* 68, 148–156.

Hayes, D.K. and Ninemeier, J.D. (2009) *Human Resources Management in the Hospitality Industry*. John Wiley & Sons, Hoboken, New Jersey.

Jong, A.D. and de Ruyter, K. (2004) Adaptive versus proactive behaviour in service recovery: the role of self-managing teams. *Decision Sciences* 35, 457–491.

References

Bamford, D. and Xystouri, T. (2005) A case study of service failure and recovery within an international airline. *Managing Service Quality: An International Journal* 15, 306–322.

Bell, C. and Ridge, K. (1992) Service recovery for trainers. *Training and Development* 46, 58–62.

Berry, L.L. and Parasuraman, A. (1992) Services marketing starts from within. *Marketing Management* 1, 25–34.

Bitner, M.J. (1990) Evaluating service encounters: the effects of physical surroundings and employee responses. *Journal of Marketing* 54, 69–82.

Bitner, M.J., Booms, B. and Mohr, L. (1994) Critical service encounters: the employee's viewpoint. *Journal of Marketing* 58, 95–106.

Bitner, M.J., Faranda, W.T., Hubbert, A.R. and Zeithaml, V.A. (1997) Customer contributions and roles in service delivery. *International Journal of Service Industry Management* 8, 193–205.

Boella, M.J. and Goss-Turner, S. (2005) *Human Resource Management in the Hospitality Industry. An Introductory Guide*, 8th edn. Elsevier Butterworth-Heinemann, Amsterdam.

Boshoff, C.R. and Leong, J. (1998) Empowerment, attribution and apologising as dimensions of service recovery: an experimental study. *International Journal of Service Industry Management* 9, 24–47.

Boulding, W., Kalra, A., Staelin, R. and Zeithaml, V.A. (1993) A dynamic process model of service quality: from expectations to behavioral intentions. *Journal of Marketing Research* 30, 7–27.

Bowen, D.E. and Johnston, R. (1999) Internal service recovery: developing a new construct. *International Journal of Service Industry Management* 10, 118–131.

Cannon, D. (2008) Contributing to employee development through training and education. In: Tesone, D.V. (ed.) *Handbook of Hospitality Human Resources Management*. Routledge, New York, pp. 373–390.

Chen, H., Lee, Y.L. and Weiler, B. (2014) Exploring perceived fairness in hotel service recovery: the case of Kingdom Plaza. *Asian-Pacific Journal of Innovation in Hospitality and Tourism* 3, 1–19.

Chuang, S.C., Cheng, Y.H., Chang, C.J. and Yang, S.W. (2012) The effect of service failure types and service recovery on customer satisfaction: a mental accounting perspective. *The Service Industries Journal* 32, 257–271.

Dick, W., Carry, L. and Carry, J.O. (2001) *The Systematic Design of Instruction*, 5th edn. Addison-Wesley, New York.

Dobbs, J. (1993) The empowerment environment. *Training and Development* 47, 55–70.

Du, J., Fan, X. and Feng, T. (2010) An experimental investigation of the role of face in service failure and recovery encounters. *Journal of Consumer Marketing* 27, 584–593.

Ennew, C. and Schoefer, K. (2003) Service failure and service recovery in tourism: a review. Available at: https://www.researchgate.net/profile/Christine_Ennew/publication/252577031_Service_Failure_and_Service_Recovery_in_Tourism_A_Review/links/00b4953604d8999e28000000.pdf (accessed 10 June 2016).

Forrester, R. (2000) Empowerment: rejuvenating a potent idea. *The Academy of Management Executive* 14, 67–80.

Grönroos, C. (1990) *Service Management and Marketing: Managing the Moment of Truth in Service Competition*. Lexington Books, Lexington, Massachusetts.

Grove, S.J., Fisk, R.P. and Dorsch, M.J. (1998) Assessing the theatrical components of the service encounter: a cluster analysis examination. *The Service Industries Journal* 18, 116–134.

Hart, C.W.L., Heskett, J.L. and Sasser, W.E.J. (1990) The profitable art of service recovery. *Harvard Business Review* 68, 148–156.

Hayes, D.K. and Ninemeier, J.D. (2009) *Human Resources Management in the Hospitality Industry*. John Wiley and Sons, Hoboken New Jersey.

Ho, W.H., Chang, C.S., Shih, Y.L. and Liang, R.D. (2009) Effects of job rotation and role stress among nurses on job satisfaction and organizational commitment. *BMC Health Services Research* 9, doi: 10.1186/1472-6963-9-8.

Hoffman, K.D. and Bateson, J.E.G. (1997) *Essentials of Services Marketing: Concepts, Strategies and Cases*. Dryden Press, Fort Worth, Texas.

Hoffman, K.D. and Kelly, S.W. (2000) Perceived justice needs and recovery evaluation: a contingency approach. *European Journal of Marketing* 34, 418–432.

Huang, M.H. (2011) Re-examining the effect of service recovery: the moderating role of brand equity. *Journal of Services Marketing* 25, 509–516.

Iacobucci, D. (1998) Services: what do we know and where shall we go? A view from marketing. In: Swartz, T.A., Bowen, D.E. and Brown, S.W. (eds) *Advances in Services Marketing and Management*, vol. 7. Emerald Group, Bingley, UK, pp. 1–96.

Johnston, R. and Michel, S. (2008) Three outcomes of service recovery. *International Journal of Operations & Production Management* 28, 79–99.

Jong, A.D. and de Ruyter, K. (2004) Adaptive versus proactive behaviour in service recovery: the role of self-managing teams. *Decision Sciences* 35, 457–491.

Kelley, S.W. and Davis, M.A. (1994) Antecedents to customer expectations for service recovery. *Journal of the Academy of Marketing Science* 22, 52–61.

Kim, J.H. and Jang, S.C. (2014) The fading affect bias: examining changes in affect and behavioral intentions in restaurant service failures and recoveries. *International Journal of Hospitality Management* 40, 109–119.

Koc, E. (2015) *Hizmet Pazarlaması ve Yönetimi*. Seçkin Yayıncılık, Ankara.

Koc, E., Yumusak, S., Ulukoy, M., Kilic, R. and Toptas, A. (2014) Are internship programs encouraging or discouraging? A viewpoint of tourism and hospitality students in Turkey. *Journal of Hospitality, Leisure, Sport & Tourism Education* 15, 135–142.

Koc, E., Ulukoy, M., Kilic, R., Yumusak, S. and Bahar, R. (2015) The influence of customer participation on service failure perceptions. *Total Quality Management & Business Excellence* 26, 390–404.

Krishna, A., Dangayach, G.S. and Jain, R. (2011) Service recovery and failure: employee perspective. *Viewpoint* 2, 19–26.

Lin, H.H., Wang, Y.S. and Chang, L.K. (2011) Consumer responses to online retailer's service recovery after a service failure. *Managing Service Quality: An International Journal* 21, 511–534.

Lorenzoni, N. and Lewis, B.R. (2004) Service recovery in the airline industry: a cross-cultural comparison of the attitudes and behaviours of British and Italian front-line personnel. *Managing Service Quality: An International Journal* 14, 11–25.

Lovelock, C.L., Patterson, P.G. and Walker, R. (2004) *Service Marketing: a South East Asian and Australian Perspective*, 3rd edn. Pearson Education, Sydney, Australia.

Lucas, R.W. (2005) *Customer Service: Building Successful Skills for the Twenty-First Century*, 3rd edn. McGraw-Hill, Boston, Massachusetts.

Lytle, R.S., Hom, P.W. and Mokwa, M.P. (1988) An organizational measure of service orientation. *Journal of Retailing* 74, 455–489.

Mattila, A.S. (1999) The role of culture and purchase motivation in service encounter evaluations. *Journal of Services Marketing* 13, 376–389.

Maxham, J.G.I. (2001) Service recovery's influence on consumer satisfaction, positive word-of-mouth, and purchase intentions. *Journal of Business Research* 54, 11–24.

Maxham, J.G.I. and Netemeyer, R.G. (2003) Firms reap what they sow: the effects of shared values and perceived organizational justice on customers' evaluation of complaint handling. *Journal of Marketing* 67, 29–45.

McLaughlin, C.P. (1996) Why variation reduction is not everything: a new paradigm for service operations. *International Journal of Service Industry Management* 7, 17–30.

Michel, S., Bowen, D. and Johnston, R. (2006) Service recovery management: closing the gap between best practices and actual practices. Available at: http://www.dienstleistungsmarketing. ch/documents/MichelBowenJohnston_Service_Recovery.pdf (accessed 10 October 2016).

Michel, S., Bowen, D. and Johnston, R. (2009) Why service recovery fails: tensions among customer, employee, and process perspectives. *Journal of Service Management* 20, 253–273.

Miller, J.L., Craighead, C.W. and Karwan, K.R. (2000) Service recovery: a framework and empirical investigation. *Journal of Operations Management* 18, 387–400.

Nguyen, D.T., McColl-Kennedy, J.R. and Dagger, T.S. (2012) Matching service recovery solutions to customer recovery preferences. *European Journal of Marketing* 46, 1171–1194.

Parasuraman, A., Zeithaml, V.A. and Berry, L.L. (1988) SERVQUAL: a multiple-item scale for measuring consumer perceptions of service quality. *Journal of Retailing* 64, 12–40.

Prasongsukarn, K. and Patterson, P.G. (2012) An extended service recovery model: the moderating impact of temporal sequence of events. *Journal of Services Marketing* 26, 510–520.

Redman, T. and Matthews, B. (1998) Service quality and human resource management: a review and research agenda. *Personnel Review* 27, 57–77.

Ro, H. and Chen, P.J. (2011) Empowerment in hospitality organizations: customer orientation and organizational support. *International Journal of Hospitality Management* 30, 422–428.

Schlesinger, L.A. and Heskett, J.L. (1991) Breaking the cycle of failure in services. *Sloan Management Review* 32, 17–28.

Seashore, C. (1968) *What is Sensitivity Training?* Available at: http://files.eric. ed.gov/fulltext/ ED025477.pdf (accessed 10 November 2016).

Shapiro, T. and Nieman-Gonder, J. (2006) Effect of communication mode in justice-based service recovery. *Managing Service Quality: An International Journal* 16, 124–144.

Smith, A.K., Bolton, R.N. and Wagner, J. (1999) A model of customer satisfaction with service encounters involving failure and recovery. *Journal of Marketing Research* 36, 356–372.

Smith, J.S., Nagy, P.F., Karwan, K.R. and Ramirez, E. (2012) The contingent nature of service recovery system structures. *International Journal of Operations & Production Management* 32, 877–903.

Stauss, B. and Seidel, W. (2005) *Complaint Management. The Heart of CRM*. South-Western Educational Publishing, Mason, Ohio.

Tax, S.S. and Brown, S.W. (1998) Recovering and learning from service failure. *Sloan Management Review* 40, 75–88.

Vera, D. and Crossan, M. (2004) Theatrical improvisation: lessons for organizations. *Organization Studies* 25, 727–749.

Warden, C.A., Huang, S.C.T., Liu, T.C. and Wu, W.Y. (2008) Global media, local metaphor: television shopping and marketing-as-relationship in America, Japan and Taiwan. *Journal of Retailing* 84, 119–129.

Weiner, B. (2000) Attributional thoughts about consumer behaviour. *Journal of Consumer Research* 27, 382–387.

Wirtz, J. and Mattila, A.S. (2004) Consumer responses to compensation, speed of recovery and apology after a service failure. *International Journal of Service Industry Management* 15, 150–166.

Yoon, S.J., Choi, D.C. and Park, J.W. (2007) Service orientation: its impact on business performance in the medical service industry. *The Service Industry Journal* 27, 371–388.

12 The Role of Empowerment, Internal Communication, Waiting Time and Speed in Service Recovery

ALI DALGIC, DERYA TOKSÖZ AND KEMAL BIRDIR

Learning Objectives

After reading this chapter, you should be able to:

- Understand and explain the importance of empowerment in relation to service recovery.
- Understand the concept and types of internal communication.
- Explain the relationship between integrated internal communications and service recovery.
- Understand the role of waiting time in service failures and recovery processes.

12.1   Introduction

Employee empowerment, communication and speed are of vital importance to minimize the frequency of service failures and increase the ability to respond to them efficiently (Boshoff, 1999; Davidow, 2000). The authority of the employee, allowing autonomy, coupled with employee empowerment training and open communication, have a significant influence on the efficiency and effectiveness of service recovery (Boshoff and Allen, 2000; Liao, 2007; Swanson and Hsu, 2011). Another important factor is internal communication. Internal communication enables employees to be more service-focused, especially when provided with relevant training (Melton and Hartline, 2010). Thus, service failures decrease and employees can effectively convey customer feedback to relevant departments (Michel *et al.*, 2009). Moreover, Gong *et al.* (2014) emphasize that personnel empowerment and communication with managers (internal communication) are important factors in the service recovery process. Another important point is waiting time (Butcher and Heffernan, 2006), which may be perceived as part of service failure and may require service recovery and speed for service improvements (Conlon and Murray, 1996; Wirtz and Mattila, 2004; Valenzuela and Cooskey, 2012). Inability to provide specified support to employees (in terms of empowerment and internal communication) and service to customers (in terms of waiting time and speed) may have a negative impact on businesses. While negative results may increase work stress and burnout and decrease business satisfaction among employees (Koc, 2015, p. 280), dissatisfaction, decrease in repurchase intentions and negative reviews from customers are also likely to abound (Boshoff and Allen, 2000; Liao, 2007; Swanson and Hsu, 2011).

12.2 Employee Empowerment and Service Recovery

Employee empowerment can be defined as a process of increasing self-efficiency among the members of an organization. Situations in which employees feel themselves power-less need to be defined and eliminated. The efficient provision of information both through informal and formal channels is of vital importance in the process of employee empowerment (Conger and Kanungo, 1988, p. 474). The provision or sharing of information together with training and encouragement are essential components of employee empowerment (Tan, 2007, p. 55). When empowered, service employees will have more power and autonomy when performing their individual tasks. Hence, empowered employees are expected to make faster decisions to meet customers' needs and expectations (Gazzoli et al., 2012, p. 5). Additionally, empowered employees will have the ability and authority to engage in recovery of service failures that may arise (Thomas and Velthouse, 1990, p. 678).

Service encounters in the tourism and hospitality sector are prone to service failures (Koc, 2013). Therefore, the empowerment of frontline employees is essential to deal with service failures (Hocutt and Stone, 1998, p. 119). Employee empowerment provides employees with the opportunity to make decisions regarding service failure recovery (Sparks et al., 1997, p. 479). Walt Disney Parks and Resorts provides employees with specialized training at the Disney Institute on service recovery. Training for service recovery needs to concentrate on three guidelines (Jones, 2015):

- Achievable: The recovery must be realistic and the individual service employee should be in a position to carry out the recovery.
- Accessible: Solutions must be readily obtainable.
- Appropriate: Recovery action should fit the particular service failure to be resolved.

Another example of employee empowerment is the Ritz-Carlton's policy of allowing each employee to spend up to US$2000 to solve a customer's problem. The Ritz-Carlton estimates that a loyal customer may spend up to US$250,000 during her/his lifetime. A similar policy is adopted at Marriott Hotels, where a service employee can spend up to US$500 to ensure customer satisfaction, and even a waiter in the restaurant has the authority to tear up a bill if s/he feels that the guest is dissatisfied with the meal (Koc, 2015, p. 284).

The above examples of employee empowerment practices require service employees to be enthusiastic and eager (Koc, 2015, p. 282). According to Carson et al. (1998) (Fig. 12.1), if the employees are empowered but unenthusiastic and reluctant, service recoveries will be ineffective. Carson et al. (1998) classify employees who may be empowered but reluctant to handle service recoveries and neglect service recovery as empowered neglecters; employees who may not be empowered but eager to handle service recoveries and avoid service recovery as learned avoiders; employees who may not be empowered but eager to handle service recoveries as recovery riskers; and finally employees who may be both empowered and eager to handle service recoveries as effective recoverers.

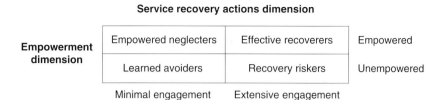

Fig. 12.1. Empowerment and service recovery dimensions. (From Carson *et al.*, 1998.)

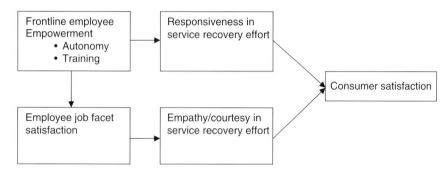

Fig. 12.2. Employee empowerment and service recovery. (From Hocutt and Stone, 1998.)

Frontline (front stage) employees in service sectors encounter service failures more frequently than other (e.g. backstage) employees (Yavas *et al.*, 2003; Yoo *et al.*, 2006) and may experience more job stress and burnout as a result (Koc, 2007). Hocutt and Stone's (1998) service recovery (Fig. 12.2) model emphasizes the role of empowerment and autonomy in job satisfaction.

In Hocutt and Stone's (1998) model (Fig. 12.2), job satisfaction will increase when employees are empowered and have autonomy. Preconditioning the employees about service compensation is another issue which increases job satisfaction (Koc, 2015, p. 282). One may say that empowerment is particularly important in this regard. Previous studies support that service recovery performance of frontline employees increases through empowerment (Boshoff and Allen, 2000; Boshoff and Staude, 2003; Yavas *et al.*, 2003; Ashill *et al.*, 2005; Yoo *et al.*, 2006; Yavas *et al.*, 2010; Nadiri and Tanova, 2016). Thus, there is a correlation between service recovery performance and customer satisfaction, intention to repurchase and also positive word-of-mouth (Boshoff and Allen, 2000; Liao, 2007; Swanson and Hsu, 2011).

The Ritz-Carlton will spend $2000 to make you happy

Known as one of the gold standards of customer service, the Ritz-Carlton has been rightly studied and dissected over the years in an attempt to find the 'secret' Ritz sauce. Entire books have been written just on the Ritz's customer service. One aspect of the Ritz's service that has received a lot of coverage is the fact that the Ritz empowers its employees to spend up to $2000 to solve customer problems without asking for a

Continued

Continued.

manager. Yes, you read that right: Ritz-Carlton employees can spend up to $2000 per incident, not per year, to rescue a guest experience. What is interesting about this famous number is that the majority of authors who mention it leave out an equally vital statistic. You see, the $2000 is always mentioned in the context of how important employee empowerment is to great customer service – as if empowering employees to excess is the key to a profitable and successful business. What the authors often leave out is this: the average Ritz-Carlton customer will spend $250,000 with the Ritz over their lifetime. Like any smart, profitable organization, the Ritz did not pull the $2000 figure out of thin air. The Ritz has studied its customer base and understands the value of the relationship with its customers and what it is willing to do to maintain those relationships. Put in that context, the $2000 does not seem so hard to conceive. Ritz-Carlton values relationships over transactions, and for anyone who has ever stayed at one of its properties, that is no secret. Knowing that your business probably doesn't have a $2000 per-incident budget for service recovery, it's important to focus on how your business can use the same principle to your advantage. It begins by embracing the idea of a relational approach over a transactional approach. When businesses do not approach customers transactionally, when they do not attempt to extract every possible advantage from their customers, those businesses are rewarded with loyalty and a customer relationship that is worth far more than any individual transaction. Far more.

Source: Toporek (2012).

12.3 Internal Communication and Service Recovery

Communication is exchange of information between a sender and a receiver. Those exchanging information have a certain channel of communication and they generally provide feedback after exchanging the information (Kalla, 2005, p. 303). While internal communication can be conceptualized as an exchange of information within the organization, it has also turned out to be a structure providing information flow (Argenti, 2009). Kalla (2005, pp. 305–307) defines this complex structure as integrated internal communication. This complex structure (Fig. 12.3) consists of four dimensions: (i) business communication in regard to all employees' communication skills; (ii) management communication in regard to all managers' communication skills and capabilities; (iii) corporate communication focusing on the formal corporate communication function; and (iv) organizational communication focusing on philosophically and theoretically oriented issues (Kalla, 2005, p. 305).

Fig. 12.3. Integrated internal communications. (From Kalla, 2005.)

A. Dalgic *et al.*

Training is an important medium that helps to structure communication components in a desired way. Information and skills gained by training contribute to the development of internal communication, which, in turn, helps employees become more service-focused (Melton and Hartline, 2010, pp. 415–416). Moreover, internal communication, which becomes more effective through training, is regarded as an important means for getting feedback from the customers regarding service failures, conveying feedback to relevant departments and providing service recovery (Michel *et al.*, 2009). Various situations, for instance a customer in a hotel finding the room dirty (Koc, 2015, p. 261) or a customer with a restaurant reservation who is told there is no vacant table, emphasize the importance of organizations' internal communication. Von Vaerenbergh *et al.* (2012) found that the forms of communication the employees establish with customers are quite important in the process starting after a service failure. They also found that effective communication developed in the recovery process has a positive effect on customers' overall satisfaction, intention to repurchase and word-of-mouth. Similarly, Komunda and Osarenkhoe (2012) found that effective communication during the service recovery process has a positive effect on customer loyalty.

The importance of communication during a business interruption

When planning for recovery, most companies' business continuity plans are so focused on recovering critical systems and people that they often overlook the importance of communication during an incident that impairs normal business. Communication is key both for continuing internal operations and for protecting the company's reputation.

Internal communications

It is important to maintain ongoing communication with management and employees in order to disseminate information regarding the situation at hand to allow for a smooth and efficient recovery effort. Ensuring the employees know the nature of the scenario, how to respond, and where to be and when, are crucial elements to make certain that everyone is on the same page and that critical time is not lost. Establishing multiple vehicles to communicate information is crucial. This may include, but is not limited to, phone trees, automatic messaging services, employee hotlines, and secure online portals/websites.

Source: Hall (2016).

12.4 Waiting Time

Time spent in the course of receiving service stands out as an important factor for customer satisfaction. Customers' perception that the waiting time is excessive could lead to many negative circumstances (Groth and Gilliland, 2001, p. 78). Waiting time may vary due to many factors, such as a queue (Fig. 12.4), a delay or a customer's early arrival for an appointment (Lin and Chang, 2011, p. 1054). As a result, the customers may have the sense of being bored, annoyed, frustrated and irritated, regardless of the quality of service they receive when their waiting time extends (Butcher and Heffernan, 2006, p. 36). For instance, Ritz-Carlton Hotels forecast customers' preferences using their own database.

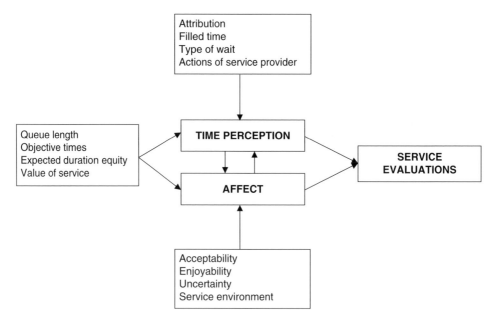

Fig. 12.4. Waiting for service. (From Taylor and Fullerton, 2000.)

In this situation, Ritz-Carlton makes preparations in advance to decrease customers' waiting time and effort. Even before customers enter their room, their preferred drink or snack (in accordance with the consumption data of the customer's previous stay) can be put in a mini bar as a complimentary gesture. In this situation, the customer won't have to phone to order the products and he won't have to wait either (Koc, 2015, p. 371).

TripAdvisor lists many complaints about waiting time in which people share their experiences. For instance, many complaints were lodged by hotel customers about the long check-in and check-out processes at a five-star hotel in Singapore. One of the best examples for the management of waiting time is the programme applied in Florida by the fast-food chain McDonald's. It guarantees that orders will be ready for delivery one minute after payment (for orders made by drive-through customers), and if it takes longer than that, the drive-through customer will have the next order free (Tuttle, 2014).

Can the customer's waiting time perception be changed?

Case study 1

Customers constantly complain about waiting for the elevator for a long period in a hotel. Hotel management want to handle the issue and think about what to do. The physical situation doesn't give the opportunity to build an additional elevator; there are operational and financial problems with demolishing and rebuilding walls. As a solution, an employee suggests that mirrors are placed on both sides of the elevator. After some time, complaints cease. The customers no longer notice the time spent waiting for the elevator

Continued

A. Dalgic *et al.*

Continued.

because they look in the mirror: they don't notice that they wait for the same duration when the time is actively spent. This enhances customers' overall satisfaction levels.

Case study 2

Passengers who get off the aircraft complain about waiting for a long time when they go to the baggage reclaim area. Airport management begin to think about where the problem stems from and how the problem can be solved. However, the management notices after studies and comparisons with other airports that the active waiting time is normal and the waiting time in their own airport is less than many airports. However, there is an important difference. When compared with other airports, the distance between the apron where the aircraft park and the luggage reclaim area is quite short. In other words, the customers feel that the waiting time is longer because they spend less time getting to the reclaim area. As a result, the airport management change the passengers' path to arrive at the reclaim area, making them follow a roundabout route in order to lengthen the distance between the apron and luggage reclaim. The customers stop complaining because the time spent walking between the apron and luggage reclaim (active time) prevents them from perceiving the waiting time negatively. An individual's boredom and dissatisfaction with waiting time is related to the individual's paying attention to elapsed time. As stated above, time spent when the person isn't engaged in an activity is perceived longer than the time when the person is engaged. TVs, magazines, newspapers and internet connection (Wi-Fi) will prevent the customers from paying attention to elapsed time and will affect customer satisfaction positively. As seen in the examples mentioned above, service businesses can change the ways their customers perceive time by means of creative and simple solutions while designing and controlling the processes.

Source: Koc (2015).

Waiting times can be examined under three groups: pre-process, in-process and post-process (Taylor, 1994, p. 56). In a restaurant business, the way employees greet customers, show them to their tables and take their orders can be exemplified as pre-process factors. Time spent in preparing the meal and serving food and beverages can be viewed as the in-process phase. Finally, asking for the bill, paying the bill and receiving change for cash payments are processes defined as post-process situations (Hwang and Lambert, 2006). There are many theories regarding waiting time. Knowing these theories and presenting solutions are of vital importance for customer satisfaction. For instance, offering appetizers to a person coming to a restaurant for dinner may be a good way to diminish the waiting time perception.

Moreover, factors resulting from being crowded and the effects of hunger on individuals' behaviours and feelings (field theory), long queues (Maister's theory) and negative factors during service procurements (attribution theory) may extend perceived waiting time and may require service recovery. These theories are briefly discussed below.

12.4.1   Field theory

Field theory states that people's behaviours and feelings are affected by some psychological forces. These psychological forces may be internal (within the individual) or external (outside the individual) (Hui *et al.*, 1998, p. 470). People usually need to cover a certain distance in order to achieve a goal. This distance becomes apparent due to an internal force or an external obstacle, which may cause a deviation from an individual's aims (Houston *et al.*, 1998, p. 738). An individual who goes to a restaurant may feel under pressure because of the crowd in the restaurant. As a result, the individual may perceive the waiting time is longer or they may not be pleased with the service they receive (Nie, 2000, p. 625). In this situation, preventing the customer from waiting idly and offering the customer something interesting to do may eliminate negative feelings and psychological pressures (Koc, 2015, p. 364).

12.4.2 Maister's theory

Maister (1984) emphasized that customers' waiting time to receive service affects their satisfaction levels and suggested taking the factors below into consideration:

- Occupied time feels shorter than unoccupied time.
- Uncertain waits seem to be longer than certain and finite waits.
- Anxiety makes waits seem longer.
- Solo waiting feels longer than group waiting.
- The more valuable the service, the longer the customer will wait.
- Unfair waits are longer than equitable waits.
- Unexplained waits are longer than explained waits.
- Pre-process waits are longer than in-process waits.

It is important that the specified situations be taken into consideration by employees and managers in order to minimize the complaints and reduce the need for service recovery. Koc (2015, p. 363) offers strategies regarding Maister's (1984) waiting situations (Table 12.1).

Applying the strategies above may eliminate customers' perception that they are waiting more than necessary (Koc, 2015, p. 363). Thus, customers' feelings of boredom, annoyance, frustration and irritation, which lead to the negative evaluation of the service, can be eliminated (Butcher and Heffernan, 2006) and businesses' service compensation may be decreased.

12.4.3 Attribution theory

Attribution theory is explained in Chapter 6 (this volume). However, attribution theory has implications in terms of waiting time and empowerment. The major argument of attribution theory is that 'people want to know the reasons or the causes for any undesirable events' (Lou *et al.*, 2004, p. 79). When individuals wait to receive a service longer than expected, they start to blame the business for the long waiting time. Studies show that any reduction in the quality of the service provided by the business will reflect on individuals' further behaviours (Nie, 2000, p. 622). Weiner (1985) underlined that there are three dimensions of attribution theory: Locus is a dimension related to the person responsible for service failure by considering internal and external reasons; stability is a dimension related to whether causal elements undergo a change and whether causal

Table 12.1. Waiting situations and strategies. (From Koc, 2015, p. 363.)

Situation	Strategy
Individual's boredom is related to individual's paying attention to elapsed time. Time when the person is not engaged in an activity is perceived as longer than the time when the person is engaged.	Placing TVs, newspapers, magazines, internet (WiFi) etc. in waiting environments to entertain the customers.
Pre-process (ordering the meal) and post-process (paying the bill) are perceived as longer than the process itself.	Making the customer feel that they are starting to get service. Bringing some appetizers and snacks (such as salad, cheese etc.) while the customer is waiting for food ordered.
Waiting in a state of worry and anxiety causes the waiting time to be perceived as longer.	Informing and explaining to customers/patients and patient's relatives in the services, especially in health services, help to relax them.
Unpredictable waiting is perceived as longer than informed and predictable waiting. If the customers don't know why they are waiting, they feel time elapses more slowly.	Customers wait more calmly if they are told what they are waiting for and why (reason for delay, if there is one) and how long they will wait. If reason for waiting is out of the business' control, the customers may tend to be more understanding of the situation. Informing the customer, calling the call centre about the customer's waiting order and average waiting time. Announcing average waiting time onscreen, e.g. in hospital waiting rooms.
Unfair waiting is perceived as longer than fair waiting.	Giving service to the customer according to the customer's sequence. Making necessary explanations to those who intend to jump the queue.
People comply with waiting when value of service increases.	By designing every factor with caution, a business which gives the service can give the feeling that the customers receive special service.
Physically uncomfortable waiting is perceived as longer than comfortable waiting.	Providing comfortable seats in waiting halls. Providing enough and clean washbasins and toilets for customers' use when needed.
Waiting alone is perceived as longer than waiting in groups.	The customer may tend to pay attention to time less when the customers are in touch with other people or observe them while waiting with others. However, waiting with the other customers may be a disadvantage at times.
Those who use a service rarely perceive the time as longer than those who use the service more frequently.	Making necessary explanations to the customers about waiting time and its reasons.

elements may be changed by the individuals; controllability is an attribution dimension about whether reasons can be controlled or not. If a customer believes that service failure occurs out of the control of a business, the customer may be more understanding and may not expect service recovery. Including the customer in service, such as self-service, may prevent complete attribution of service failure to the business, while use of technology by the business may both decrease the possibility of service failure and prevent the complete attribution of service failure to the business (Koc, 2015, p. 256).

12.5 Speed of Service Recovery

Solving the problems arising from service failure swiftly is of vital importance for customer satisfaction (Koc, 2013). In Boshoff's (1999) scale for measuring customer satisfaction in service recovery, organizational responses include six dimensions: communication, empowerment, feedback, atonement, explanation and tangible. Davidow (2000) emphasizes that service mistakes result in a variety of customer behaviours represented by six dimensions. These dimensions are timeliness, facilitation, redress, apology, credibility and attentiveness. The timeliness dimension may be defined as the perceived speed of an organization's handling of and response to the complaint (Davidow, 2003, p. 232). The post-complaint behaviour model by Davidow (2000) is detailed below (Fig. 12.5).

Conlon and Murray (1996) indicated that the speed of service recovery has a positive relationship with a customer's intentions to repurchase, and lower service recovery time leads to a higher repurchase ratio. Davidow (2000) also suggests that service recovery time has an impact on the business–customer relationship and a positive association with customers' intentions to repurchase. Moreover, service recovery time decreases negative word-of-mouth if service recovery is fast. Swanson and Kelley (2001) reiterate that time spent during service recovery has an effect on satisfaction, intention to repurchase, positive perceptions of recovery and word-of-mouth. Wirtz and Mattila (2004) observed that speed is important for recovery after service failure. According to the researchers, when service speed is combined with an apology and recovery, customers' intentions to repurchase increase and negative word-of-mouth decreases (Wirtz and Mattila, 2004). Chebat and Slusarczyk (2005) concluded that accomplishing service recovery swiftly may decrease customers' negative feelings. For example, Valenzuela and Cooskey (2012) highlighted that customer complaints about handling time and their service failure recovery time had a big impact on service delivery. Hyatt Hotels was given an award in 2016 for its efficiency in responding to and resolving complaints. Hyatt Hotels continually enhances its customer portfolio by responding to complaints made on Twitter within an eight-minute timeframe (Shortyawards, 2016). Disney managers follow a method that includes five steps in order to recover service failures. This method is composed of a range of steps: hear (listening to customers carefully), empathize (employees imagining themselves in a

Fig. 12.5. Post-complaint behaviour model. (From Davidow, 2000.)

A. Dalgic *et al.*

customer's situation), apologize (apologizing for service failures), resolve (providing service compensation as soon as possible) and diagnose (faultlessly carrying out service compensation) (Jones, 2013).

Justice theory posits that employees must respond efficiently to service recovery (Mattila and Ro, 2008; Fig. 12.6). Justice theory is concerned with whether a situation, behaviour or decision is fair with regard to individuals (Ha and Jang, 2009, p. 319). It comprises three dimensions: distributive justice, procedural justice and interactional justice (Wirtz and Mattila, 2004, p. 151). Distributive justice can be defined as justice perceived in outputs at the end of the service recovery process by the customers (e.g. offering free beverages due to slow service in a restaurant). Procedural justice can be defined as justice perceived during the course of service failure recovery (quick service of food to the customer by the employee); interactional justice can be defined as justice emerging from service providers' behaviours against the customers (service provider employee's respectful behaviour; being sensitive to customers) (Sparks and McColl-Kennedy, 2001, p. 211; McColl-Kennedy and Sparks, 2003, p. 253). Distributive justice embodies situations such as discounts, coupons, free gifts and apologizing. Procedural justice includes process control, timing/speed, flexibility and accessibility. Finally, interactional justice incorporates components such as honesty, empathy and kindness (Tax *et al.*, 1998, p. 63).

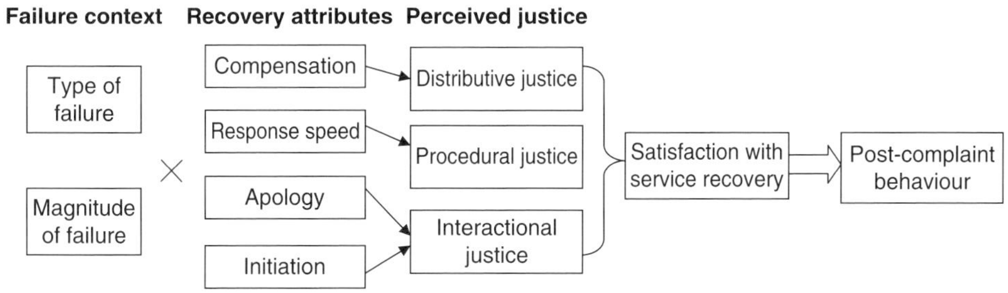

Fig. 12.6. Perceived justice on service recovery. (From Mattila and Ro, 2008.)

How Disney leaders recover from a service failure

As a consumer, sometimes the most frustrating aspect of a service failure isn't the problem, but rather the organization's inability to fix the problem. But even when service is built into your organization's foundational thinking, the reality is that the best-designed service processes will sometimes fail. This is an opportunity for organizations to strengthen their relationship with the customer. When service failure occurs, emotions become heightened – customers will likely care as much or more about how they are treated as they do about the outcome itself. This is why you must see the person, not just the issue. At Disney, we recognize that a service failure may not always be our fault, but it is our problem. For that reason, Disney Institute recommends using the following method as a means of providing consistent service recovery:

Hear: And more specifically, listen. Give the customer the opportunity to tell their complete, uninterrupted story.

Continued

Continued.

Empathize: Empathy creates an emotional connection, a trust that is crucial to demonstrating an authentic willingness and ability to help the customer. Consider using phrases like 'If I were in your shoes...' and 'Your reactions are completely normal...' to validate the customer's feelings.

Apologize: Sometimes, this is all the customer is looking for. The power of a sincere apology should never be underestimated. You must take ownership and remember, the manner in which you apologize matters greatly – apologies cannot be scripted.

Resolve: Speed is critical to recovery and is best achieved when the maximum amount of authority possible is delegated to employees.

Diagnose: Seek perfection, settle for excellence. Remove any personal guilt and examine the processes related to the service failure. Returning customers will appreciate your efforts to improve the experience.

The next time your customer experiences a service failure, make sure you hear, empathize, apologize, resolve and diagnose.

Source: Jones (2013).

12.6 Conclusions

This chapter stressed the importance of employee empowerment and internal communication within the context of service recovery. Waiting time and speed of service recovery, which are critical for both businesses and customers, were also discussed. Employees become more competent through training and gain authority and autonomy as a result of employee empowerment (Gazzoli *et al.*, 2012). Thus, service failures can be minimized or recovery strategies can be applied quickly after service failures (Thomas and Velthouse, 1990). Another important point is the effective use of internal communication. Many service failures can be prevented and service recoveries can be applied through effective internal communication (Michel *et al.*, 2009). Thus, effects such as decrease in work stress, increase in business satisfaction and decrease of burnout syndrome may occur (Koc, 2015). Additionally, increase in customer satisfaction, intention to repurchase and positive word-of-mouth are among the possible outcomes (Boshoff and Allen, 2000; Liao, 2007; Swanson and Hsu, 2011).

Waiting time, which can be perceived as an important facet of service failure, may require service recovery. Feelings of boredom, annoyance, frustration and irritation associated with waiting time may seriously endanger customer satisfaction (Butcher and Heffernan, 2006). An equally important point is the speed of service recovery. Justice theory highlights service recovery as a vital part of its procedural justice dimension (Sparks and McColl-Kennedy, 2001). An increase in customer satisfaction, intention to repurchase and positive word-of-mouth will be accomplished if waiting time is perceived as lower than expected by the customers and service recovery is performed swiftly (Boshoff and Allen, 2000; Liao, 2007; Swanson and Hsu, 2011). Combining these elements and articulating them into the service strategies of a firm seem to be crucial for a business to remain competitive in today's highly globalized business world.

A. Dalgic *et al.*

Questions

1. Why is employee empowerment important in service recovery?
2. Why is the speed of service recovery important? What are the consequences if service recovery is late?
3. Explain Maister's theory in terms of waiting time.
4. What is internal communication and the relationship between internal communication and service recovery?
5. Explain Hocutt and Stone's model in terms of service recovery.
6. What kinds of practices can be made to reduce the waiting time and the perceived waiting time in a service business?

Further Reading

Carson, P.P., Carson, K.D., Eden, W. and Roe, C.W. (1998) Does empowerment translate into action? An examination of service recovery initiatives. *Journal of Quality Management* 3, 133–148.

Hocutt, M.A. and Stone, T.H. (1998) The impact of employee empowerment on the quality of a service recovery effort. *Journal of Quality Management* 3, 117–132.

Melton, H.L. and Hartline, M.D. (2010) Customer and frontline employee influence on new service development performance. *Journal of Service Research* 13, 411–425.

References

Argenti, P.A. (2009) *Strategic Corporate Communication: A Global Approach For Doing Business in the New India*. McGraw-Hill, New York.

Ashill, N.J., Carruthers, J. and Krisjanous, J. (2005) Antecedents and outcomes of service recovery performance in a public health-care environment. *Journal of Services Marketing* 19, 293–308.

Boshoff, C. (1999) RECOVSAT: an instrument to measure satisfaction with transaction-specific service recovery. *Journal of Service Research* 1, 236–249.

Boshoff, C. and Allen, J. (2000) The influence of selected antecedents on frontline staff's perceptions of service recovery performance. *International Journal of Service Industry Management* 11, 63–90.

Boshoff, C. and Staude, G. (2003) Satisfaction with service recovery: its measurement and its outcomes. *South African Journal of Business Management* 34, 9–16.

Butcher, K. and Heffernan, T. (2006) Social regard: a link between waiting for service and service outcomes. *International Journal of Hospitality Management* 25, 34–53.

Carson, P.P., Carson, K.D., Eden, W. and Roe, C.W. (1998) Does empowerment translate into action? An examination of service recovery initiatives. *Journal of Quality Management* 3, 133–148.

Chebat, J.C. and Slusarczyk, W. (2005) How emotions mediate the effects of perceived justice on loyalty in service recovery situations: an empirical study. *Journal of Business Research* 58, 664–673.

Conger, J.A. and Kanungo, R.N. (1988) The empowerment process: integrating theory and practice. *Academy of Management Review* 13, 471–482.

Conlon, D.E. and Murray, N.M. (1996) Customer perceptions of corporate responses to product complaints: the role of explanations. *Academy of Management Journal* 39, 1040–1056.

Davidow, M. (2000) The bottom line impact of organizational responses to customer complaints. *Journal of Hospitality & Tourism Research* 24, 473–490.

Davidow, M. (2003) Organizational responses to customer complaints: what works and what doesn't. *Journal of Service Research* 5, 225–250.

Gazzoli, G., Hancer, M. and Park, Y. (2012) Employee empowerment and customer orientation: effects on workers' attitudes in restaurant organizations. *International Journal of Hospitality & Tourism Administration* 13, 1–25.

Gong, T., Yi, Y. and Choi, J.N. (2014) helping employees deal with dysfunctional customers: the underlying employee perceived justice mechanism. *Journal of Service Research* 17, 102–116.

Groth, M. and Gilliland, S.W. (2001) The role of procedural justice in the delivery of services: a study of customers' reactions to waiting. *Journal of Quality Management* 6, 77–97.

Ha, J. and Jang, S.S. (2009) Perceived justice in service recovery and behavioral intentions: the role of relationship quality. *International Journal of Hospitality Management* 28, 319–327.

Hall, T. (2016) The importance of communication during a business interruption. Available at: https://www.wolfandco.com/insight/importance-communication-during-business-interruption (accessed 10 October 2016).

Hocutt, M.A. and Stone, T.H. (1998) The impact of employee empowerment on the quality of a service recovery effort. *Journal of Quality Management* 3, 117–132.

Houston, M.B., Bettencourt, L.A. and Wenger, S. (1998) The relationship between waiting in a service queue and evaluations of service quality: a field theory perspective. *Psychology & Marketing* 15, 735–753.

Hui, M.K., Thakor, M.V. and Gill, R. (1998) The effect of delay type and service stage on consumers' reactions to waiting. *Journal of Consumer Research* 24, 469–479.

Hwang, J. and Lambert, C.U. (2006) Customers' identification of acceptable waiting times in a multi-stage restaurant system. *Journal of Foodservice Business Research* 8, 3–16.

Jones, B. (2013) How Disney leaders recover from a service failure. Available at: https://disneyinstitute.com/blog/2013/08/how-disney-leaders-recover-from-a-service-failure/187/ (accessed 10 October 2016).

Jones, B. (2015) Customer service 101: three tips for empowering speedy service recovery. Available at: https://disneyinstitute.com/blog/2015/08/customer-service-101-three-tips-for-empowering-speedy-service-recovery/369/ (accessed 10 October 2016).

Kalla, H.K. (2005) Integrated internal communications: a multidisciplinary perspective. *Corporate Communications: An International Journal* 10, 302–314.

Koc, E. (2007) Assessing all-inclusive pricing from the perspective of the main stakeholders in the Turkish tourism industry. *Advances in Culture, Tourism & Hospitality Research* 1, 273–288.

Koc, E. (2013) Power distance and its implications for upward communication and empowerment: crisis management and recovery in hospitality services. The *International Journal of Human Resource Management* 24, 3681–3696.

Koc, E. (2015) *Hizmet Pazarlaması ve Yönetimi. Global ve Yerel Yaklaşım*. Seçkin Yayınevi, Ankara, Turkey.

Komunda, M. and Osarenkhoe, A. (2012) Remedy or cure for service failure? Effects of service recovery on customer satisfaction and loyalty. *Business Process Management Journal* 18, 82–103.

Liao, H. (2007) Do it right this time: the role of employee service recovery performance in customer-perceived justice and customer loyalty after service failures. *Journal of Applied Psychology* 92, 475–489.

Lin, H.Y. and Chang, T.Y. (2011) The customer's perspective on waiting time in electronic marketing. *Social Behavior and Personality: An International Journal* 39, 1053–1062.

Lou, W., Liberatore, M.J., Nydick, R.L., Chung, Q.B. and Sloane, E. (2004) Impact of process change on customer perception of waiting time: a field study. *Omega. The International Journal of Management Science* 32, 77–83.

Maister, D.H. (1984) *The Psychology of Waiting Lines*. Harvard Business School, Boston, Massachusetts.

Mattila, A.S. and Ro, H. (2008) Customer satisfaction, service failure, and service recovery. In: Oh, H. (ed.) *Handbook of Hospitality Marketing Management*. Elsevier, Amsterdam, pp. 297–323.

McColl-Kennedy, J.R. and Sparks, B.A. (2003) Application of fairness theory to service failures and service recovery. *Journal of Service Research* 5, 251–266.

Melton, H.L. and Hartline, M.D. (2010) Customer and frontline employee influence on new service development performance. *Journal of Service Research* 13, 411–425.

Michel, S., Bowen, D. and Johnston, R. (2009) Why service recovery fails: tensions among customer, employee, and process perspectives. *Journal of Service Management* 20, 253–273.

Nadiri, H. and Tanova, C. (2016) What factors influence employee service recovery performance and what are the consequences in health care? *Quality Management in Healthcare* 25, 162–175.

Nie, W. (2000) Waiting: integrating social and psychological perspectives in operations management. *Omega* 28, 611–629.

Shortyawards (2016) How Hyatt uses social customer service to better care for guests. Available at: http://shortyawards.com/8th/hyatt-best-in-class-social-customer-servcie (accessed 10 October 2016).

Sparks, B.A. and McColl-Kennedy, J.R. (2001) Justice strategy options for increased customer satisfaction in a services recovery setting. *Journal of Business Research* 54, 209–218.

Sparks, B.A., Bradley, G.L. and Callan, V.J. (1997) The impact of staff empowerment and communication style on customer evaluations: the special case of service failure. *Psychology & Marketing* 14, 475–493.

Swanson, S.R. and Hsu, M.K. (2011) The effect of recovery locus attributions and service failure severity on word-of-mouth and repurchase behaviors in the hospitality industry. *Journal of Hospitality & Tourism Research* 35, 511–529.

Swanson, S.R. and Kelley, S.W. (2001) Attributions and outcomes of the service recovery process. *Journal of Marketing Theory and Practice* 9, 50–65.

Tan, M.K. (2007) Antecedents and outcomes of employee empowerment: an empirical study of British managers. Doctoral dissertation, Cardiff University, Cardiff, UK.

Tax, S.S., Brown, S.W. and Chandrashekaran, M. (1998) Customer evaluations of service complaint experiences: implications for relationship marketing. *The Journal of Marketing* 62, 60–76.

Taylor, S. (1994) Waiting for service: the relationship between delays and evaluations of service. *The Journal of Marketing* 58, 56–69.

Taylor, S. and Fullerton, G. (2000) Waiting for service: perceptions management of the wait experience. In: Teresa A.S. and Iacobucci, D. (eds) *Handbook of Service Marketing and Management*. Sage, Thousand Oaks, California, pp. 171–189.

Thomas, K.W. and Velthouse, B.A. (1990) Cognitive elements of empowerment: an 'interpretive' model of intrinsic task motivation. *Academy of Management Review* 15, 666–681.

Toporek, A. (2012) The Ritz-Carlton's famous $2,000 rule. Available at: http://customersthatstick.com/blog/customer-loyalty/the-ritz-carltons-famous-2000-rule/ (accessed 10 October 2016).

Tuttle, B. (2014) McDonald's guarantees one-minute drive-thru service or you get free food. Available at: http://time.com/money/3082429/mcdonalds-drive-thru-guarantee-minute-free-food/ (accessed 10 October 2016).

Valenzuela, F.R. and Cooskey, R. (2012) Customer perception of time and complaint outcome during the service recovery process. *International Review of Business Research Papers* 8, 1–19.

Van Vaerenbergh, Y., Larivière, B. and Vermeir, I. (2012) The impact of process recovery communication on customer satisfaction, repurchase intentions, and word-of-mouth intentions. *Journal of Service Research* 15, 262–279.

Weiner, B. (1985) An attributional theory of achievement motivation and emotion. *Psychological Review* 92, 548–573.

Wirtz, J. and Mattila, A.S. (2004) Consumer responses to compensation, speed of recovery and apology after a service failure. *International Journal of Service Industry Management* 15, 150–166.

Yavas, U., Karatepe, O.M., Avci, T. and Tekinkus, M. (2003) Antecedents and outcomes of service recovery performance: an empirical study of frontline employees in Turkish banks. *International Journal of Bank Marketing* 21, 255–265.

Yavas, U., Karatepe, O.M. and Babakus, E. (2010) Relative efficacy of organizational support and personality traits in predicting service recovery and job performances: a study of frontline employees in Turkey. *Tourism Review* 65, 70–83.

Yoo, J.J.E., Shin, S.Y. and Yang, I.S. (2006) Key attributes of internal service recovery strategies as perceived by frontline food service employees. *International Journal of Hospitality Management* 25, 496–509.

A. Dalgic *et al.*

13 Cross-Cultural Aspects of Service Failures and Recovery

ERDOGAN KOC

Learning Objectives

After reading this chapter, you should be able to:

- Understand the implications of inseparability from the perspective of social exchange and interaction.
- Understand the importance of social interactions and exchange from the perspective of service encounters.
- Explain the influence of culture on service encounters, service failures and recovery.
- Explain the main dimensions of culture and their influence on service encounters, service failures and recovery.
- Understand the role of intercultural sensitivity on service encounters, service failures and recovery.

13.1   Introduction: Social Interaction and Exchange in Services

The inseparability of services implies that the production and consumption of services take place at the same time, i.e. with the participation of both customers and service personnel. Although certain preparations can be made beforehand, in most service situations the customers and service providers need to engage in an interaction or exchange for the service performance to take place. Hence, these service encounters can be viewed as social interactions and exchanges (Barker and Härtel, 2004; Scott *et al.*, 2008; Gruber *et al.*, 2009; Koc, 2010; Koc and Bozkurt, 2017).

As mentioned in Chapter 1 (this volume), tourism and hospitality services often require constant and intense interactions between customers and service personnel, so they are usually referred to as *people businesses* (Kim *et al.*, 2007; Dolnicar *et al.*, 2011; Koc, 2013). The quality of these social interactions is extremely important because customers usually base their service quality evaluations on these interactions and exchanges alone (Koc, 2006; Prayag and Ryan, 2012; Rauch *et al.*, 2015) and make their various decisions based on these evaluations, such as whether to continue with the same service provider or not. According to research, customers' perceptions of service interactions significantly influence their satisfaction and service quality evaluations (Kim *et al.*, 2010). Moreover, depending on the quality of social interactions, service personnel in tourism and hospitality establishments can be used as a significant marketing communications tool (Koc, 2003).

Based on the social interaction experience during the service encounters, the tourism and hospitality customers may or may not wish to continue their relationship with the same tourism and hospitality business. As explained in Chapter 1 (this volume), while 14% of the causes of customer switching may be attributed to products (tangible products and services), i.e. aspects of technical quality, 67% may be attributed to dissatisfaction with social exchanges between the customer and service personnel (Doyle, 2008), i.e. functional aspects of quality. Perhaps for this reason, many service quality elements in service quality models (as in SERVQUAL or SERVPERF) are based on relational aspects or social interactions that take place between the customer and service personnel.

According to research, in a limited number of instances, certain customers may not switch even after they have encountered service failures (Jones *et al.*, 2007; Nagengast *et al.*, 2014; Koc, 2017), because of:

1. Procedural costs (i.e. the time and effort required for searching for, finding and adapting to the new service provider) (Bloch *et al.*, 1986).
2. Loss of privileges (i.e. benefits, privileges and advantages in the form of special discounts, collected points, etc., which are lost when the customer switches service providers).
3. Social costs (i.e. the loss of personal social relationships developed with the service personnel) (Burnham *et al.*, 2003; Jones *et al.*, 2007; Nagengast *et al.*, 2014; Koc, 2017).

Jones *et al.* (2007) showed that customers who did not switch because of the first two costs (i.e. procedural costs and loss of privileges) did not tend to develop affective commitment since they stayed because they had to, and tended to engage in negative word-of-mouth communication about the service provider. However, customers who did not switch because of social costs were the customers who had affective commitment and did not tend to engage in negative word-of-mouth communication about the service provider. This is because these customers preferred to stay with the same service provider. Arising from this ability to choose or prefer, or the feeling of control (or illusion of control) (Koc, 2016), positive social relationships based on social interactions with service providers may be conducive to reducing dissatisfaction and the intention to complain and switch service providers (Goodwin and Verhage, 1989; Coulter and Ligas, 2000; Koc, 2017).

13.2 Culture and Social Interactions

Culture can be defined as all the patterns of thinking, feeling and behaviour shared by the members of a society (Schwartz, 1997). As culture shapes people's thoughts, feelings and behaviour (Mosquera *et al.*, 2011), social interactions and exchanges taking place between service personnel and customers can be strongly influenced by the culture of service personnel and customers. Moreover, customers' evaluations of service encounters in international service settings are influenced by their perceptions of the service failure and recovery, which are strongly influenced by their cultural orientations (Wong, 2004).

Research shows that cultural values and norms influence service quality expectations of customers (Donthu and Yoo, 1998; Koc, 2013). This is because culture influences the ways people react and engage in both social and business interactions (Zhao and Lin, 2014; Hofstede, 2015; Budhwar *et al.*, 2016). As tourism and hospitality activities are increasingly becoming international in nature (Mihalič and Fennell, 2015), a better understanding of culture in tourism and hospitality is of paramount importance. In 2015 about 1.2 billion international tourists engaged in international tourism, resulting in revenue generation of about US$1.5 trillion (World Tourism Organization, 2015).

Norms and codes

In Europe, particularly in the UK, when a guest in a hotel or a restaurant finishes eating, s/he is expected to place his knife and fork side by side on the right side of the plate in the 4 o'clock position. A guest from outside of Europe not knowing this norm may not place her/his knife and fork accordingly after finishing her/his starter and may wait unnecessarily for the main course to be served. As a result the guest may get angry and think that the service personnel are not responsive.

13.3 The Relationship Between Cultural Dimensions and Service Encounters

Studies on services in general, and tourism and hospitality research in particular, have so far concentrated on Hofstede's (1984) cultural dimensions of power distance, risk aversion, individualism–collectivism and femininity–masculinity. The literature shows that studies have investigated topics as diverse as the influence of cultural dimensions on the perceptions and service quality expectations of customers (Li *et al.*, 2011; Pookulangara and Koesler, 2011), perception and evaluations of the nature of service encounters (Sizoo, 2007, 2008; Koc, 2010; Montoya and Briggs, 2013; Park *et al.*, 2014; Sharma *et al.*, 2015), the strength and nature of relationships with customers (Gopalan and Narayan, 2010; Kokkranikal *et al.*, 2011) and the referral of customers based on their evaluations of service encounters (Patterson *et al.*, 2006; Luoh and Tsaur, 2007).

Table 13.1 explains Hofstede's (1984) cultural dimensions in general terms. However, interpretations of the dimensions of culture are not simple because a specific culture may have different scores in all cultural dimensions. Moreover, there may be other factors outside these cultural dimensions (e.g. personality, education, income, etc.) that may influence how people think and react in various contexts.

As the explanations in Table 13.1 are general, there is a need to analyse the literature for research findings demonstrating the implications of these dimensions. The analysis of cultural dimensions from the perspective of service failures and recovery in tourism and hospitality has important implications for almost all business functions, ranging from human resource management to marketing.

Activity

Identify five countries whose culture you may be interested in. Then visit Hofstede's web page (https://geert-hofstede.com/countries.html) and compare countries' cultural dimension scores.

Table 13.1. Cultural dimensions. (From Author.)

Cultural dimension	Explanation	Examples of cultures/countries
Power distance	The extent to which members of a society accept that power is distributed unequally in the society.	High in power distance: France, Mexico, Hong Kong and Turkey. Low in power distance: the USA, Sweden and Austria.
Individualism and collectivism	While people in individualistic cultures tend to place more importance on the welfare and interests of the individuals, in collectivist societies people tend to place more importance on the interests and welfare of the society as a whole.	High individualism: the USA, the UK, Sweden, Italy and the Netherlands. Low individualism (i.e. high in collectivism): Venezuela, China, Singapore, Japan, Taiwan and South Korea.
Risk aversion/uncertainty avoidance	The degree to which members of a society feel uncomfortable with uncertainty and avoid risk.	High in risk aversion: Japan, Turkey, Poland, Portugal, Spain and Uruguay. Low in risk aversion: Jamaica, Singapore, Denmark and Sweden.
Masculinity and femininity	Masculine societies tend to display a preference for achievement, assertiveness and material success and display a strong belief in gender roles. Feminine societies place more emphasis on the quality of life, welfare of others, care for others and equality, more especially between sexes.	High in masculinity: Japan, Hungary, Italy, Switzerland and the USA. Low in masculinity: Sweden, Norway, the Netherlands, Finland and Denmark.

E. Koc

13.3.1 Research findings relating to power distance

Customers from a larger power distance culture are more likely to perceive unsatisfactory goods and services as a fact of life and are less likely to complain when they encounter service failures (Au *et al.*, 2010). In general, customers from low power distance cultures may expect a higher performance in SERVQUAL dimensions of reliability and responsiveness (Donthu and Yoo, 1998). Furrer *et al.* (2000) showed that customers from high power distance cultures did not place much importance on reliability and responsiveness.

In high power distance cultures, customers tend to place more importance on the status of the employee in the service business, e.g. the status of an employee apologizing after a service failure, as people in these cultures do not value equality as much as people in low power distance cultures. On the other hand, customers from low power distance cultures do not tend to pay much attention to the status of the personnel apologizing after a service failure (Patterson *et al.*, 2006). This means that when offering an apology to a customer from a high power distance culture, the customers may appreciate it if that apology comes from a high-status employee, e.g. a manager, rather than a lower ranking member of staff such as a receptionist or a waiter (Patterson *et al.*, 2006; Koc, 2016).

Moreover, customers from high power distance cultures may have higher expectations than customers who are from low power distance cultures. For instance, due to their high level of expectations, Turkish domestic tourists tend to be less satisfied with their holidays than tourists from the Netherlands, the UK and Denmark, i.e. customers from low power distance cultures, who stay at the same holiday establishment (Koc, 2017).

In terms of service personnel, employees in a high power distance culture may be more likely to resort to avoiding and accommodating strategies in situations of conflict (Koc, 2010), causing a delay in the diagnosing and handling of conflicts among service personnel. Power distance also influences the way service personnel behave and interact with their peers, subordinates and superiors. For instance, Koc's (2013) study on service failures and recovery found that hospitality employees in the UK, a country with a relatively low power distance score, responded to the same service failure scenarios more quickly and directly than the hospitality employees in Turkey, a country with a relatively high power distance score. While Turkish employees used mitigated speech in communicating the problem to their superiors, employees in the UK used a more direct approach when communicating the problem to their superiors.

Heung and Lam's (2003) research showed that Chinese customers (i.e. people from a high power distance culture) tended to adopt an unassertive style of communication approach when encountering failures. When a failure is recovered, Chinese customers are more likely to end up being silent and avoiding further friction.

13.3.2 Research findings relating to individualism and collectivism

Customers from individualistic cultures are more likely to demand more efficient, prompt and error-free service than customers from collectivist cultures (Furrer *et al.*, 2000). Additionally, customers from individualistic cultures are also more likely to expect service personnel to show more respect, care, attention and empathy, and personalized treatment, than customers from collectivist cultures (Donthu and Yoo, 1998; Au *et al.*, 2010). On the other hand, customers from collectivist cultures value consistency more than individual attention and personalized treatment.

Moreover, customers from an individualistic culture are more likely to complain to the service business itself or to a third party than customers who are from a collectivist society. On the other hand, customers from a collectivist culture tend to warn friends and relatives after experiencing service failures (Blodgett *et al.*, 2008). As people in collectivist cultures value harmony more and tend to avoid confrontation, customers from collectivist cultures tend to express their dissatisfaction to friends and relatives rather than making formal complaints to the tourism and hospitality establishment (Akkawanitcha *et al.*, 2015). For this reason the establishment and operation of customer feedback and complaint systems for tourism and hospitality establishments serving customers from collectivist cultures are significantly more important. In Chapter 1 (this volume), it was stated that 96% of all dissatisfied customers switched to other providers without making a complaint (TARP, 2007). This may mean that switching to other service providers may be higher among customers from collectivist cultures. It must also be kept in mind that in collectivist cultures the role of word-of-mouth communication in customer retention is significantly higher (Wong, 2004; Kong and Jogaratnam, 2007).

Additionally, people from individualistic cultures are more likely to make a fundamental attribution error than people from collectivistic cultures in the event of a service failure. In general, while people from individualistic cultures tend to attribute a person's behaviour to his internal factors, e.g. dispositional factors, people from collectivistic cultures tend to attribute a person's behaviour to his external factors, e.g. situational factors (Choi *et al.*, 2003; Um and Lee, 2014). According to research (Choi *et al.*, 2003; Um and Lee, 2014), people from individualistic cultures are more likely to engage in self-serving bias than people from collectivistic cultures (Yuksel *et al.*, 2006). On the other hand, people from collectivist cultures tend to engage in self-effacing bias. Self-effacing bias is the opposite of self-serving bias and it causes an individual to attribute success to external factors and blame failure on internal factors, i.e. to herself/himself (Choi *et al.*, 1993, 2003; Um and Lee, 2014). For instance, the Japanese culture is characterized as a traditionally humble culture, so people from Japan are more likely to attribute success to external factors and failure to internal factors (Bergiel *et al.*, 2012).

13.3.3 Research findings relating to risk aversion

As mentioned above, the consumption of hospitality services involves a high level of uncertainty and risk (Namasivayam and Hinkin, 2003). The heavy reliance on human service providers and near impossibility of quality inspections prior to consumption (Zeithaml *et al.*, 1990; Chan *et al.*, 2007) make hospitality services inherently variable (Chan *et al.*, 2007).

In risk-averse cultures, customers may place more value on control offered by the service business (Patterson *et al.*, 2006; Koc, 2017) as a risk reduction strategy. Customers who feel in control usually appear to be happier, and when control is threatened they tend to attempt to reinstate it (Brehm, 1956; Langer, 1975; Chen *et al.*, 2017). All-inclusive holidays offer cognitive control and are purchased largely by risk-averse customers. Hence, offering control (whether cognitive, decisional and behavioural) may increase customers' involvement and participation in the purchasing and consumption of services, and hence they may respond more mildly to particular types of service failures (Koc, 2017). Table 13.2 shows how three types of control may be used by tourism and hospitality managers to develop strategies for reducing customers' perception of risk.

Furthermore, people from high risk-averse cultures tend to express their emotions more openly and tend to attach more importance to seeking safety and stability. On the other hand, people from less risk-averse cultures tend to be less emotional and more contemplating (Triandis *et al.*, 1995). It is also expected that a high level of uncertainty avoidance will have a strong influence on customers' repurchase intensions, regardless of the service recovery actions. For instance, no matter what the real cause of the service failure, people from risk-averse cultures may be more likely to attribute a significant proportion of blame to the service business (Patterson *et al.*, 2006; Koc, 2017).

Table 13.2. Types of control. (From the author.)

Type of control	Explanation	Strategies
Cognitive control	Predictability of future events, having sufficient information about future events and being free from negative surprises.	Providing customers with detailed information about the various aspects and components of service such as price. Offering standard packages with standard prices (as in all-inclusive holidays). Ensuring the standardization of services.
Decisional control	The ability to make free choices allows customers to have decisional control.	Allowing customers to design their service products. Offering customers sufficient choices. Allowing customers to make their choices freely.
Behavioural control	Enabling customers to cancel a transaction at any point in time without incurring any significant costs.	Offering customers opportunities to cancel their purchase with a refund.

13.3.4 Research findings relating to masculinity and femininity

Research shows that customers from highly masculine cultures are more likely to report dissatisfaction and complain when they encounter service failures (Crotts and Erdmann, 2002). As the role of men is distinct and different from that of women in masculine cultures, tangibles would be relatively more important than empathy in these cultures (Furrer *et al.*, 2000). In other words, while people from a masculine culture may value distributive justice more, people from a feminine culture may value interactional and procedural justice more. In cultures with a high degree of masculinity, the relative importance attached to each service quality dimension may be different because they are more likely to attach more value to the tangibles. Moreover, the role expectations of customers from a masculine culture may be different than the role expectations of customers from a feminine culture. For instance, customers from a masculine culture expect male service personnel to be professional, more reliable and more responsive than female service personnel. On the other hand, these customers may expect female service personnel to be more empathetic than male service personnel (Furrer *et al.*, 2000). Moreover, customers from a highly masculine culture tend to be more perfectionist and expect things to be more straightforward. This may result in more complaints to the service management as well as to third parties (Blodgett *et al.*, 2008).

13.4 Long-Term Orientation and Indulgence–Restraint Dimensions

The long-term orientation and indulgence–restraint dimensions are the least studied of Hofstede's dimensions. This is probably due to the fact that long-term orientation is frequently misunderstood (Newman and Nollen, 1996; Fang, 2003; Abubakar *et al.*, 2014). On the other hand, the indulgence–restraint dimension is relatively new and has not been researched extensively. Although it is relevant, there has been almost no research on the indulgence–restraint dimension in tourism and hospitality.

13.4.1 Long-term orientation

A review of the literature shows that long-term orientation is the least examined of Hofstede's culture dimensions. As stated above, this is probably due to the fact that it is frequently misunderstood (Newman and Nollen, 1996; Fang, 2003; Abubakar *et al.*, 2014). However, this dimension is significant from the viewpoint of social interactions and trust (Hofstede, 1983). Trust and relational bonds between people are promoted by long-term orientation through emphasis on social sanctions (Hofstede, 1983; Coelho and Henseler, 2012). Customers with long-term orientation and values are more likely to choose long-term relationships with tourism and hospitality businesses than a customer with short-term orientation and values (Patterson *et al.*, 2006; Kantsperger and Kunz, 2010; Narteh *et al.*, 2013).

In effect, a customer who has long-term orientation norms and values may be more likely to choose a long-term relationship with a tourism and hospitality service provider than a customer who has a short-term orientation culture (Hofstede, 1991; Patterson *et al.*, 2006; Kantsperger and Kunz, 2010; Narteh *et al.*, 2013). Most south-east Asian countries such as China, Hong Kong, Taiwan and South Korea score high on the long-term orientation due to their Confucian traditions, resulting in persistence, ordering relationships by status and observing this order. In short, while long-term orientation is about sustainability and long-term success, short-term orientation is about immediate gratification (Ayoun and Moreo, 2009). It is expected that in long-term-oriented cultures tourism and hospitality managers would concentrate more on sustainability and long-term well-being of the business. This may mean that in long-term-oriented countries tourism and hospitality businesses may be more likely to establish stronger service quality systems.

13.4.2 Indulgence and restraint dimension

The indulgence–restraint paradigm was added in 2010 to the original five dimensions of Hofstede. Minkov and Hofstede (2010) explain that indulgence is the tendency of people to satisfy their basic and natural desires freely and enjoy their lives. On the other hand, restraint is a conviction that basic and natural desires and enjoyment in life need to be controlled and regulated by strict social norms. Table 13.3 shows that a significant number of the characteristics of indulgence and restraint cultures (Minkov and Hofstede, 2010) may have implications for service failures and recovery.

The indulgence–restraint dimension was inspired by Inglehart's (2003) dimension of well-being versus survival (Minkov, 2007). According to Hofstede *et al.* (2010), the indulgence–restraint dimension explains why poor people in the Philippines are happier than rich people in Hong Kong. This means that people living in a poor country may have more positive attitudes, or be generally happier in life, than those living in a wealthier country.

Customers from restraint-oriented cultures (e.g. from Bulgaria, Russia, Poland, Portugal, and relatively from Turkey and Japan) tend to place less value on fun, leisure and other desires, and hedonic activities. As tourism and hospitality are primarily hedonic experiences, the dimension of indulgence and restraint may have significant implications for tourism and hospitality. Service encounters and interactions may be strongly influenced by the indulgence–restraint dimension because this dimension may influence the attitudes and behaviour of both service personnel and customers.

As customers from high-indulgence cultures (e.g. the USA, the UK, Canada, Switzerland and Austria) attach more importance to leisure, they may be expected to be more involved in their purchase and consumption activities of tourism and hospitality products/services. This may mean that tourism and hospitality customers from high indulgence cultures may engage in more extensive information collection and analysis processes. Hence, customers from indulgence cultures may be more astute in their holiday and leisure related decision-making and may have more, and more specific, expectations from the service business. This may mean that tourism products such as package

Table 13.3. Indulgence and restraint cultures. (From the author.)

Indulgence cultures	Restraint cultures
A perception of personal life control	A perception of helplessness
Higher importance of leisure and fun	Lower importance of leisure and fun
Higher importance of having friends	Lower importance of having friends
More likely to remember positive emotions	Less likely to remember positive emotions
Less moral discipline	Moral discipline
Positive attitude	Cynicism
More extroverted personalities	More neurotic personalities
Higher optimism	More pessimism

holidays or events and destinations targeting customers from cultures with high indulgence scores need to be better designed.

As customers from an indulgence-oriented culture collect and analyse more information regarding their holidays, they may be expected to be more interested in authenticity and the relevancy of the features of the touristic product or destination. Due to their high level of involvement, customers from a high-indulgence culture would be more knowledgeable about their holiday and leisure experiences. For instance, customers/tourists from an indulgence culture would know that an African safari would entail fewer luxuries and hence would develop their expectations accordingly, no matter how expensive that holiday may be. According to Koc (2016), Turkish domestic tourists tend to be less satisfied with their holidays than visitors from the Netherlands, the UK and Denmark who stay in the same holiday establishment: the indulgence figures for Turkey, the Netherlands, the UK and Denmark are 49, 68, 69 and 70, respectively.

Moreover, it could be argued that, because of the inability to understand and internalize fun and leisure activities (for instance, tourism and hospitality activities), service personnel in restraint cultures may lack the basic skills to display service-oriented behaviours. This in turn may be expected to result in more service failures and poorer recovery systems and recovery attempts. Additionally, it is also important that people from high-indulgence cultures are more likely to remember positive emotions and experiences, while customers from restraint cultures are more likely to remember negative experiences. This means that the indulgence–restraint orientation of customers may have significant implications in terms of their post-service evaluations.

Finally, from the supply-side perspective, as people from indulgence cultures tend to be more involved in leisure and pleasure activities, service employees in these cultures may be in a better position to understand and internalize customers' expectations and thus have a deeper understanding of their needs, wants and expectations. This may mean that people from indulgence cultures may be able to design tourism and hospitality products and services more efficiently and effectively than people from restraint cultures.

13.5 Intercultural Sensitivity

The explanations so far have shown that understanding other cultures is highly important from the perspective of service quality, service failures and recovery. Thus, the recruitment of service personnel who have the right knowledge and skills to interact with other cultures may reduce service failures and enable a more efficient and effective recovery of service failures.

Resembling emotional intelligence, described in Chapter 4 (this volume), intercultural sensitivity is an intercultural ability of noticing and experiencing cultural differences. People with this ability demonstrate sensitivity to the importance of cultural differences, and to the points of view of people from other cultures (Hammer *et al.*, 2003). Intercultural sensitivity of employees can be measured by using Chen and Starosta's (2000) Intercultural Sensitivity scale. This scale comprises five dimensions:

- intercultural interaction engagement;
- respect for cultural differences;

- intercultural interaction confidence;
- intercultural interaction enjoyment; and
- intercultural interaction attentiveness.

Interculturally sensitive employees tend to perform better than those who are interculturally insensitive (Sizoo, 2008). Research shows that interculturally sensitive employees are better at providing efficient service to international customers (Sizoo, 2008; Sharma *et al.*, 2015; Khan *et al.*, 2016; Stauss, 2016). This is because service personnel with higher intercultural sensitivity are able to adapt more rapidly and cope with customers who are from different cultures (Kriegl, 2000). Hence tourism and hospitality businesses may ensure functional quality and satisfy the needs of their international customers better by recruiting service personnel who have a higher level of intercultural sensitivity.

Additionally, service personnel with a high level of intercultural sensitivity are more likely to score significantly higher on many measures of service aspects, including interpersonal skills, service attentiveness, revenue contribution, job satisfaction and social satisfaction, because they relate to cross-cultural encounters (Sizoo, 2008).

It is important to note that intercultural sensitivity is a type of ability that can be taught, learned and improved (Ouellet, 2002; Bennett and Bennett, 2004). Previous research shows that participation in educational programmes in other countries (e.g. participating in student exchange programmes such as ERASMUS and work and travel programmes, or exposure to other cultures through international travelling and working abroad) can improve intercultural sensitivity (Anderson *et al.*, 2006; Patterson, 2006; Yashima, 2010; Salisbury, 2011; Stebleton *et al.*, 2013; Guo, 2015).

The emotions customers and service personnel develop during intercultural service encounters have their bases in role theory (Biddle, 1979, 1986), social identity theory (Tajfel and Turner, 1986) and the similarity-attraction model (Byrne, 1971). According to role theory, human beings tend to behave in ways that are often different and predictable, depending on their particular social identities and the nature of the particular situation they are in (Biddle, 1986). Although both role theory and script theory, explained in Chapter 3 (this volume), use the theatrical metaphor, role theory is more to do with a set of learned behaviour patterns used in social interactions (by customers and employees), while script theory is more to do with a service script specifying behaviour sequences of employees and customers during service encounters. In the theatre, the actors and actresses have their own individual roles/parts or scripts. In real-life situations, i.e. in business and social contexts, people have behavioural expectations of others in line with their roles (Biddle, 1986). Service failures may arise due to behaviours that do not comply with roles expected from service employees. For instance, after a service failure, a customer expects service personnel to be empathetic and take quick action to recover the failure.

Social identity theory may also be helpful in understanding intercultural service encounters, service failures and recovery. The theory proposes that the in-group will discriminate against the out-group to enhance their image and increase their gains (Tajfel *et al.*, 1971; Hopkins *et al.*, 2005). The categorization of people into an in-group may cause the individual to exaggerate the perceived differences among the groups and favour in-group members (people from the same culture) at the expense of out-group members (people from other cultures) (Tajfel *et al.*, 1971; Sharma *et al.*, 2012, 2015).

For instance, despite many problems associated with all-inclusive holidays, they result in fewer intercultural conflicts because the number and intensity of social interactions with locals are lower (Koc, 2007).

A final theory that may be associated with intercultural service interactions, service failure and recovery is the similarity-attraction theory (Byrne, 1971). According to this theory, people are more likely to be attracted to people who are similar to themselves (Byrne, 1971; Sharma *et al.*, 2012, 2015). As people generally perceive similar people as less threatening (Koc, 2016), they are more likely to be attracted to other people who are similar to themselves. For instance, during a service encounter, service employees may not respond as expected towards customers from other cultures and may avoid interaction with these customers.

13.6 Conclusion

This chapter has investigated the role and influence of culture in service encounters, service failure and recovery in tourism and hospitality settings. It has mainly concentrated on Hofstede's (2015) cultural dimensions and explained how each dimension may influence the perception and behaviour of both customers and service employees. In addition to Hofstede's dimensions, the dimensions and components suggested by scholars such as Hall (1959), Trompenaars (1993) and House *et al.* (2004) can also be used to understand service encounters in more depth. The chapter has also explained the theory of intercultural sensitivity and other relevant theories such as role theory, social identity theory and similarity-attraction theory, which may provide good insights into the understanding of service encounters, service failures and recovery.

Questions

1. Why are interaction and social exchange important in tourism and hospitality?
2. Why do certain customers not leave a service business even after they have experienced a service failure?
3. What is the role of culture in service encounters?
4. What are the main dimensions of culture and how may they relate to service encounters, service failures and recovery?
5. Explain the concept of intercultural sensitivity. Why would it be a good idea to recruit service personnel with a high level of intercultural sensitivity?

Further Reading

Barker, S. and Härtel, C.E. (2004) Intercultural service encounters: an exploratory study of customer experiences. *Cross Cultural Management: An International Journal* 11, 3–14.
Minkov, M. and Hofstede, G. (2010) The evolution of Hofstede's doctrine. *Cross Cultural Management: An International Journal* 18, 10–20.
Sharma, P., Tam, J.L.M. and Kim, N. (2012) Intercultural service encounters (ICSE): an extended framework and empirical validation. *Journal of Services Marketing* 26, 521–534.

E. Koc

Sharma, P., Tam, J.L. and Kim, N. (2015) Service role and outcome as moderators in intercultural service encounters. *Journal of Service Management* 26, 137–155.

Sizoo, S. (2008) Analysis of employee performance during cross-cultural service encounters at luxury hotels in Hawaii, London and Florida. *Asia Pacific Journal of Tourism Research* 13, 113–128.

References

Abubakar, M.M., Mokhtar, S.S.M. and Abdullateef, A.O. (2014) The role of long-term orientation and service recovery on the relationships between trust, bonding, customer satisfaction and customer loyalty: the case of Nigerian retail banks. *Asian Social Science* 10, 209–220.

Akkawanitcha, C., Patterson, P., Buranapin, S. and Kantabutra, S. (2015) Frontline employees' cognitive appraisals and well-being in the face of customer aggression in an Eastern, collectivist culture. *Journal of Services Marketing* 29, 268–279.

Anderson, P.H., Lawton, L., Rexeisen, R.J. and Hubbard, A.C. (2006) Short-term study abroad and intercultural sensitivity: a pilot study. *International Journal of Intercultural Relations* 30, 457–469.

Au, N., Law, R. and Buhalis, D. (2010) The impact of culture on ecomplaints: evidence from Chinese consumers in hospitality organisations. In: Gretzel, U., Law, R. and Fuchs, M. (eds) *Information and Communication Technologies in Tourism*. Springer, Vienna, pp. 285–296.

Ayoun, B. and Moreo, P. (2009) Impact of time orientation on the strategic behavior of Thai and American hotel managers. *Journal of Hospitality Marketing & Management* 18, 676–691.

Barker, S. and Härtel, C.E. (2004) Intercultural service encounters: an exploratory study of customer experiences. *Cross Cultural Management: An International Journal* 11, 3–14.

Bergiel, E.B., Bergiel, B.J. and Upson, J. (2012) Revisiting Hofstede's dimensions: examining cultural convergence of the United States and Japan. *American Journal of Management* 12, 69–79.

Bennett, J.M. and Bennett, M.J. (2004) Developing intercultural sensitivity: an integrative approach to global and domestic diversity. In: Landis, D., Bennett, J. and Bennett, M. (eds) *Handbook of Intercultural Training*, 3rd edn. Sage, Thousand Oaks, California, pp. 147–165.

Biddle, B.J. (1979) *Role Theory: Expectation, Identities, and Behaviors*. Academic Press, New York.

Biddle, B.J. (1986) Recent developments in role theory. *Annual Review of Sociology* 12, 67–92.

Bloch, H.P., Sherrell, D.L. and Ridgway, N.M. (1986) Consumer search: an extended framework. *Journal of Consumer Research* 13, 119–126.

Blodgett, J.G., Bakir, A. and Rose, G.M. (2008) A test of the validity of Hofstede's cultural framework. *Journal of Consumer Marketing* 25, 339–349.

Brehm, J. (1956) Post-decision changes in the desirability of alternatives. *Journal of Abnormal and Social Psychology* 52, 384–389.

Budhwar, P.S., Varma, A. and Patel, C. (2016) Convergence-divergence of HRM in the Asia-Pacific: context-specific analysis and future research agenda. *Human Resource Management Review* 26, 311–326.

Burnham, T.A., Frels, J.K. and Mahajan, V. (2003) Consumer switching costs: a typology, antecedents, and consequences. *Journal of the Academy of Marketing Science* 31, 109–126.

Byrne, D.E. (1971) *The Attraction Paradigm*. Academic Press, New York.

Chan, H., Wan, L.C. and Sin, L.Y. (2007) Hospitality service failures: who will be more dissatisfied? *International Journal of Hospitality Management* 26, 531–545.

Chen, G.M. and Starosta, W.J. (2000) Intercultural sensitivity. In: Samovar, L.A. and Porter, R.E. (eds) *Intercultural Communication: A Reader*. Wadsworth, Belmont, California, pp. 406–413.

Chen, C.Y., Lee, L. and Yap, A.J. (2017) Control deprivation motivates acquisition of utilitarian products. *Journal of Consumer Research* 43, 1031–1047.

Choi, I., Dalal, R., Kim-Prieto, C. and Park, H. (2003) Culture and judgment of causal relevance. *Journal of Personality and Social Psychology* 84, 46–59.

Choi, S.C., Kim, U. and Choi, S.H. (1993) Indigenous analysis of collective representations: a Korean perspective. In: Kim, U. and Berry, J.W. (eds) *Indigenous Psychologies: Research and Experience in Cultural Context*. Sage, Newbury Park, California, pp. 193–210.

Coelho, P.S. and Henseler, J. (2012) Creating customer loyalty through service customization. *European Journal of Marketing* 46, 331–356.

Coulter, R. and Ligas, M. (2000) The long good-bye: the dissolution of customer service provider relationships. *Psychology and Marketing* 17, 669–695.

Crotts, J. and Erdmann, R. (2002) Does national culture influence consumers' evaluation of travel services? A test of Hofstede's model of cross-cultural differences. *Managing Service Quality* 10, 410–419.

Dolnicar, S., Grabler, K., Grün, B. and Kulnig, A. (2011) Key drivers of airline loyalty. *Tourism Management* 32, 1020–1026.

Donthu, N. and Yoo, B. (1998) Cultural influences on service quality expectations. *Journal of Service Research* 1, 178–186.

Doyle, P. (2008) *Value-Based Marketing. Marketing Strategies for Corporate Growth and Shareholder Value*, 2nd edn. John Wiley & Sons, Chichester, UK.

Fang, T. (2003) A critique of Hofstede's fifth national culture dimension. *International Journal of Cross Cultural Management* 3, 347–368.

Furrer, O., Liu, B.S.C. and Sudharshan, D. (2000) The relationships between culture and service quality perceptions: basis for crosscultural market segmentation and resource allocation. *Journal of Service Research* 2, 355–371.

Goodwin, C. and Verhage, B. (1989) Role perceptions of services: a cross-cultural comparison with behavioural implications. *Journal of Economic Psychology* 10, 543–558.

Gopalan, R. and Narayan, B. (2010) Improving customer experience in tourism: a framework for stakeholder collaboration. *Socio-Economic Planning Sciences* 44, 100–112.

Gruber, T., Szmigin, I. and Voss, R. (2009) Handling customer complaints effectively: a comparison of the value maps of female and male complainants. *Managing Service Quality* 19, 636–656.

Guo, L.H. (2015) Intercultural communicative competence, language proficiency, and study abroad. *International Journal of Research Studies in Education* 4, 57–67.

Hall, E.T. (1959) *The Silent Language*, Vol. 3. Doubleday. New York.

Hammer, M.R., Bennett, M.J. and Wiseman, R. (2003) Measuring intercultural sensitivity: the intercultural development inventory. *International Journal of Intercultural Relations* 27, 421–443.

Heung, V.C.S. and Lam, T. (2003) Customer complaint behaviour towards hotel restaurant services. *International Journal of Contemporary Hospitality Management* 15, 285–289.

Hofstede, G. (1983) The cultural relativity of organizational practices and theories. *Journal of International Business Studies* 14, 75–89.

Hofstede, G. (1984) Cultural dimensions in management and planning. *Asia Pacific Journal of Management* 1, 81–99.

Hofstede, G. (1991) *Cultures and Organizations – Software of the Mind*. McGraw-Hill, New York.

Hofstede, G.J. (2015) Culture's causes: the next challenge. *Cross Cultural Management: An International Journal* 22, 545–569.

Hofstede, G., Hofstede, G.J. and Minkov, M. (2010) *Cultures and Organizations: Software of the Mind: Intercultural Cooperation and its Importance for Survival*. McGraw-Hill, New York.

Hopkins, S.A., Hopkins, W.E. and Hoffman, K.D. (2005) Domestic inter-cultural service encounters: an integrated model. *Managing Service Quality: An International Journal* 15, 329–343.

House, R.J., Hanges, P.J., Javidan, M., Dorfman, P.W. and Gupta, V. (eds) (2004) *Culture, Leadership, and Organizations*. Sage, Thousand Oaks, California.

Inglehart, R. (2003) *Human Values and Social Change: Findings from the Values Surveys*. Brill, Leiden, The Netherlands.

Jones, M.A., Reynolds, K.E., Mothersbaugh, D.L. and Beatty, S.E. (2007) The positive and negative effects of switching costs on relational outcomes. *Journal of Service Research* 9, 335–355.

Kantsperger, R. and Kunz, W.H. (2010) Consumer trust in service companies: a multiple mediating analysis. *Managing Service Quality* 20, 4–25.

Khan, M., Ro, H., Gregory, A.M. and Hara, T. (2016) Gender dynamics from an Arab perspective: intercultural service encounters. *Cornell Hospitality Quarterly* 57, 51–65.

Kim, H.J., Shin, K.H. and Umbreit, W.T. (2007) Hotel job burnout: the role of personality characteristics. *International Journal of Hospitality Management* 26, 421–434.

Kim, M.G., Wang, C. and Mattila, A.S. (2010) The relationship between consumer complaining behavior and service recovery: an integrative review. *International Journal of Contemporary Hospitality Management* 22, 975–991.

Koc, E. (2003) The role and potential of travel agency staff as a marketing communications tool. *Tourism Analysis* 8, 105–111.

Koc, E. (2006) Total quality management and business excellence in services: the implications of all-inclusive pricing system on internal and external customer satisfaction in the Turkish tourism market. *Total Quality Management & Business Excellence* 17, 857–877.

Koc, E. (2007) Assessing all-inclusive pricing from the perspective of the main stakeholders in the Turkish tourism industry. In: Woodside, A.G. (ed.) *Advances in Culture, Tourism & Hospitality Research*, vol. 1. Elsevier, Amsterdam, pp. 273–288.

Koc, E. (2010) Services and conflict management: cultural and European integration perspectives. *International Journal of Intercultural Relations* 34, 88–96.

Koc, E. (2013) Power distance and its implications for upward communication and empowerment: crisis management and recovery in hospitality services. *The International Journal of Human Resource Management* 24, 3681–3696.

Koc, E. (2016) Food consumption in all-inclusive holidays: illusion of control as an antecedent of inversionary consumption. *Journal of Gastronomy and Tourism* 2, 107–116.

Koc, E. (2017) *Hizmet Pazarlaması ve Yönetimi, Global ve Yerel Yaklaşım*. 2 Baskı. Seçkin Yayıncılık, Ankara.

Koc, E. and Bozkurt, G.S. (2017) Hospitality employees' future expectations: dissatisfaction, stress and burnout. *International Journal of Hospitality and Tourism Administration* (article in press).

Kokkranikal, J., Wilson, J. and Cronje, P. (2011) Human empowerment, management and tourism. In: Moutinho, L. (ed.) *Strategic Management in Tourism*, 2nd edn. CAB International, Wallingford, UK, pp. 158–181.

Kong, M. and Jogaratnam, G. (2007) The influence of culture on perceptions of service employee behavior. *Managing Quality* 17, 275–297.

Kriegl, U. (2000) International hospitality management. *Cornell Hotel and Restaurant Administration Quarterly* 41, 64–71.

Langer, E.J. (1975) The illusion of control. *Journal of Personality and Social Psychology* 32, 311–328.

Li, X.R., Lai, C., Harrill, R., Kline, S. and Wang, L. (2011) When east meets west: an exploratory study on Chinese outbound tourists' travel expectations. *Tourism Management* 32, 741–749.

Luoh, H.F. and Tsaur, S.H. (2007) Gender stereotypes and service quality in customer waitperson encounters. *Total Quality Management and Business Excellence* 18, 1035–1054.

Mihalič, T. and Fennell, D. (2015) In pursuit of a more just international tourism: the concept of trading tourism rights. *Journal of Sustainable Tourism* 23, 188–206.

Minkov, M. (2007) *What makes us different and similar: a new interpretation of the world values survey and other cross-cultural data*. KlasikaiStil, Sofia.

Minkov, M. and Hofstede, G. (2010) The evolution of Hofstede's doctrine. *Cross Cultural Management: An International Journal* 18, 10–20.

Montoya, D.Y. and Briggs, E. (2013) Shared ethnicity effects on service encounters: a study across three U.S. subcultures. *Journal of Business Research* 66, 314–320.

Mosquera, R.P.M., Uskul, A.K. and Cross, S.E. (2011) The centrality of social image in social psychology. *European Journal of Social Psychology* 41, 403–410.

Nagengast, L., Evanschitzky, H., Blut, M. and Rudolph, T. (2014) New insights in the moderating effect of switching costs on the satisfaction–repurchase behavior link. *Journal of Retailing* 90, 408–427.

Namasivayam, K. and Hinkin, K. (2003) The customer's role in the service encounter. *Cornell Hotel & Restaurant Administration Quarterly* 44, 26–36.

Narteh, B., Agbemabiese, G.C., Kodua, P. and Braimah, M. (2013) Relationship marketing and customer loyalty: evidence from the Ghanaian Luxury Hotel Industry 22, 407–436.

Newman, K.L. and Nollen, S.D. (1996) Culture and congruence: the fit between management practices and national culture. *Journal of International Business Studies* 27, 753–779.

Ouellet, F. (2002) Quelle formation interculturelle en éducation? In: Dasen, P.R. (ed.) *Pour quoi des approaches interculturelles en sciences de l'éducation?* De Boeck Université, Brussels, pp. 243–260.

Park, G.S., Kim, K. and O'Neill, M. (2014) Complaint behavior intentions and expectation of service recovery in individualistic and collectivistic cultures. *International Journal of Culture, Tourism and Hospitality Research* 8, 255–271.

Patterson, P. (2006) Effect of study abroad in intercultural sensitivity. Unpublished doctoral dissertation. University of Missouri, Columbia, Missouri.

Patterson, P.F., Cowley, E. and Prasongsukarn, K. (2006) Service failure recovery: the moderating impact of individual-level cultural value orientation on perceptions of justice. *International Journal of Research in Marketing* 23, 263–277.

Pookulangara, S. and Koesler, K. (2011) Cultural influence on consumers' usage of social networks and its impact on online purchase intentions. *Journal of Retailing and Consumer Services* 18, 348–354.

Prayag, G. and Ryan, C. (2012) Visitor interactions with hotel employees: the role of nationality. *International Journal of Culture, Tourism and Hospitality Research* 6, 173–185.

Rauch, D.A., Collins, M.D., Nale, R.D. and Barr, P.B. (2015) Measuring service quality in midscale hotels. *International Journal of Contemporary Hospitality Management* 27, 87–106.

Salisbury, M.H. (2011) The effect of study abroad on intercultural competence among undergraduate college students. Unpublished doctoral dissertation. University of Iowa, Iowa City, Iowa.

Schwartz, S. (1997) Values and culture. In: Munro, M.S., Schumaker, J.F, and Carr, S.C. (eds) *Motivation and Culture*. Routledge, New York, pp. 69–84.

Scott, N., Laws, E. and Prideaux, B. (2008) Tourism crises and recovery strategies. *Journal of Travel and Tourism Marketing* 23, 1–13.

Sharma, P., Tam, J.L.M. and Kim, N. (2009) Demystifying intercultural service encounters: toward a comprehensive conceptual framework. *Journal of Service Research* 12, 227–242.

Sharma, P., Tam, J.L.M. and Kim, N. (2012) Intercultural service encounters (ICSE): an extended framework and empirical validation. *Journal of Services Marketing* 26, 521–534.

Sharma, P., Tam, J.L. and Kim, N. (2015) Service role and outcome as moderators in intercultural service encounters. *Journal of Service Management* 26, 137–155.

Sizoo, S. (2007) The effect of intercultural sensitivity on cross-cultural service encounters in selected markets: Hawaii, London, and Florida. *Journal of Applied Management and Entrepreneurship* 12, 47–66.

Sizoo, S. (2008) Analysis of employee performance during cross-cultural service encounters at luxury hotels in Hawaii, London and Florida. *Asia Pacific Journal of Tourism Research* 13, 113–128.

Stauss, B. (2016) Retrospective: 'culture shocks' in inter-cultural service encounters? *Journal of Services Marketing* 30, 377–383.

Stebleton, M.J., Soria, K.M. and Cherney, B. (2013) The high impact of education abroad: college students' engagement in international experiences and the development of intercultural competencies. *Frontiers: Interdisciplinary Journal of Study Abroad* 22, 1–24.

Tajfel, H. and Turner, J.C. (1986) The social identity theory of intergroup behaviour. In: Worehel, S. and Austin, W.G. (eds) *The Psychology of Intergroup Relations*. Nelson Hall, Chicago, Illinois, pp. 7–24.

Tajfel, H., Billig, M.G., Bundy, R.P. and Flament, C. (1971) Social categorization and intergroup behaviours. *European Journal of Social Psychology* 1, 149–178.

TARP (Technical Assistance Research Programs Institute) (2007) *Consumer Complaint Handling in America: An Update Study*. White House Office of Consumer Affairs, Washington, DC.

Triandis, H.C., Chan, D.K.S., Bhawuk, D.P., Iwao, S. and Sinha, J.B. (1995) Multimethod probes of allocentrism and idiocentrism. *International Journal of Psychology* 30, 461–480.

Trompenaars, F. (1993) *Riding the Waves of Culture*. Brealey, London.

Um, N.H. and Lee, W.N. (2014) Does culture influence how consumers process negative celebrity information? Impact of culture in evaluation of negative celebrity information. *Asian Journal of Communication* 25, 327–347.

Wong, N.Y. (2004) The role of culture in the perception of service recovery. *Journal of Business Research* 57, 957–963.

World Tourism Organization (2015) *Annual Report 2015*. Available at: http://cf.cdn.unwto.org/sites/all/files/pdf/annual_report_2015_lr.pdf (accessed 1 December 2016).

Yashima, T. (2010) The effects of international volunteer work experiences on intercultural competence of Japanese youth. *International Journal of Intercultural Relations* 34, 268–282.

Yuksel, A., Kilinc, U. and Yuksel, F. (2006) Cross-national analysis of hotel customers' attitudes toward complaining and their complaining behaviours. *Tourism Management* 27, 11–24.

Zeithaml, V.A., Parasuraman, A. and Berry, L.L. (1990) *Delivering Quality Service: Balancing Customer Perceptions and Expectations*. Collier Macmillan, New York.

Zhao, D. and Lin, I.Y. (2014) Understanding tourists' perception and evaluation of inter-cultural service encounters: a holistic mental model process. *International Journal of Culture, Tourism and Hospitality Research* 8, 290–309.

14 Disappointment in Tourism and Hospitality: the Influence of Films on Destinations

ANNA IRIMIÁS, GÁBOR MICHALKÓ, DALLEN J. TIMOTHY AND MARIANGELA FRANCH

Learning Objectives

After reading this chapter, you should be able to:

- Understand the role of films as marketing communications tools in developing images about a tourist destination.
- Explain the concept of disappointment as an emotion.
- Understand the communications gap occurring as a result of film-induced tourism.
- Understand how consumers respond to service failures and express their disappointment.

14.1 Introduction

When sons of the aristocracy, on returning from the Grand Tour, unwrapped the canvases purchased as souvenirs of Venice, Canaletto's fascinating views of the city of lagoons amazed the public. The landscape artist majestically used two-point linear perspectives to create the illusion of space. His highly refined detailing of the Venetian architecture aimed to recreate the city's unique milieu. In the 18th century, the Italian painter engaged his public in a virtual journey, nurturing their desire to visit Venice personally. Canaletto, long before the era of tourism, managed to turn the attention of the world to his city. Two centuries later, film, a new visual technology, has contributed to Venice's international fame. As Fernand Braudel asserts in his volume on Venice, 'films, more than literature, are the best introduction to the city' (2013, p. 34). Venice's popularity as a tourism destination has increased by hundreds of thousands of tourists over the last decade. Since the era of on-location filming (for example, *Othello*, released in 1951), Venice has also become a popular location for films, such as *Death in Venice* (1971) by Luchino Visconti, *Indiana Jones and the Last Crusade* (1989), *The Merchant of Venice* (2004), *Casino Royale* (2006) and *The Tourist* (2010), starring Johnny Depp and Angelina Jolie.

In addition, since 1932 the Italian city has hosted one of the world's most prestigious film festivals. Each year, La Biennale creates a symbiosis between the film industry and tourism, conveying the festival's appeal to attract thousands of tourists and film

---

fans. But does every tourist perceive Venice as portrayed in Canaletto's canvases or Orson Welles's and Michael Radford's films? Or have significant numbers of tourists remained disappointed by their experiences with 'the Queen of the Adriatic'? Only assumptions can be formulated regarding the number of disappointed tourists, and little is known about them, like other tourists who are disappointed in their experiences because their hyper film-induced expectations of a popular movie location were far different from reality.

14.2   Service Failures and Communication Gaps

Numerous studies in tourism have explored consumer behaviour in terms of the stages prior to purchase, consumption and post-purchase (Foster, 1999; Franch *et al.*, 2005). In consumer surveys, respondents are frequently asked about their motivations and factors that influenced them to visit a particular destination. The aim of this approach is to detect the pool of resources that elicit a desire to travel. Although media such as television, newspapers or magazines are listed among travel-inspiring sources, the influence of feature films as tourism motivators has been largely overlooked (Del Bosque and San Martìn, 2008; Beeton, 2016). Films can convey a wide variety of messages about various issues and help develop, intentionally or unintentionally, positive or negative attitudes among the target audience. By developing positive or negative attitudes about a tourist destination, films can influence tourists' decisions to visit or avoid that particular locale. Hence, films may act as an influential marketing communications tool to develop positive intentions about a particular destination.

The analysis of tourist satisfaction and dissatisfaction is mainly based on the contributions of psychology to tourism and hospitality studies (Pearce and Packer, 2013; Xin *et al.*, 2013). One result of this research interest is to measure perceived value and its implications for tourism marketing. The perceived value of a destination, prestige, and its culturally determined brand image, influence consumers' purchase and consumption processes. For example, while the James Bond filming locations are usually associated with luxury, the recent film *La La Land* (2016) depicts Los Angeles as a destination for entertainment. The measurement of consumer behaviour in a destination usually concentrates on the positive features rather than the negative ones. Unless it is a specific film aimed at political propaganda, the negative factors that may generate disappointment in destinations are largely overlooked (Rátz and Puczkó, 2002; Fuchs and Weiermair, 2003). Volo (2008) argues that the negative factors and potential risks pertaining to a destination should also be communicated.

Most customers develop expectations and attitudes regarding the service and the quality of service they hope to receive in a destination (Kenesei and Stier, 2016). However, problems arise when service providers' performance falls below the expectations of customers. These instances can be classified as service failures. Customer dissatisfaction occurring as a consequence of a service failure can seriously threaten the survival and growth of destinations and various stakeholders (Koc *et al.*, 2017), ranging from accommodation establishments to restaurants. As described by Parasuraman *et al.* (1991, pp. 337–338), service quality problems or service failures occur due to the following service quality gaps:

- The knowledge or perception gap: the difference between the customers' service expectations and service managers' perceptions of the customers' service expectations.
- The standards gap: the difference between service managers' perceptions of customer expectations and the service procedures, standards and specifications established.
- The delivery gap: the difference between service quality specifications and the actual service delivered to the customers.
- The communications gap: the difference between what is communicated to the customer and the actual service delivered.

The communications gap, which is the difference between what is communicated to the customer and the actual service delivered, is to do with developing infeasible expectations through marketing communications or promotional materials such as films. When used as promotional materials for destinations, feature films or television series can seriously widen this gap and cause serious customer dissatisfaction due to unmet expectations (Hudson and Ritchie, 2006; Koc, 2016).

In fact, movies usually do not make intentional promises about the film location and destination. However, films that involve emotional storytelling implant an image of a destination in movie-goers' minds. Feature films and television series might induce tourists to visit a certain destination, making film-induced tourism one of the fastest developing and most dynamic marketing communications tools for destinations (Beeton, 2016). Destinations are increasingly recognizing the promotional potential of films. Hence, movies and television series can be considered powerful promotional material for a destination (Hudson and Ritchie, 2006). In this vein, specialized destination marketing strategies have been developed to broaden the visitor base and to reduce seasonality (Volo and Irimiás, 2016).

Service failures in film-induced tourism can generate negative impacts that might lead to tourists' disappointment. If high expectations are developed by movies or television series that do not match the reality of a destination, customer disappointment and negative word-of-mouth may be inevitable, especially with the popularization of social media and traveller-generated information on destination rating websites. A better understanding of negative emotional attributes through investigating the causes, factors and consequences of tourists' disappointment is required to avoid service failures and word-of-mouth communication (Michalkó *et al.*, 2015). The working definition of a service failure, in this context, is any pitfall occurring during the service provision processes that elicits negative feelings and generates tourists' disappointment. In short, a service failure is the inability of service providers to meet tourists' expectations (Koc *et al.*, 2017).

As a consequence, film tourism destinations should be managed carefully to avoid consumer dissatisfaction, although this process is challenging since high expectations were nurtured by films and not by destination managers' actions. In this chapter, destination management is studied from the viewpoint of disappointed film tourists, and the concept of disappointment management is further explored (Michalkó *et al.*, 2015). Disappointment management can be defined as a managerial philosophy and an operative practice that aims to reduce tourists' negative emotional experiences caused by service failures and to host tourists with empathy. In this chapter the focus is only on film tourism destinations because movie-induced tourism is one of the best examples to show that disappointment caused even by small errors in service performance projects negative feelings towards the whole destination. However, the concept is based on the notion that identifying sources of disappointment and strategies to reduce and compensate for disappointment generated by service failures can be applied to any tourism product.

14.2.1   Causes and sources of disappointment in tourism

The term 'disappointment' is defined in the *Oxford English Dictionary* as 'sadness or displeasure by the non-fulfilment of one's hopes or expectations' (see also Smith *et al.*, 2003). As described in Chapter 4 (this volume), all emotions, including disappointment, are formed based on external stimuli (such as the feeling of disappointment or anger after a service failure) and internal stimuli (Picard, 2012) such as body conditions (e.g. pain or hunger). Service failures may act both as external stimuli or internal stimuli, such as in the case of a tourist who is shocked and gets angry when s/he meets rude service staff in a destination, contrary to what was depicted in a film.

The affective states of consciousness and emotions influence thought and behaviour, and can be defined as brief but intense experiences (Beesley, 2005). In tourism contexts, disappointment may arise due to unrealistic ideas and expectations developed about places, people and services. All of these causes of disappointment can be described as service failures. Service failures, such as the lack of entertainment options promised in promotional materials for a destination, rude staff in hotels or poor hospitality services, might challenge tourists' levels of frustration tolerance in different ways (Michalkó *et al.*, 2015).

14.2.2   External and internal sources of emotions

The glorification of places in promotional materials, web pages, magazines and brochures makes people believe that on arrival they will have wonderful experiences (Edelheim, 2007). These marketing messages as extrinsic sources act as the forces outside an individual's self that influence her/his expectations about a destination (Alegre and Garau, 2010) and widen the communications gap between consumers and service providers. External stimuli are usually linked to elements of the tourist's surrounding environment. However, tourism marketing messages, no matter how much they clearly target potential specific tourist segments, may be misinterpreted by individual tourists (McKercher *et al.*, 2002). This misinterpretation may be caused by tourists' intrinsic sources, such as the level of their self-awareness about their needs and desires and their attitudes and past experience. Internal sources or stimuli, like fantasies or psychological baggage, might become sources of disappointment. The creation of place meaning is not contingent solely on destination managers or tourists; rather it is an interactive process involving both parties. External and internal sources usually act together to form expectations and to boost illusions and become sources of disappointment (Fig. 14.1).

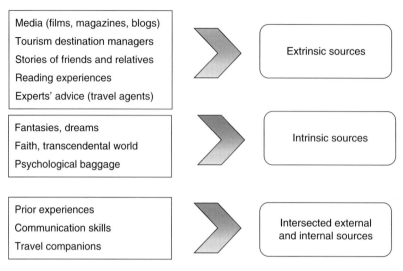

Fig. 14.1. Sources of disappointment. (From the author.)

Tourism marketing aims to convince potential tourists to choose a destination by developing anticipations and expectations, as noted above. But the previously described communication gap can be so wide it may cause a strong feeling of disappointment and anger. The phenomenon of 'Paris Syndrome' has been studied since the 1990s. This psychological condition relates mainly to Japanese tourists, who after arriving in Paris experienced culture shock and a high level of disappointment. As a consequence, these people suffered serious psychological distress in the 'city of love'. This syndrome is characterized by acute delusional states and anxiety arising from the collective idealized image of Paris, combined with language and cultural barriers and travel stress (Picard, 2012). Similarly, tourists from the USA often complain that Florence and Siena in Italy do not look as they imagined; the buildings are too old and the streets are too narrow. Thus, mental images of a destination might be rather different from reality.

Tourists' prior travel experience, formed by a combination of extrinsic and intrinsic variables, may also provide an overlapping source of disappointment. The emotional experiences lived on a journey (e.g. in childhood, for a graduation celebration or on a honeymoon) may paint a relatively idealistic picture of the previously visited place, but the inability to revitalize journeys without that earlier particular emotional state may cause long-standing expectations to fade away.

Service failures can reflect a negative perception of the journey, and bad memories will not just be linked to service providers, but to the whole destination (Fig. 14.2). Unpredictable crises such as particularly bad weather conditions or unforeseen difficulties in transportation or infrastructure can lead to the renegotiation of prior beliefs.

Disappointment in tourism may involve different processes. The time dimension of facing unfulfilled expectations depends on the duration of the cause of disappointment. If the problem is quickly resolved, tourists' disappointment might quickly vanish, but permanent disappointment caused during a vacation may last a longer period of time. The place, time and the people responsible for the disappointment (e.g. the tourist him/

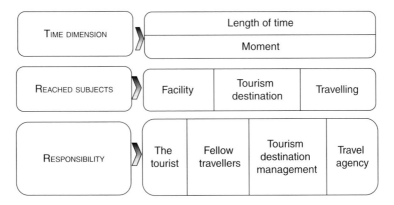

Fig. 14.2. Aspects of service failure in destination. (From Michalkó *et al.*, 2015, p. 88.)

herself, fellow travellers, service providers or even destination managers) may have different influences on tourists' experiences.

14.2.3 Negative word-of-mouth

When tourists become disappointed, they may complain either directly to service providers or indirectly to friends and relatives, or by writing on user-generated content sites such as TripAdvisor or booking.com. Given that tourists increasingly depend more on the comments and advice of other tourists, service providers need to pay special attention to managing service failure processes, the ensuing disappointment and the potential negative word-of-mouth communication that tourists may engage in.

Visitors' satisfaction and positive word-of-mouth, along with positive comments on web sites such as TripAdvisor, booking.com and other similar user-generated content sites, are crucial in developing a good reputation and a strong brand image (Munar, 2011). On the other hand, negative comments posted as a consequence of service failures may damage not only a particular service provider's reputation, but also the reputation and image of the destination as a whole (Litvin *et al.*, 2006). Yet, it should be borne in mind that consumers' online complaints can provide valuable insights into the root causes of service failures. Later in the chapter some of the examples of comments posted by tourists on various websites are provided to demonstrate additional insight into tourists' disappointment in a destination.

14.3 Films as Sources of Disappointment in Destinations

Mass media, such as films, television series and reality shows, have become major story-tellers in society, communicating social and cultural ideals to consumers, as well as enhanced images of places (Cooper *et al.*, 2010). Although it may not be the movie-makers' intentions, movies can enhance destinations' perceived image and might function as destination marketing tools to increase the number of visitors to a destination. Film viewers may associate the depicted destination with a particular atmosphere and embedded brand narrative(s) (Hudson and Ritchie, 2006). Destination marketing and management activities involve a wide variety of stakeholders who may capitalize on the popularity of films set in certain destinations. Thus, service destination managers and other stakeholders need to have a better understanding of film-induced tourism.

14.3.1 Definition of film-induced tourism

The term film tourism refers to tourism activity generated in a destination that hosted a successful movie production (Beeton, 2016). Film tourists choose a particular destination to find some form of stimuli that may overlap with their interests about the filming location. Locations of popular films, such as the case of New Zealand for *The Lord of the Rings* (2001–2003) saga, and television series like *Game of Thrones* (2011–present), set in Northern Ireland and Dubrovnik, induce significant tourism visitation with the promise of being part of that fantasy world. However, this definition might seem restrictive (Tzanelli, 2010). In fact, film-induced tourism, in a broad sense, includes visits to film studios and film-related theme parks. Movies that reflect an authentic image of the destination, capture the essence of places and enhance scenery and local culture tend to be more successful in attracting film tourists (Tooke and Baker, 1996; Iwashita, 2006; Kim, 2010).

> **Activity**
>
> Think about one of your favourite movies filmed in a destination you have been to. Explain to your colleagues the potential scenes that may cause disappointment for visitors.

14.3.2 Film topics to increase desire to visit a destination

Popular culture that continually renews stories often reflects contemporary social changes, making tourism one of its topics. Even in childhood, young consumers are exposed to travelling figures, and to amazing rural and urban landscapes like in the classic children's programmes *Around the World with Willy Fog* (1981), *The Wonderful Adventures of Nils Holgersson* (1962) or in more recent animation productions such as *UP* (2009), *Frozen* (2013) and *Finding Dory* (2016). The purchase power of 4–8-year-old children and their role in the decision-making processes involving holidays have been studied (Fodness, 1992), but not the effects of disappointment caused by service failures. However, it might be that children compensate themselves and rebalance feelings (Izard, 1977), even if their expected experience in a destination is far from being met in reality.

In the case of experienced travellers, brand narratives imbued with identity and lifestyle ideals depicted in films might lead to a more complex construction of expectations. Further, it is more difficult to compensate film-fan tourists once disillusions occur. Cinematic images invite film viewers to experience the places and lifestyles of characters. Illusions, like beautiful, deserted beaches in Thailand as in the movie *The Beach* (2001), elicit emotions that enhance the perceived value of a destination. Some popular film topics illustrate well the possible communications gaps generated by films with an impact on a destination that could create overly exaggerated tourism expectations. This list of categories is not exhaustive but illustrates how film narratives fuel the desire to visit a certain destination.

- *Luxury*: Films set in luxurious hotels like Ciragan Palace Kempinski Hotel in Istanbul (Turkey) in *Skyfall* (2013) or set on huge and comfortable airplanes such as *Flightplan* (2005) are capable of creating high expectations from service providers. But following the footsteps of Daniel Craig in Istanbul while staying in a bed and breakfast or flying economy class on intercontinental flights might bring disappointment to those travellers who associated the journey with luxury and extra comfort.
- *Romance and love*: Several romantic movie productions have been set in the Mediterranean (e.g. *Mamma Mia!* 2008), dominated by sun–sea–sand images. Taking a romantic journey with a loved one is associated with happy relationships and such romantic environments with expectations for similar emotional experiences. However, not all expectations can be fulfilled in such idealized destinations. *Amélie* (2001) and *Eat, Pray, Love* (2006) are examples of other films credited for creating a romantic image of Paris and Indonesia, resulting in many disappointed tourists.
- *Career success*: Movie productions about successful businesspeople, artists or athletes depict these individuals spending most of their time on comfortable airplanes and in nice hotels (e.g. *I Don't Know How She Does It*, 2011). This hectic lifestyle is presented as being compensated by a quick and successful career. But in real life this is far from the truth.
- *Adventure, excitement*: Film plots comprised of well-structured drama (e.g. *The Da Vinci Code*, 2006; *Angels and Demons*, 2009) suggest that a historical destination with a rich socio-cultural environment provides adventure and excitement. In most cases, this level of intense adventure is only relived in visitors' minds when they recall their most memorable movie scenes.
- *Alternative sites, runaway productions*: Many productions are not filmed in the location where they are set. For example, *Evita* (1996) was set in Buenos Aires, Argentina, but it was filmed in Budapest, Hungary. In the case of Hollywood films, runaway productions are frequent because cheaper locations significantly reduce budget costs. But when tourists seek the locations they see on screen, they can be disappointed.

Activity

Choose a destination you are familiar with and prepare a brief script for a short film which may be useful in helping to avoid visitor disappointment.

14.4 Disappointment Caused by Service Failures

Although the above examples demonstrate how the media can influence tourists' perceptions about a destination, movies are hardly ever the sole motivation for tourists visiting a destination. Three different examples of film tourism service failures are provided below. These examples were selected particularly to provide better insight into the concept, both in terms of scope and depth. For this reason, the examples cover: (i) services targeted at different film tourism segments (e.g. families, enthusiastic film fans and theme park visitors); (ii) attractions situated in different geographical areas (an island in the UK, a private property in New Zealand and a theme park in Dubai); and (iii) disappointed tourists expressing their disappointment and dissatisfaction (e.g. by posting comments on TripAdvisor).

The first example evidences service failures on the Isle of Mull, UK, where the popular pre-school television programme *Balamory* was set. Balamory is the fantasy name of the town, but could easily be identified with the picturesque port of Tobermory. In the case of family travel, children's satisfaction is one of the key goals (Connell, 2005). The following review taken from TripAdvisor shows some of the service failure factors causing disappointment.

Balamory – Family trip to Balamory, Sep 16, 2007

We have just got back from a week on Mull with our kids (aged 8 and 5). We went to visit Tobermory and it is a perfectly nice little fishing village (with a most fantastic chip van) but **you must go not expecting to be going to 'Balamory'**. Our kids were not at all disappointed as they understood that **it was just the place where it used to be filmed** (they stopped filming there a couple of years ago) and I certainly would not describe the place as dilapidated. There are a couple of little gift shops selling Balamory associated goods **but there is not much else to keep young children entertained.** All the tourist attractions for children on Mull I would describe as 'scaled down' and didn't represent great value for money compared with what you get in England. However, the kids enjoyed it all.

(https://www.tripadvisor.com/ShowTopic-g551869-i10742-k1456992-Family_trip_to_ Balamory-Tobermory_Isle_of_Mull_The_Hebrides_Scotland.html)

Disappointment here derives from the illusion these film tourists had about 'Balamory' before their visit (communication gap). Clear reference to service failures such as poor gift shops selling film memorabilia and the lack of entertainment services is evidence that the destination failed to prepare for the family tourist segment, especially young children.

Other meaningful examples can be found in such popular film destinations as Matamata in New Zealand, the location of 'Hobbiton'. Hobbiton was constructed as a film set on a private farm for *The Lord of the Rings* (2001–2003) and *The Hobbit* (2012–2014) trilogy. The property housing the former movie set has been developed into a post-filming tourist attraction (Beeton, 2016). The worldwide popularity of the Peter Jackson films and the identification of Middle Earth with New Zealand have boosted film tourism to the country. But not everyone is satisfied by the attraction, as one reviewer from Malaysia explained in his/her TripAdvisor comment on Hobbiton. The visitor's previous expectations were not fulfilled by the site. This negative word-of-mouth communication suggests that film tourists, while expecting to live their 'once in a lifetime experience', did not have their expectations met and were therefore disappointed. Triggered by service failure and ensuing disappointment, the visitor posted the following comment on TripAdvisor.

'Disappointed and Sad'

Reviewed January 2017

It is one of those days you prebook your ticket and looking forward to this. No doubt the place is nice and the pull factor is there because of the movie and it seems **to be a must see place but the experience for me is bad**. Sadly. I felt ticket overpriced at 79NZ because it was a touch and go experience, restricted, a bus with around 20–30 people with a tour guide will allow you minimal time to experience and take photos. **Is a quick tour where you are rush and not allow to enjoy fully**. We had to follow closely the tour guide and is very rush as the next tour bus would be coming like just a 5 mins apart. **too crowded** and hence **you would not able to take photos whenever you want it.** Add to It **The tour guide don't understand that** and just rush us through the tour. not worth the money. The only more time given is 10 min during whole duration of tour is where we are put at the bar to have complimentary drinks. even that is a rush. **Is just a money-making movie set.**

I think they knew is a one off visits hence the overprice and rushing. But seriously my friend only wanted to take one photo where the scene capture Frodo run in and shout **he want have adventure of lifetime but yet the guide said she was not allowed to do so because another bus load of people coming in**. So is like telling you either u walk pass it miss it too bad you can't have the photos taken. So remember to be quick when want take photos because u only have one chance as you cannot walk back same spot even though is just 5 feet away!

(https://www.tripadvisor.co.za/ShowUserReviews-g3395240-d1382525-r452908064-Hobbiton_Movie_Set_Tours-Hinuera_Waikato_Region_North_Island.html#)

In this comment posted by a visitor, service failures such as overpriced tickets, crowded and rushed guided tours, limited time to take pictures, lack of tour guide empathy and destruction of the 'fantasy atmosphere' by crowded buses pouring into the site are evident. Service providers at Hobbiton should consider re-designing their services and establish appropriate recovery systems to prevent tourist dissatisfaction.

The last example is a new Bollywood-themed park (opened to the public in November 2016), a unique film tourism attraction targeting Bollywood film fans in Dubai, United Arab Emirates. Studio theme parks can be significant attractions for movie destinations. As Beeton argues, 'theme parks celebrate populist films that are set anywhere and can be viewed anywhere in the world' (2016, p. 222). These theme park attractions aim to satisfy film tourists' demands without considering the park's geographical appropriateness or its socio-cultural relationships to the theme. Service failures caused disappointed film tourists to write negative comments, as the quote demonstrates:

'What a rip-off.....', Reviewed in December 2016

I bought 5 tickets online in the UK for our trip. **We're all Bollywood fans and were expecting something special**. Based on the website and the adverts this was meant to be amazing. **How completely wrong we were. This place is poor**. Firstly, **nothing is signposted**, so the taxi driver just drops you off anywhere nearby … I travelled with my 2-year-old daughter and had to walk a considerable distance to get to the park, and this was after asking someone working on the construction site.

When we got to the park I was expecting queues of people wanting to get in. To my amazement, not even a line of 2 people waiting to get in, we walked straight in (The website actually gives you an option to buy a quick pass that avoids the queues!) Then just as I wanted to start to look **around I get harassed by the parks photographers** offering to take pictures, I don't mind one or two during my experience but I collected over 20 photo tokens.

They also **charged full price for a park that clearly is not ready,** half the rides were not even open. And the rides that open are not really very good. I was told they will open in the future … no use to me. **The shops around the complex are still being built.** Whilst walking out **I was asked by a staff member to give feedback. When we all gave him our opinion even he agreed that the park wasn't very good.** What does that say about it? He also said a lot of people complained.

I have written to the park and asked for a response from the park that wasn't the usual standard reply … and guess what … I got the standard reply … I'm not surprised in anyway. **Clearly this place is** all about making money and **nothing about satisfying the customer.**

(https://www.tripadvisor.it/Attraction_Review-g295424-d11880048-Reviews-Bollywood_ Parks_Dubai-Dubai_Emirate_of_Dubai.html#review_444068028)

Such obvious service failures, lack of access and directional information, harassment by service providers, closed rides and shops yet to be built in a newly opened film-based tourist attraction could be extremely costly for the establishment. Moreover, as evident from the previous quotation, these failures have already generated deficient employee performance and low morale (see the reference to the staff member asking for tourists' feedback). These examples of film tourist disappointment generated by service failures show that every journey is a complex process wherein tourists' expectations can remain unfulfilled by a variety of factors. Some of these factors could be eliminated or at least reduced by the combined effort of service providers and destination managers. Destination managers do not have any influence on the film genre or on the storyline of a film set in the destination, but several actions could be undertaken to avoid service failures, to reduce the communications gap and, consequently, the disappointment felt by film tourists:

- communicate clearly about movie-based attractions and entertainment services, and avoid glorifying the place;
- implement orientation assistance with appropriate and informative signs about film locations, while maintaining community residents' privacy;
- provide sufficient information about attractions and accessibility;
- display and keep opening hours of shops and attractions;
- calculate plenty of time for visits;
- provide appropriate conditions for visitors to take pictures at meaningful film locales;
- verify information about pre-announced programmes and provide information on schedule changes; and
- train staff and tour guides to manage tourists' disappointment with empathy (Michalkó *et al.*, 2015).

A better understanding of film tourists' expectations would enable service providers and destination management organizations to enact appropriate policies and plan better for visitor management. To enrich this policy, disappointment management should be applied. Disappointment management is based on studies of consumer behaviour and destination management and embraces the managerial philosophy of hosting tourists with empathy while also safeguarding local communities. Several factors causing disappointment can be eradicated by attentive planning, but unpredictable incidents will still happen. In such cases, possible compensation should be considered as an important part of planning and policy decision-making.

Activity

Visit the TripAdvisor website and identify three negative comments regarding a destination you have been to. Do you agree with those comments? Why? What should the stakeholders in the destination do to avoid visitor disappointment?

14.5   Conclusions

Nowadays, travellers are more experienced, informed and interconnected to each other than ever before. In consumer society, tourism is not only a leisure activity but also a source of learning and an act of self-fulfilment and cultural identification. Expectations of tourist experiences are enhanced by various media, especially films and television series. Film-induced tourists are eager to experience the locations seen on screen by travelling to the destinations that are depicted through storytelling and visual imagery. Emotions and affective variables influence behavioural intentions in the tourism context (e.g. positive online word-of-mouth, willingness to return or to pay more for a service) and to reduce negative emotions; thus, destinations should have clear managerial policies and practices (Bigné and Andreau, 2004).

Research shows that unpleasant incidents and service failures occur quite often in hospitality and service environments (Mattila and Ro, 2008; Brunner-Sperdin and Peters, 2009; Brunner-Sperdin *et al.*, 2012). The impact and consequences of such undesired events must be detected, understood and managed by all stakeholders involved. In the long term, not recognizing tourists' disappointments might lead to serious difficulties not only for individual service providers but for destinations as well (Alegre and Garau, 2010). Disappointment management is a concrete operational practice to intervene on pre-travel, travel and post-travel experiences to reduce unrealistic expectations and to inform tourists appropriately in order to minimize potential disappointment.

Questions

1. What are service failures and disappointment management in film-induced tourism?
2. List the sources of disappointment in tourism. Which of these sources should be managed by service providers and destination management organizations?
3. How could service failures in the examples provided have been avoided and services recovered?

Acknowledgements

This study is part of a three-year (2016–2019) research programme titled 'The role of cultural industry in the innovative territorial development: A complex geographical analysis', supported by the Bolyai János Scholarship of the Hungarian Academy of Sciences awarded to the first author.

Further Reading

Beeton, S. (2016) *Film-Induced Tourism*, 2nd edn. Channel View, Bristol, UK.

Hudson, S. and Ritchie, J.R.B. (2006) Film tourism and destination marketing: the case of *Captain Corelli's Mandolin*. *Journal of Vacation Marketing* 12, 256–268.

Michalkó, G., Irimiás, A. and Timothy, D. (2015) Disappointment in tourism: perspectives on tourism destination management. *Tourism Management Perspectives* 16, 85–91.

Tooke, N. and Baker, D. (1996) Seeing is believing: the effect of film on visitor numbers to screened locations. *Tourism Management* 17, 87–94.

Volo, S. and Irimiás, A. (2016) Film tourism and post release marketing initiatives: a longitudinal case study. *Journal of Travel and Tourism Marketing* 33, 1071–1087.

References

Alegre, J. and Garau, J. (2010) Tourist satisfaction and dissatisfaction. *Annals of Tourism Research* 37, 52–73.

Beesley, L. (2005) The management of emotion in collaborative tourism research settings. *Tourism Management* 26, 261–275.

Beeton, S. (2016) *Film-Induced Tourism*, 2nd edn. Channel View, Bristol, UK.

Bigné, J.E. and Andreau, L. (2004) Emotions in segmentation: an empirical study. *Annals of Tourism Research* 31, 682–696.

Braudel, F. (2013) *Venezia*. Il Mulino, Bologna, Italy.

Brunner-Sperdin, A. and Peters, M. (2009) What influences guests' emotions? The case of high quality hotels. *International Journal of Tourism Research* 11, 171–183.

Brunner-Sperdin, A., Peters, M. and Strobl, A. (2012) It is all about the emotional state: managing tourists' experiences. *International Journal of Hospitality Management* 31, 23–30.

Connell, J. (2005) 'What's the story in Balamory?' The impacts of a children's TV programme on small tourism enterprises on the Isle of Mull, Scotland. *Journal of Sustainable Tourism* 13, 228–255.

Cooper, H., Schembri, S. and Miller, D. (2010) Brand-self-identity narratives in the James Bond movies. *Psychology and Marketing* 27, 557–567.

Del Bosque, I.R. and San Martin, H. (2008) Tourist satisfaction: a cognitive-affective model. *Annals of Tourism Research* 35, 551–573.

Edelheim, J. (2007) Hidden messages: a polisemic reading of tourism brochures. *Journal of Vacation Marketing* 13, 5–17.

Fodness, D. (1992) The impact of family life cycle on the vacation decision-making process. *Journal of Travel Research* 31, 8–13.

Foster, D. (1999) Measuring customer satisfaction in the tourism industry. *Third International & Sixth National Research Conference on Quality Management*. The Centre for Management Quality Research at RMIT University, Melbourne, Australia.

Franch, M., Martini, U., Novi Inverardi, P.L. and Buffa, F. (2005) Comportamenti e scelte del turista fai-da-te nelle Dolomiti. *Sinergie* 66, 153–180.

Fuchs, M. and Weiermair, K. (2003) New perspectives of satisfaction research in tourism destinations. *Tourism Review* 58, 6–14.

Hudson, S. and Ritchie, J.R.B. (2006) Film tourism and destination marketing: the case of *Captain Corelli's Mandolin*. *Journal of Vacation Marketing* 12, 256–268.

Iwashita, C. (2006) Media representations of the UK as a destination for Japanese tourists: popular culture and tourism. *Tourist Studies* 6, 59–77.

Izard, C.E. (1977) *Human Emotions*. Springer Science, New York.

Kenesei, Z. and Stier, Z. (2016) Managing communication and cultural barriers in intercultural service encounters: strategies from both sides of the counter. *Journal of Vacation Marketing* doi: 10.1177/1356766716676299.

Kim, S. (2010) Extraordinary experience: re-enacting and photographing at screen tourism locations. *Tourism and Hospitality Planning Development* 7, 59–75.

Koc, E. (2016) *Tüketici Davranışı ve Pazarlama Stratejileri, Global ve Yerel Yaklaşım*. 7 Baskı. Seçkin Yayıncılık, Ankara.

Koc, E., Ulukoy, M., Kilic, R., Yumusak, S. and Bahar, R. (2017) The influence of customer participation on service failure perceptions. *Total Quality Management & Business Excellence* 28, 390–404.

Litvin, S., Goldsmith, R.E. and Pan, B. (2006) Electronic word of mouth in hospitality and tourism management. *Tourism Management* 29, 458–468.

Mattila, A. and Ro, H. (2008) Discrete negative emotions and customer dissatisfaction responses in a casual restaurant setting. *Journal of Hospitality & Tourism Research* 32, 89–107.

McKercher, B., Ho, P., du Cros, H. and So-Ming, B.C. (2002) Activities-based segmentation of the cultural tourism market. *Journal of Travel and Tourism Marketing* 12, 23–46.

Michalkó, G., Irimiás, A. and Timothy, D. (2015) Disappointment in tourism: perspectives on tourism destination management. *Tourism Management Perspectives* 16, 85–91.

Munar, A.M. (2011) Tourist-created content: rethinking destination branding. *International Journal of Culture, Tourism and Hospitality Research* 5, 291–305.

Parasuraman, A., Berry, L.L. and Zeithaml, V.A. (1991) Perceived service quality as a customer-based performance measure: an empirical examination of organisational barriers using an extended service quality model. *Human Resource Management* 30, 335–364.

Pearce, P. and Packer, J. (2013) Minds on the move: new links from psychology to tourism. *Annals of Tourism Research* 40, 386–411.

Picard, D. (2012) Tourism, awe and inner journeys. In: Picard, D. and Robinson, M. (eds) *Emotions in Motion: Tourism, Affect and Transformation*. Routledge, New York, pp. 1–21.

Rátz, T. and Puczkó, L. (2002) *The impacts of tourism: an introduction*. Häme Polytechnic, Hämeenlinna, Finland.

Smith, E., Fredrickson, B., Loftus, G. and Nolen-Hoeksema, S. (2003) *Atkinson and Hilgard's Introduction to Psychology*. Thomson-Wadsworth, Belmont, California.

Tooke, N. and Baker, D. (1996) Seeing is believing: the effect of film on visitor numbers to screened locations. *Tourism Management* 17, 87–94.

Tzanelli, R. (2010) The Da Vinci node: networks of neo-pilgrimage in the European cosmopolis. *The International Journal of the Humanities* 8, 7–28.

Volo, S. (2008) Communicating tourism crises through destination websites. *Journal of Travel and Tourism Marketing* 23, 83–93.

Volo, S. and Irimiás, A. (2016) Film tourism and post release marketing initiatives: a longitudinal case study. *Journal of Travel and Tourism Marketing* 33, 1071–1087.

Xin, S., Tribe, J. and Chambers, D. (2013) Conceptual research in tourism. *Annals of Tourism Research* 41, 66–88.

Index

Note: Page numbers in **bold** type refer to **figures**
Page numbers in *italic* type refer to *tables*

technology (*continued*)
    newly emerging issues in 89
    and satisfaction with services 85–88
    wearable 91, **92**
    see also self-service technologies
technology acceptance model 84
thankfulness 76
theme parks 220, 223
third-party justice 30, 130
timeliness 190
tour guide 166
tourism, film-induced 220
tours 74, 93
training 129
    attitude 166
    and attribution **163**
    for customer recovery 172–173
    for effective service recovery **165**
    emotional intelligence 154
    for employee recovery 167–171
    improvisation 169
    on intercultural sensitivity 207
    practices for effective service
        recovery 162–173
    process **161**
    programmes 161
    for service failures 5–6, 160–176
    simulation 174
    techniques 175–176
    to influence customer attribution 162
travel 136, 207
    group 137
travel-inspiring sources 215
travellers, experienced 225
triangulation of data 46
TripAdvisor 70, 87, 219, 222, 223

trust 60, 61, 204
truth, moments of 10
Turkey 143

unavailable service failure 15
uncertainty 202
unfairness 130
unsure responses 109
urgency 18
utilitarian cultural model 32
utilitarian-style customers 111

value, emotional 139
values 198
variability 12
Venice 214
virtual reality 89–91, **90**
voice, likelihood of 112
voucher 164

waiting time 181, 185–190, **186**, 192
    in hotels 186–187
    perceptions of 186–187
    in restaurants 187
    situations and strategies *189*
wearable technology 91, **92**
win-win principle 173
word of mouth 22, 57, 140, 141, 190
    negative 219
wrong customers 170

Yelp 17, 87